SOUTHWEST
ADVENTURES

FRASER BRIDGES

An On-Route Communications Book

PRIMA PUBLISHING

© 1995 by On-Route Communications

PRIMA PUBLISHING, ROAD TRIP ADVENTURES, and their
respective colophons are trademarks of Prima Communications, Inc.

Maps: Andrew Stone and Fraser Bridges
Travel research and editorial assistance: Joyce Williams

Library of Congress Cataloging-in-Publication Data

Bridges, Fraser.
  Southwest adventures / Fraser Bridges—1st ed.
    p. cm.
  Includes index.
  ISBN 0-7615-0134-7

  1. Southwest, New—Guidebooks.
  2. Automobile travel—Southwest, New—Guidebooks. I. Title.

  F785.3.B74 1995

  917.904'33—dc20   95-10894
                         CIP

95 96 97 98 99 AA 10 9 8 7 6 5 4 3 2 1
Printed in the United States of America

How to Order:
Single copies may be ordered from Prima Publishing, P.O. Box 1260BK,
Rocklin, CA 95677; telephone (916) 632-4400. Quantity discounts are
also available. On your letterhead, include information concerning
the intended use of the books and the number of books you wish
to purchase.

Contents

Contents

The Road Trip Adventures series of books were created to provide as much information as possible on the finest scenic drives and the destinations along these touring routes. The books are also meant to encourage you to leave your car, frequently, to enjoy the wonders of nature, and to soak up the atmosphere of the Southwest: the history, the land, and the people who live in the region today.

The Southwest is perfect for the driving traveler. What better way is there to experience the vastness of the deserts of the Southwest than to spend several hours driving through fields of saguaro cactus in Arizona, or the fragrant sage of Nevada? Stopping along the way to enter the desert and to look around is, for me, a necessity when crossing the open desert. Oddly enough, most of the scenic drives in this book on the Southwest involve some mountain driving. Newcomers find that the Southwest is a land of contrasts, not just flat desert.

For the sake of brevity, we have used several short forms and special terms throughout the book. B & B refers to bed and breakfast accommodations; either a B & B home in which the hosts offer overnight accommodation in their bedrooms, and breakfast, or a B & B inn, which is a more elaborate form of bed and breakfast place—usually a historic house that is operated as a small hotel and often offering such additional amenities as a hot tub and evening wine and cheese.

The term RV is used throughout the book as a general term covering all the varieties of self-propelled recreational vehicles, including motor homes, and pickups with campers attached. We try to warn RV drivers and people with trailers when campgrounds do not have suitable sites for long motor homes and trailers. Additionally, when directing you on a sideroad or backroad, we've made an effort to let you know when these roads cannot accommodate long vehicles and trailers.

Drives & Destinations

The book is divided into regional chapters, each covering a single state. In the cases of California and Utah, the book deals with the southern portion of these states.

Scenic Drives

Each chapter begins with a number of drives that explore the most exciting scenic highways and byways, including several that have been designated as national scenic byways. We have excluded almost all interstate highways and have concentrated on U.S. and state roads, which provide more scenery and services en-route.

Each drive description includes an overview that leads to the **Strip Map and Highway Log** for the drive, which is designed to be used while driving from Point A to Point B. We've tried to include all of the interesting places along the drive, including picnic parks, campgrounds, fishing spots, walking trails, and water-sport locations. You will also find the location of gas stations, cafes, motels, resorts, park and forest ranger stations, ferry landings, and commercial tourist enterprises such as theme parks, marinas and scenic boat rides.

Destinations

Following the drive descriptions are Destinations pages, which cover the major towns and cities on the drives as well as significant historic sites, state parks, and national parks and monuments. Some of these destinations are on the scenic drive, and some are a short drive from the scenic routes.

You'll find our recommendations on places to eat and a digest of things to do and see. Included is as much historical background as we could include to put your visit within a cultural and historical context. These pages are designed to help you in planning your trip—deciding what to see and how to budget your time.

Places to Stay

Each chapter ends with a selective list giving short descriptions of recommended motels, hotels, resorts, campgrounds, and RV parks. We have tried to find unique inns, lodges, guest ranches, and resorts that offer the traveler something different from the standard-issue chain motel. Cost ranges ($ to $$$+) are included for making reservation decisions.

Using This Travelguide

Recommendations

Places to Stay Pages

You'll find a broad selection of places to stay in each chapter. Whether you're traveling deluxe or on a tight budget, there are recommended resorts, motels, inns, lodges, guest ranches, RV parks, and private and public camping places.

Accommodations

Deluxe accommodations are found in unique and specialized resort hotels, inns, and lodges. We have included these but also have listed budget inns and resorts as well as moderately priced B & B homes.

The Southwest is blessed with resorts, old and new. From the five-star Wigwam Resort near Phoenix, a golfer's paradise, to the Rancho de los Caballeros at Wickenburg, the resorts of the West provide something for every vacation need. Many of these fine resort and guest ranch operations are included.

Price Ranges

The cost ranges for overnight accommodations are based on double occupancy and are marked with dollar signs:

- Inexpensive
  under 65 dollars ($)
- **Moderate**
  66–99 dollars ($$)
- **Deluxe**
  100 dollars and up ($$$)
- **Super Deluxe**
  you don't care about the cost ($$$+)

Camping

There are many campgrounds and RV parks in the Southwest. Public campgrounds (national, state, and county parks; national forests and BLM sites) often have minimal facilities, often with pit toilets and without hot water (sometimes without drinking water).

Private campgrounds and RV parks have hookups, hot water, showers, flush toilets, water piped to sites and electrical supply. Prices for government campgrounds range from $4 to $10. Privately owned facilities run from $10 to $20.

Generally, for the extra dollars, you trade natural solitude for comfort, convenience, and facilities such as recreation buildings, barbecue pits, stores, and children's playgrounds.

vii

Using This Travelguide

Recommendations

Places to Eat

The Southwest is food-lovers' heaven, particularly Arizona and New Mexico. In recent years, Southwest cuisine has set the standard for American dining, and if you're RVing or camping, you can purchase the fresh peppers and other ingredients along the way and cook it yourself.

Restaurants

Roadside cafes and taverns are listed in the highway logs. Other suggestions for dining, including restaurants which feature fine dining as well as cheaper places with local atmosphere and cuisine, are found in the Destinations pages.

Many of the more convenient restaurants are to be found in hotels or attached to motels along the highways, and these are identified in the hotel and motel listings found at the end of each state chapter.

On the other hand, we have made an effort to include the smaller, more interesting local eating places that serve regional cuisine. Throughout the Southwest there are many local restaurants that are standouts. These are listed under Where to Eat in the Destinations pages for each chapter.

A selection of neighborhood bars or taverns that serve meals is included. We have found that bars and saloons often serve simple and nourishing meals that are usually less expensive than the meals in standard restaurants.

Price Ranges

Three price ranges are listed for recommended places to eat:

• **Inexpensive**
4–6 dollars per entree for evening meals. ($)

• **Moderate**
7–11 dollars per entree for evening meals ($$)

• **Expensive**
more than 11 dollars per entree for evening meals ($$$)

Picnicking

As always, we encourage you to picnic along the way. Hundreds of scenic roadside picnic parks are listed in the highway logs. Many picnic areas are found in the state and county parks and campgrounds on or near the scenic routes. These are listed in the logs and also in the Destinations pages.

H aving grown up in a land far distant from the American Southwest, my first travels in Utah, Arizona, and New Mexico resulted in culture shock and astounding desert revelations.

In no other portion of North America is there the profound influence of three major cultures, nor is there the stupendous variety in geological history and the natural environment. From the high mountains—capped with glaciers—to the low desert, the Southwest provides vacation opportunities which are unmatched.

The recent emergence of Southwest cuisine as a dominant force in American cooking and eating is merely the latest of the gifts which this part of America has given the rest of America and the world. Earlier in the 1900s, eastern American artists flocked to the region, particularly to New Mexico, to absorb the confluence of culture that is so pervasive. In the nineteenth century, settlers and transients in Arizona created the modern myth of the Wild West. Much earlier, the ancient people called the Anasazi moved into the area of the Four Corners, creating amazing community structures which still remain as a major influence on home design throughout the region. Although their cultural traditions live on through the modern pueblo communities, the Anasazi are long gone, remaining for only a few hundred years but infusing the Southwest with a sense of place that is seen in places such as Santa Fe, Taos, and Albuquerque.

Into the midst of this longstanding native tradition came the Spanish. They tried, but failed, to destroy the cultural spirit of the Southwest natives. But the Spanish, too, left their cultural traditions, which have greatly influenced the modern Southwest. Their successors—from Mexico—added to the stew (figuratively and literally). The more recent arrivals have wisely chosen to honor these traditions.

1

The presence of nature—in all its variety—is also a hallmark of the Southwest. In the northeastern corner of New Mexico, the southernmost section of the Rocky Mountains slopes into the arid hills near Santa Fe, a haven for hiking, fishing, riding, and winter sports. The two deserts—high and low—range throughout the whole region, nurturing wildlife habitats of amazing variety. Picture the San Pedro River in Arizona, perversely flowing northward under the most prolific flyway in the American interior, providing sanctuary for hundreds of varieties of resident and traveling birds and offering birdwatchers unparalleled opportunities for observation.

Out in the desert, the saguaro stand tall. These huge cacti are only the largest of the scores of desert plants that provide shelter and food for yet another adaptive group of animals and birds.

And in between are the transition zones, which are found in the oddest places: pinyon pine forests that range from Nevada to Utah and New Mexico; far southern mountains (the San Francisco Range near Alamogordo) where snow dusts the peaks only a few miles from the white dunes and burning desert; the valley oaks in the hills of the Mule Mountains near Bisbee, seemingly transplanted from northern California but a native species in the Wild West country of Arizona.

And above them all, the ancient bristlecone pines—the oldest living things on earth—clinging to the peaks of the highest mountains in Nevada.

As with the other books in this series, our driving tours wander off the freeways as much as possible, onto roads that reveal the true beauty of the southwestern countryside and lead to outstanding outdoor adventure across this superb landscape. From the Rocky Mountains to the Sonoran, Chihuahuan, and Colorado deserts, there's a tour for everyone—lasting from a few hours (the Apache Trail and Benson to Bisbee) to several days (Death Valley, the Grand Canyon). There are the earth's mysteries to explore (Bryce Canyon, Arches National Park, and Sunset Crater) and a host of wildlife to see (Tombstone to Nogales, the North Rim of the Grand Canyon). The following pages outline some of the high points of a southwestern tour.

Introduction

Southwest Standouts

Great Vistas

1. Bryce Canyon (Utah)

A staggering group of several amphitheaters—not a canyon—Bryce exhibits centuries of work by rain, snow, and wind. The soft limestone has been eroded into spires, pinnacles, and fins, surrounded by the "canyon" walls, which have also been eroded into dramatic shapes. What is most striking here is the color of the rock, ranging from deep red to light salmon, accented in winter with caps of snow perching on the pinnacles.

Thirteen overlooks provide exceptional views of this geological fairyland, and an 18-mile drive leads along the rim. From two viewpoints (Rainbow Point and Yovimpa Point) one can view the attractions of the entire park. The park lies along the eastern edge of the Paunsaugunt Plateau in south-central Utah, on high country where, on most days, the views extend as far as 200 miles.

2. Grand Canyon (Arizona)

There is one Grand Canyon but there are two national park sections, separated by 12 miles (across the canyon) but by a road trip of 210 miles. The canyon is certainly the most majestic of America's natural attractions, as eons of natural history are revealed on the mile-deep walls carved by the Colorado River. Choosing which part of the park to visit takes some thinking and planning. If you like people—lots of people—and want to stay in modern lodgings or in a serviced RV park, the South Rim is for you. The North Rim offers something different: a quiet forest environment atop the Kaibab Plateau, wildlife, waterfalls, a grand old lodge, and a network of rim trails.

3. Monument Valley (Arizona)

Straddling the Utah/Arizona border, the monuments march across the landscape—giant icons of the Navajo Nation. Standing singly or in groups, the great rock pillars are sentinels in this vast, silent land. You may have seen Monument Valley in countless movies and TV commercials, but you never are able to get the same awe inspiring effect unless you're actually there.

Great Cities

4. Santa Fe (New Mexico)

Readers of *Conde Nast Traveler* magazine have voted Santa Fe the top city on their vacation dream lists. Drive, do not walk, to this wonderful community—of Indian, Spanish, and Mexican influences; of food which spans these cultures and more; of art and crafts; of the history of the Pueblo people and the immigrants who followed and made this city the regional capital of three nations. Add to all this the Santa Fe Opera, a year-round festival ambience, chili peppers, cathedrals, fine hotels, and B & B inns. You get the picture. If you've been there, you want to return. If you haven't visited Santa Fe, put it at the top of your own list.

5. Tucson (Arizona)

A truly civilized city on the Sonoran desert, like Santa Fe a city of different cultures but with a relaxed western lifestyle. Playing golf, guest ranching, museum going, visiting nearby nature preserves, driving along mountain roads, hiking canyon trails, you could easily spend a week or two of vacation activity in Tucson without retracing the same road.

6. Bisbee (Arizona)

This little old town in the Mule Mountains is one of the largely undiscovered gems of Arizona. Not far from the Mexico border, surrounded by groves of oak trees, Bisbee is the mining town that refused to die—unlike nearby Tombstone, which also refused to die and became a caricature of itself—but just kept on living as it did during its mining days at the turn of the century. Visitors can stay in an authentic Victorian hotel (or two), take a mine tour, visit little museums, and stroll through a cactus garden. It's a getaway without pretensions.

Ten Best Places

Natural Wonders

7. Great Basin National Park (Nevada)

The bristlecone pines say everything there is to say about fighting natural adversity and staying alive. For thousands of years, these stunted, dead-looking trees have weathered cold, the whipping winds, and the summer heat and have become amazingly adapted to holding on to life. The pines are near the top of Wheeler Peak, reached by a steep drive and then a hike. Under the mountain are the Lehman Caves, and surrounding the park is the high desert of eastern Nevada. Talk about an ecosystem!

8. Death Valley (California)

The mystery and the wonder of Death Valley are legend: searing heat in summer; the chill and flash floods of winter; the absolute aridity of it all! Death Valley is a prized destination for foreign visitors, but most Americans have never seen this amazing landscape of salt pan, sand dunes, foul springs (at Badwater, the lowest spot in America), brilliant colored mud formations and volcanic outcroppings, high mountains, and low desert. Death Valley is simply unforgettable.

9. Red Rocks at Sedona (Arizona)

Surrounding the town, the rock formations inspire wonder at the natural beauty and have generated a cultlike obsession that something more is happening here. You may take a Jeep tour to an energy vortex of your choice, but I recommend spending time gazing at the wonderful red rock canyons, pillars, and peaks. Just down the road is the verdant Verde Valley, with rivers and forests in contrast to the russet geology of Sedona.

Wild Places

10. Gila Wilderness (New Mexico)

The first-ever wilderness forest area to be proclaimed and protected by Congress, the Gila Wilderness offers silent hikes through mountain valleys and along cascading rivers to hot spring pools. You can also travel by horseback rides to remote campsites. Found in the Mogollon Mountains of southwestern New Mexico, this superb area is an outdoor-lover's Xanadu.

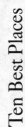

Ten Best Places

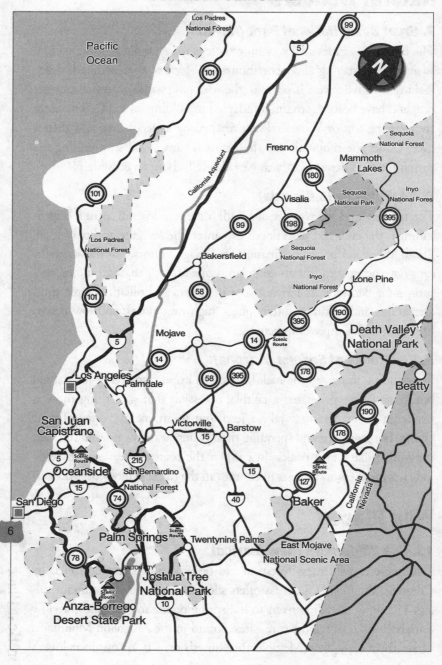

F our drives are featured here and all are routes to and from the major desert regions of California: the Mojave (high) and Colorado (low). All of the drives can be taken in one day, although you will probably wish to spend several days on each trip. We have not included coastal routes in this book, leaving the Pacific Coast to its own book of scenic drives. All four drives combine desert adventure with mountain scenery. The Palm Desert Drive leads through the **Santa Ana and San Jacinto ranges**, between San Juan Capistrano and Palm Springs. The Anza-Borrego Desert Drive crosses the **Vallecito Mountains** east of San Diego.

Three wonderful preserves offer a thorough exploration of California's prime desert regions. **Anza-Borrego Desert State Park** is at the far southern edge of the state on the Colorado Desert. Here, badlands lie near lush palm canyons and the open sandy desert, offering a bewildering variety of landscapes as well as the many desert plants and animals that survive in this harsh climate.

Joshua Tree National Park straddles the high and low deserts. This unique region of mountains, dry valleys, Joshua tree forests, and jumbled rock formations is only a short drive from the pleasure palaces and golf courses of Palm Springs.

The drive to **Death Valley** provides the ultimate desert experience, starting with a northward route beside the usually dry remains of the Amargosa River to Death Valley Junction, and then descending to the lowest place in the hemisphere—now a national park—with its scorching summer heat and amazingly colorful geological displays. Death Valley is at its most comfortable in the winter season but a summer drive through the valley offers a body- and mind-searing vacation experience you'll never forget.

Palm Desert Drive

San Juan Capistrano to Palm Springs

The normal fast route between the Los Angeles area and Palm Springs is Interstate 10, providing an easy 2-hour drive to the Coachella Valley. If you're prepared to spend an extra 90 minutes on the road, there's a much more interesting drive that crosses two mountain ranges through two national forests, with some of the most dramatic views to be found in southwestern California. Be prepared to explore sideroads to rustic mountain towns and to stop frequently at vista points and lakeside parks. Highway 74 West leads through the town of San Juan Capistrano for 2 miles, and then the scenic highlights begin.

Along the Drive

• Santa Ana Mountains

The **Cleveland National Forest** covers this small mountain range, and at the boundary the first climb begins. Just before leaving the valley, R. W. Caspers Wilderness Park, operated by the County, offers a leafy refuge. On the climb toward the summit, there are two forest campgrounds and a shady picnic park. The Lookout, a roadhouse at the summit, is a handy place for lunch.

The national forest offers a woodsy loop drive north from Hwy. 74. Begin the loop by turning onto **Long Canyon Road,** passing the El Cariso Picnic Area and Blue Jay Campground. Then turn east on **North Main Divide Road** to return to the highway.

The main route descends the eastern slope of the Santa Anas, providing several views of Lake Elsinore. The reservoir is a popular recreation area ringed with campgrounds and beaches.

• San Jacinto Mountains

After passing through Hemet—an unexciting crawl for several miles through strip development—we enter the **San Bernardino National Forest**. This is an area of mountain resorts, peaceful forest campgrounds, and rustic lodges, a favorite vacation area for Angelenos. The highway climbs through the mountains to the tiny crossroads community of Mountain Center. Five miles north of the junction (via Highway 243) is the resort town of **Idyllwild**. The side trip is time well spent and you may wish to continue north of Idyllwild to **Mt. San Jacinto State Park**, which boasts five campgrounds, including the Stone Creek site located on the highway north of Idyllwild. Farther north are several additional campgrounds, operated by the Forest Service in the **Black Mountain Scenic Area**, which includes Lake Fulmor (fishing and picnicking). The small community of Alandale is nearby. There are several trailheads near Idyllwild for trails that lead into the beautiful **San Jacinto Wilderness**.

Highway 74 continues east to the Keen Camp Summit. **Hurkey Creek County Park** offers campsites near the summit. There's a private RV park beside Lake Hemet, with a public picnic area nearby. This is the Garner Valley area. Thomas Mountain is located 4 miles off the highway, via Forest Road 6S13.

The **Pacific Crest Trail** has an access point off a parking lot beside the highway. Should time permit, a side trip along Santa Rosa Mountain Road is worthwhile. This forest route leads south from the highway for 9 miles to the **Santa Rosa Springs** area where there are three forest campgrounds. Near this junction is the trail to **Palm Canyon**, providing hiking opportunities with views of desert environments including several unique plant communities.

The main road descends into the **Santa Rosa Mountains National Scenic Area** after passing the road to the Pinyon Flats Campground. There's a wonderful view at the **Cahuilla Tewanet Vista Point,** to the south of the highway, where a short interpretive trail leads from a parking lot.

There are more pulloffs as the highway winds its way down the mountainside through Deep Canyon, with views of the Coachella Valley which lies just below. The highway passes the Bighorn Golf Course on the way into Palm Desert, one of the resort communities which line the Coachella Valley. Palm Springs is to the north, via Highway 111, with Indian Wells, Indio, Coachella, and the Salton Sea to the south.

Drives

Highway Log

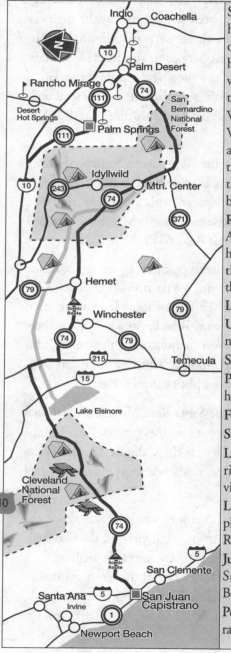

San Juan Capistrano Gas, motels, hotels, restaurants, stores. This city offers several attractions, including the historic mission. Capistrano Beach is west of the city with San Clemente to the south via Interstate 5.

We begin the drive to the Coachella Valley at the junction of Interstate 5 and Highway 74. Take Hwy. 74 east through town. The highway leads through the San Juan Creek Valley before beginning the climb.

Ronald W. Caspers Wilderness Park A county park, to the north of the highway. The route now crosses the Santa Ana Mountains, through the **Cleveland National Forest.**

Lower San Juan Picnic Area

Upper San Juan Campground To the north of the hwy. in a live oak grove.

San Juan Loop Trail North of hwy.

Picnic Area Under the trees across the highway from the ranger station.

Forest Campground

Summit (el. 2,666 ft.)

Lookout Roadhouse Good views and ribs. The road descends with more views of Lake Elsinore and the valley.

Lake Elsinore A popular recreation place with beaches, campgrounds and RV parks.

Junction–Interstate 15 Leads south to San Diego and north to San Bernardino.

Perris Town with gas, motels, cafes, railway museum, stores.

125 miles—3 hours

Junction–Highway 215 Take I-215 south briefly, to rejoin Hwy. 74 West.

Exit–Hwy. 74 East Take Hwy. 74 to continue the drive to Palm Desert and Palm Springs.

Junction–Hwy. 79 Leads east to Winchester, Murietta Hot Springs, and Interstate 15.

Hemet (el. 2,000 ft.) City with gas, motels, cafes, stores. There's a long and often slow drive along the highway through the town's business section. There's camping to the north of town on Warren Rd. (at the west end of Hemet).

The highway ascends from Hemet through the **San Bernardino National Forest.**

McCall Park Horse camping only.

Mountain Center Store and cafe.

Junction–Highway 243 This scenic route leads north to the rustic mountain resort town of **Idyllwild** (gas, cafes, motels, B & B homes, stores, forest ranger station). Idyllwild is 5 miles from the junction at Mountain Center and is an interesting place to visit (and to eat). Hwy. 243 continues past Idyllwild to the town of Banning & Interstate 10 (31 miles from Mountain Center).

Keene Creek Summit (el. 4,917 ft.)

Hurkey Creek Park Camping, for tenters & RVs, beside highway (county park).

Lake Hemet Private campground plus a forest picnic area beside reservoir.

Banana Trail To the south of the highway.

Junction–Hwy. 371 To Anza & San Diego (leads southwest).

Pacific Crest Trail Access just off the highway beside a parking lot in the burn area.

Santa Rosa Mtn. Road To Santa Rosa Springs (9 miles).

Palm Canyon Trail Via road north from the highway.

Pinyon Flats Campground Via backroad, 1,000 feet from highway to north. **Cactus Spring Trail**, via road to south.

Sugar Loaf Cafe Atop the mountain, with telephone.

Santa Rosa Mtns. Nat. Scenic Area The road winds along and down this mountain preserve.

Cahuilla Tewanet Vista Point 100 yards from a parking area. Picnic tables over the canyon.

Viewpoint At the pulloff, with the Coachella Valley on view, on the descent to Palm Desert.

Palm Desert One of the Coachella Valley towns, situated between Palm Springs and Indio. Hotels, motels, restaurants, golf, stores. To reach **Rancho Mirage**, **Palm Springs**, and **Desert Hot Springs**, drive northwest on Highway 111.

Anza-Borrego Desert Drive

Oceanside to the Salton Sea

Another of the mission towns of the California coast, Oceanside provides a launching point for a drive east on California Highway 78, through the Colorado Desert to the Salton Sea. The drive ends in Salton City (not a city) at Highway 86, which leads north toward Indio and Palm Springs and south through Brawley to the Mexican border and Mexicali. The major attraction is **Anza-Borrego Desert State Park**, a remarkable piece of geography that surrounds the town of Borrego Springs. This desert park is one of southern California's finest natural attractions and is one of its least-known treasures.

Along the Way

• Mission San Luis Rey

The town of Oceanside—with its foggy mornings and coastal breezes—is home to this old mission, which is tucked into a valley a few miles from the coast. This is the eighteenth of the 21 Spanish missions to be built in the 1700s and was founded by the Franciscan order. It is a national historic landmark, with a sunken garden, arched colonnade, and picnic grounds.

• Cleveland National Forest

Our drive to the low desert begins at the junction of Interstate 5 and California Highway 78. The first part of the trip is unexciting, traveling on a divided highway as far as the town of Escondido (25 miles from the coast). The drive becomes more interesting as Highway 78 passes through the San Pasqual Valley and the community of Ramona and then enters the forest. A ranger station is conveniently located at the eastern end of the small town.

• Julian

This a picturesque old community at the edge of the desert, with several historic buildings including the Julian Hotel, which has operated continuously since the Butterfield Stage stopped across the street almost a hundred years ago. Julian was a gold mining camp following discoveries in the area in 1870. The town boasted 15 hotels during its boom days, but only the Julian has survived. It's now an excellent B & B inn with a true Victorian ambience.

• Desert Hills

Highway 78 departs from Hwy. 79, which leads north to Lake Henshaw (an alternate route to Borrego Springs) and we continue on Hwy. 78, climbing again past **Cuyamaca Ranch State Park**, which features camping. Winding through a rocky, yucca-clad canyon, the highway enters the desert.

A historical side trip is available via County Road S-2, which leads south toward Interstate 8. Nineteen miles down this road is the site of one of the original Butterfield Stage stations. By driving north on the same road, you have yet another alternate route to Borrego Springs and Anza-Borrego Desert State Park.

• Anza-Borrego Desert State Park

By staying on Highway 78, we reach the turnoff to County Road S-3, which leads across Yaqui Pass, through the Borrego Valley and the town of Borrego Springs.

The park headquarters looks out onto a beautiful desert setting and a short self-guided trail leads through the flat dry landscape. You're likely to be accompanied by jackrabbits and more than a few lizards as you stop to look quietly at the desert plants. We suggest that, rather than return to Highway 78 for an uneventful drive to Brawley, you could drive due east from Borrego Springs, through the park on County Road S-22. The route leads through the Borrego Badlands, including the Arroyo Salado canyons, a prime feature of this stark region.

After proceeding through the badlands, a glint of white is apparent, and the strong odor of salt affects your nose. We're now about 10 miles from the Salton Sea, California's largest lake and a briny body of water indeed. Created by a diversion from the Colorado River, it's now a home for millions of tiny brine shrimp and little else. The highway comes to an end at the tiny crossroads of Salton City. Palm Springs is 46 miles to the north via Highway 111.

Highway Log

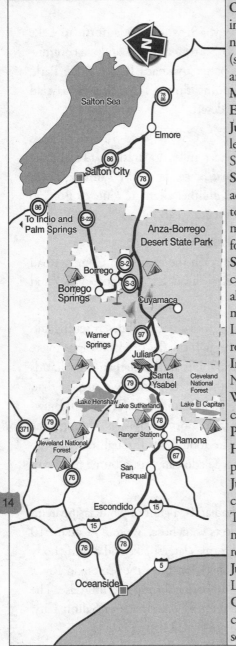

Oceanside The drive begins at the intersection of Interstate 5 and California Highway 78. The road is a divided (six-lane) roadway between Oceanside and Escondido, passing through **San Marcos** (16 miles from the start). **Escondido** is 25 miles from I-5.

Junction–Interstate 15 This freeway leads north to Riverside and south to San Diego.

San Pasqual Valley The highway runs across the valley, passing by the small town of **Ramona**, which has cafes, a motel, gas, stores and a ranger station for the Cleveland National Forest.

Santa Ysabel Small town with gas, cafes, store. **Hwy. 79** leads north, an alternate route to Borrego Springs (32 miles) via County Roads S-2 & S-22. Lake Henshaw is 11 miles along this road. Hemet is 61 miles.

Inaja Picnic Area In the Cleveland National Forest.

Wynola Springs A tiny village with a cafe and fruit market.

Pine Hills Road Leads south. **William Heise County Park** (campground and picnic area).

Julian Town (pop. 1,320) with gas, cafes, store, bar, deli, B & Bs, motel. The Julian Hotel is an historic landmark, now a B & B inn with a respected dining room.

Junction–Highway 97 Leads north to Laske Henshaw & south to Cuyamaca.

Cuyamaca Rancho State Park Located on Hwy. 97, about 20 miles south of Julian, with camping.

110 miles—2¼ hours

The road climbs into mountains again and then descends through a canyon into the desert.

Agua Caliente County Park 21 miles off the highway with camping. Closed from June 1 to September 1.

Junction–County Road S-2 Leads south to Ocotillo and Interstate 8. It passes the historic Butterfield Stage Station (19 miles) and Agua Caliente Springs. By driving north on Rd. S-2, you can take another desert route to Borrego Springs.

Anza-Borrego Desert State Park The highway crosses the park boundary as it runs through the canyon formed by San Felipe Creek.

Junction–County Road S-3 To Borrego Springs and the Anza-Borrego Park Headquarters. Turn north for the park facilities and Borrego Springs services. The park visitor center is 16 miles from the junction.

Tamarisk Grove Campground Just off the highway to the east.

Yaqui Pass (el. 1,750 feet) There is a camping (parking) area to the east of the highway, at the pass.

Borrego Springs The town is spread across the valley, with a golf resort at the southern end, and the county road continues northward to the business center of town. The road ends in a circle with a picnic park in the middle. Stores, cafes, motel, resort hotel, banks, RV park, and gas station.

Park Facilities There is a campground

in the Palm Canyon section of the park, a few minutes' drive from the visitor center.

East via County Road 22

Our drive continues for another 30 miles east via County Road S-22, passing through the Borrego Badlands. An alternate route to the Salton Sea is via County Road S-3 south, retracing our way in, and then along Highway 78 to Elmore and Brawley.

Our preferred route via S-22 provides a shorter drive to the Coachella Valley (Palm Desert, Palm Springs, etc.).

The road passes through bizarre and fascinating badlands, including the stark canyons of Arroyo Salado, which are seen to the south of the road. There is a campground at Arroyo Salado, suitable for tents and pickups.

Salton City Far from being a city, this community is basically a few stores, a cafe and a motel at the highway junction.

Junction–Highway 86 This is the route along the west shore of the briny Salton Sea, with Brawley to the south and the towns of the Coachella Valley to the north.

Indio is 23 miles from the junction.

Palm Springs is 46 miles from Salton City via Highway 86 and then Highway 111.

Joshua Tree Circle Drive

Palm Springs to Joshua Tree National Park & Return

As a result of the temblors that shook the Yucca Valley/Landers area in 1992, this drive provides an extra attraction—earthquake dodging. Seriously, there are few (if any) reminders of the great earthquakes of 1992 in either Yucca Valley or Landers, and even though small aftershocks have rumbled through the Mojave, Yucca Valley residents live a normal life, apparently getting their "sea legs" as time progressed. Waiting for another aftershock is the least exciting part of a tour of Joshua Tree National Park.

Along the Way

• Desert Hot Springs

There are two ways to exit Palm Springs on your way to the Joshua Tree National Monument. One route uses Interstate 10 west for a short distance before catching Highway 62. The alternate route leads through Desert Hot Springs via Indian Canyon Drive (from downtown Palm Springs). This route provides views of the northern end of the Coachella Valley and Palm Springs. The pools of the Desert Hot Springs Hotel aren't hard to take, either.

• Joshua Tree (the town)

The small town of Joshua Tree lies just 9 miles east of Yucca Valley. Park Boulevard leads south from town to the national park boundary and enters the park at the west entrance. You can continue through the park on Quail Springs Road to the Hidden Valley area and continue on a loop drive through the Queen Valley, driving north to Twentynine Palms. This is a shorter loop, which can be accomplished from Palm Springs in a morning's drive. Back on Highway 62 east of Joshua Tree, Indian Cove Road provides another entrance to the park, although this is a short road that ends at the Indian Cove campground and picnic area.

• Twentynine Palms Oasis

Reaching the town of **Twentynine Palms**, we turn onto **Utah Trail**, which becomes the main north/south route through the national park. The **29 Palms Oasis** (Oasis of Mara) is located beside the

California

park visitor center. A short walk will show you the palms remaining from the 29 which ringed the long-time Indian oasis.

• Joshua Tree National Park

To take the recommended drive, enter the park at the 29 Palms gate and drive south along Utah Trail until reaching the junction of the road to the Queen Valley (a loop to Joshua Tree). Turn west onto this road to drive by the Jumbo Rocks formations and Ryan Mountain. There are campgrounds here, beside the first of the Joshua tree forests.

Turn left at the next junction (to Keys View) and drive through Lost Horse Valley. Atop this valley are the remains of the old Lost Horse Mine which is reached by taking a backroad for 1 mile and a steep walking trail for 2 miles. The fullest of the Joshua tree forests is located on both sides of the road in this valley. At the end of the road is **Keys View**. Above the parking area is a promenade from which you'll catch wonderful views of the Coachella Valley and the San Bernardino Mountains.

The drive is retraced through the Lost Horse and Queen valleys, meeting Utah Trail and turning south for the descent to the Colorado Desert. Along the way into the low desert, the road passes through a transition zone, where the plant species and rock formations change. The **Cholla Cactus Garden** is seen to the west of the road at the southern edge of this transition zone. A short self-guiding trail wanders through the "garden," showing typical plants and (sometimes) animals of the Colorado Desert. Park rangers suggest stopping and quietly observing lizards, rabbits, and other animal life in the observation circle around you.

The highway continues to descend, past the **Ocotillo Patch** to the Cottonwood Visitor Center, where you'll find a campground and sheltered picnic area beside the small **Cottonwood Oasis**. **Lost Palms Oasis** is found at the end of a 4-mile hike through a series of desert washes. Contained in a canyon, this is the largest of the oases in the park. Interstate 10 is just south of the park gate for the 54-mile return drive to the Coachella Valley and Palm Springs.

17

Drives

Highway Log

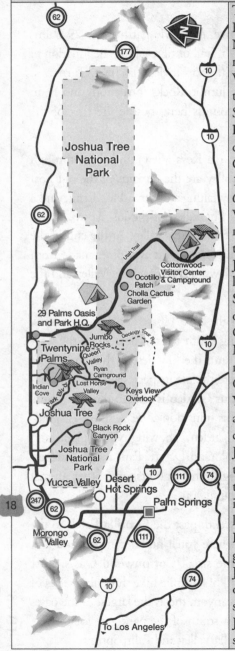

This drive provides a day-trip from Palm Springs, entering Joshua Tree National Park at the town of Twentynine Palms. We take a side trip to Keys View Overlook and then descend to the low desert, returning to Palm Springs on Interstate 10.

Palm Springs Beginning the drive in downtown Palm Springs, take Indian Canyon Drive northwest to Interstate 10. Drive west on I-10 to the Highway 62 exit and drive north toward Yucca Valley and 29 Palms. For an alternate route, continue on Indian Canyon Dr. to Hwy. 62.

Junction–Pierson Blvd. This road leads east to the town of **Desert Hot Springs**, a resort town that lies on a hill overlooking Palm Springs and the Coachella Valley.

Morongo Valley This roadside community is spread out for several miles. Gas, cafes, stores.

Yucca Valley (el. 3,334 ft.) This town is a regional trading center, with gas, cafes, stores, and motels.

Junction–Highway 247 Leads north to Landers, Lucerne Valley, and Victorville (66 miles). There's an interesting series of rock formations on the hill leading north from the town. **Black Rock Canyon** is a national park campground, 5 miles south via Joshua Lane.

Joshua Tree Small town, 9 miles east of Yucca Valley. Gas, cafes, B & B inn, stores.

Junction–Park Blvd. This road leads south through Joshua Tree National

177 miles—4½ hours

Park, providing a short loop drive through the park, returning to the highway at 29 Palms. We continue east for a more complete tour of the park.

Junction–Indian Cove Road A national park campground is located south of town.

Junction–Canyon Road Leads south to 49 Palms Oasis, one of several oases in the park. A 1.5-KM trail leads through the oasis.

29 Palms Town, 15 miles east of Joshua Tree. Gas, cafes, motels.

Junction–Utah Trail This is the main north/south road through Joshua Tree National Park. The **park head-quarters and visitor center** is located beside the 29 Palms Oasis (Oasis of Mara). There is a short trail around the palms that remain from the old Indian oasis. We take this road south for 10 miles.

Junction–Quail Springs Road Turn right and drive west through the Queen Valley, home of one of the park's Joshua tree forests. Park features on the 16-mile side trip are described below.

Side Trip to Keys View

Jumbo Rocks There are two picnic areas (on both sides of the road) and a campground in this area filled with rock formations.

Geology Tour Road This 4WD road leads south through the park for 18 miles (29 KM), connecting with Dillon

Road which goes south to I-10. This dirt road provides splendid views of the desert landscape.

Queen Valley The road leads through the forest at an elevation of 4,460 feet.

Ryan Campground At the base of Ryan Mountain. The main trail through the park from Black Rock Canyon is found here.

Junction–Rd. to Keys View Turn left (south) for the lookout.

Lost Horse Valley (el. 4,384 ft.) Another forest. The old Lost Horse Mine is reached via a 1-mile road and a 2-mile hike.

Keys View Overlook Walk up the steps from the parking area to the viewpoint for fine views of the Coachella Valley and the San Bernardino Mtns., including Mt. San Gorgonio.

Back on Utah Trail

We now drive south toward I-10, descending through the park to the low desert. There are two campgrounds (Belle and White Tank) just south of the junction. The **Cholla Garden** & **Ocotillo Patch** are found to the west.

Cottonwood Campground and Picnic Area Lost Palms Oasis is four miles from the visitor center. Continue to Interstate 10 for the return drive to the Coachella Valley, Indio and Palm Springs.

Death Valley Drive

Baker to Beatty (Nevada)

Billions of years of history have made Death Valley what it is today: an untamed land of salt pan—200 square miles of it—with outlandish colors in its hills and mountains; shifting sand dunes, dry creeks, and washes; salty springs, rugged, steep mountains; searing summer temperatures; and the lowest spot in the Western Hemisphere. Yet in all of this desert desolation, Death Valley has a thriving plant and animal life that has adapted to this land of extremes. Over the years, I have met and talked to many Californians, and most have never visited Death Valley. Yet, this amazing landscape should be on everyone's list of places to visit—in the cooler winter (the high season here) and—yes—in the 120-degree summer months when visiting the valley is a true adventure.

Along the Way

Our suggested drive through the valley hits most of the high (and low) points and short side trips will take you to all of the valley's attractions. To get there, we tour the equally amazing Amargosa Desert with its trailer communities and famed opera house.

- **The Mojave**

    Our preferred route begins at **Baker**, south of Death Valley at the junction of Interstate 15 (the short route from the L.A. and Las Vegas areas) and California Route 127. The road leads northward, past long-dry lakes and into Inyo County just south of Tecopa. This hamlet and the neighboring hot springs community are two of the desert trailer villages that see a flood of RV people and trailerites during the winter months—attracted by the winter warmth and the hot springs. There's a large county RV park across the road from the public hot springs pools, and there are several private RV parks with their own hot springs facilities.

- **The Amargosa**

    So far, the drive has been over the Mojave Desert, through a series of washes. Eight miles north of Tecopa is the small community of Shoshone, where you come across the first vestiges of the Amargosa

River, at least what is left of it. Now a series of desert washes leading north to south on both sides of the highway, the once-mighty Amargosa is a dry reminder of an era when the climate was dramatically different from the dusty present. An alternate route into Death Valley leads west from Shoshone (69 miles to Furnace Creek and the park visitor center).

- **Death Valley Junction**

  What used to be a mining town is now a basic white-colonnaded motel attached to the Amargosa Opera House. Here dancer Marta Becket performs her one-woman show as she has done for decades, on most nights during the winter season and on Saturdays during the summer.

Death Valley

Our drive now turns to the west via Highway 190, past Pyramid Peak (el. 1,703 ft.) to the boundary of Death Valley National Park. The route quickly descends into the valley through Furnace Creek Wash. From the turnoff to Dante's View, a sideroad climbs the Black Mountains for the most impressive overview of Death Valley.

Highway 190 continues down the wash, past Zabriskie Point with its famed yellow mud badlands, and along the one-way loop drive through Twenty Mule Team Canyon. The highway reaches the valley floor, passing the Furnace Creek Inn, a deluxe resort hotel at the junction with Highway 178. For park details, see page 40.

There are two junctions that provide access to Beatty, Nevada. The southern junction offers the Beatty Cutoff, saving several miles of driving farther north in the valley. Highway 190 continues north for 7 miles before turning east beside the sprawling sand dunes, passing the lodge and other services at Stovepipe Wells. The highway leads into the Owens Valley and runs to Lone Pine. However, for further exploration of Death Valley, take the road north for another 32 miles to Scotty's Castle, the strange ranch house at the extreme north end of the valley. Back at the main junction near Stovepipe Wells, Route 374 leads 27 miles north through Daylight Pass, past Rhyolite—a ghost town—to Beatty, Nevada.

Drives

Highway Log

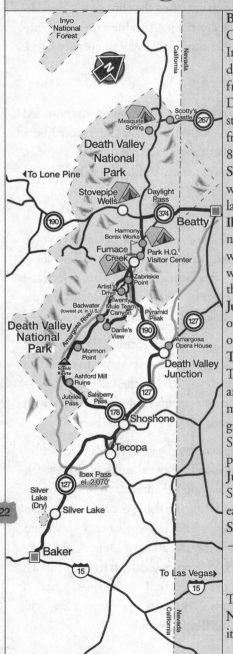

Baker Gas, cafe, store. This southern California town lies at the junction of Interstate 15 and Highway 127. Our drive begins by taking Hwy. 127 north from Baker toward Shoshone and Death Valley Junction. There is an ice store just north of town. The distance from Baker to Death Valley Junction is 85 miles.

Silver Lake This dry lake bed to the west is the first of several such former lakes along the route.

Ibex Pass (el. 2,070 feet) The highway now descends through a series of desert washes in the Greenwater Valley. The washes are subject to flooding during the short "rainy" season.

Junction–Old Spanish Trail This road offers a short loop drive to the village of **Tecopa** (4 miles) and then left to **Tecopa Hot Springs** (another 2 miles). There's gas, a store, a cafe, a laundry, and a bar in Tecopa, and the county maintains pools and a large campground and RV park at Tecopa Hot Springs. There are also private hot pools and RV parks.

Junction–Hwy. 178 Just south of Shoshone, this backroad leads northeast to Pahrump, Nevada (27 miles).

Shoshone Gas, cafe, store, motel.

Alternate Route into Death Valley

This road leads into **Death Valley National Park,** entering the valley near its southern end. **Badwater**, the lowest spot in America, is 55 miles. **Furnace Creek** is 72 miles. Because this route is long, crosses two mountain passes, and leads north almost the full length of the valley, we choose to drive further north on Hwy. 127. However, if it's not too hot, you may wish to take this scenic road into Death Valley.

Back on Highway 127

Amargosa River The channels of this mostly dry river are seen beside the highway as the route leads toward Eagle Mountain.

Death Valley Junction Now with only a motel and the famous Amargosa Opera House, this is where you turn west to enter Death Valley. Highway 127 continues north to Stateline (gas), Lathrop Wells, Nevada, and Highway 95.

Junction–Highway 190 Take this road west toward Death Valley, through the northern edge of the Greenwater Valley. Furnace Creek (the park headquarters) is 29 miles.

Death Valley National Park Just beyond the boundary are an information kiosk and toilet. Park fees are taken at the Furnace Creek Visitor Center, next to the ranch resort.

Road to Dante's View This road leads to the left and up to the top of the Black Mountains for a truly impressive view of Death Valley and other mountain ranges to the west. It's best to do this drive in the early morning if you're a summer traveler.

Twenty Mule Team Canyon This one-way loop road leads through an old borax mining area where transport was powered by the renowned mule teams.

Zabriskie Point The famous yellow mud badlands offer eerie views at any time of day but are best at daybreak or nightfall.

The road descends through the Furnace Creek Wash, past the **Furnace Creek Inn** (not open during the hottest months).

Junction-Hwy. 178 This road leads south to several attractions, including Badwater, Mormon Point, and the Ashford Mill ruins, and on through Jubilee and Salsberry passes to Shoshone.

Furnace Creek Facilities The Furnace Creek Ranch, Furnace Creek Inn, golf course, and park visitor center are located here, with the visitor center north of the entrance to the ranch. There are lodgings at the inn and ranch, plus a store, restaurants, ice, pool, camping, and RV parking.

Junction–Beatty Cutoff This is the short route to Beatty, Nevada, meeting Hwy. 374 west of Daylight Pass.

Junction-Hwy. 190 Leads to the east across the valley to Stovepipe Wells & on to Lone Pine.

Junction–Hwy. 374 To Beatty, Nevada (27 miles) through Daylight Pass and past Rhyolite ghost town.

23

Other Death Valley Drives

• Highway 178—South to Badwater

This road leads south from the junction with Highway 190 within view of Furnace Creek Inn. This trip is a must, for it leads to the lowest piece of land in the United States and the lowest driveable point in the Americas. Badwater is a set of brackish pools fed by a spring and set on salty flats that are unbearably hot on the feet during the summer months. The route also provides access to several other points of interest including Artist's Drive (a loop tour with brilliantly colored volcanic rock on display), Mormon Point, and the ruins of Ashford Mill. This highway exits the national park near Jubilee Pass and runs east to join Highway 127 near Shoshone.

• To Scotty's Castle

This route leads up the valley from the junction with Highway 190 near the sand dunes and Stovepipe Wells. Between Furnace Creek and the junction lie the remains of the Harmony Borax Works—the first borax mining operation in the valley—and a salt marsh. There is access to the dunes just north of the Hwy. 190 intersection. The road continues north to two major points of interest: Ubehebe Crater and Scotty's Castle. The crater is an impressive sight with a rim 5 miles in diameter and is accompanied by several smaller craters. The eccentric Scotty's Castle was built as a vacation ranch by a wealthy easterner but was largely occupied by Walter Scott, a garrulous drifter who became known as "Death Valley Scotty." Tours of the building are provided daily. The round trip from Furnace Creek to Scotty's Castle covers 120 miles.

• Highway 190—West to Lone Pine

This is an alternative entrance route to Death Valley, with the highway linking the valley to the eastern Sierra Nevada and the Owens Valley. Past Stovepipe Wells, the route climbs over the Panamint Range and plunges into the Panamint Valley. It then climbs again, over the Inyo Range, and joins Highway 395 beside the dry "shores" of the late, lamented Owens Lake. A shortcut via County Road 136 leads directly to the town of Lone Pine.

California

Anza-Borrego Desert

nza-Borrego Desert Following the winter rains, the southern desert is carpeted with tiny flowers, and then the cacti come into bloom. The largest state park in the Lower 48, Anza-Borrego's 600,000 acres include mountains higher than 6,000 feet, palm-covered canyons, badland areas, and some of the most wondrous desert wildlife in all of California. The park is less than 2 hours' drive from San Diego and 3½ hours from Los Angeles. The park is the main feature of our scenic drive, which starts in Oceanside, north of San Diego, and ends at the Salton Sea.

The town of Borrego Springs is surrounded by the park and is the main access point for the park's attractions. The **State Park Visitor Center** is located at the north end of Palm Canyon Drive, the town's main street (Road S-22). This is definitely the place to begin a visit to the park. Children will enjoy reading the *Junior Naturalist* handbook, available here, and a short trail leads through the desert in front of the visitor center, which is buried in the desert scape. Because of the intense heat of the summer months, the park's interpretive program starts each year in November and ends during May. However, the park facilities are open year-round.

Anza-Borrego is one of the nation's foremost fossil and bone yards. Thousands of fossils have been collected in the park area and are now catalogued and stored in the fossil library. Most are fossils of small (and some very, very small) animals. However, more than 100 species of large animals have been unearthed in the park, including the giant ground sloth, bison, llama, ancient dog, American lion, zebra, horse, dromedary camel, mammoth, and many reptiles. These animals once thrived in what is now the Borrego Badlands, where waving seas of grass grew to the edge of an ancient sea.

Tours of the Daniel Laboratory and the fossil library are conducted during the prime season. A score of other interpretation events take place on a regular basis, including discovery hikes to the Coyote Badlands, at the 17 Palms Oasis, and through Box Canyon and several driving tours to more remote locations accessible only by 4WD vehicles.

What to See & Do
• Scenic Areas & Park Trails

Hiking is a major activity in the park and there are several excellent trails to explore. Many of the park's million visitors each year take off across the ridges and through the more remote canyons. If you're considering backpacking in the open desert, you should notify the visitor center staff of your intentions.

The most popular section of the park is the **Borrego Palm Canyon** area, which has its own campground. A trail (3 miles round trip) leads through the canyon to a native palm grove and a stream which runs year-round. A brochure is available for this hike and a slightly longer alternate return trail provides fine views of the Borrego Valley.

The **Tamarisk Grove Area**, 13 miles from the visitor center, contains additional trails including the short (1-mile) Cactus Loop Trail which provides panoramic views of San Felipe Wash and nearby mountains. This trail starts across the road from the Tamarisk Grove Campground. Another trail leads .8 mile to Yaqui Well, a desert water hole that frequently attracts wildlife.

The **Blair Valley** and **Bow Willow** areas of the park are located southeast of Borrego Springs on County Road S-2, south of Highway 78. Blair Valley is a 28-mile drive from town, while Bow Willow is another 27 miles south. There are three short trails in Blair Valley including a hike to the remains of an old home on top of Ghost Mountain, where two writers, Marshal and Tanya Smith, lived and raised a family during the 1930s and '40s. Another trail (Morteros) leads to granite boulders, where one can see Indian grinding holes. The morteros in the rocks are about 10 inches deep and 3 inches across. The third trail in this area (Pictograph) leads 1 mile to pictographs painted on a boulder by Diegfueño Indians. Farther along the trail is Smuggler Canyon and a waterfall with fine views of the Vallecito Valley and a restored stage station.

Two trails in the Bow Willow area lead to Mountain Palm Springs Canyon, which has a pygmy palm grove and a group of elephant trees. The second trail leads along the north fork of the canyon to more palms including another pygmy grove. A map of this area is available at the visitor center and at the Bow Willow Campground.

• Campgrounds

There are three developed campgrounds plus a group campground. There are additional primitive campgrounds. Of the two developed car campgrounds, **Borrego/Palm Canyon** has an RV and trailer hookup campground that does not permit tent camping. There is also a campground without hookups in this area. **Tamarisk Grove Campground**, south of Borrego Springs, has tent and RV camping with no hookups. Four other primitive campgrounds accommodate trailers and RVs, and three are suitable for tents and pickup campers. Unlike most parks, this park has an open wilderness camping policy.

One of the benefits for tent campers (and car campers as well) is the park's open camping policy. It's possible to drive along a sideroad, park beside the road, and walk into the desert to camp. Reservations for open camping are not required. You just seek out a place and set up camp for an unusual, private, overnight experience.

To make reservations for the developed campgrounds, phone 800-444-7275. When making reservations, you'll save time by using the following campground designations:

- Borrego/Palm Canyon Hookup Area
- Borrego/Palm Canyon Non-Hookup Area
- Tamarisk Grove Campground
- Vern Whitaker Horseman's Camp (located 8 miles north of town in Coyote Canyon).

Destinations

• Borrego Springs

This desert town is what many people say Palm Springs was like 40 years ago, before the transformation to chic took place. The business section of town is built around and near a traffic circle, which features a park with palm trees and a picnic area, close to the state park headquarters and visitor center.

Borrego Springs is a relaxed retirement and resort town with several good hotels including the deluxe **La Casa Del Zorro** and the slightly less expensive **Palm Canyon Resort**. Summers are very hot (daytime average of 106 degrees during August, and 75 degrees at night). Winter and spring temperatures are wonderfully comfort-able—day and night. The park provides a reason to stay in Borrego Springs, and, other than the park, there is little for a visitor to do in town except enjoy the resort facilities, which include pools and tennis courts. But who's complaining? There's also an executive 18-hole golf course at the **Roadrunner Golf and Country Club**, a mobile home community.

You can also rent a home in town for anywhere from $145 to $240 per day. There are several sets of luxury condominium accommo-dations that are available to travelers. These include Villas Borrego and Rams Hill, which has a championship 18-hole golf course, a good restaurant, and a lounge. Palm Canyon Resort has both supe-rior hotel accommodations and a large RV park, complete with swimming pool and bar and grill. See the Places to Stay pages for information on Borrego Springs resorts, motels, and private camp-grounds.

While in the Anza-Borrego area, you should explore the old mining town of **Julian**, located at the junction of Highways 78 and 79. The last remaining hotel (of 15 operating during the gold rush days) is the Julian Hotel, still in operation as a quaint, Victo-rian-era B & B inn.

Where to Eat

The dining facilities in **La Casa Del Zorro** are excellent, including pool-side service and barbecues (**$$ to $$$**). I usually avoid airport restaurants, but Borrego Springs has a good one, the **Whifferdil,** which serves lunch and dinner Tuesday through Sunday, with breakfast served on Sunday as well. There is a lounge beside the restaurant with fine mountain views ($$ to $$$). The **El Mexicali Cafe #3**, at 747 Palm Canyon Drive (closed Tuesdays) serves up Mexican dishes and seafood ($ to $$). **George & Ernie's Little Italy,** in The (shopping) Center, serves Italian and American dishes ($$ to $$$).

Barstow

A city of 60,000 people, Barstow has from its founding been a railroad town. In 1888, the Santa Fe Railroad arrived in town and a splendid station was built. The town was named after the president of the Santa Fe Railroad, William Barstow Strong, and it soon became a service center for the gold and silver mines that surrounded the community.

Before all this feverish activity in the late 1800s, the Mojave Desert had been occupied by Indian tribes who (2,000 years ago) lived beside the immense lakes that covered most of the Mojave. Today, the landscape is dry, and Barstow is a service center at the junction of Interstate Highways 15 and 40, on the routes between Los Angeles, Las Vegas, and Flagstaff. The station has been converted into a restaurant and shops.

What to See & Do
- **California Desert Information Center**
  Anyone interested in exploring the region's natural attractions should head first to this multi-agency center, located on Barstow Ave. just a block north of I-40. Operated by the Bureau of Land Management (BLM) and the local chamber of commerce, this center has displays of desert life and much information on the Mojave Desert: campgrounds, old wagon trails, wildlife, and natural history. You'll find a full range of maps, brochures, books, and desert guides.

- **Calico**
  The second place to visit is Calico ghost town. Walter Knott, founder of Knott's Berry Farm, provided the money to restore this

29

Destinations

old mining camp, now a San Bernardino County regional park. In the 1800s, Calico was a bustling silver town. Contained within a picturesque canyon, Calico boasts wooden sidewalks, shops, restaurants, and tunnels to be explored in Maggie's Mine. A railroad car takes visitors to mine workings north of the ghost town. There's a modern campground and RV park with 110 units in a wooded canyon near Calico, where hookups are available. The park is open every day except Christmas, and parking costs $4. There are special festival-style events on Palm Sunday weekend and a Mother's Day weekend music celebration. Columbus Day in October features a Wild West parade and gunfights, and on the first weekend in November there's an Old West celebration and Indian fine arts show.

The most prominent historic site in Barstow is the original Harvey House building, across the street from the old train station. Railroad riders streamed from the trains to be served by the famous Harvey Girls, a special breed of western pioneer.

• On the Desert

North of town, via Ft. Irwin Road, is **Rainbow Basin**, where well-preserved fossils are found on ancient lake beds. The basin has been turned into a highly colored landscape, eroded by wind and water over millions of years. Fossil collecting is prohibited now and the area is a national natural landmark. A narrow 4-mile loop drive winds through the basin. The road is suitable for small vehicles only; not for trailers and motor homes.

The BLM campground at **Owl Canyon** (1 mile east of the loop road) is a fine place to stop for a picnic. There are several developed campgrounds in the BLM country surrounding Barstow (check with the Desert Information Center), with private RV parks in the Calico ghost town area.

Where to Eat

The historic **Santa Fe Railroad Station** is now a shop and restaurant complex, in downtown Barstow. Menus are varied ($ to $$$).

California

Coachella Valley/Palm Springs

California's des0ert playground is the Coachella Valley, the narrow strip of land just east of the Little San Bernardino Mountains. An easy 2-hour drive from either Los Angeles or San Diego, Palm Springs and its equally ritzy neighbors provide a warm, dry refuge for the rich and famous during winter months, with more golf courses per acre than any other urban area in the world (more than 80 in the valley). The area is also highly landscaped with row upon row of fan palms and lush evergreen shrubbery. All of this takes a lot of water, which comes from a large aquifer lying under the valley, some of it transported to the surface by the springs that brought native Indians to the area in the first place.

The city of **Palm Springs** lies at the northwestern end of the valley, with **Desert Hot Springs** located on a ledge to the north of Palm Springs, nestled against the slopes of the Little San Bernardino Mountains. East of Palm Springs are the neighboring communities lying along Highway 111: **Cathedral City**, **Rancho Mirage**, **Palm Desert**, **Indian Wells**, **La Quinta**, **Indio**, and **Coachella**. All except Coachella are golfers' paradises, with Palm Desert and Indian Wells just about wall-to-wall with championship courses, many of them linked to resort hotel operations. The famed PGA West course is in La Quinta, and the most exclusive course of them all is ambassador and philanthropist Walter Annenberg's huge estate at the corner of Bob Hope Drive and Frank Sinatra Drive. The spread includes a strictly private, nine-hole course outfitted with 18 tees. The Annenberg house sprawls over an area of about 35,000 square feet.

All of this opulence would lead one to believe that the Coachella Valley is only for the very rich. Well, it is possible to bring your trailer or RV into the valley and hook up for a week or more, and it's possible to stay in a souped-up Motel 6 (with pool) for $40 a night for two. Most visitors stay in the many fancy resort hotels, which cost $120–$250 for two people, per night. Some of the hotels attached to golf courses include the Westin Mission Hills Resort in Rancho Mirage (at Dinah Shore and Bob Hope Drives), surrounded by the deluxe Mission Hills Country Club with two courses, and the Marriott Rancho Las Palmas Resort in Palm Springs. There are some bargains including the Spa Hotel and Mineral Springs in downtown Palm Springs, boasting the original hot springs that made the area famous. The hotel's rates range from $55 in summer months to $115 in the winter season. Families with children should consider a stay at the Oasis Waterpark, which has condo-style accommodations and a huge waterslide park on Gene Autry Trail. There's even a clothing-optional motel in Palm Springs, the Treehouse Too on North Palm Canyon Drive. For Palm Springs and Coachella Valley accommodations, see the Places to Stay listings starting on page 57.

For additional information on Coachella Valley attractions, hotels, golf courses, and a myriad of other things to do and see, phone or visit the Palm Springs Visitors Information Center at 2781 N. Palm Canyon Drive, (619) 778-8418. The central hotel reservation number is 800-34-SPRINGS.

Things to See & Do
• Coachella Valley Preserve
In the Indio Hills lies one of the most amazing and accessible desert nature preserves in California. This unique ecosystem was created by its fortunate geography. Lying atop the San Andreas Fault, it is the last undisturbed watershed in the Coachella Valley. From deep in the earth, water seeps to the surface through the fault line, providing a constantly bubbling supply of nourishment for the palms in three oases, the largest of which is the Thousand Palms oasis. Also nestled in the hills are the Willis and Indian Palms Oases. Together they contain more than 1,200 California fan palms along with marsh grasses and other vegetation. The desert that surrounds the oases is seen in sharp contrast.

The dunes are ever-shifting as strong winds whistle down from the Little San Bernardino Mountains, bringing gravel and sand into the hills along wide alluvial fans. The constant supply of new sand nourishes an astonishing diversity of life.

The preserve was established in 1984 when The Nature Conservancy purchased 1,920 acres, including Thousand Palms Oasis. Government agencies joined the movement to acquire the remainder of the preserve. The area comprises two major habitats: palm

California

oasis woodland and blow-sand fields created by periodic flooding that washes rainwater down the fans through Thousand Palms Canyon. The primary plants in the preserve (other than the palms) are creosote bush, smoke tree, burrobush, encelia, and desert lavender. One hundred eighty animal species reside in the preserve including birds—both resident and migratory. The Coachella fringe-toed lizard is an endangered species. Other animals include the Coachella round-toed squirrel and the giant palm-boring beetle. Birds include the greater roadrunner, American questrel, northern and hooded orioles, phoebes, gnatcatchers, and several varieties of owl: burrowing, great horned, long-eared, barn, and screech. Mammals range from the coyote and deer to pocket mice, bobcats and bighorn sheep.

The McCallum trail system winds through the preserve to the Thousand Palms Oasis, then passes along a ridge and through a wash to McCallum Grove. The one-way distance is about a mile. On this short walk, you'll see the San Andreas fault system at work, providing water to the desert plants and animals, plus lots of desert reptiles, desert pupfish in a pond and the wonderful palm environment. The endangered pupfish are not native to this area. They exist naturally in only two small streams which feed into the Salton Sea and were placed here to save them from extinction.

• Museums & the Arts

Besides golfing, there are many attractions throughout the valley that are recreational and also educational. Most of the Palm Springs attractions are included in the pages on that city. Other highlights include the **Palm Springs Desert Museum** (101 Museum Drive, Palm Springs), which has a permanent collection as well as changing exhibitions.

The **Living Desert** (47-900 Portola Ave. in Palm Desert) is a desert animal park whose attractions include botanical gardens, displays of Indian culture, hiking trails, and animals including birds of prey and endangered species such as bighorn sheep, Grevy's zebra, and the Arabian onyx.

Those interested in warfare, particularly desert warfare, will enjoy visiting the **General Patton Memorial Museum**, located off Interstate 10, about 30 miles east of Indio at Chiriaco Summit. The site was the entrance to the World War Two desert training center set up and commanded by General George Patton prior to his departure for the decisive North African campaign. Open hours are 9 AM to 6 PM, daily.

The **McCallum Theatre for the Performing Arts** in the Bob Hope Cultural Center (73-000 Fred Waring Dr., Palm Desert) has a full range of concerts and other events during the year.

• Outdoor Activities

Summer months feature Class-A baseball with the **Palm Springs Angels**, affiliated with Gene Autry's California Angels (major league) team. Gene Autry is a prominent name in the area.

Horse riders will enjoy taking a trail ride from the **Ranch of the 7th Range**, located behind the PGA West Golf Club in La Quinta (off Ave. 58). The trails lead to panoramic views of the Coachella Valley and the Salton Sea, and through the foothills of the Santa Rosa Mountains. Evening events at the ranch include hayrides, western music, and dancing.

Where to Eat

Several Palm Springs favorites are included in the pages that follow but don't neglect the neighboring communities. They too have fine places to eat, for each is a resort town on its own. Rancho Mirage is particularly blessed with fine dining places and some restaurants and bistros that are less formal. The latter include the **Cactus Club** (71-730 Highway 111), a bar and grill with southwestern decor with the piano bar opening at 4:30 and dinner selections including barbecued ribs, steak, and seafood ($$$). **Ristorante Mamma Gina** (73-705 El Passe, Palm Desert) serves what the name suggests, a long list of pastas, plus veal dishes and other Italian delicacies (there's a piano bar here too). The restaurant opens at 5:15 PM ($$ to $$$). **Tutti Gusti Ristorante** features wood-oven pizza as its specialty—the crust is very crisp. For people who don't fancy pizza, the place serves a selection of other dishes (mostly of the "light" variety). There's a

34

patio for al fresco eating and a very large TV screen in the lounge ($$). For those who like the ambience of an oyster bar and less formality than in the posh hotel dining rooms, try **Hank's Fish House**, next to the Holiday Inn at 155 S. Belardo in Palm Springs. It's open for all three meals each day ($$).

Desert Hot Springs

Sitting in foothills above the valley floor, the folk who live in Desert Hot Springs look down on the busy life of the rich and famous and say "who cares." This is a relaxed spa town, supplied with abundant streams of hot mineral water that come to the surface to fill the pools of hotels and spa resorts here. Besides, the most exclusive resort hideaway in California is in Desert Hot Springs—but they're not telling. **Cabot's Old Indian Pueblo**, a striking adobe building with 35 rooms, was built by one man, Cabot Yerxa, between 1939 and 1965. It's now a museum which is open daily except Tuesdays.

Things to See & Do
• **Outdoor Attractions**
With the large number of hotels and motels—many of them reasonably priced—Desert Hot Springs makes a good place from which to visit the nearby desert, particularly **Joshua Tree National Park**, which is just across the Little San Bernardino Range; it's a drive of under an hour to the entrances in Joshua Tree and Twenty-nine Palms. The **Mission Lakes Country Club** features an 18-hole golf course and is located on Clubhouse Drive, at the northwest end of town on the way to Joshua Tree National Park.

• **Spas**
For hot springs fans, this town is Xanadu. Since developers found the springs in the area (long after the Agua Caliente Indians found them first), it has been a mecca for vacationers who want to soak in what they believe to be curative waters. Hotels with pools were built, a townsite was laid out, and the people came—thousands every winter, many of them Canadians getting away from their harsh climate.

35

Destinations

For details on accommodations, see page 54. Many of the resort's hotels are located along Hacienda Avenue. **Desert Hot Springs Hotel and Spa** has an impressive array of pools, its own hot water supply from underground, and a comfortable feeling in its 50 rooms and large but relaxing pool area. In fact, most of the hotels and motels have their own thermal wells, from the **Royal Fox Inn** with 115 units to the diminutive **Cactus Springs Lodge** with 11 standard rooms.

Two Bunch Palms is a resort so exclusive and private that there is no sign telling you it's there, and it's not listed in any of the town's tourist brochures. Reputedly built by Al Capone as a secure hideaway in the 1930s, this resort complex is built around a palm oasis with a deluxe restaurant, two hot mineral pools, a spa program, and spectacularly beautiful grounds—including the old oasis palms. There are tennis courts, a swimming pool, and more.

Where to Eat

Desert Hot Springs is not known as a place for fine dining unless you're guesting at Two Bunch Palms, although you can obtain a good meal at the **Sunshine Cafe and Dining Room** in the Desert Hot Springs Hotel & Spa at 10-805 Palm Drive (**$$ to $$$**). **Mission Lakes Country Club** also has a full-service restaurant in a scenic setting (**$$ to $$$**).

Palm Springs

For more than 2,000 years, the Agua Caliente Indians have occupied much of the Coachella Valley, centered in the Indian Canyons where water and vegetation were plentiful. Early inhabitants used the natural hot springs pool and lived a hunter-gatherer existence. Mexican expeditions first came to the area in 1774, and in 1853 a U.S. government survey party mapped Palm Springs and established a wagon route through San Gorgonio Pass. Smallpox killed thousands of natives in 1863, and the Southern Pacific Railway arrived in 1877. The dispossessed Agua Caliente band finally achieved victory in the U.S. Supreme Court to retain their land allotments but had to wait until 1959 to profit from their heritage and hard-earned achievements.

California

Today, many of Palm Springs' important buildings—including the convention center—sit on land leased from the Indian band.

Palm Springs was—and is—a desert oasis, and to me that is what makes this famous resort town and the whole Coachella Valley such an interesting vacation spot. Quite unlike its Nevada counterpart, Las Vegas, Palm Springs is relaxed, less formal, and very friendly. It has high style without neon glitz and gaudy architectural theatrics. After two or three days of exploring Palm Springs and the natural environment around the town, one comes away with a feeling that here is a region of unique beauty—with the nearby desert ready to enchant you at any time of day, particularly at sunrise and sunset. The town (which they call The Village) has parks, mountain recreation, trendy boutiques, excellent restaurants, and museums—all offered in an unstressful manner.

This is not just a vacation town for the very rich and famous. Among the more than 150 hotels and motels in Palm Springs, there are the deluxe resort hotels and spas which attract the wealthy, but there are also ordinary but less expensive motels, old-fashioned bungalow courts and several small, cozy bed and breakfast inns which offer personalized service at a reasonable price. The most accessible Visitor Information Center is located on Palm Canyon Drive at the north end of Palm Springs. Hotel reservations may be made here, and the center has a variety of local maps and brochures.

What to See & Do

The original hot spring is now part of the **Spa Hotel**. This is the place to stay if you're a hot springs fanatic. For accommodations, see page 57.

The Palm Springs area is big on golf. More than 80 golf courses create green splotches on the valley, with most of them open to the public year-round. There are tennis courts everywhere, and with 8,000 swimming pools in town, you should be able to find at least one to suit your needs. This is beginning to read like a tourist brochure, but it's all true!

As fine as the town is for vacationers, it's the out-of-town experience that should catch your full attention. The **Indian Canyons** offer the largest natural oasis on the continent. The area is home to many birds, reptiles,

37

Destinations

and other animals and thousands of plant species, which thrive along the canyon streams. There are three canyons—Andreas, Murray and Palm—with a trading post, hiking trails, horse riding, and picnic areas.

Close to the town center, **The Living Desert** is a commercial desert wildlife park with exhibits of desert plants, animals, and birds and guided tours. The **Palm Springs Aerial Tramway** takes you up the side of Mt. San Jacinto, the mountain that dominates the Palm Springs skyline, up to the 8500-foot level where the tramway stops in **San Jacinto State Park**. Here are hiking trails, mountain meadows, and attractions including a restaurant and lounge, a movie show, horse and mule rides, and campsites, with great views of the nearby mountain ranges and the valley. During winter months, this is a prime cross-country ski area. The summit of the mountain is at 10,831 feet.

Back on the valley floor, **Moorten's Botanical Gardens** features nature trails through cacti, trees, succulent varieties, and flowers. The nursery here is an excellent place for desert plant lovers to buy cacti and succulents to take home. There are well-designed and executed collections of western American art and artifacts in the **Palm Springs Desert Museum**, at 101 Museum Drive. The Annenberg Theater here provides a full schedule of performances.

A local tour company—Desert Adventures—provides excursions into the nearby desert, including tours of the Indian Canyons and off-road Jeep rides. The company also offers longer tours to the mountain resorts and down the valley to the Salton Sea. For information, call (619) 324-3378.

The **Agua Caliente Heritage Festival**, an affair that includes chili cook-offs, native singing and dancing, hay rides, and Indian art and crafts sales, is held on the first weekend after Easter. Food served includes Indian fried bread, tamales, and stew; pig roasts and barbecues are featured. The event is a major fund-raiser for the Agua Caliente band's planned Heritage Museum, and is held at Andreas Ranch near the Indian Canyons—a 5-minute drive from town.

On Thursday evenings, Palm Canyon Drive becomes a pedestrian mall with street musicians, farmers' market, food booths, antique vendors, and

California

craftspeople selling their work. It's called **VillageFest**. On Friday nights, the northern part of Palm Canyon Drive features the **Canyon Stroll**, with much the same atmosphere, except that car traffic continues on the street.

Day-Trips

Within an hour or so from town, there are several outdoor locations that attract visitors. East of Palm Springs, via Highway 74, the **San Jacinto Mountains** offer great scenery. The little town of **Idyllwild** is a rustic community with several crafts studios and shops and good restaurants. Lake Hemet is a good place to stop on the way to Idyllwild for fishing and a picnic.

The mountain resorts in the San Bernardino Mountains are about a 90-minute drive away. At Big Bear and Lake Arrowhead there is boating, water skiing in the summer, and downhill skiing in winter with resort accommodations, restaurants, and shops.

Joshua Tree National Park, via Highway 62 (see the scenic drive, page 47), is a superb wilderness in the desert with an amazing collection of jumbled rocks, historic sites, and wildlife.

Where to Eat

All of the deluxe resort hotels have chic restaurants where celebrity watching is as much of the action as dining. This game is pursued at such places as the **Terrace Restaurant** at the Hilton Resort and **Bono**, the restaurant Sonny used to run at the Riviera Resort & Racquet Club. Both are in the $$$ range.

Hank's Fish House (155 S. Belardo) serves breakfast, lunch, and dinner. At night it's a loud, busy place with entertainment ($$ to $$$). Lunch or dinner with a view is available in the cafeteria at **Mountain Station**, which is at the top of the aerial tramway on Mt. San Jacinto. This is a family favorite ($ to $$).

One of the most charming of the long-time cafes in Palm Springs is **Las Casuelas**. This Mexican cafe is at 368 N. Palm Canyon Drive, opening daily at 10 AM with indoor tables and patio dining beside the street. The newer **Las Casuelas Terrace** is at 222 S. Palm Canyon, open from 4 PM. ($ to $$).

Destinations

Death Valley National Park

From our earliest years, the tales of Death Valley and the Amargosa captivated our imaginations. Ronald Reagan tried his best to further the treacherous mystique of the area in the TV series "Death Valley Days." The pictures of the 20-mule teams pulling wagons of borax to a more civilized part of the desert are forever imprinted on our minds. It's a dry, salty sink that captures the imagination becuse of its desolation and serene starkness.

Yet the valley has a history that includes lakes covering the valley floor, one (Lake Manly) existing as recently as 20,000 years ago. Another small lake covered part of the valley about 2,000 years ago. The rains were more frequent then, and, although scientists aren't sure of this, the lakes in the valley may have been linked to the Amargosa River, which used to flow just east of Death Valley.

Whatever happened, the floor of the valley is now mostly covered with a deposit of salt that in some places is close to 3,000 feet deep. In the sun, the valley floor shimmers as the heat rises from the hot salt pan. North of the salt marshes, sand dunes blow and shift in the strong winds that whip across the landscape. And all around, high mountain cliffs enclose the valley, providing irridescent volcanic deposits, steep upthrusting granite walls, and badlands formed of mud hills: yellow, orange, mustard, and gray, reflecting the sunlight in brilliant, shifting displays as the sun moves from east to west.

Amidst the desolation of Death Valley, wildlife has adapted to the extremes of the area. More than 600 varieties of plants survive in the park, in ecosystems varying from the alluvial fans that have washed down through mountain gullies onto the valley floor to the heights of the mountain peaks. Four major climatic zones are experienced in the park; they range from 200 feet below sea level (at the Badwater springs) to 11,049 feet above sea level (at the top of Telescope Peak).

At the bottom, the creosote bush and desert holly predominate. At the top, there are ancient bristlecone pine trees, the oldest living things on earth. In between, pickleweed surrounds the pan at Salt Creek, and the

California

strange plant called arrowweed—in the Devil's Cornfield—clings to mounds of sandy earth at sea level and below. Mesquite is found on the sand dunes a mile to the north of the Devil's Cornfield.

While the valley plants are brown during the hot months, everything comes to life for a short time following the spring rains, and for a few days the valley is covered with flowers that quickly seed and then die until the next year.

Animals, too, survive the harshness of the landscape and the climate. The desert bighorn sheep is well adapted to life on the mountainsides. Sidewinders slither along the salt pan, especially in the mesquite groves on the alluvial fans. Coyotes pick their way across the salty wastes, looking for their food—rodents and lizards. Roadrunners also dine on lizards, of which there are many varieties; the chuckwalla is the largest. Even the desert tortoise lives here, digging in for the hottest periods of the summer.

Think of Death Valley as a gigantic natural theme park, as wild and wonder-full as any Disney World or Magic Mountain—formed by volcanoes and earthquakes, with four billion years of geological history on display. It is truly one of the most fascinating places on earth to visit and never fails to excite the traveler, whatever the time of year.

Few North Americans visit Death Valley during the hottest months, and that's too bad. The valley is a growing summer destination for Japanese, Germans, and the French tourists, who come to experience the valley's attractions at this most extreme time of year. With air conditioning and swimming pools to cool you, there is no reason not to be comfortable, at least while you're inside or in the pool. Furnace Creek Ranch and Stovepipe Wells Village both offer a range of air-conditioned accommodations during the summer, with restaurants and a saloon.

Death Valley Climate

The climate ranges from sublime comfort between November and the end of March to scorching heat during the summer months. The prime tourist season in Death Valley is the winter when the temperature ranges from 40 degrees at night to a maximum of 80 degrees around five o'clock in the afternoon. By the end of May the daytime temperatures rise to about 100 degrees, and by August the thermometer often registers over 120 degrees—in the shade—with ground temperatures around 150 degrees. Occasionally, winter storms bring rain, and travelers should be aware of the flash flooding that can occur at these times. On occasion, roads are damaged by water racing down the washes.

Some caution is urged while traveling through Death Valley in the summer. Water should be carried at all times, and only short drives should be taken to valley attractions during the hottest hours.

It should be pointed out that off-road travel inside the park is prohibited. On the way north from Furnace Creek is a set of ruts from wagons that crossed the valley almost 100 years ago. It takes a long time for the desert to recover from even the most minor disturbance. The best time for a day-trip in July and August is very early in the morning, when temperatures are in the 80s. Extended hikes should not be taken in these months. Otherwise, summer is a good time for adventurers to experience the uniqueness of Death Valley. You'll never feel so hot again!

Orientation

To get an overview of park activities, visit the park's main **Visitor Center**, at Furnace Creek. Open from 8 AM, the center has an introductory 15-minute film on Death Valley and a range of brochures on various attractions including several day-trips to scenic and historic areas within the park. There are topographic maps and hiking guides available. Park rangers conduct daily activities from the center including talks on desert animal and plant life and presentations on the human history of the valley. The evening programs in the center begin at 5 PM, and the building closes at 6. The center is located just north of the Furnace Creek Ranch, on Highway 190.

Day-Trips

Four drives can be taken for access to just about all of the attractions in the national park:

- **Zabriskie Point & Dante's View**
  A half-day trip up the Furnace Creek Wash is best done at sunrise, driving east along Highway 190 from Furnace Creek. The first

42

California

point of interest is **Zabriskie Point**, the colorful badlands area composed of yellow mud that reflects the light in mysterious ways. From the parking lot, walk up to an overlook which will give you a great view of one of the strangest places on earth—the backdrop (and title) of Antonioni's 1970 cult movie. Continuing eastward on Hwy. 190, take the loop road through **Twenty Mule Team Canyon**, through a series of mudstone hills where prospectors looked for borax. The loop is 2 miles long. Farther east is the turnoff to **Dante's View**, which is 13.3 miles from the junction. The road climbs to the top of the Black Mountains. The final ¼ mile is not recommended for trailers and long RVs. There's a parking lot here, with another at the top. The view from the ridge is spectacular, looking down into the desolate valley and to the mountain ranges to the west. Temperatures at the crest tend to be cool, and with the usual stiff breeze blowing, you'll need a jacket.

• South to Badwater & Artist's Drive

Another half-day round trip leads south from Furnace Creek, past the Highway 190 junction on Badwater Road. A tour pamphlet (50 cents) is available from a box at the junction. Twelve miles from the intersection is the turnoff to the **Devil's Golf Course**, where the salt pan has been sculpted into jagged pinnacles.

Badwater is 5 miles farther down the road. Here, springs create brackish pools of water at the lowest spot you can drive to in the Americas. The lowest point in the hemisphere (282 feet below sea level) is several miles west of the road. A sign on the rock above Badwater shows sea level.

On the return drive, turn right for a loop trip along **Artist's Drive**. The road winds through several small canyons and across hills near the face of the mountain. The highlight is the **Artist's Palette**: hillsides of garish, colored volcanic deposits. The loop returns to Badwater Road for the northward return toward Furnace Creek. The final event along this route is the Golden Canyon Trail—to the east. This 1-mile trail leads through a rock cleft with brightly colored walls. The trail is self-guiding.

• North to the Dunes & Mosaic Canyon

This tour (another half-day drive) leads north from the Furnace Creek area to the midsection of the valley and the sand dunes area. First, Highway 190 passes the historic **Harmony Borax Works**, the site of the first borax mining operation in the valley. Parts of the old adobe-block buildings remain, with rusted pieces of equipment used in mining the "cotton ball" borax deposits. Further north is the sideroad to **Salt Creek**, where desert pupfish have adapted to the briny waters of the salt marsh. There's a half-mile boardwalk looping through this area. Drive north again, taking the road toward Scotty's Castle, and turn left on a sideroad labeled **Sand Dunes**. There are no trails into the dunes, but you can just walk into the area. The highest dune, a popular destination, is about 2 miles from the parking lot. There's a picnic area here. Once you've had enough sand, drive back to the highway junction and turn west to Stovepipe Wells, a man-made oasis where there is a motel, restaurant, and bar. Just beyond the village is **Mosaic Canyon**. The trail up the canyon is the valley's most popular walk. You'll see marble canyon walls as the canyon narrows, and about 2 miles from the beginning—at the end of the trail—is a dry waterfall.

• All the Way North to Scotty's Castle

Our fourth day-trip—one that will take a full day and take you to Scotty's Castle—heads north again from Furnace Creek, past the Stovepipe Wells junction. You'll pass the Sand Dunes road and begin climbing through the Kit Fox Hills badlands. If there is time, take **Titus Canyon Road** (north on an alluvial fan) until reaching the mouth of Titus Canyon. There, the road becomes a one-way drive for westbound travel only. There's a parking lot and you can walk a short distance into the canyon. Return to the Scotty's Castle Road. The highway continues to climb, passing the Grapevine Entrance Station. Drive up Grapevine Canyon for another 3 miles to **Scotty's Castle**. Imagine building a vacation home in Death Valley! Yet that's what Albert Johnston did in the early 1900s. The building, part of Death Valley Ranch, was named for Johnston's friend Walter Scott, known as Death Valley Scotty.

California

On a guided tour of the castle you'll learn Scott's story and much more. It's important to register for a tour as soon as you arrive at the site. There may be a wait of about an hour for the next tour, and fees are charged ($6 for adults, $3 for seniors and children 6 or over). There is a snack bar, as well as a gift shop and gas station at the castle. The site is usually open at 8:30 AM and tours begin at 9. Returning south from the castle, turn right onto the road that leads to **Ubehebe Crater**, 5 miles from the junction. This explosion pit is 5 miles wide, 750 feet deep, and less than a thousand years old. The large crater is flanked by several small craters that were more recently formed. The total round trip from Furnace Creek to Scotty's Castle is 120 miles.

Hikes

There are day hikes and then there are backcountry hikes. The latter are mostly strenuous and designed for only the most fit and experienced. The most strenuous hike leads from the Mahogany Flat Campground, climbing 3,000 feet to Telescope Peak, the highest spot in the park. A more moderate backcountry route leads through Jayhawker Canyon, starting on Highway 190 (2.3 miles past Emigrant Junction, at the 3,000-foot elevation sign). This trail was used by gold seekers in 1850 and some signed their names on a large boulder about 2 miles from the trailhead. The trail runs 5 miles to the base of Pinto Peak.

There are many shorter day hikes to explore including the Mosaic Canyon Salt Creek and Golden Canyon trails mentioned previously. To add to the experience in Golden Canyon, continue past the marked end of this trail, taking the path over the badlands to Gower Gulch. It's possible to hike to Zabriskie Point from here, or down the gulch to return to Golden Canyon.

High above the valley floor is the **Keane Wonder Mine** (reached by driving up the Beatty Cutoff Road north of Furnace Creek). There is a very steep, winding trail from the ruins of the mill to the mine site, which is 2,000 feet above the mill. There are wonderful views of Death Valley from this area, and the trail's length is 1 mile (each way). To make it seem easier, I'll point out that it takes far less effort coming down than it does

Destinations

walking up. An easier walk from the same Keane Mill parking lot follows a pipeline north along the base of the mountain to some sulphurous springs (**Keane Wonder Springs**) that feature travertine mounds. The remains of an old cabin and stamp mill are just beyond the springs.

Where to Stay & Eat

All accommodations and food services are provided by national park concessionaires at three locations. You'll find several restaurants, all but one informal, at Furnace Creek Ranch. Furnace Creek Inn provides more upscale dining, while Stovepipe Wells Village has a saloon-style restaurant. Other than these locations, the best place to get a good meal is at your own campsite. Indoor accommodation (of high quality) is available at the **Furnace Creek Inn** and **Furnace Creek Ranch**, as well as at **Stovepipe Wells Village**. The ranch also has cabin-style accommodation at moderate cost and sections for trailer and RV parking. The inn is open from October 1 to May 15. The other accommodations are available year-round. For inn and ranch reservations, phone (619) 786-2345. For Stovepipe Wells Village reservations, phone (619) 786-2387.

Camping

Facilities are available year-round, although there are few campers during the hottest months and some park campgrounds are closed during the summer period. Death Valley National Park operates nine campgrounds, and all campsites are available on a first come, first served basis except for the Furnace Creek Campground from October through April.

To reserve your Furnace Creek site, phone Mystix reservations at 800-365-CAMP. Reservations can be made eight weeks in advance for the October through April period.

46

The first come, first served campgrounds are located at **Texas Springs** & **Sunset** (both just south of Furnace Creek), **Stovepipe Wells** (mid-valley), **Emigrant** (9 miles west of Stovepipe Wells), **Mesquite Spring** (4 miles south of Scotty's Castle), **Wildrose** (near the western edge of the valley), **Thorndike** (8 miles east of Wildrose—no campers or motor homes), and **Mahogany Flat** (9 miles east of Wildrose and suitable only for high-clearance cars).

Joshua Tree National Park

If ever there was a piece of public land which should have been designated a national park, Joshua Tree National Monument was that place. It is now a national park, thanks to the California Desert Protection Act. This unique series of ecosystems is one of the foremost treasures of the American Southwest, serving to provide a dramatic link between the two great California deserts.

Sitting just east of Palm Springs, the northwestern half of the park is in the high Mojave Desert. The eastern and southern portions are in the low Colorado Desert. Dividing them is a remarkable transition zone which is a mixture of the two—sharing plants, animals, and birds. A drive through the park offers possibly the finest overview of our western desert landscape. For a tour of the park, see the scenic drive on page 16.

Covering 850 square miles, the park is accessible from several northern entrances and one in the south, via Interstate 10. The communities of Joshua Tree and Twentynine Palms offer nearby overnight accommodations and the two northern gates to the park are at these towns. The Parks Service operates nine campgrounds, and all but one are a short drive from the two communities.

The preserve is named for the Joshua tree forests that are located in the northern regions, at about 4,000 feet elevation. The best places to see these forests are in the Queen Valley and Lost Horse Valley, both accessible by the loop that connects Joshua Tree and Twentynine Palms. The twisted trees, members of the agave family (cousins to the lily species), stand in unorganized array in the western part of the park. The trees provide the basis for an amazing food chain. Birds nest in the trees, insects infest the wood, night lizards live in the toppled, dead remains of the trees, and worms and termites turn the wood back into soil. Jackrabbits and kangaroo rats are there too, caught and eaten by coyotes, bobcats, hawks, and eagles. This desert is deceptively busy.

Aside from the dry desert ecosystems, Joshua Tree is blessed with several palm oases, each of which harbor wildlife. At the northern edge of the Park is the 29 Palms Oasis (the Oasis of Mara) next to the main visitor

47

Destinations

center and park headquarters. This was a classic Indian oasis that became a stopping point for prospectors and desert pioneers at the turn of the century. Also to the north is the 49 Palms Oasis, on a spur road which leads into the park between the two towns. A trail of middling difficulty leads 1.5 miles from the end of Canyon Road to this oasis.

The two southern oases in the Colorado Desert are located near the Cottonwood Visitor Center and Campground. The largest oasis in the preserve (Lost Palms) is reached by driving on a backroad southeast from Cottonwood (which has its own small oasis) and then walking through a series of desert washes for 4 miles.

The low desert is more barren, but the short transition zone offers several fascinating features. The Cholla Garden, at the southern edge of the transition zone along the road to Cottonwood, offers a short walk through a display of cactus. A grove of ocotillo (the sticklike shrub) is situated slightly south and at a lower elevation. The prime flowering season for yucca, wildflowers, and cacti is March and April.

As in Death Valley, the desert scene is punctuated with alluvial fans, which have brought rock and soil from the hills to the desert floor along with desert varnish on the rocks and granite formations. What makes Joshua Tree special are the large jumbled formations made up of boulder piles that are scattered over the northern valley landscape. This is prime rock-climbing country.

There are several picnic areas: in the Queen Valley, in Hidden Valley south of the town of Joshua Tree, and at Cottonwood, at the southern edge of the preserve.

Joshua Tree Hikes

Areas of the preserve were mined during the lust for gold and silver during the first half of the century. A trail to the Lost Horse Mine is a relatively easy 2-mile climb from the end of a 1-mile road. The historical gem of the park is the Desert Queen Ranch, a mill and homestead during the teens and 20s, and the home of Bill Keys, who raised a family here. Because of the fragility of the site, permits are required to walk into the ranch, which is in a canyon off the Queen Valley. Guided tours are given

California

during the high season (October through March), and our suggestion is to phone the park office (619-367-7511) in advance of your visit to try to catch a group tour. Now that the preserve is designated a national park, this area should be opened to the public in the future, with the proper protections and interpretation program in place.

Other hikes are available, the longest being the **Boy Scout Trail** which leads 15 miles (25.1 KM) through the Wonderland of Rocks area east of the Quail Springs picnic area. Backcountry hiking and camping are permitted with camping no closer than ¼ mile from water sources.

Camping
The campground at **Black Rock Canyon** provides 100 sites with flush toilets, fireplaces, water, and a dump station. This is the only campground for which reservations are taken. To reserve your individual site or to inquire about group camping, phone 800-365-2267. Other campgrounds are filled on a first come, first served basis. The Queen Valley has three campgrounds: **Jumbo Rocks**, **Ryan Mountain**, and **Sheep Pass** (group camping). These are all situated in the midst of twisted rock formations. The **Hidden Valley Campground** (on Quail Springs Rd.) has 39 sites with water, tables, and fireplaces. The **Belle** and **White Tank** campgrounds (no water) are situated on the road that leads south to Cottonwood. **Indian Cove Campground** (13 sites) serves groups only. At **Cottonwood**, there is a campground with 62 sites and an adjacent picnic area. There is water here, in addition to flush toilets, but there are no showers in the park. Horses are permitted at Ryan and Black Rock Canyon campgrounds.

Needles

Another of the old Route 66 towns, Needles is not noted for spectacular scenery or exciting tourist attractions. However, it's not far from a whole panoply of recreational areas and historic sites, which makes it at least a good lunchtime stopover, and a handy overnight place if you're interested in gambling (24 miles north), ghost towns (25 miles northeast), the Colorado River (it's here), riverside wildlife marshes (to the south), mountain wilderness (in every direction), or Lake Mead (to the north).

Destinations

The topographical highlight of the area is the little range of peaks called the Needles. The Sacramento Mountains are 5 miles west of town. More interesting and important to the environment is the Havasu Wildlife Refuge, which is situated along the Colorado River between Needles and Lake Havasu. The refuge includes Topock Marsh, a 4,000-acre wonderland of sloughs, bays, and channels filled with cattails and bulrushes. Beaver, waterbirds, and quail inhabit the marsh. South of the marsh, the river enters Topock Gorge.

A float trip down the river from Needles to Lake Havasu—a ride of 30 miles—not only offers the sight of a deep red canyon but gives close-up views of wildlife. Providence Mountains State Recreation Area is found 17 miles north of town at the 4,300-foot level, featuring Mitchell Caverns, which has guided tours, and the Mary Beal Nature Trail as well as picnic areas and hiking trails.

Recently restored as a 4WD trail, the old Mojave Road gives Jeepers a ride along the Colorado River, on what was once a footpath used by local Indians and then a wagon road used by prospectors and emigrants. A guide to the Mojave Road is available (on a loan basis) from the BLM office in Needles.

Northwest of town on the old Route 66 is the near-ghost town of Oatman, where wild burros will eat out of your hand on what used to be the main street of the old gold mining town. There are 100 people living here, and a few businesses are in operation including the historic Oatman Hotel, a two-storey adobe structure.

There are six RV parks in Needles and several standard motels (see the Places to Stay pages). The town operates an 18-hole golf course, and there are four launch ramps for Colorado River boating. The town's tourist information center is at Front and G Streets.

Where to Eat

You can eat at the Burger King, Carl's Jr., or Irene's Drive In, or (better still), at **Rita's Mexican Food** at 1901 Broadway ($ to $$). The **Hungry Bear** at 1906 W. Broadway (next to a Travelodge) serves up steak and lobster (a fine desert delicacy) and the best pie in town ($$ to $$$).

California

BAKER

Bun Boy Motel
I-15 and State Route 127
P.O. Box 130
Baker CA 92309
(619) 733-4363

There's not much to choose from in this small desert town. In fact, the Bun Boy is just about it, but it's a good launching point for a trip to Death Valley. This is a standard motel beside the interstate, with showers, TV with movies, and a 24-hour restaurant with all-night room service ($).

BARSTOW

Holiday Inn
1511 E. Main St.
Barstow CA 92311
(619) 256-7581

With full services, this is one of the larger and quieter hotels in Barstow—away from the busy highways. There's a heated pool, whirlpool, exercise room with a restaurant nearby ($ to $$).

Desert Villa Motel
1984 E. Main St.
Barstow CA 92311
(619) 256-2146

A Best Western motel, the Desert Villa has 97 units, pool, whirlpool and laundry. Suites & rooms with kitchenettes are available. There's a cafe open from 4:30 PM to 9 PM. 1/2 mile west of I-15—exit at Montara ($ to $$).

Quality Inn
1520 E. Main St.
Barstow CA 92311
(619) 256-6891

One of the few motels in Barstow to accommodate pets, this chain motel is 1/4 mile from I-15 (via the Main St. exits). There's a heated pool and laundry, with a dining room open from 6 AM to 10 PM. There's a coffee shop across the street. Deposit required and 7-day refund notice ($ to $$).

Barstow/Calico KOA Campground
P.O. Box 967
Yermo CA 92398
(619) 254-2311

This large campground with RV hookups is located 7 miles northeast of Barstow, next to the Calico ghost town. There are shaded sites, dump station, pool, play-ground, store, laundry, and propane.

There are two additional BLM recreation sites with camping: at Owl Canyon next to the Rainbow Basin Geological Area and at Afton Canyon. These campgrounds are primitive.

BORREGO SPRINGS

La Casa Del Zorro Resort
P.O. Box 127
Borrego Springs CA 92004
(619) 767-5323
or 800-824-1884

This desert resort operation has been here for many years and is conveniently close to the Anza-Borrego Desert State Park visitor center. With 77 units and attractive grounds, the resort boasts suites and villas, three heated pools, whirlpools, a putting green, tennis courts, and an exercise room. The rates start at about $100 and private villas can cost as much as $500 in the top season (winter). There's a dining room plus lounge and entertainment ($$$).

Palm Canyon Resort
P.O. Box 956
Borrego Springs CA 92004
(619) 767-5341
or 800-242-0044

With both a motel and an RV park, this operation is inside the state park boundary, on State Route S-22 (221 Palm Canyon Dr.). There are 44 units with heated pool, laundry, whirlpool, and a suite with whirlpool ($$). The restaurant is open from 11 AM to 10 PM (weekends from 7 AM). The campground has 142 sites with a store and dump station.

Oasis Motel
P.O. Box 221
Borrego Springs CA 92004
(619) 767-5409

Your basic motel, the Oasis has only seven units, one mile west of the town center on S-22 (366 Palm Canyon Drive), with pool & whirlpool. Two of the units have kitchens. Weekly rates are available. Three-day refund notice ($ to $$).

Anza-Borrego Camping

Anza-Borrego Desert State Park operates a campground in Palm Canyon. There are 117 sites. Unlimited primitive camping is permitted across the park expanse. The limit for RVs in the organized campground is 31 feet. There is a 30-day limit in the campground. For information on the various campgrounds inside Anza-Borrego Desert State Park, see page 27.

California

DEATH VALLEY JUNCTION

Amargosa Hotel
Death Valley Junction
CA
92328
(619) 852-4441

The stark white motel is just about the only remaining relic in what used to be a larger town—when the borax mines were active in the area. The famed Amargosa Opera House is part of the motel and staying in a motel room gets you a ticket to Marta Becket's performances (mid-October through early May. ($).

DEATH VALLEY NATIONAL PARK

Furnace Creek Ranch Resort
P.O. Box 1
Death Valley CA 92328
(619) 786-2345
or 800-528-6367

The year-round ranch resort with deluxe motel and connected cabin-style units is located at the palm oasis next to the park headquarters on State Route 190. There is a golf course, tennis courts, riding, archery range, large pool, saunas, and whirlpool. The complex includes the fascinating Borax Museum, and you can buy dates fresh off the palms. The ranch has several restaurants including a cafeteria and coffee shop. Deposit required ($$ to $$$).

Furnace Creek Inn
P.O. Box 1
Death Valley CA 92328
(619) 786-2361

This grande dame of a resort hotel is perched on a hillside overlooking the depths of Death Valley. Palms shade the garden terrace. There are 67 rooms, a heated pool, saunas, whirlpool, and lighted tennis courts. Not open during the torrid summer months, the inn is just the place for winter socializing with visitors from around the world. There are two dining rooms. The Sunday brunch is a Death Valley tradition ($$$+).

Stovepipe Wells Village
Death Valley, CA
92328
(619) 786-2387

The quasi-rustic resort complex is near the sand dunes, 24 miles from the ranch on State Route 190. There are 82 units with full baths, and shower units, a hot spring pool, store, and service station. The restaurant and bar are open from 7 AM to 2 PM and 5:30 PM to 9 PM ($$).

53

Places to Stay

DESERT HOT SPRINGS

Desert Hot Springs Spa Hotel
10805 Palm Dr.
Desert Hot Springs
CA 92240
(619) 329-6495

The hot springs at this location are the reason for the development of this growing spa town. This good-sized hotel (50 rooms) is also open to the public and features three natural hot mineral pools, a wading pool, saunas, and mineral water whirl-pools. The low-slung motel-style units border the large pool deck area. This place has anything a hot springs fanatic could wish for unless you're an habitué at Two Bunch Palms (see below). There's a dining room and coffee shop (**$ to $$**).

Linda Vista Lodge
67-200 Hacienda Dr.
Desert Hot Springs
CA 92240
(619) 329-6401

This unpretentious motel with 42 units is built around a hot mineral pool and three hot whirl-pools (two indoor and one outdoor). The rates are very reasonable. Rooms have showers or com-bination baths. There are 28 efficiency units and one two-bedroom unit. Weekly and monthly rates (**$**).

Two Bunch Palms
67-425 Two Bunch
Palms Trail
Desert Hot Springs
CA 92240
(619) 329-8791

An exclusive resort on a 28-acre palm oasis, with a subtly disguised and patrolled entrance, truly won-derful grounds with two hot mineral pools, and spa facilities including saunas, massage services, a swimming pool, and tennis courts. The retreat has a history that becomes embellished with the pass-ing years. It's said to have been the hideaway of Al Capone, with a gambling casino and a lookout tower for security. Today, there's a renowned restau-rant and the privacy that attracts important people from near and far (**$$$+**).

Sam's Family Spa
(campground)
70-875 Dillon Rd.
Desert Hot Springs
CA 92240
(619) 329-6457

This large campground is located on 40 acres, 7 miles southeast of town. Aside from the 225 sites—all with hookups—there are two natural hot pools, a swimming pool, laundry, playground, store, and restaurant. Monthly rates are available, and for weekends a two-night stay is required. There is a small motel as well, with reasonable rates (**$ to $$**).

California

Royal Fox
Campground and Inn
14500 Palm Dr.
Desert Hot Springs CA
92240
(619) 329-4481

This campground, 1.5 miles south of the town center on Palm Drive, is the closest camping spot to the main hot pool action. Registration is at the Royal Fox Inn. There are 34 sites with a pool, sauna, whirlpool and restaurant. The inn has 115 units, 10 with a small hot spring pool (**$ to $$**).

JOSHUA TREE
NATIONAL PARK

There is no indoor accommodation inside the park, but there are eight places to camp. These campgrounds are listed in the Joshua Tree National Park section of this book, beginning on page 47. For additional information on campsites, contact the national park headquarters at (619) 367-7511. There are motels in nearby 29 Palms and Yucca Valley.

JULIAN

Julian Hotel
P.O. Box 1856
Julian CA 92036
(619) 765-0201 or
800-734-5854

This wonderful bed and breakfast inn is a very well preserved hotel, built 100 years ago. The Victorian era speaks from every nook and cranny including the "necessary rooms" for ladies and gentlemen at the end of the hall. The hotel has separate units, Patio Cottage and Honeymoon House, in which to celebrate special occasions. A full breakfast is served (**$$ to $$$**).

Julian Lodge
P.O. Box 1930
Julian CA 92036
(619) 765-1420

A little more than a standard motel—with 23 units—south of Main Street (the highway) on C Street. The units have air conditioning and restaurants (including the one in the Julian Hotel) are nearby (**$$**).

MOJAVE

Western Inn
16200 Sierra Hwy.
Mojave CA 93501
(805) 824-3601

One of several small motels in this desert crossroads town, there are 23 air-conditioned units plus a pool and whirlpool. The coffee shop is open from 7 AM to 10 PM (**$**).

55

Places to Stay

Scottish Inn
16352 Sierra Hwy.
Mojave CA 93501
(805) 824-9317

This chain motel has 25 units, some with microwave oven and refrigerator. Small pool and whirlpool. As with the above motel, this one provides basic accommodation ($).

NEEDLES

Colorado River Inn
2371 Needles Hwy.
Needles CA 92363
(619) 326-4562

This highway town has a jumble of chain and local motels scattered along I-40 and the business loop. One of the newest is this 62-unit Best Western operation, which is not really near the river (about a mile) but is comfortable and modern. It has an indoor pool, sauna, and whirlpool. There's a restaurant next door. Exit from I-40 via W. Broadway ($ to $$).

Days Inn
1111 Pashard Street
Needles CA 92363
(619) 326-5660

A reliable place to stay and not much more in cost than some far less suitable motels in this desert way-station of a town, this Days Inn has 60 units plus pool, whirlpool, and sauna. From Interstate 40, take the W. Broadway exit ($ to $$).

Overland Motel
712 Broadway
Needles CA 92363
(619) 326-3821

A Best Western motel, the Overland has 41 units, is downtown on the Hwy. 40 business loop and has a variety of rooms and suites, plus a pool. The coffee shop is open from 5:30 AM to 9 PM ($).

OCEANSIDE

Marty's Valley Inn
3420 E. Mission Ave.
Oceanside CA 92054
(619) 757-7700
or 800-528-1234

This Best Western motel is on State Route 76 (East Mission Ave.), with standard rooms and suites, a heated pool, free continental breakfast, restaurant, and lounge. It is centrally located within easy reach of the ocean and golf clubs in the area ($$).

Oceanside Inn
1680 Oceanside Blvd.
Oceanside CA 92054
(619) 722-1821

Another Best Western, the inn is built around a large pool area, and some of the first-floor rooms open to the poolside. There are 80 units in all, sauna, whirlpool and free continental breakfast. The motel is handy to Interstate 5 ($ to $$).

California

Casitas Poquitos RV Park
1510 S Hill Street
Oceanside CA 92054
(619) 722-4404

Spread over 9 acres, the 139 sites here all have hookups. There's a store and laundry, as well as a heated pool, whirlpool, and playground. From I-5, take the Oceanside Blvd. exit, drive for 3⁄4 mile and turn onto S. Hill Street. Deposit required.

Paradise by the Sea RV Park
1537 S. Hill Street
Oceanside CA 92054
(619) 439-1376

A neighbor to the above RV park, located a 2-block walk from the beach and with the same types of features including a pool, grocery store, etc. The 102 sites have hookups and concrete patios. Seven-day refund notice.

PALM SPRINGS & THE COACHELLA VALLEY

Palm Springs and area offer hundreds of lodgings, from posh resorts costing upwards of $250 per day to modest locally owned operations and chain motels. Below are several places that we consider to be unusual or reasonably priced.

Spa Hotel & Mineral Springs
100 N. Indian Cyn. Rd.
P.O. Box 1787
Palm Springs CA 92263
(619) 325-1461

The springs that bubble beneath this hotel mark the site of the original oasis that brought native Indians to the region. The Spa Hotel has had several remodelings and now has 230 units, including a few efficiencies. There are outdoor and indoor hot mineral pools, whirlpool, and a health spa with steam room. The hotel is close to Palm Springs shopping and restaurants. It has its own restaurant and lounge (**$$ to $$$**).

Riviera Resort & Racquet Club
1600 N. Indian Cyn. Rd.
Palm Springs CA 92262
(619) 327-8311

This hotel with recreation facilities is one of the best bargains in Palm Springs, particularly if you're a AAA member. Off-season rates are particularly low, and even at the height of the winter period, they're reasonable compared to those of many other resorts. The hotel has a large pool deck (two pools), tennis courts, volleyball, basketball and croquet. Kids have a supervised camp. Shopping and restaurants are nearby, including Bono—Sonny's former place—which is on the site (**$$ to $$$**).

57

Places to Stay

Orchid Tree Inn
261 South Belardo
Road
Palm Springs CA
92262
(619) 325-2791

This unusual apartment-motel operation has rooms, suites, and Spanish bungalows with kitchens, set amidst gardens next to the San Jacinto Mountains. There are two heated pools and a whirlpool on the landscaped grounds. Most of the units have kitchens. A minimum stay of two nights is required ($ to $$$).

Autry Resort Hotel
4200 E. Palm Canyon
Dr.
Palm Springs CA
92264
(619) 328-1171

This famous hotel has been here since Palm Springs grew into a major destination resort, attracting stars such as Gene Autry to the desert society scene. There are posher resorts and more expensive ones, but the Autry has some history to it and a feeling of permanence with its superbly landscaped grounds. The rates are reasonable compared to those of some of the newer resort hotels. There are three heated pools plus whirlpools, tennis courts (fee), and an exercise room. The dining room is open from 7 AM to 11 PM, and the cocktail lounge features entertainment ($$ to $$$).

Westin Mission Hills Resort
Dinah Shore and Bob
Hope Drives
Rancho Mirage CA
92270
(619) 328-5955

If you want to (and can afford to) stay in one of the newer resort hotels, this Westin hotel is one of the best. With golf courses in every direction (including at the hotel door), the Mission Hills offers swimming and pool-side deck lounging (three pools), tennis, fitness training, and—of course—golfing on the two courses designed by Gary Player and Pete Dye. There's a supervised activity center for the kids. Eight restaurants and lounges, exercise room, facials, massage. Live it up! ($$$ to $$$+).

Rancho Las Palmas Resort
41000 Bob Hope
Drive
Rancho Mirage CA
92270
(619) 568-2727

The rates for this Marriott golf resort hotel are a little lower than for the Mission Hills, and the hotel's Spanish style provides a soft decor. The rooms are built around palm groves and garden terraces. A 27-hole golf course is adjacent, and 25 courts satisfy tennis buffs. Two pools, sundeck, whirlpool, restaurants and lounges ($$ to $$$).

California

Palm Springs Camping

Several resort-style parks accommodate RVers. The largest is **Outdoor Resorts/Palm Springs**, at 69-411 Ramon Rd., Cathedral City CA 92234. This huge landscaped area features 620 grassy sites with concrete pads, store, laundry, restaurant, eight heated pools, whirlpools, saunas, par-3 golf, and tennis courts. (619) 324-4005.

De Anza Palm Springs Oasis RV Resort (36-100 Date Palm Drive, Cathedral City CA 92234) has 140 sites, all with hookups, with a heated pool, whirlpool, laundry, tennis, and 18-hole golf course nearby.

Happy Traveler Recreation Vehicle Park (211 West Mesquite Ave., Palm Springs CA 92264) has 138 sites with hookups, just a block from Palm Canyon Drive. Check for age restrictions here. Pool, whirlpool, recreation room, playground, laundry. (619) 325-8518.

Pinyon Flats Campground (national forest) has primitive facilities 14 miles southwest of Palm Desert on State Route 74. RVs are limited to 15 feet. No showers; pit toilets. Nature trails and a store are available.

SAN JUAN CAPISTRANO

The following motels are recommended in case you're using this town near the sea as a staging place for a drive to Palm Springs (see page 8).

Capistrano Inn
27174 Ortego Hwy.
S. J. Capistrano CA
92675
(714) 493-5661

One of only two motels in town, this is a Best Western motel, 1/2 block removed from Interstate 5. A few of the 108 rooms are efficiencies. Heated pool, whirlpool, free breakfast, and evening drinks on weekdays. ($$).

Travelodge
28742 Camino Capistrano
S. J. Capistrano CA
92675 (714) 364-0342

This chain motel is close to I-5 (exit via Avery Parkway). All rooms have a whirlpool tub, and there is a coin laundry on site ($ to $$).

Places to Stay

TECOPA

This is truly one of the strangest places to stay in the nation, but hundreds do every winter. **Inyo County Tecopa Hot Springs Campground** covers 40 acres across the road from the two public bathhouses that are fed from the springs. The community is 5 miles south of Shoshone, 3 miles off U.S. Hwy. 127, (619) 852-4264. There's a store and tavern in Tecopa. Las Vegas is 100 miles away. The nearest motel is in Shoshone, and there's another farther north in Death Valley Junction plus more lodging in Death Valley National Park.

29 PALMS

Best Western Gardens Motel
71487 29 Palms Hwy.
29 Palms CA 92277
(619) 367-9141

There are 71 units in this motel on State Route 62, an easy drive to the entrance to Joshua Tree National Park. Heated pool, whirlpool, eight units with kitchen ($).

Circle C Motel
6340 El Rey Ave.
29 Palms CA 92277
(619) 367-7615

This is a small, non-chain motel with eleven units, a pool, whirlpool and laundry. Refrigerators are available. The motel is 1.5 miles west of town, via State Route 62 and then one block north on El Rey ($$).

29 Palms Inn
73950 Inn Avenue
29 Palms CA 92277
(619) 367-3505

Since the late 1920s, this unusual desert inn has entranced visitors. Spread over 70 acres are rustic adobe cottages—each with its own name—with fireplaces and antique furnishings. There is a pool, restaurant, and lounge ($$).

29 Palms Camping

29 Palms RV Resort is located at 4949 Desert Knoll Ave. on 20 acres. The park has close to 200 sites, all with hookups. Some sites are on the eighth fairway of the Roadrunner Dunes golf course. There is a pool with laundry, sauna, whirlpool, tennis court, recreation room, exercise room, shuffleboard, horseshoes and volleyball. The golf course is open to the public—another bonus from a stay at this resort.

California

YUCCA VALLEY

Oasis of Eden Inn
56377 Twentynine
Palms Hwy.
Yucca Valley CA
92284 (619) 365-6321

There are standard units and suites in this motel with landscaped grounds, a heated pool and whirlpool. There are two efficiency suites. The motel is 1/2 mile east of town on State Route 62 (**$ to $$**).

Yucca Inn
7500 Camino Del
Cielo
Yucca Valley CA
92284 (619) 365-3311

This motel is 1 mile west of town via State Route 62 and then one block north of the highway. There are 72 units in all, including 17 one-bedroom suites with kitchen. Heated pool, whirlpools, exercise room, restaurant open from 7 AM to 2 PM (Friday–Sunday from 7 AM to 9 PM). Lounge ($).

Desert View Motel
57471 Primrose Drive
Yucca Valley CA
92284
(619) 365-9706

This smaller standard motel has a pool with deck area and a one-storey building. The motel is slightly out of town. Drive 2 miles east on State Route 62, then turn south on Airway Ave. Drive one block and turn onto Primrose. Free coffee in room ($).

Yucca Valley Camping

Nearby campgrounds are located in Joshua Tree National Park, south of the town of Yucca Valley. **Hidden Valley Campground** is 14 miles south of town (via Park Boulevard). **Ryan Campground** is 16 miles southeast of Yucca Valley (also via Park Boulevard). Both are primitive campgrounds with pit toilets, no showers and no drinking water. Additional campsites are located in Joshua Tree National Park.

Places to Stay

Nevada

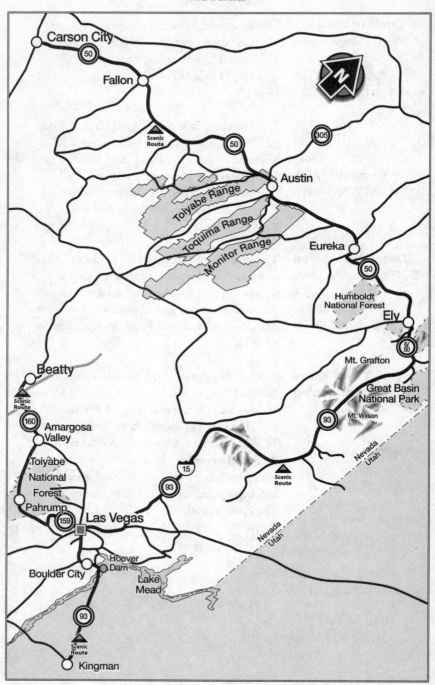

O ver the past 6 years I have crossed Nevada more than 20 times, first in driving between California and the Rocky Mountain regions to research the book on scenic drives in that area, and more recently in aid of writing this southwestern odyssey. What I considered would be a boring pain has been a constant pleasure and the land I had imagined as a desolate wasteland soon proved to be an intriguing area of mountains and forests as well as the "endless" high desert for which the state is most well known.

Life magazine's famous description of Highway 50 as "The Loneliest Road in America" has helped to set this theme of emptiness in people's minds. I hope the pages which follow will tell the opposite story, for Nevada is a mosaic of changing landscapes; muted but varying colors; dry sandy lake beds ringed by high, snow-clad mountains; and varying altitudes, which bring vast changes in topography and ecosystems. There's an incredible difference between the Amargosa Desert and Great Basin National Park, and I hope the four drives that follow will lead you down the road to dispelling Nevada's myth of boredom and emptiness. Even when the land seems to be empty, it is actually full of life.

Tucked into the mideastern side of the state, Great Basin National Park is a recent addition to the national parks system and offers a drive from the Great Basin Desert to above the tree line—an amazing leap in space and time. Near the mountain peaks stand bristlecone pines, the oldest living things on earth. These stark trees have endured on the slopes of Mount Wheeler for more than 3,000 years, and some may be as old as 4,000 years.

The whole of Nevada is like the ancient bristlecones: an enduring and endlessly facinating landscape carved by the forces of nature.

Red Rock Canyon Drive

Beatty to Las Vegas

This route could be called the backroad route between Death Valley and Las Vegas, although it uses paved highways. It can be used as a continuation of the previous drive, which leads from Baker through Death Valley to Beatty.

There is a shorter route to Las Vegas, using Highway 95 for the entire trip, but 95 tends to be boring and travelers shouldn't pass up a chance to visit the Red Rock Canyon National Conservation Area. This route also runs across the southern edge of the Spring Mountain Range, providing visual contrast to a desert experience.

Along the Way

- **Rhyolite**

  Before leaving Beatty, you should see this Nevada ghost town, located just south of town via Highway 374 (the route to Death Valley). Silver was discovered in the valley in 1905, and Rhyolite quickly grew into a sizeable town. Several of the buildings are there today—in a state of disrepair—including the mission-style railroad station and a bottle house. You'll see the remaining walls of the mining company buildings, among other ruins.

- **Amargosa Dunes**

  Our drive to Las Vegas begins by using Highway 95, passing through the Amargosa Valley, where the former river is but a series of desert washes. There's a bridge over the old river just east of Beatty. Farther along, you'll see the dunes west of the highway. A backroad across the desert will take you closer to the shifting sands, formed from the silt that lined the bed of an ancient inland sea.

- **Side Trips**

  We pass the junction village of Lathrop Wells (Amargosa Junction) with an access route to Death Valley Junction and the Amargosa Opera House. If for some good reason you're staying in this area, a side trip to see Marta Becket and her one-woman show in this tiny showplace is highly recommended.

64

Nevada

We now turn onto Highway 160 to continue our drive. Those staying in this area (for no good reason) are probably staying at Crystal—not on the maps (for good reason) but just off Highway 160; Madam Butterfly's and Mabel's are the only reasons for this village's existence. These are only two of a number of adult "theme parks" that dot Nevada's outback. Some of the state's most renowned brothels are just down the highway in the next town (Pahrump).

• Toiyabe National Forest

There are fine recreational opportunities along Wheeler Pass Road which leads east from Pahrump into the Spring Mountains. These are lands within the Toiyabe National Forest. The Lee Canyon area is a popular ski resort. During the summer, the national forest is used for camping and hiking.

• Red Rock Canyon

The major attraction along this road is Red Rock Canyon National Conservation Area, a preserve administered by the Bureau of Land Management (BLM). This recreation area covers 62,000 acres. It's a wonderful scenic region of red rock cliffs and deep canyon oases filled with fan palms—perfect for relaxed sightseeing. The conservation area includes a modern visitor center and features a 13-mile loop drive that is paved and leads to the edges of the cliffs that tower 2,000 feet above the floor of the valley. There are burros and wild horses in the area, as well as bighorn sheep, foxes, and raptors. In the areas with water, there's an amazing variety of amphibians and reptiles. The high sandstone cliffs are part of the Keystone Thrust Fault, which was thrown up about 150 million years ago (give or take a few years). There is a scenic picnic area at Willow Spring. Lost Creek Canyon is a riparian zone that fosters abundant animal and bird life. You'll find brochures on the various attractions in the visitor center.

65

From Red Rock Canyon, downtown Las Vegas is a 30-minute drive. Charleston Blvd. takes you through the suburbs to the action.

Drives

Highway Log

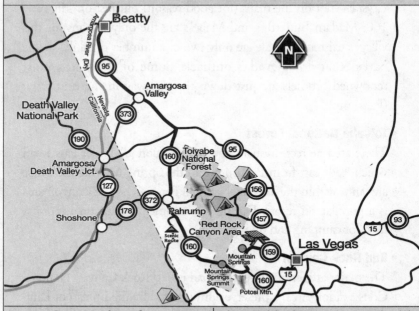

Beatty Gas, motels, cafes, casinos, stores. The ghost town of Rhyolite is 3 miles west of Beatty via Hwy. 374 (the road to Daylight Pass and Death Valley). Our drive begins by taking U.S. Highway 95 south from Beatty. One mile south of town, the highway crosses what used to be the Amargosa River, now a dry wash.

Lathrop Wells Village at junction with gas, cafes and store.

Junction–Highway 373 This road leads south to Amargosa Valley and Death Valley Junction.

Junction–Highway 160 Turn south on Highway 160 to continue this drive to Pahrump, abd Red Rock Canyon.

Turnoff to Crystal A backroad leads to a community that's not on any map—two brothels and a saloon. The dirt road leads west across a dry lake bed, past a mining operation.

Johnny A ghost town (pop. 5) with a pack of burros roaming the sageland.

Sideroad to Death Valley Junction Leads past Devil's Hole National Monument.

Pahrump A town with gas, motels, casinos, cafes, golf courses, RV parks, stores, and other services. Most cafes and motels are located along the highway, with others in the "downtown" area on the Loop Road.

Junction–Highway 372 This road leads southwest to meet Highway 127.

Wheeler Pass Road Leads north from the highway into the Spring Mountains and **Toiyabe National Forest** recreation sites. This is an area filled with canyons and during winter months, the Lee Canyon area is a popular ski facility.

Backroad to Tecopa Leads west from the highway, 10 miles south of Pahrump. There are hot springs at the end of the road, with more than 500 trailer and RV parking spaces.

Twenty miles after leaving Pahrump, the highway curves to the east and enters the Spring Mountains, ascending to **Mountain Springs Summit** (el. 5,493 feet).

Lowell Canyon Road To a ski hill.

Mountain Springs Small community at the summit with restaurant/saloon.

Potosi Mountain (el. 8,504 ft.) is the castellated peak to the east.

Junction–Highway 159 Take this highway north for Red Rock Canyon and Las Vegas. Las Vegas is 25 miles from the junction. Hwy. 160 continues west to meet Interstate 15, 9 miles south of Las Vegas.

Blue Diamond A small community, off the highway.

Red Rock Canyon Recreation Area This outstanding preserve has exciting geology and several recreation sites and trails.

Bonny Springs Road Leads west to Old Nevada, a western mining town re-creation (theme park).

Spring Mountain Ranch State Park To the west of the highway. There are picnic areas in the park, and during summer months the park is the site of concerts and plays.

First Creek Trailhead Leads to the red rock hills.

Red Rock Overlook Pulloff to the north with geological & historical markers, plus good views of the rock cliffs.

Red Rock Canyon Visitor Center–Operated by the BLM, with displays and other information on the recreation area.

Side Trip–Calico Hills
The **Scenic Loop Drive** begins beside the Red Rock Canyon Visitor Center, ending at the highway. The road runs for 13 miles through the Calico Hills, providing vista points for views of wooded canyons and easy walks to the sandstone walls. Picnic sites are available at Red Spring and Willow Spring.

Back on Highway 159
Road to Calico Basin and Red Spring Leads west from the highway toward the red rock formations. Highway 159 continues in a westerly direction, toward the outskirts of Las Vegas.

Approaching Las Vegas–The highway becomes Charleston Blvd., reaching the downtown area of Las Vegas near the Casino Center. Charleston Blvd. intersects Interstate 15 in the downtown area. Las Vegas Blvd. is the famous casino "Strip."

67

Hoover Dam Drive

Las Vegas to Kingman (Arizona)

With the White Hills and the Cerbat Mountain Range dominating the eastern skyline, Highway 93 provides an interesting if not particularly thrilling drive. For the hundreds of thousands of tourists who drive this road between Kingman and Las Vegas each year to reach their favorite casinos, it must become pretty ordinary. However, it's not what's beside the highway, but the attractions a few miles off the highway, that will provide the real thrills that come from a trip through the Lake Mead region. The drive south from Las Vegas starts with the Las Vegas suburbs folding into the industrial town of Henderson, the major supplier of manganese to the war effort during World War Two. It's now a center for chemical industries. The prosaic nature of the region disappears by the time you get to Boulder City and Lake Mead.

Along the Way

• Lake Mead & the Hoover Dam

Located just down the Colorado River from the Grand Canyon, Lake Mead is the result of the greatest power project in the nation, the building of the Hoover Dam in the early 1930s. Above the dam is a wonderful lake and recreation area managed by the National Parks Service. From access points including several resort communities on both the Nevada and Arizona sides of the lake, Lake Mead offers something for everybody: boating, fishing, relaxing in modern/rustic lodges, and marinas. The lake is 105 miles long with 822 miles of wandering shoreline. The water is usually placid and attracts anglers and boaters (including many houseboaters who rent boats at the lake) as well as waterskiers and those who prefer to look at the water from their lakeside campsites. The lake is encircled by the Lake Mead National Recreation Area, which includes Lake Mojave and the Black Canyon.

The dam is an attraction in itself. The highway runs across the dam and there is a parking area at the Hoover Dam Information Center, which stages regular daily tours of the dam and the powerhouse with its huge turbines. There are vista points on both sides of the

Nevada

dam with good views of the dam, of the lake which lies to the
north, and into the Black Canyon.

• Lake Mojave

Below Hoover Dam is another Colorado River canyon, and the
water then flows into Lake Mojave, another widening of the river
behind Davis Dam, built in the 1940s. The highway log that follows points out these distractions from the main highway, and you
are advised to be distracted for a while. If you're a boater, there is
the possibility of a lengthy vacation ahead of you, exploring these
two lakes.

• Arizona Attractions

The highway climbs away from the dam, into Arizona. There are
two access roads to the Arizona side of Lake Mead. One road leads
through Dolan Springs—a retirement community lying at the base
of Mt. Tipton (el. 6,900 feet)—and on for a total of 36 miles to
the community of Meadview. Access to the lake is 9 miles north of
Meadview, at South Cove. The other access point is reached by
taking the more northerly road to Temple Bar, a resort community
that offers a full range of accommodations (motels, a lodge, and
campgrounds). Both Temple Bar and South Cove offer an easy
boat ride to the western end of the Grand Canyon.

There are two resort communities south of Hoover Dam and west
of the main highway. Willow Beach, at the south end of the Black
Canyon, offers boating with lodge and motel accommodations.
Katherine Landing—farther south on Lake Mojave near Bullhead
City, Arizona, and Laughlin, Nevada—provides services for lake
activity, including a large marina, lodge, motel, restaurant, and boat
ramp. Willow Beach is four miles from the highway.

Katherine Landing is 30 miles via Highway 68, which crosses the
Davis Dam above Bullhead City and leads to Laughlin, the fast-
growing Nevada casino town. The drive ends in Kingman, once a
major stopping point on Route 66 and now a service town for
Interstate 40 travelers.

Drives

Highway Log

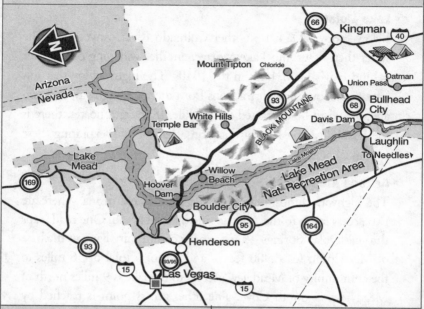

This is close to the shortest drive in this book, but you could spend several days along this route, visiting various points on Lake Mead and Lake Mojave, as well as poking around several ghost towns and enjoying hotel and casino life in Laughlin, Nevada.

Las Vegas From the downtown casino district, take Highway 93/95 (a divided roadway) toward Henderson & Boulder City. The road passes through the Las Vegas suburbs.

70

    Henderson This is the chief industrial town in Nevada, known for its chemical production and other industries.

Junction–Lake Mead Drive This road skirts the western side of the **Lake Mead National Recreation Area**, with several access roads leading to the lake.

Valley Fire State Park is located along Highway 169, off Lake Mead Drive.

Junction–Highway 95 This road runs south to the riverside resort town of Laughlin and the "point" of Nevada, then past the state boundary to Interstate 40 at Needles, California. We continue eastward on Highway 93, toward Lake Mead.

Boulder City Gas, motels, casinos, restaurants, stores. Thirteen miles from Henderson, this is home for the people who work at the Hoover Dam and in the Lake Mead area.

Junction–Lakeshore Road An access road leading along the southwest shore of the lake, joining Hwy. 147 (Lake Mead Dr.) and Northshore Road, which continues to the upper sections of the lake & Valley of Fire State Park.

Hoover Dam The highway crosses the dam (726 feet high), with viewpoints along the way. A tour of the dam and powerhouse is available.

Road to Willow Beach Leads west to the Colorado River and the Lake Mead National Recreation Area. Camping, motel, restaurant.

Road to Temple Bar This road runs north from the highway for 30 miles to Temple Bar, on Lake Mead. This resort community has motels, restaurant, campground, and boat rentals. The shoreline leads all the way into the Grand Canyon.

White Hills Backroads Leading north from the highway, a backroad leads for 3 miles to a fork. Take the left fork for a longer drive into the mountains.

Road to Meadview This road leads northeast through the Hualapai Valley and its Joshua tree forest. There is camping as well as other visitor facilities in the community of Meadview and the road continues, to give access to Lake Mead just a few miles from the mouth of the Grand Canyon.

Dolan Springs is 5 miles from the main highway. It's 36 miles to Meadview and another 6 miles to South Cove (on Lake Mead).

Road to Lake Mojave Leads west for 18 miles to Lake Mojave, a widening of the Colorado River, in the Lake Mead National Recreation Area.

Loop Road to Chloride This near-ghost town is a former mining camp.

The road leads northeast from the highway—a loop of 12 miles. **Junction–Highway 68** Gas, cafe, store at the junction.

Side Trip on Highway 68
Highway 68 runs west for 30 miles, crossing the Davis Dam with access to Bullhead City (AZ) and Laughlin (NV). This is also an opportunity to take a loop drive back to Las Vegas.

Just before the Davis Dam, a sideroad leads north to **Katherine Landing**, a favorite of boaters for recreation on Mojave Lake. Operated by the National Parks Service, Katherine has a motel, restaurant, campground, RV parking, marina, and boat ramp.

Bullhead City also has full visitor facilities and provides free ferry rides across the river to the Laughlin casinos. While it's an 8-mile drive over the Davis Dam to Laughlin, it takes about 2 minutes on the free ferries. Continuing across the Davis Dam, the highway intersects with a road leading south to the Laughlin casino strip, where there are large high-rise hotels.

Kingman This desert stopover city has full visitor services and a regional tourist center on Andy Devine Lane. The late beloved actor lived here and has long been the town's "patron saint" since Route 66 days.

71

Great Basin Drive

Las Vegas to Ely

Eastern Nevada is known for its mountains, lakes, and open rangeland and contains several popular state parks. Leading north from the Las Vegas area, Highway 93 passes through several old pioneer towns including Pioche, Caliente, and Ash Springs. Our drive is designed to take you to Ely on Highway 50 (The Loneliest Road) or to Great Basin National Park which lies southeast of Ely.

Along the Way

• Nevada Lake Country

Sixty miles north of Las Vegas, the highway passes Maynard Lake (to the east) and enters the Pahranagat Lakes region. This is a meadowland which provides wildlife with a superb environment. The two lakes (Upper & Lower Pahranagat) are fine canoeing lakes with adjacent marshes and many birds to see. There are several picnic areas in the Pahranagat Lakes region, as well as convenient campgrounds. At the north end of the upper lake is the village of Alamo, and another 7 miles north is Ash Springs. The warm spring here provides an old-fashioned swimming hole, and a handy RV park is located near the spring.

• Caliente & Pioche

The highway veers due east just north of Ash Springs, climbing over Pahroc Summit. Twelve miles south of the highway—on a backroad—is the ghost town of Delamar. A further climb takes you to Oak Springs Summit (el. 6,237 feet). The town of Caliente was named for the hot springs that feed pools at several Caliente motels. The highway passes the impressive mission-style railroad depot, which was constructed in 1923. Caliente's big annual festival is Meadow Valley Days, held in September.

Thirty-eight miles east of town is Beaver Dam State Park—32 miles of the road is gravel, and this is a pleasant drive during the summer. There's a small reservoir in the park, and the fishing is said to be good here. The campground is situated in a pinyon pine grove.

72

Nevada

The major town on this drive is Pioche, located 25 miles north of Caliente. Pioche is reputed to have been just about the wildest mining camp in Nevada during its peak days in the mid-1870s. At one time, 12,000 people called Pioche home; there are 600 people living there today. The pioneer cemetery provides an interesting stroll. Legend has it that with hordes of people bursting into town and no peacekeepers to be found, more than 75 people were dispatched to their maker by gun before a single person died of natural causes. Today, Pioche is the county seat. The Lincoln County Museum features displays and artifacts of the untamed days of the silver era. The county courthouse (dubbed the "million-dollar courthouse") cost almost $1 million because of corruption and bribery. A tour takes you through this well-restored building.

• State Parks

There are more state parks in this stretch of eastern Nevada than in the rest of the state combined. Three are located only short distances from Pioche. Just south of town is Cathedral Gorge State Park. The gorge is a striking eroded canyon that offers climbs and hikes, camping, and picnicking at a gorge-top picnic park off the highway north of the main section of the park. Spring Valley State Park and Echo Canyon State Recreation Area are about a half-hour's drive east of Pioche. Both areas have reservoirs and feature fishing, hiking, picnicking and camping. North of Pioche the highway parallels Patterson Wash, which can be seen to the east of the road. The highway climbs to 6,100 feet at the Lake Valley Summit and then heads up a wide valley that is framed by the Egan Range (on the west) and the Wilson Creek Range (to the east).

Those wishing to drive to Great Basin National Park (or into Utah to reach Delta) should turn east onto Highway 6/50 at Major's Junction. The side trip to one of America's newest national parks is detailed in the highway log that follows. The trip provides a chance to drive along Osceola Road, through a former gold mining area.

Drives

Highway Log

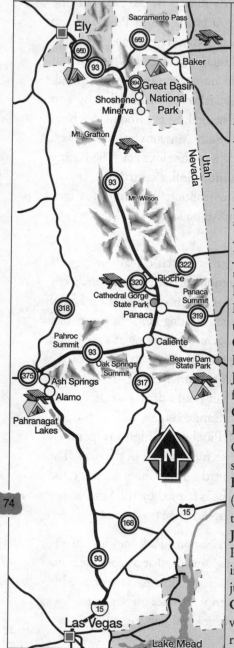

Las Vegas Take Interstate 15 east from the Las Vegas downtown area. Drive east for 20 miles.

Junction–Highway 93 Leads due north toward Ash Springs. Take this exit for the drive to Ely.

Junction–Hwy. 168 To **Glendale**

Junction–Backroad

Pahranagat Lakes Scenic lakes, wildlife refuge, camping areas.

Picnic Area In a cottonwood grove.

Alamo Town with gas, motel, cafes, store.

Ash Springs Gas, store, cafe, RV park.

Junction–Hwys 375 and 318 Continue east on Hwy. 93.

Pahroc Summit (el. 4,961 feet)

Backroad to Delamar (ghost town—12 miles south)

Oak Springs Summit (el. 6,237 feet) Picnic table.

Junction–Highway 317 Leads east from highway to state park.

Caliente Town with gas, cafes, motels, RV park. Hot springs pool at motel. City Hall located in historic Spanish-style former railroad station.

Backroad to Beaver Dam State Park (38 miles from highway) Camping, trails, picnicking.

Junction–Highway 319 To Panaca, Panaca Summit (el. 6,715 feet) and on into Utah and Cedar City. Gas, cafe at junction.

Cathedral Gorge State Park Camping, viewpoints, and trails through the rugged canyon.

Picnic Site and Viewpoint Stairway to bottom of Cathedral Gorge. Two miles north of main park road.

Junction–Hwy. 320 Loop road around Pioche. Access to the town.

Junction–Highway 322 Leads east to Echo Canyon Dam and state rec. area.

Pioche Historic silver mining town with gas, motels, stores, Lincoln County Museum.

Junction–Highway 320 This road loops northward around the town of Pioche and rejoins the main highway. There are several exits to Pioche.

Marker Ghost town of Jackrabbit.

Back Country Byway to Mt. Wilson.

Pony Springs Picnic Area

Backroad Leads west to Cave Valley.

Lake Valley Summit (el. 6,100 ft.)

Backroad Leads east to Atlanta.

Picnic Area At pulloff to the west.

Junction–Hwy. 894 To Shoshone and Minerva.

Junction–Hwys. 6 and 50 (Major's Junction) Hwy. 6/50 leads east toward Baker, Great Basin National Park, and further east to Delta, Utah.

Side Trip to Great Basin N. P.

Drive east on Hwy. 6/50.

Osceola Ghost town (1877), off the highway. Osceola Road is a winding and scenic backroad through old gold mining country, joining the highway beyond Sacramento Pass. We suggest taking this road from the other end as

the route descends past the former mine sites.

Sacramento Pass (el. 7,154 feet)

Osceola Road The other end of this scenic backroad route.

Picnic Area

Junction–Road to Baker Gas, cafe, small store, RV parking.

Baker Small town with rustic motel, minimal campsites, gas, store, deli, cafe, bar. Take the road west to the park gate.

Great Basin National Park Lehman Caves, campground near the park entrance. Mt. Wheeler Scenic Drive also has campgrounds along the road and at the top. Trail to Mt. Wheeler Summit and ancient bristlecone pine forest. Cafe, gift shop.

Back on the Route to Ely

Hwy. 6/50/93 (at Major's Junction)

Picnic Area Off large pulloff at Connor's Pass (el. 7,723 feet).

Junction–Taylor Backroad to Charcoal Ovens Leads west for 7 miles to the Ward Ovens (historic site) and ghost town of Ward (9 miles).

Road to Cave Lake State Park (7 miles off hwy.) Camping, fishing, boating.

Cave Valley Rd. Backroad to west of the highway, a mining road. The Egan Range lies to the west with the Schell Creek Range to the east.

75

The Loneliest Road

Carson City to Ely

Highway 50 leads east from Sacramento, California, and crosses the High Sierra just south of Lake Tahoe. It descends through the eastern Sierra to Nevada's capital, Carson City. Then, it becomes The Loneliest Road in America. It was given this moniker by *Life* magazine in July 1986. The story advised that drivers come equipped with survival skills and indicated that there were no points of interest or attractions along the route.

The people of Fallon, Austin, Eureka and Ely (and points between) didn't get mad—they got even! Communities along the highway got together and developed a Highway 50 Survival Kit that includes a "passport" to be validated along the route and a bumper sticker identifying "survivors." The state helped out by declaring Highway 50 The Loneliest Road in America, and appropriate signs were installed. It was the best thing to have happened to the highway and the communities along this fascinating stretch of central Nevada roadway. The hype worked, and more than 300,000 highway kits have been distributed. Of course there was a lot there to begin with, and the publicity has introduced the historic mining towns of the region to additional tourists. The route is filled with scenic highlights and recreation opportunities.

Along the Way

• Sand Mountain & Pony Express Station

Beyond Fallon there is a dry salty lake bed, and to the north is the 400-foot Sand Mountain—a huge sand dune formed by the strong winds which whistle across Lake Carson, whipping up sand and blowing it into a shallow canyon that traps the sand. There is a BLM recreation area here, and the dunes are popular with off-roaders. In this same area is the first (and best-preserved) of several pony express stations. On a nature trail through the desert at Sand Springs, the old lava rock express station has been unearthed and reconstructed to its original shape, with roofless rooms (with a fireplace) for the riders and rock corrals for their horses. For visitors, this is a trip back in time to the romantic days of gold discoveries and western settlement.

Nevada

• To Austin

Far from being lonely, the highway passes watering holes such as Cold Springs (a cafe and bar) and then (after two mountain passes) arrives in Austin—one of Nevada's prominent mining towns of the late 1880s. Today, Austin has three remarkable pioneer churches, historic buildings along the highway, and ruins of many of the town's original buildings (see page 81).

• Toiyabe National Forest

Between Austin and Eureka, a distance of 70 miles, the road crosses the Toiyabe Range through the Toiyabe National Forest. There are campgrounds and picnic parks near the Austin and Hickison Summits. The recreation area at Hickison Summit offers a picnic area in a pinyon pine forest and a short walk to an Indian petroglyph site. After 15 minutes, the highway descends into long, flat valleys with many dry lake beds.

• Eureka

Eureka is the second of three major mining towns: a nineteenth-century Wild West town with a restored county courthouse, a theater with restoration in progress, and a museum in the former *Eureka Sentinel* building, one block off the highway (see page 87). The 77 miles between Eureka and Ely provide some more "lonely" experiences. This is mostly open grazing land, with cattle often feeding on the more juicy vegetation along the highway. There's lots of sage in the valleys, and after a short rainstorm the smell of the land is remarkably pungent.

• Ely

A modern town with historic overtones, Ely has casinos and modern motels. The old railway station is now a railway museum. It also serves as the station for the Nevada Northern Railway, which offers short-line rides through the countryside on most weekends and always during the three summer holiday weekends. An hour's drive south of this pioneer outpost, Great Basin National Park offers access to the bristlecone pines atop Mt. Wheeler, in addition to camping, caves, and hiking trails.

Drives

Highway Log

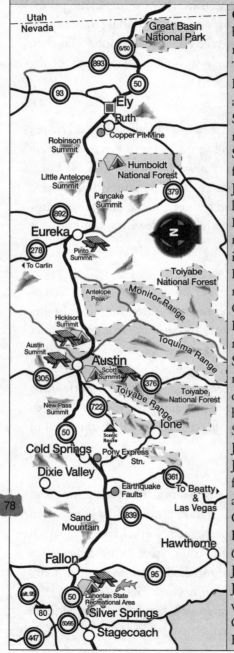

Carson City The state capital, at the base of the High Sierra, with hotels, motels, gas, stores, and restaurants. Take Highway 50 east.

Dayton Gas, cafes, motels. Small town at edge of Carson Valley.

Sideroad to Virginia City Leads east, 5 miles beyond Dayton.

Silver Springs Small town, 35 miles from Carson City. Gas, motel, store.

Junction–Alt. Hwy. 50/95 This road leads north to Fernley & Interstate 80.

Lahontan State Recreation Area Ten miles west of Fallon. Camping, boating, fishing, picnicking.

Fallon Agricultural town with large naval air base, 61 miles from Carson City. Motels, gas, cafes, RV parks.

Petroglyph Site At Grimes Point, north of highway via sideroad.

Sand Mountain Huge sand dune, north of highway about 20 miles east of Fallon. Closer to the highway is the historic pony express station and the Sand Springs desert nature trail.

Junction–Dixie Valley Rd. (Hwy. 121)

Junction–Rd. 839 To the south, paved for 20 miles and then gravel for another 58 miles. Leads past Pilot Cone to Hawthorne and Highway 95.

Backroad to 1954 Earthquake Faults 6 miles off highway to the south.

Junction–Hwy. 361 To Beatty.

Junction–Rd. 722 Former main highway is now a scenic loop drive over Carroll Summit & Railroad Pass. Joins Hwy. 50 just west of Austin.

241 miles—5 hours

Pony Express Station Rock remains of old station & telegraph repeater.
Cold Springs Gas and bar.
Old Stage Station Another in the series of stage stops.
New Pass Summit (el. 6,348 feet)
Mt. Airy Summit (el. 6,979 feet) The road now descends into the Reese River Valley.
Marker–Pony Express Trail To north.
Marker–Jacobsville The first settlement in the area, from 1860.
Backroad to Ione Follows course of the Reese River south for 44 miles.
Big Creek Rd. Leads south to camping (12 miles).
Junction–Rd. 722 Eastern end of the old highway route.
Junction-Hwy. 278. Leads north to Interstate 80 and town of Battle Mountain. Forest ranger station just north of junction.
Austin Silver mining town, founded 1862. Gas, motels, cafes, stores, museum. The highway now climbs to the **Austin Summit** (el. 7,484 ft.).
Picnic Area To north of the highway.
Scott Summit (el. 7,267 ft.)
Mt. Scott Campground North of the summit. Picnic tables.
Junction–Rd. 376 Leads south to Round Mtn. and Tonopah.
Hickison Summit (el. 6,564 ft.)
Campground Just west of summit, to north of the highway at Petroglyph Recreation Site. Campsites in pinyon pine forest, picnic tables.

Picnic Area North of highway halfway across the valley.
Picnic Area On Bean Flat Road.
Backroad Leads south past Antelope Peak.
Junction–Highway 278 Leads north to Carlin and Interstate 80.
Eureka Historic mining town. Gas, cafes, bars, casinos, motels.
Picnic Area At pullout.
Pinto Summit (el. 7,376 feet)
Backroad Leads south to Rd. 379 & village of Currant.
Junction–Hwy. 892 Leads north for 54 miles, to the hamlet of Strawberry & the loop to Eureka.
Pancake Summit (el. 6,517 feet) Leads to another vast valley of sage and sand with dry lake.
Little Antelope Summit (el. 7,433 ft.)
Campground South of highway on Illepah Reservoir.
Road to Ruby Marshes A scenic backroad leads along eastern edge of Ruby Mountains (Humboldt National Forest). Rd. leads north to Hwy. 229 & to Wells & I-80.
Robinson Summit (el. 7,607 ft.)
Garnet Hill Recreation Site Via sideroad north from hwy. (3 miles).
Junction–Sideroad to Ruth & Open Pit Mine Visitor parking, viewpoint.
Ely Town with motels, hotels, stores, casinos, restaurants, scenic railway, RV parks & campgrounds. The old train station is a block north of Hwy. 50.

Other Nevada Drives

- **Toiyabe National Forest**

  Less than an hour north of Las Vegas, via Highway 95, are the eastern slopes of the Spring Mountains, including the **Mt. Charleston Recreation Area** and **Floyd Lamb State Park**. There are **Toiyabe National Forest campgrounds** in the mountains, as well as hiking and nature trails. Drive west from Highway 95 on Nevada Hwy. 157 and a loop drive that leads from Hwy. 157 onto Hwy. 158. Hwy. 156 will take you back to Highway 95. One doesn't think of southern Nevada as an outdoor recreation area, but the Spring Mountains will quickly dispel this myth.

- **South of Ely**

  Highway 95 leads south from Ely—the main north/south route to Las Vegas from the northeastern part of the state. There are several points of interest just off this stretch of highway, particularly the **Ward Charcoal Ovens Historic Site**, reached by a backroad leading west. Much charcoal was used in the copper smelting process in the late years of the 1800s, and six large beehive-shaped ovens were built from native stone in the 1870s. **Cave Lake State Park** is 20 miles southeast of Ely, with a 32-acre reservoir offering swimming, picnicking, boating, fishing, and camping.

- **Sideroads to Death Valley & Tecopa**

  There are several backroad routes between Hwy. 95 and the California desert. A dirt road across the Amargosa Desert provides access to Death Valley Junction, where Hwy. 95 meets Hwy. 160. The road passes Devil's Hole National Monument.

  Ten miles south of Pahrump is a backroad leading east to **Tecopa**, California. During the winter months, Tecopa (including the nearby hot springs area) is awash in trailers. There's a huge Inyo County campground across from the public hot spring pools, in addition to several private RV and hot spring resorts. Altogether, there are more than 500 trailer & RV spaces in this tiny pair of communities, and the place is jammed during the high season.

Nevada

Austin

Austin Located midway along The Loneliest Road in America and at the geographical center of Nevada, Austin was the largest of 30 busy mining camps in this region of the state in the 1860s and 1870s.

It was silver that brought more than 10,000 people to the city following an accidental discovery of the mineral by a pony express rider (at least that's one of the stories). The Nevada Central Railroad ran down the main street, at the end of 92 miles of track from Battle Ground. Fifty million dollars in silver was produced in this town, which was named after Austin, Texas. The town has some fascinating stories: The International Hotel was moved—board by board—from its original site in Virginia City. Emma Wixon, the daughter of a prominent pioneer Austin doctor, went to Europe as Emma Nevada and found fame as an opera singer. Mining financier Anson Phillips Stokes used part of his wealth to build a three-story "tower" as his summer home—the replica of a tower outside of Rome. Three churches built in the 1860s and 1870s stand today, as reminders of the days when churches in Nevada were funded with donated mining stocks and pipe organs were shipped "around the horn" from Europe. Austin today is a town that reflects these early days, along its main street and in other parts of town. Many of the old buildings remain in various states of decline, decay and restoration.

Austin is set in the middle of a fine recreation area that includes parts of the Toiyabe National Forest. There are many forest and BLM campgrounds in the region, including an excellent campground in the Bob Scott recreation area east of town along Highway 50. Seventy million-year-old remains of huge fossils are found in Ichthyosaur State Park, which also preserves the substantial remains of the Berlin ghost town—one of the many mining camps of the 1860s. The park and ghost town are 60 miles southeast of Austin at an elevation of 7,000 feet. There are campgrounds in the park, which is reached by taking Nevada Highway 21.

The Reese River Valley, extending south from Austin, is a prime fishing area with more campgrounds operated by the Forest Service. Spencer Hot Springs is located 21 miles east of town on Monitor Road. Water at 140 degrees pours into a concrete tub. Wooden bathtubs were used by early miners and Austin townsfolk. South of the springs is Toquima Cave, with Indian pictographs and a primitive campground. Diana's Punch Bowl, farther south, is an old geyser.

Beatty

Beatty is the closest town to Death Valley National Park and is only a half-hour's drive from the valley floor.

If Beatty had an official town animal, it would have to be the burro. During the gold rush era in the 1800s, prospectors came to the Amargosa Valley with their belongings on the backs of sturdy burros (usually one burro to a miner). Realizing that the gold fields of California were far away, they hiked over the mountains, leaving their burros behind. The little pack animals thrived in the desert, breeding thousands of descendants. By 1950, there were so many herds of wild burros around Beatty and in Death Valley that a program to export burros was begun, and it continues today. However, you'll still see plenty of burros grazing in the desert, paying no attention to highway traffic.

Beatty was the railroad service center for the Bullfrog Mining District in 1900. Nearby Rhyolite, the mining camp, was a booming town of 10,000. Today, Rhyolite is a ghost town (although a new gold mine and mill operate near the old townsite), and Beatty is a casual highway stopping point for travelers to Death Valley. Rhyolite is worth the short drive south of town. The wind has knocked down many of the buildings on the old mining town's main street, and only a few walls remain. The mission-style railroad station still stands, as does a bottle house that was constructed with 50,000 liquor and beer bottles by a miner, Tom Kelly.

Some of the features of the old town are to be restored by the Friends of Rhyolite, a nonprofit society recently formed. The bottle house is high on their list of priorities.

With six campgrounds and RV parks, Beatty provides a cooler place to camp than Death Valley during summer months. There also several motels, as well as casinos, bars, and cafes. One campground is at Bailey's Hot Springs, located 6 miles north of Beatty on U.S. 95. The hot springs resort has a picnic area and offers swimming in addition to providing campsites for overnight visitors.

The highway drive to Death Valley (via Highway 374) passes through Daylight Pass. Travelers during the winter season—October to June—may wish to take the Titus Canyon backroad, an extremely scenic one-way route that crosses the Amargosa Range and reaches Death Valley to connect with the road to Scotty's Castle, near the north end of the valley. Ubehebe Crater is also in this northern area.

Southwest of Beatty are the Amargosa Dunes, huge hills of sand open to the public for hiking, off-road driving, and picnicking. Conventional vehicles (even 4WD vehicles) are not suitable for driving on the dunes: ATVs or dune buggies are required. The dunes are just a small part of what constitutes the Amargosa Desert, a vast tract that lies in the valley of the old Amargosa River. The river is now a series of dry washes. Many backroads lead through Bureau of Land Management lands.

• A Low-Level Day-Trip

The Amargosa must be savored—close up and not just not driven past—and a day-trip provides the full impact of the desert and this fascinating region, with a drive through the Amargosa plus a tour of parts of Death Valley.

Start at Beatty and drive southeast along U.S. Highway 95. Turn south at Lathrop Wells (46 miles from Beatty) and drive across the desert to Death Valley Junction (the site of the fabled Amargosa Opera House). Continue west, descending into Death Valley through the Furnace Creek Wash. Drive north, exiting Death Valley via Highway 374.

Destinations

Boulder City

Boulder City holds a considerable distinction. It is the only city in Nevada without gaming; it was created for the construction of the Hoover Dam, and has developed into a green, friendly, vacation and retirement city. The community services the needs of more than one million visitors who are attracted by Hoover Dam and Lake Mead each year. The point of all this is just to emphasize that Boulder City makes a fine place to stay—even if you're commuting to a casino in Las Vegas, only 19 miles away. The Gold Strike Casino is on the highway much closer to Boulder City, if you get desperate. This is a getaway town with great recreation facilities along Lake Mead, all close to the city center via North Shore Road.

Boulder City, a modern and totally planned community, is blessed with more than its share of parks. The town was actually built by the federal government to house the people who built the dam and then came to run it and the recreation area. There's a free movie about the building of the dam shown in the visitor's bureau, at 441 Nevada Highway. The town has a golf course. A thriving artists' community provides a good selection of small galleries and crafts shops. Hoover Dam is 7 miles east of Boulder City. The highway crosses the dam with viewpoints offering lake and canyon scenes. Guided tours of the dam and power plant are given daily, except Christmas Day. You can take a cruise on Lake Mead. The Desert Princess operates popular cruises daily throughout the year from 11:30 AM, with a special early Sunday breakfast cruise at 9 AM. The sternwheeler tours the southern part of the lake, passing between islands and sailing close to Hoover Dam.

The Lake Mead National Recreation Area is located both north and south of town. The northern edge of Lake Mead has seven marinas with boat rentals (including houseboats). There are campgrounds with 290 spaces for tents, RVs, and trailers, as well as additional private RV parks in the area. For accommodations information, see page 101.

Farther south, via U.S. Highway 93, is the southern section of the national recreation area, which includes the canyons just south of the

Nevada

Hoover Dam and Lake Mojave. It stretches along both sides of the Colorado River to just north of Laughlin. This part of the river is popular with rafters. Organized raft trips leave from just beneath Hoover Dam and float through the Black Canyon—past riverside hot springs and waterfalls—to Willow Beach or on to Lake Mojave. Canoe trips may also be arranged. See the visitor's bureau for schedules.

Where to Eat

Lake Mead Lodge and Marina (322 Lake Shore Rd.) has places to eat in a scenic setting beside the water. Menus are wide-ranging (**$$ to $$$**).

For Mexican food, try **Casa Flores Restaurant** (930 Nevada Highway). Like most Boulder City restaurants, this is a casual place without pretensions (**$$**).

You can get traditional steak and eggs breakfasts at the **Gold Strike Inn & Casino** (on Highway 93, out of the city near Hoover Dam). This, too, is not a fancy spot, and casino noises intrude on dining (**$ to $$**). The **Railroad Pass Hotel and Casino** (Hwys. 93 and 95, north of town) serves the same kinds of casino fare (**$ to $$**). Otherwise, there are the standard fast-food joints including the **Snacketeria** at Hoover Dam (**$**).

Ely

The gateway town to Great Basin National Park, Ely is a mining town that is a rarity: it still has a working mine, the huge open copper pit just west of town. The "glory hole" is so big that in its expansion, it consumed the old townsite of Ruth. An overview offers a good look at the largest open pit in the western U.S.

Ely is pronounced Eee-Lee. It's the seat of White Pine County, a desert and mountain region near the eastern boundary of the state. To the south and also to the north, there are state parks, wildlife preserves, and recreation sites operated by the Bureau of Land Management and the Forest Service. These include the **Ruby Marshes** (north) and **Cave Lake State Park** (south). Ely offers what many railroad buffs think are three (not one, but three) of the finest short-line scenic railway experiences in the country.

Destinations

The Nevada Northern Railway, inaugurated in 1906, was a necessity for copper mining around Ely. It connected the mines with the Southern Pacific Railroad line, 130 miles to the north. It provided passenger service until 1920 and provided local service until 1983, when the line was donated to a nonprofit foundation. The Nevada Northern Railway Museum is the old Ely Station. It's a museum and a station—where you catch the short-line passenger rides into the countryside.

The most nostalgic ride is what they call The Ghost Train of Old Ely. A classic Baldwin 10-wheeler steam engine pulls an 1890 Pullman coach and a slightly younger (1907) baggage car. The Ghost Train passes through Ely's downtown and then through Robinson Canyon to Keystone—a ghost town site. The Highliner uses an ore-line diesel engine to climb through the foothills over the Steptoe Valley. This trip is 22 miles long with McGill the destination.

Offered on Saturdays, a diesel excursion on the Twilight Special travels both the Keystone and Highline routes during the late afternoon and twilight hours. Rates for rides range from $8 to $14. You can even rent an engine and be your own engineer (with supervision) for a 140-mile round trip— for $175 (diesel) or $350 (steam). For all those who wanted to be railroad engineers in their youth, this is the ultimate! For reservations, phone (702) 289-2085.

Ely has a selection of motels—some attached to casinos—an RV park, and a fine B & B place, the Steptoe Valley Inn. See page 102 for Ely accommodations. The White Pine Chamber of Commerce, the visitor center, is in an office on the main street (Hwy. 50). The BLM office, with plenty of good information on recreation sites and backroads, is just north of town on Hwy. 93.

Day-Trips from Ely

Great Basin National Park is just an hour's drive southeast of Ely via Highway 6/50. The park's scenic drive will take you from desert flatland up the slopes of Mount Wheeler, to a campground and a trail that leads to the peak. Also accessed by a trail is an ancient bristlecone pine forest. Cave Lake State Park is located south of Ely on Success Summit Road.

Nevada

Past the park, the road is unpaved and suitable only for 4WD and high-clearance vehicles. This is a fascinating 32-mile loop route with deer and elk to be seen (evenings are best) and several primitive camping areas along Success Creek. The dirt road ends in Duck Creek Basin (Forest Service campgrounds), with the end at Highway 93, near McGill.

Eureka

Now a town of 1,500 people, Eureka boasted a population of 9,000 after the lead and silver discoveries of the 1860s. At one time, around 1880, the city had several dozen gambling houses, more than a hundred saloons, an opera house, several "modern" hotels, and sixteen nearby smelters. The town was built so quickly that buildings were moved from several other communities including Elko, Carlin, and Treasure City.

One of the best-preserved of the old mining towns of Nevada, Eureka is quite an historic treasure. The county court house and post office date from the late 1800s, as do many of the other buildings along Main Street (Highway 50). Fire destroyed many of the original wooden buildings and the second stage of construction used brick and volcanic tuff. There are still several buildings with volcanic rock walls. The last of three large fires occurred along Main Street in 1884, and most of the current buildings date from construction after that fire. New mines have opened in recent years, and Eureka is again a mining town.

The first place one should visit when arriving here is the Historical Museum on Monroe Street, one short block from Main Street. The building used to house the *Eureka Sentinel* newspaper, and the museum contains several old printing presses, left in position. The museum also serves as the local visitor information center.

The Eureka County Historical Society has a self-guiding tour map of the town available at the museum, and this provides an excellent guide for walking the town and visiting the historic Victorian buildings. One prominent building on Main Street is the Eureka Theatre. Originally the Opera House, its name was changed when silent movies came to town in

1913. It has been in a state of disrepair for many years and is now under restoration. St. James Episcopal Church—on Spring Street—was the first church building in town, built in 1872.

Eureka was settled by many Cornish miners, and the church was built to accommodate the Cornish people and other English immigrants. Built of stone, it survived the fires of the 1880s. Five cemeteries are located on the west side of town in an area known alternatively as Graveyard Flat and Death Valley.

There's an RV park in town (Cottage RV Park) in addition to a bed and breakfast inn (the Parsonage House) and several rudimentary motels (see page 102 for accommodations). There's a scenic picnic spot at Pinto Summit, a few miles east of town on The Loneliest Road in America (Highway 50).

Backroad Trips from Eureka

Eureka is midway between the Toiyabe and Humboldt mountain ranges and public campgrounds are at a premium in the area close to town. BLM lands in the area have recreation sites with primitive campsites.

The best backroad adventure in the area is a drive beginning by taking Road 892 north from Hwy. 50—15 miles east of Eureka. The paved road becomes a dirt surface after 30 miles, and this backroad leads through a long valley to the east of the Diamond Mountains.

Although this road continues north toward Elko, turn left toward Railroad Pass (el. 5,896 ft.) and after crossing the summit, the road curves south through another valley with the Diamond range now to the east, returning to Eureka. There are several BLM sites along the loop and the scenery includes fine views of both sides of Diamond Peak (el. 10,614 ft.).

Fallon

We don't think of Nevada as an agricultural state, yet some of the most productive farmland in the West is at Fallon, a high-desert town located on Highway 50, The Loneliest Road in America—featured in our drive across Nevada, on page 76. This is cantaloupe country.

Nevada

Fallon has a fascinating history, which is evident as you drive around the town. **Churchill County Museum** features extensive exhibits on Indian and pioneer life in the area. There's a reproduction of a Paiute tule hut and a tour through the Hidden Cave. Many of the pioneer displays focus on the people who traveled the overland emigrant trail that passed close to Fallon. Beginning in the late 1840s, thousands of emigrants walked and rode this trail, which led through the High Sierra gold rush country and on to the coast.

Fallon is also pony express territory, and the famed but short-lived mail service was followed by the Overland Telegraph. Churchill County still operates what is the nation's only telephone system owned by a county. You'll see Navy jets criss-crossing the sky above Fallon. The Naval Air Station here is one of the top pilot training facilities in the nation, and the air base has provided Fallon with a stable economy.

Lahontan Lake, a large reservoir west of Fallon, is a favorite recreation area. **Stillwater Wildlife Management Area** and the **Lahontan Marshes** attract thousands of migratory geese and ducks which use the marshes as a resting point on their annual flyways. Fishing is good in Lahontan Lake, the Harmon and Sheckler Reservoirs, and the Carson River.

One of the most interesting scenes in the area is east of Fallon, a half-mile off the highway. **Sand Mountain** is 2 miles long, a mile wide, and more than 600 feet high. This perfect hill of fine bleached sand has blown into a box canyon over thousands of years from the flats of Lake Lahontan, an ancient sea now dry. The huge pile of sand is available to ATV enthusiasts, who buzz up and down the dune, with the constant winds covering the tracks in short order.

A short desert trail leads from the foot of Sand Mountain to the tumble-down site of one of the original pony express overnight stations, where the riders came to rest themselves and their horses. Visiting this spot gives you a good feeling for the hardship and many privations faced by these fearless riders.

There are two areas that geology and history lovers will find interesting. **Grimes Point County Park** is located a few miles east of town, with an

Destinations

Indian burial ground and displays of petroglyphs, as well as several bat caves. Hidden Cave is considered to be one of the country's most important archeological finds. East of the park along Highway 50, the base of the Fairview Mountains has jumbles of semiprecious stones, including geodes, agates, calcite, and jasper, which are there for the picking. On the eastern slopes of the range are more chances for rock-hounding. This is the location of a well-defined fault line.

Where to Eat

While there are several rather ordinary cafes in town, the **Stockyard Cafe** at 1025 Allen Rd. offers an unusual venue for a restaurant—at Gallagher's Livestock Yard. They serve breakfast and lunch, and Basque dinners on Wednesday and Friday evenings ($ to $$). The **Bonanza Inn and Casino** gives you food while you gamble ($$). **The Depot** is the former 1906 railroad station, moved to 875 Williams Ave. ($$ to $$$).

Great Basin National Park

The Great Basin of the American West is a vast, under-appreciated region that stretches from the Rocky Mountains to the Sierra Nevada, and from southern Nevada and Death Valley in the south to Oregon (and even southern Canada) to the north. The Great Basin includes more than 160 mountain ranges, and not one of the rivers and creeks draining these mountains flows into the ocean. The water drains into the desert, where it evaporates or soaks into the ground. Two highways cross this high-desert region from west to east: Interstate 80 (in northern Nevada) and Highway 50, which runs from Carson City to Ely..

The first explorer to map and describe the region was John C. Fremont, who traveled across the basin in 1843–44. Fremont put to an end the theory that the Great Salt Lake was an arm of the Pacific Ocean and, for the first time, proved the idea of the basin as a region unto itself. His name is remembered across the West.

One of the benefits of taking the Loneliest Road (Highway 50) across the middle of Nevada is that it passes Great Basin National Park, located near the village of Baker at the eastern edge of the state. Great Basin, one of the newest national parks, preserves and protects a significant piece of the region centered around Mt. Wheeler, an impressive mountain rising from the desert to an elevation of 12,067 feet.

The park is 50 miles southeast of Ely, Nevada. To get there, take Highway 6/50 leading south from Ely and turn west at Major's Junction. A turnoff to the small community of Baker also leads to the park.

• Park Attractions

The park area has seen several incarnations over the past 100 years. Mt. Wheeler has been part of the Humboldt National Forest, and the national forest still encases the park on the west, south, and north sides. One of the park's major attractions, the Lehman Caves, has been a national monument for many years. The caves may have been discovered by prospectors before the 1860s when Absalom S. Lehman moved to the area and explored the series of caves under the Snake Range. Taking time from his ranching activities, he led tours through the caves until he died in 1891. A trail runs through the caves. Pools of water on the floors have built miniature dams that have terraced the caves. Stalagmites, stalagtites, silvery crusts, and helictites (the popcornlike lumps) have grown throughout the caves. No two rooms in the cave series are alike. Daily tours are conducted through the caves, on a 2/3-mile (1 kilometer) pathway with stairs. The temperature averages about 50 degrees F (10 degrees C), and jackets are advised. The cave entrance is adjacent to the park visitor center and a snack bar. The visitor center is the natural place to begin a visit to the park.

Mt. Wheeler itself is the second major attraction. Drivers may take an exciting tour up the mountain on the Mt. Wheeler Scenic Drive, which winds its way up the eastern slope through the Lehman Creek Valley. There are several viewpoints at pulloffs along the way. The first turnoff is at the remains of the Osceola gold mining ditch, which took water from Lehman Creek to the Osceola mining camp several miles to the north. The Mather and Peak overlooks provide superb views of the peak. There are campsites beside the drive at a parking area and near the summit.

From the entrance to the top campground, a trail leads to a grove of bristlecone pine trees. You can take the hike on your own or join a guided hike with a park ranger. These 3-hour hikes are offered in the summer (from mid-June to Labor Day, starting at 9 AM).

• Park Trails

Other hikes and nature walks are available from various points in the park. The **Lehman Creek Trail** connects the upper Lehman Creek Campground and Wheeler Peak Campground over a distance of 4 miles, with an elevation change of more than 2,000 feet. The **Mountain View Nature Trail**, starting near the visitor center, is a 1/2-mile self-guided loop walk that begins near the Rhodes Cabin and a picnic area. A trail leaflet is available.

In other parts of the park: The **Baker Creek Trail** begins at the end of Baker Creek Road and winds 5 miles beside Baker Creek to Baker Lake, a fine spot to relax for a picnic. There are excellent views of the Snake Range peaks from this trail. The **Johnson Lake Trail** begins at the end of Snake Creek Road, following an old mining road for 6.5 miles, climbing about 1,000 feet and ending at Johnson Lake. Snake Creek Road is reached by taking Highway 487 south from the town of Baker.

Camping

There are are four campgrounds in the park and three are located along Wheeler Peak Road. All are operated on a first come, first served basis.

Lower Lehman Creek Campground has 11 sites, open year-round, with water, pit toilets, and pull-through sites for small RVs and trailers (elevation, 7,500 feet). **Upper Lehman Creek Campground** has 24 sites, with water, pit toilets, pull-through sites for small RVs and trailers, and a group picnic site, at an elevation of 7,800 feet.

Wheeler Peak Campground has 37 sites, with water and pit toilets, 12 miles from the visitor center at the top of the scenic drive, at an elevation of 9,950 feet.

Baker Creek Campground has 32 sites, with water and pit toilets. It is 3 miles from the visitor center.

Nevada

Las Vegas

The Glitz and the Glitter!

Las Vegas is best seen at night as miles of neon tubing glows, gleams, flashes, and snakes along the sides of the Strip casinos, lighting up the town. Red imitation volcanoes flow, a pirate ship fires on a British man-of-war, palm trees have their own spotlights, as do the aging entertainers who perform in the casino theaters that hark back to another day.

The economy of Las Vegas, and indeed the entire Nevada casino industry, has seen better days. Not as many gamblers are showing up, and those who do don't spend as much money as they once did. More than one Las Vegas casino has declared bankruptcy in recent years, as did the city's most prominent resident entertainer, Wayne Newton. A sorry pass for the city that Bugsy Siegel built!

However, all is not lost (except for gambling money). Huge new hotels have just been built, with more to come with the retooling of the city as a major family destination resort. Room prices can be had for little more than a song (at the right time of year), and food is still the best bargain in this town of perpetual gambling and buffet service. And you can still play nickel slots (my self-imposed limit). New museums have opened to join Liberace's piano collection as side-attractions to the main casino economy. Best of all, Lake Mead is but a half-hour drive to the east. The city also has a historical side, which is well worth exploring.

Las Vegas is still the place to go for the ultimate escape—to a world completely alien from the ordinary humdrum working life we normally lead. So Wayne Newton is broke. He still lives in his mansion and has only joined the crowd who lose their shirts in Las Vegas every night—and most gambling tourists think that's quite OK.

Las Vegas is doing all right. There's still lots of power flowing from Hoover Dam to keep the neon blinking, and there is a not-so-subtle shift taking place in Las Vegas, toward offering more of an all-around family vacation experience. Excalibur—that huge new hotel—started the trend, and there are more hotels combined with theme parks being constructed at this moment. The newest additions now operating include the MGM

Destinations

Grand, Treasure Island, and Luxor. Circus Circus, the first of the family-oriented casino-hotels, has added Grand Slam Canyon.

In addition to the attractions of Las Vegas, the city is just 140 miles from the middle of **Death Valley** and only 20 miles from **Red Rock Canyon**—a wonderful conservation area that offers an archeological loop drive. The city is 50 miles from **Valley of Fire State Park**, where 1,500-year-old Indian rock paintings are found amidst great vistas. North of town, **Mt. Charleston** offers a cool retreat from the bustle of Las Vegas with recreation sites operated by the Forest Service. It's only 40 miles away. You can take a canoe or raft trip down the Colorado River, below the Hoover Dam through the Colorado's **Black Canyon** to **Lake Mojave**. Even the **Grand Canyon** is less than a day's drive from Las Vegas.

This is a university town with several good museums, including the **Clark County Museum** (1830 South Boulder Hwy. in nearby Henderson), the **Las Vegas Art Museum** (3333 W. Washington), the **Las Vegas Natural History Museum** (990 Las Vegas Blvd.), and the **Nevada State Museum** (700 Twin Lakes Drive). The University of Nevada at Las Vegas (UNLV) has two fine cultural attractions to visit: the **Museum of Natural History** and the **Alta Ham Fine Art Gallery,** both at 4505 S. Maryland Parkway. The city's **Zoo** is located at 1775 North Rancho and is open daily from 9 AM to 5 PM. Commercial museums include the **Liberace Museum** and the newer attraction next door, the **Bethany Celebrity Doll Museum**—think of it as a miniature wax museum. They're located at Tropicana Blvd. and Spencer St.

Where to Eat

There was a day when eating in Las Vegas meant suffering an overdose in a casino's buffet restaurant. There's a lot more variety today, as the hotels have developed a more sophisticated approach to dining. All of the major casino operations have several restaurants including family-style cafes, and several of the newer (and classier) places have fine dining. Caesars set the tone by putting a branch **Spago** in the Forum Shops. The MGM followed with Mark Miller's **Coyote Cafe,** serving the same kind of food as the original in Santa Fe. Wolfgang Puck, not to be outdone with only one restaurant in town, opened **Cafe California** in the MGM Grand. On the

Nevada

other hand, you can engage in fine dining without a big name attached at the Golden Nugget in downtown Las Vegas. The restaurant is called **Stefanos**, and it is one of four restaurants in the venerable and deluxe hotel. All of the above are in the $$$ range.

There are several independent restaurants where one can get away from the bustle of casino life and thoroughly enjoy a good meal. **Andre's Restaurant**, at 401 South Sixth Street, serves French cuisine and does it with a flair every day from 6 PM ($$$). Reservations are advised, call (702) 385-5016. **Ruth's Chris Steak Houses** are renowned and incredibly popular restaurants, at 3900 Paradise Road on the Eastside (702-791-7011) and at 4561 W. Flamingo Rd. on the Westside (702-248-7011). Steaks and accompaniment is the theme here, but (unlike most steak houses) this double-name cafe has an excellent wine list. There's a late-night menu from 11 PM ($$ to $$$).

On the other hand, buffets are still popular, and there is one available at most casino-hotels, from **Balley's** to **The Mirage** and **Luxor**. For those who treasure the idea of the truly cheap buffet as part of a Las Vegas vacation, **Harrah's** has breakfast for $3.79, lunch for $4.49, and dinner for $5.99. **Circus Circus** has the same prices (at press time). There are cheaper buffets in the downtown Casino Center area, but they are skimpy and uninteresting tables indeed, with food that's been waiting too long on steam tables.

A Day-Trip from Las Vegas

The north end of Lake Mead offers a fascinating day-trip through the Moapa Valley. In 1864, Mormons settled this area along the Muddy River. Their town was named St. Thomas. Later, Overton, Logandale, and Kaolin sprang to life. Lake Mead was formed by the waters backed up from the Hoover Dam, and both St. Thomas and Kaolin succumbed to the flooding. The Lost City Museum is located in Overton, containing collections from Pueblo Indian cultures that existed in the valley long before the Mormons arrived. Moapa, north of Glendale, is an old railroad town with many historic buildings. Along this same route is the Valley of Fire. Formed from shifting sand dunes over millions of years, this is a stark area full of brush and desert wildlife. The state park has picnic areas.

95

Destinations

One of the striking scenes along this route is the Overton arm of Lake Mead. This bay of deep blue water offers boating, waterskiing, fishing, and relaxing in a marina restaurant. There are picnic parks along the arm, and an RV park is located at the marina.

To get there, drive west from Las Vegas on the Boulder Highway (Hwys. 93/95) and turn north onto Lake Mead Drive (Hwy. 169), at Henderson. Drive north along the shore of Lake Mead past Valley of Fire State Park to Overton. Drive to Glendale and return to the city via I-15, or continue on Hwy. 168 (beside the Muddy River) and return to Las Vegas via Highway 93 South and Interstate 15.

Laughlin

A little more than a decade ago, what is now Laughlin was a gas station and bait shop with a couple of small casinos beside the Colorado River—at the bottom tip of the state. Don Laughlin, an entrepreneur who developed the first casino, decided that the little village required a new name. It was originally called South Pointe. A basic fellow, Laughlin wanted to call the place Casino, but the post office demurred. It became Laughlin, and now it's a casino center—the third largest in the state, bowing only to Las Vegas and Reno.

Large casino hotels have been built along a riverside walkway, and tourists come from Arizona, California, and farther afield to enjoy relaxed and inexpensive resort vacations. Laughlin was developed as a low-cost casino resort center, and that policy paid off remarkably. The Hilton Flamingo has joined a Golden Nugget, and a Harrah's. A new Ramada is on the scene. The hotels now offer more than 7,200 rooms. Don Laughlin's hotel, the Riverside, is a major casino operation. The Colorado Belle, a casino shaped like a paddle steamer, is close by.

South of town is Laughlin's 18-hole Desert Target Club, a PGA championship golf course. There's a nine-hole course across the river in Bullhead City, Arizona. A major side-attraction to gaming is taking a ride on the *Little Belle*, a paddle wheeler. Another is touring the Colorado River to the Davis Dam, which separates the town from Lake Mojave. Free ferry

Nevada

boats buzz across the Colorado to Bullhead City. RV owners park their vehicles in a large RV park close to the casinos and the river.

Summer in Laughlin is a time of extreme heat, and the Colorado River flies, more like gnats, are somewhat of a pesky nuisance. Winter offers perfect temperatures with no flies, the highs hovering around 75 or 80 and the lows suitable for a good night's sleep. However, the summer temperatures are made more comfortable by dipping into the large resort hotel pools. Lake Mojave is just north of town, offering boating, swimming, and other water activities. There are three marinas north of the dam, and the Lake Mead National Recreation Area offers camping and boating access.

Day-Trips from Laughlin

There are two ghost towns that offer glimpses of the Old West. Forty-six miles northeast of Laughlin (across the Davis Dam) is Chloride, an 1860s silver mining town. Melodramas are staged every first and third Saturday at 10:30 AM and 2:30 PM. Giant rock murals have been painted by western artist Roy Purcell. Oatman, also in Arizona, is 30 miles south of Laughlin. This authentic gold mining town has been preserved with museums, shops, and cafes. On weekends, gunfighters stage Wild West shows on Oatman's main street, which was part of historic Route 66.

Grapevine Canyon offers a walk through a desert wash and into a canyon containing Indian petroglyphs. Farther up the canyon is a surprising growth of wild grape vines, and then hikers encounter small waterfalls (if there has been enough rain). The canyon is accessed by Christmas Tree Pass Road, off Hwy. 163, 6 miles west of the Davis Dam.

Red Rock Canyon Conservation Area

This federally operated site offers superb geological views and opportunities for hiking and scenic touring. About 65 million years ago a strong earthquake rumbled under the southern Nevada desert, and two of the earth's plates collided with such force that part of one plate was shoved up over much younger sandstone formations. The result is the Keystone Thrust Fault—part of which is seen at Red Rock Canyon, a spectacular

Destinations

piece of geology, 20 miles west of Las Vegas. The conservation area, administered by the Bureau of Land Management, offers many opportunities for walking nature trails along the cliff face or hiking through narrow canyons to desert springs where bighorn sheep and other wildlife are seen. A modern visitor center overlooks the recreation area, with information on the geology and wildlife of the preserve.

Things to See & Do
• Loop Drive

You will enjoy taking a 13-mile loop drive through the preserve. The paved, one-way road begins next to the visitor center and heads along the Calico Hills, with two pulloffs offering vistas of the crossed-bedded Aztec sandstone. There are short trails to the rock face from each of the vista points. A good place to stop and walk to the base of the sandstone is at the Sandstone Quarry parking lot (about one third of the way along the drive). Here, huge blocks of stone provide evidence of the extensive quarrying that took place in the early 1900s.

Picnic sites are located at two of the springs in the area: Willow Spring and Red Spring. There are more pulloffs along the route, providing views of wooded canyons and desert washes (at Icebox Canyon, Pine Creek Canyon, and Red Rock Wash). Flash floods occur following downpours, and you should be wary of crossing low places when the water is running.

• Red Rock Canyon Trails

There are several short hikes that provide diversions along the loop drive. **Icebox Canyon** features a maintained trail for almost a mile. The end of the canyon (called Icebox because it's cool in the shade there) is reached by continuing on over the rocks. Another popular trail leads into **Pine Creek Canyon**. This 2-mile round trip leads to the ruin of an old homestead situated near a creek and tall ponderosa pines.

Nevada

AUSTIN

Lincoln Motel
28 Main Street
Austin NV 89310
(702) 964-2698

This is one of two standard motels in this historic mining town. Rooms are air conditioned and there is coffee available in the units ($).

Pony Canyon Motel
P.O. Box 86
Austin NV 89310
(702) 964-2605

Located on Highway 50, this motel has queen beds in otherwise standard units. The motel is near cafes and services ($).

Austin Camping

Austin RV Park (Austin NV 89310) is a commercial RV campground, located beside Highway 50 in Austin. For reservations, call (702) 964-2393. Most camp sites in the area are located in the national forest, or on BLM land.

Bob Scott Campground is at the mountain summit beside Highway 50, 9 miles east of Austin. **Kingston Campground** is farther from town: 12 miles east on U.S. 50, then south on State Route 376 for 16 miles and finally 6 miles on Forest Road 20012. RV length limit: 22 feet. Primitive camping.

BAKER & AREA

Baker is a small town (a village) near the entrance to Great Basin National Park in eastern Nevada. While there is a gas station and store in Baker, motels and private campgrounds are located some distance from town, around Ely and to the east, at the Utah border.

Border Inn
P.O. Box 548
Baker NV 89311
(702) 234-7300

This motel is located 13 miles from the national park entrance, on the Utah/Nevada border. There are 15 rooms here, in addition to a restaurant and bar, laundry, showers, and gambling ($).

The "Y" RV Park
Box 75
Baker NV 89311
(702) 234-7223

This basic RV park has 10 sites with hookups plus other sites without hookups. It's located 10 miles from Great Basin National Park. This is an RV park without much in the way of facilities, but next door are showers, a laundry, and gas service plus a restaurant and bar.

There are campgrounds inside Great Basin National Park—near the entrance and at several elevations on the way along the Mt. Wheeler Scenic Drive. For details, see page 92.

BEATTY

Exchange Club Motel
P.O. Box 97
Beatty NV 89003
(702) 553-2333

Easily found on U.S. Highway 95, this basic motel has 44 units (one with whirlpool bath), a coin laundry, and 24-hour coffee shop. There's also a small casino here ($ to $$).

Burro Inn
P.O. Box 7
Beatty NV 89003
(702) 553-2225

Just south of the main part of town—at Third Street on U.S. 95—the Burro Inn has 62 rooms, laundry, a 24-hour cafe, lounge, and casino ($).

Beatty Camping

The town has several private RV parks, including an RV park at the **Burro Inn** (see above). There are 42 sites here, with hookups and laundry (and a casino to attract or distract you). For reservations, call (702) 553-2225 or 800-843-2078. **Bailey's Hot Springs**, 6 miles north of Beatty, has 14 sites with hookups as well as swimming—(702) 553-2395. The largest RV park in the area is the **Rio Rancho RV Park**, with 58 sites (with hookups), laundry, and playground. For reservations, call (702) 553-2238 or 800-448-4423.

Death Valley National Park (an hour's drive to the west) has campgrounds operated by the National Parks Service. For information on campground locations, see page 46.

Nevada

BOULDER CITY

Lighthouse Inn
110 Ville Drive
Boulder City NV 89005
(702) 293-6444

This Best Western operation is just a mile east of downtown via State Route 93. There are 70 rooms, some offering views of Lake Mead. Pool, whirlpool, laundry (**$ to $$**).

El Rancho Boulder Motel
725 Nevada Highway
Boulder NV 89005
(702) 293-1085

Located on U.S. Highway 9, this motel with a Spanish theme has 39 rooms including 9 two-bedroom units and 16 with kitchens. There is a pool, and a coffee shop is nearby (**$ to $$**).

Boulder City Camping

The campgrounds near Boulder City are under the administration of the Lake Mead National Recreation Area. There are six campgrounds in the area. The closest to town is the **Hemenway Campground**, 5 miles northeast of downtown on State Route 166. As with the other camping areas, there are no showers. There is a boat ramp here. **Boulder Beach Campground** is 6 miles northeast of Boulder City on State Route 166. There is a restaurant at this location, plus rental boats and a boat ramp. The **Las Vegas Wash Campground** is 15 miles north of town, also via State Route 166. Reservations are not accepted at these or the other Lake Mead sites.

CARSON CITY

Trailside Inn
1300 N. Cardon Rd.
Carson City NV 89701
(702) 883-7300

There are 67 units in this Best Western motel, located 1/2 mile north of downtown on U.S. 395. Many of the rooms have refrigerators, and there is a modest swimming pool. Rates vary with the seasons. (**$ to $$**).

Motel Orleans
2731 S. Carson Street
Carson City NV 89701
(702) 882-2007

This small, regional, family-owned motel chain is a cut above the other super-budget motels for about the same price. This one is just over a mile south of the downtown area at U.S. 50 and U.S. 395. There's a small pool plus a whirlpool (**$**).

101

Places to Stay

Ormsby House
P.O. Box 1890
Carson City NV 89702
(702) 882-1890

This large casino hotel is found at 600 South Carson Street (Hwy. 395) in the middle of downtown Carson City. The place hums 'round the clock (like any casino) with a restaurant and coffee shop (including a buffet operation), and the pool is open from early June through September. Because it's a casino, the rates are reasonable, and the age of the hotel provides an ambience that many of the more modern casinos can't touch ($).

Carson City Camping

Comstock Country RV Resort has many pull-through sites and is equipped with a pool, whirlpool, tennis court, playground, and recreation room. All 156 sites have hookups. Located at 5400 S. Carson Street, it's less than a mile from the center of town, off U.S. 395 near U.S. 50 (702) 882-2445.

Davis Creek Park is a county operation with 63 sites on Old U.S. 395, 12 miles north of downtown. There are 200 acres with fishing, dump station, and nature trails. RVs and trailers are limited to 26 feet.

Camp-N-Town is closer to Carson City, on U.S. 395. There are 74 sites with pull-throughs, hookups, dump station, laundry, pool and recreation room (702-883-1123).

ELY

Fireside Inn
Star Route 1, Box 2
Ely NV 89301
(702) 289-3765

You'll find this motel and casino 3 miles north of Ely on U.S. 93. There are standard rooms and two-bedroom units, and there is an Italian restaurant on-site ($).

Steptoe Valley Inn
P.O. Box 151110
Ely NV 89301
(702) 289-8687

A fine bed and breakfast inn with five rooms above a restored 1907 grocery store, at 220 East 11th Street in the downtown area. Rooms have small private balconies and the yard is nicely landscaped. Some rooms have showers ($ to $$).

102

Nevada

Copper Queen Motel
701 Avenue I
Ely NV 89315
(702) 289-4884

Located on the Pioche Highway (Hwy. 50/93 South), the Copper Queen is close to casinos, the station for the scenic railroad, and the downtown area. The motel has a restaurant on-site, and there are others nearby (**$ to $$**).

Ely Camping

KOA of Ely is almost 3 miles south of town on U.S. 50/93. With 110 sites, the operation has pull-through spaces, hookups, dump station, laundry, store and propane. There is also a recreation room, horse boarding, and playground.
Cave Lake State Recreation Area is south of town via the same route and then east on State Route 486 (Success Summit Rd.). There are no showers here, but the park covers 1,240 acres, with swimming, boat ramp, and fishing and ski trails during the colder months (a good part of the year in this high altitude).

EUREKA

Alpine Lodge
P.O. Box 69
Eureka NV 89316
(702) 237-5365

There are few places to stay in this historic mining town and this is one of them, a motel located at Clark and Main streets. Rooms are basic (**$**).

**Parsonage House
Bed & Breakfast**
P.O. Box 99
Eureka NV 89316
(702) 237-5765

This historic bed and breakfast home is located at Spring and Bateman (Highway 50). It is definitely the place to stay if you're not inclined toward standard motel rooms and it makes a fine stopping place on the Loneliest Road. It's also a good place to get breakfast in a town where the cafes are basic (**$ to $$**).

FALLON

**Bonanza Inn
and Casino**
P.O. Box 1530
Fallon NV 89406
(702) 423-6031

This is where the casino action is, and you can stay here too. This Best Western motel is at 855 Williams Street in Fallon, and the services, including a restaurant and lounge, are open 24 hours (**$ to $$**).

Places to Stay

Comfort Inn
1830 Williams Ave.
Fallon NV 89406
(702) 423-5554

Probably the most comfortable place to stay in town, this chain motel has 49 units, a pool, whirlpool; six of the units have whirlpools. There's a coffee shop nearby. ($).

Lariat Motel
Box 649,
Fallon NV 89406
(702) 423-3181

This is very basic accommodation, at 850 W. Williams Ave. There are 18 units here, many with refrigerators. The rooms have showers only. There's a small pool, and a restaurant is across the street ($).

Fallon Camping

Fallon RV Park, 6 miles west of town on U.S. 50 (5787 Reno Hwy.), has 10 acres of space with 45 sites including pull-through sites. Laundry, gasoline, store, and propane (702-867-2332). **Lahontan State Recreation Area** has a campground at Churchill Beach on the Carson River. There are 11 sites here plus unlimited camping along the beach. Dump station, flush and pit toilets, swimming, and boat ramp. The campground is 18 miles west of Fallon via U.S. 50.

LAS VEGAS

Casino Hotels

Increasingly, Las Vegas is becoming a major family destination resort with new casino/theme park operations built along Las Vegas Boulevard (the Strip.) There are two groups of casino hotels in Las Vegas: those on the Strip and those in the downtown area clustered near Fremont and Main Streets. You'll find the newer "theme" hotels (Excalibur, Circus Circus, The Mirage, Luxor, etc.) along Las Vegas Blvd. along with Caesars, the Tropicana, and the Flamingo on the Strip.

The hotels in the downtown casino center are of the older era, and most are less expensive than the Strip hotels, with the exception of the Golden Nugget—one of the finest hotels in all of Las Vegas, and one we highly recommend. A few of the more interesting casino hotels follow, with non-casino places to stay and camping resorts on the city's outskirts.

Nevada

Golden Nugget Hotel
P.O. Box 2016
Las Vegas NV 89125
(702) 385-7111

Built around a central pool and relaxation area, the Golden Nugget is one of the earlier large hotels in Las Vegas, and one of the best. At 129 E. Fremont Street in the downtown Casino Center, this hotel has a fine dining room and three additional restaurants, pool, whirlpool, movie theaters, bowling alley, steamroom, health club, and casino. The nightclub often has name entertainers. There are standard rooms plus one- and two-bedroom suites ($$ to $$$+).

The Mirage
P.O. Box 9193
Las Vegas NV 89109
(702) 791-7111

This is the place that started the current trend toward theme park–style hotel operations. This Polynesian resort hotel is at the high end of the comfort (and price) scale, in the midst of the neon Strip action. A flood-lit volcano flows outside the front entrance. The shows inside are among the most popular and long-running in town. The grounds are sumptuous, and the hotel has two heated pools, a wading pool, whirlpools, a health club, a fine dining room, seven restaurants (including a buffet), and coffee shop. Accommodations include rooms plus one-&-two bedroom suites which are on the ultra-expensive side ($$ to $$$+).

Luxor
3900 Las Vegas Blvd.
Las Vegas NV 89109
(702) 262-4000
or 800-262-4444

Staying inside a pyramid has its benefits and drawbacks. Among the benefits are the deluxe rooms and suites (more than 2,500) and the Egyptian-themed attractions and specialized restaurants. The slanted ride on the pyramid's elevators may result in queasy stomachs, but many say it's just another of the rides available at this ultimate theme park/hotel ($$ to $$$).

MGM Grand Hotel
3799 Las Vegas Blvd.
Las Vegas NV 89109
(702) 891-1111
or 800-929-1111

The largest hotel in the U.S. (5,005 rooms), the MGM Grand is a "mega-resort" with four casinos and a 33-acre adventure theme park. It has signature restaurants, including the Coyote Cafe, and hosts spectaculars in the Grand Garden Events Center ($$ to $$$+).

Places to Stay

**Debbie Reynolds'
Hotel, Casino and
Hollywood Movie
Museum**
305 Convention
Center Dr.
Las Vegas NV 89109
(702) 734-0711
or 800-633-1777

This recent addition to the Las Vegas scene is actually an old casino that went belly-up and was bought by the movie star and friends as a showcase for Ms. Reynolds' collection of movie memorabilia. She appears in the nightly show. The hotel has 197 rooms, with some Jacuzzi suites. All the rooms have balconies, and there are two restaurants, a sauna and whirlpool, and low prices that match the general quality of the hotel. For movie fans and Debbie Reynolds fans in particular, staying here is quite worth a few inconveniences ($ to $$).

Circus Circus
P.O. Box 14967
Las Vegas NV 89114
(702) 734-0410

The Circus Circus group, which includes Excalibur (see below), set the pace for lower-priced accommodations and food with unusual entertainment themes. Their original hotel is at 2880 S. Las Vegas Blvd. (the Strip), containing more than 2,700 rooms, three pools, whirlpool, circus entertainment from 11 AM. Three restaurants, coffee shop and casino ($).

**Excalibur Hotel &
Casino**
P.O. Box 96778
Las Vegas NV 89193
(702) 597-7777

Located at the south end of the Strip, at 3850 Las Vegas Ave. (at Tropicana). This huge, 4,000-room hotel has a medieval castle theme with a large cavernous casino, children's arcade and play area (downstairs), medieval showroom with jousting and other olde-fashioned entertainments, and reasonably priced rooms. Two heated pools, whirlpool, a dining room plus five restaurants (including buffet), and coffeeshop ($).

**Desert Inn Hotel
and Casino**
3145 S. Las Vegas
Blvd.
Las Vegas NV 89109
(702) 733-4444

One of the older resorts on the Strip, the Desert Inn has managed to keep up with the crowded competition with regular remodeling and its golf course and country club atmosphere. The hotel grounds are beautifully landscaped, and besides the 18-hole golf course (extra fees) the hotel boasts ten tennis courts, a jogging track, pool, whirlpools, spa, and health club. There's a fine-dining room plus two restaurants and a coffee shop ($$ to $$$).

Nevada

Non-Casino Accommodations

Some visitors to Las Vegas prefer to stay in motels and hotels without the busy casino action. Following are several medium and lower-priced places to stay.

Sheffield Inn
3970 Paradise Road
Las Vegas NV 89109
(702) 796-9000
or 800-777-1700

This modest motel has rooms and suites, some with microwave ovens and refrigerators. There's a barbecue area with tables, free continental breakfast, pool, whirlpool, and a shuttle bus to the Strip. It's almost a mile south of the Convention Center and a half-mile from the Strip ($ to $$).

Plaza Suite Hotel
4255 S. Paradise Rd.
Las Vegas NV 89109
(702) 369-4400

This Howard Johnson hotel has 202 units (most with refrigerators), a pool, sauna, whirlpool, and exercise room. The restaurant is open from 6 AM to midnight. Rates as at other Vegas hotels, vary as to the season ($ to $$$).

Emerald Springs Inn
325 E. Flamingo Road
Las Vegas NV 89109
(702) 732-9100

This newish non-casino hotel has 150 units (rooms and suites), with whirlpools in some units. There's a pool, whirlpool, exercise room, restaurant open from 6:30 AM to 2 AM, and lounge ($ to $$$).

Courtyard by Marriott
3275 Paradise Rd.
Las Vegas NV 89109
(702) 791-3600 or
800-321-2211

Located near the Desert Inn and one block from the Convention Center, the Courtyard has 149 rooms with pool, whirlpool, exercise room (minigym), laundry, restaurant, and lounge. The restaurant opens at 6:30 AM, closes between 2 and 5, and closes for the night at 10 PM ($$).

Boomtown Hotel and Casino
3333 Blue Diamond Rd.
Las Vegas NV 89109
(702) 263-7777 or
800-588-7711

For anyone who has visited the Reno-area casinos, this will be a familiar kind of place. It is a western theme hotel and casino with 300 rooms which makes it just about the smallest casino hotel around (and that ain't all bad). Motor home owners will appreciate the 460 RV spaces with hookups (another Reno innovation). There are two restaurants and gold panning is offered as an additional attraction ($$).

Places to Stay

Las Vegas Camping

Las Vegas KOA
4315 Boulder Hwy.
Las Vegas NV 89121
(702) 451-5527

The KOA is located 5 miles southeast of town and is reached via U.S. 93 and U.S. 95, then 1/2 block south off Desert Inn Rd. There are RV and tenting sites here, pull-through sites, dump station, laundry, store and propane, two pools, a wading pool, whirlpool, and playground—all the normal KOA facilities. There is a free shuttle to the casinos.

**Sam's Town
RV Parks**
5225 Boulder Hwy.
Las Vegas NV 89122
(702) 454-8055

This huge RV-only (no tents) facility has 500 sites, including pull-throughs, laundry, dump station, two pools, whirlpool, and recreation room. It is found 8 miles southeast of town via U.S. 93, U.S. 95, and Nellis Blvd.

**Nevada Palace
Trailer Park**
5325 Boulder Hwy.
Las Vegas NV 89122
(702) 451-0232

This resort-style place, which calls itself the Nevada Palace VIP Travel Trailer Park, has a 14-day limit. Many of the 168 availabilities are pull-through sites. The operation covers 10 acres and has a pool and dump station.

**McWilliams
Campground**
c/o Las Vegas Ranger
Dist.
550 E. Charleston
Las Vegas NV 89104
(702) 477-7782

For those who like to camp in natural surroundings, this national forest campground has 31 sites, and is located northwest of Las Vegas in the Toiyabe National Forest. To get there, take U.S. 95 north for 29 miles and then turn onto State Route 156 and drive for another 18 miles. There are pit toilets and dump station but no showers. The stay limit is 16 days. Nine units are reserved through MISTIX. This is one of several national forest campgrounds in this mountain area.

LAUGHLIN

**Flamingo Hilton
Hotel**
P.O. Box 30630
Laughlin NV 89029
(702) 298-5111

This is one of the newest of the riverfront Laughlin casino hotels, with two bedroom towers (2,000 rooms) and a neon-lit casino in between. There is a large pool deck overlooking the river and the Arizona hills beyond, whirlpool, tennis courts, two restaurants, buffet, and coffee shop ($ to $$).

Nevada

Edgewater Hotel
P.O. Box 30707
Laughlin NV 89029
(702) 298-2453

This large casino hotel, near the Hilton on the riverwalk, is one of two Circus Circus operations here (the other is the Colorado Belle). Room rates are extremely reasonable at the Edgewater, which has 1,450 rooms, a pool, whirlpool, river cruises departing from the hotel dock (extra fee), a dining room, and a large buffet operation, that offers unlimited grub for hungry families around the clock ($).

Riverside Resort
P.O. Box 500
Laughlin NV 89029
(702) 298-2535

When Don Laughlin bought the little Riverside Casino a little more than 20 years ago, it brought major changes to the sleepy little desert village. Now a major gaming town, Laughlin has concentrated on family and lower-priced accommodations, competing well with its northern neighbor Las Vegas. The Riverside is now a large slab-sided high-rise with more than 650 rooms, two pools, dining room, restaurant, and buffet. There's a casino and a club with name entertainment. Don Laughlin also operates a smaller motel on the Arizona side of the river (River Queen Resort), with a short boat ride joining the two ($ to $$).

Golden Nugget–Laughlin
2300 S. Casino Dr.
Laughlin NV 89029
(702) 298-7111
or 800-237-1739

This tropical theme hotel has waterfalls, a miniature rain forest, jungle birds, and 300 rooms and suites. The Golden Nugget generally keeps to the standards set by its Las Vegas parent. There are three restaurants, including a high-quality buffet. Other amenities include a pool, whirlpool, and Tarzan's Lounge ($$ to $$$).

Places to Stay

Utah

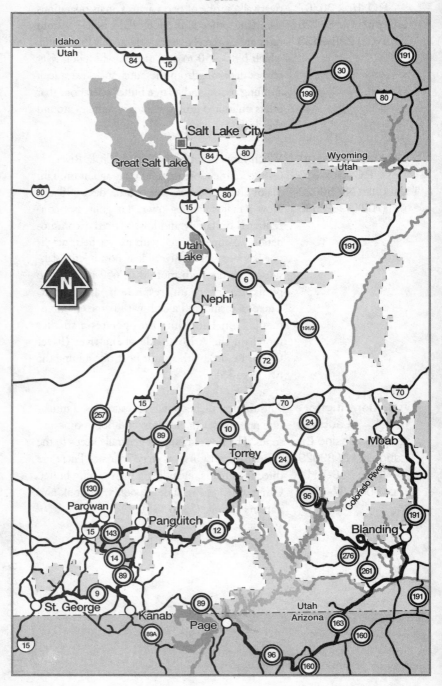

The geological wonderland that is southern Utah can't help but inspire and lift you (psychologically speaking as well as in altitude). In the span of 3 or 4 days, the visitor can visit five national parks and four national monuments or recreation areas—the largest concentration of national scenic preserves in the nation. This landscape is the result of sandstone having been eroded over millions of years by rain, rivers, and wind, leaving immense stands of hoodoos, rocky domes, ever-deepening canyons, and amphitheaters. From Arches to Zion, this is an area of natural and national treasures which often defy description, although I will do my best.

The six scenic drives that follow provide a motoring tour of southern Utah attractions, beginning at St. George in the southwestern corner of the state. Our route moves in a more or less clockwise direction through the national parks and monuments, ending in Monument Valley—monumental, but only a small part of the huge Navajo Indian Reservation that straddles the boundaries of Utah, Arizona, Colorado, and New Mexico.

Along the way, between the major attractions, are a score of state parks—mostly historic sites and geological oddities—that only add to the sense of wonder. The "goosenecks" of the San Juan River curl back and forth near the Utah/Arizona border on our way to Monument Valley. The Coral Pink Sand Dunes (in a state park) are just that. Newspaper Rock State Park includes some of the earliest graffiti produced in America. Kodachrome Basin (named by the National Geographic Society) holds a fine collection of red rock spires as well as slick rock displays in a semidesert environment.

Visitors have the choice of staying in lodges within several national parks or in comfortable lodges and motels near these attractions.

Zion National Park Drive

St. George to Kanab

By normal standards, the Virgin River is not much of a stream. Except during winter and spring runoff months, it's not much more than a creek, and after filling several small reservoirs it peters out as a desert wash before its official end at the edge of Lake Mead in Nevada. Along the way, the Virgin is interrupted by a series of dams. This development and the threat of more such interference with nature has placed this river on the slate of endangered rivers published by the American Rivers organization. Seeing Zion is an intense experience. With a dramatic background of steep red cliffs, the river flows down fragile waterfalls and through narrow cuts in the rock (where it is necessary for humans to walk up the river) then cascades into the more accessible valley where the park's visitor services are located.

Along the Way

- **St. George**

  Called Utah's Dixie, St. George is a pleasant city with eight golf courses that offer fine views whether you're playing golf or not. The 18-hole Green Spring course is particularly scenic. There's an historic courthouse, and the Dixie National Forest is located a few miles north of town, accessed by taking Utah Route 18 (which also takes you to Snow Canyon State Park).

- **Quail Creek State Park**

  Year-round camping is featured in this park that sits beside the Quail Creek Reservoir, located off Highway 9 (our route to Zion, 3 miles west of the Interstate 15 exit). The bass fishing is good here, and boating is permitted. There are 23 campsites and two covered picnic pavilions as well as open picnic tables.

- **Side Trip on Kolob Terrace Road**

  This is a scenic summer drive north from the village of Virgin. Although you can drive all the way north to Cedar City, the major attraction is the Kolob Terrace and Lava Point portion of Zion National Park. From Virgin, the road leads along North Creek for

Utah

more than 15 miles to near Spendlove Knoll (el. 6,895 feet). The route veers to the east, past Firepit Knoll (el. 7,265 feet) and then over a long switchback as it climbs to the Upper Kolob Plateau with a campground elevation of 7,890 feet. These dirt roads are impassable and closed during winter months and are sometimes closed during rainy periods in other months. Check on road conditions with the rangers at Zion National Park, (801) 772-3256.

• Springdale

This town sits at the entrance to Zion Canyon, at the park boundary. There are several motels and bed and breakfast homes in Springdale, along with gas stations, rock shops, and stores which have camping food and other supplies for a stay in Zion National Park.

• Zion Canyon

The centerpiece of Zion National Park—the drive in the canyon—begins at the park visitor center that is just inside the southern gate to the park (at Springdale). The Zion Canyon Scenic Drive leads along towering cliffs, stark monoliths, waterfalls, and other features, including the Court of the Patriarchs, the Emerald Pools, the Grotto, and (at the end of this short drive) the Temple of Sinawava. Zion Lodge, with motel and lodge accommodations, is located along the drive in the Grotto area. For park details, see page 159.

• Zion/Mt. Carmel Highway

Highway 9 runs through the park. Following the turnoff for the park scenic drive, it quickly climbs the walls of Pine Creek Canyon by a series of switchbacks and goes through a tunnel. Just past the tunnel is the Canyon Overlook, which offers fine views of Pine Creek Canyon and beyond—into Zion Canyon.

The route continues eastward across a high plateau, past slickrock formations of white, orange, and red and the unusual Checkerboard Mesa—a sandstone mountain carved with striations resembling the lines on a checkerboard.

Drives

Highway Log

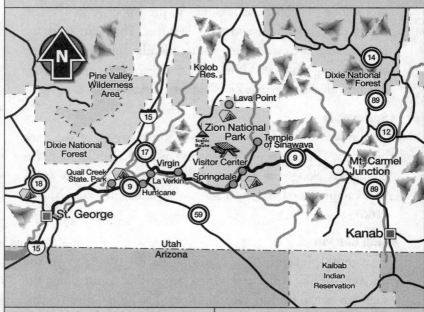

St. George The drive begins by taking Interstate 15 north (toward Salt Lake City) for 9 miles. Turn off the Interstate onto Utah Route 9 (exit 16).
Quail Creek State Park To the west via Utah Route 318 with camping, fishing and picnicking. There is also a private RV park in the **Quail Lake Recreation Area** which is along the same sideroad.
Hurricane Valley Hwy. 9 now runs through this valley, with several RV parks, with overnight hookups beside the highway. Gas, store.
Hurricane Small town with gas, store, cafes, motels.
Pah Tempe Hot Springs A resort beside the Virgin River, east of town.
La Verkin Small village.
Junction–Highway 17 North This road leads to Toquerville and Interstate 15. Hwy. 9 now climbs into the hills with a panoramic view to the left.
Virgin Village with trading post.

Side Trip—Kolob Terrace Road
This backroad leads north from the town of Virgin to Kolob Reservoir and, on the way, into Zion National Park. To reach the Lava Point Campground inside the park, follow the road that runs beside North Creek and becomes a gravel road. Then turn right (southeast) at the Lava Point sign. The backroad continues north to the reservoir and beyond.

Back on Highway 9
North of Virgin, Hwy. 9 follows the path of the Virgin River, leading east.
Rockville Gas, B & B home.

Springdale Gas, restaurants, rock shops, Indian trading post, motels, B & B homes, campground and RV park. This town serves the needs of Zion park staff and visitors. This is the place to buy camping supplies before entering the park and a good place to stay while visiting Zion.

Zion National Park

The park gate is just beyond Springdale. A road to the right—just inside the park gate—leads to two campgrounds. The **Watchman Campground** is the larger (keep to the right). The **Watchman Trail** offers a 2-mile (round trip) walk ending at a viewpoint with views of the lower Zion Canyon, Pine Creek Canyon, and the town of Springdale.

The **South Campground** is at the end of the left fork, off the sideroad.

Nature Center This education facility is to the right of the highway beyond the campground road. There is an amphitheater here.

Visitor Center To the left of the highway, beyond the nature center. Restrooms, maps, books, etc.

One mile beyond the visitor center is the **Zion Canyon Scenic Drive** (turn left). This road runs down the deep canyon past several trailheads and ends at the **Temple of Sinawava** after a 13 mile (20 KM) route. Halfway along the drive is **Zion Lodge** (cabins, motel units, restaurant, picnic area).

Hwy. 9 continues eastward through the park, climbing quickly with several sharp switchbacks after the junction with the Zion Canyon Scenic Drive, running through Pine Creek Canyon. The first tunnel is 1.1 miles in length, followed by a parking area for the Canyon Overlook.

Canyon Overlook Trail Leaving from the Overlook, this trail provides an easy 1-mile round trip over a self-guided route, with steep terrain below the trail. It ends with fine views of lower Zion Canyon and Pine Creek Canyon. The altitude is now 5,000 feet. There is a second (shorter) tunnel and a one-lane bridge beyond the Overlook.

Checkerboard Mesa Viewpoint Below the unusual rock formation, to the left of the highway. The mesa is to the right (el. 6,670 feet).

Trailhead for the East Entrance Trail The trail wanders across high country, running northwest, joining the network of park trails including a trail through Echo Canyon, and ending in Zion Canyon.

Park Entrance Fee gate for those entering the park from the west.

The highway begins its descent to Mount Carmel Junction. Past the junction (gas, store, motel) U.S. Hwy. 89 leads south to the town of Kanab (17 miles) and north to Panguitch.

115

Cedar Breaks (South) Drive

Kanab to Parowan

While much of southern Utah is desert-like, the region offers the chance to climb to the top of several exceedingly high plateaus where thick forests of ponderosa pine are studded with clear lakes and spotted with little meadowed clearings. This drive is the first section of a two-part trip (almost a full circle) that touches Cedar Breaks National Monument at both its southern and northern approaches. The next drive, starting on page 120, covers the northern route from Parowan to Panguitch.

The combined tour weaves across high country through the Dixie National Forest, where there are many opportunities for hiking, camping and, in the winter, snowmobiling and skiing: downhill and cross-country. For ease in getting overnight accommodation, this drive begins in Kanab, a small town just north of the Arizona border and a convenient stopping place after visiting Glen Canyon or Zion National Park.

The route leads north along U.S. 49 for 40 miles, through Mt. Carmel Junction to Long Valley Junction, where we catch Utah Route 14, running east, up a steep climb onto the Markagunt Plateau approaching Cedar Breaks National Monument. A few miles past the sideroad to the park, the Zion Overlook provides a wonderful vista spanning the miles between the plateau and Zion National Park, which is seen to the south. The highway descends through a narrow canyon to reach Cedar City, an agricultural town that is the home of the renowned summer Shakespeare festival. The last leg of the drive follows Interstate 15 (a short exception to our general rule of driving no interstates) for only 18 miles, until reaching the Parowan exit.

Along the Way

• Coral Pink Sand Dunes State Park

This odd landscape of pinky sand is situated off Highway 89, just north of Kanab. The dunes are in the state park of the same name, where you'll also find a campground with pull-through sites, restrooms with showers, and plenty of space for walking or riding over the sand in an off-road vehicle.

Utah

• Long Valley Junction

Not much of a town, this little village serves as the launching point for the drive up (and I mean UP) the side of the mountain on Highway 14, to the top of the wide plateau from which you can reach Cedar Breaks National Monument and several forest recreation sites, as well as rustic lodges and trails. There is a motel here, plus a store and gas station. Please heed the warnings about long loads and winter precautions before traveling on Hwy. 14.

• Dixie National Forest

Our route passes through only one of four large sections of this national forest, each of which have many recreation sites: campgrounds, picnic areas, hiking trails, riding trails and snowmobiling areas. Along the way, on or near Utah Route 14, you'll find the Swain's Creek site, Uinta Flat, Strawberry Point (south, off the highway), and the Zion Overlook. A campground is located just before leaving the Dixie National Forest.

• Cedar Breaks National Monument

This impressive amphitheater sits below the plateau, with Utah Route 143 leading along the rim for the entire length of the park. The "cedar" in the name refers to the native juniper found here (juniper/pinyon pine forest). Atop the Markagunt Plateau is a lush forested landscape of spruce, fir, and quaking aspen, where spring flowers carpet the high meadows (late June is tops) and bristlecone pines outlive any other living thing—here or anywhere else. For Cedar Breaks details, see page 146.

• Side Trip—Scenic Backroad to Kolob Reservoir

A dirt road—muddy in rainy months and closed during the winter—wanders across the Kolob Plateau. It departs from Hwy. 14 just east of Cedar City, passing the Kolob Reservoir and entering the northwestern section of Zion National Park (Kolob Terrace area).

There's a park campground at Lava Point, near a fire lookout. The road meanders all the way south to Virgin, near the south entrance to Zion National Park.

Drives

Highway Log

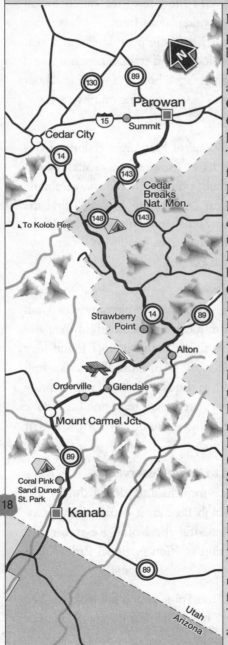

Kanab Town with motels, cafes, RV park, stores, museum. Our drive begins by taking U.S. Highway 89, north toward Mt. Carmel Junction and Panguitch.

Coral Pink Sand Dunes State Park Off the highway via a sideroad to the left (west). Camping, scenic landscape. There is a second road to the park, a few miles north of this one.

Mt. Carmel Junction (17 miles from Kanab) Gas, motels, store, cafes. Our drive continues north on Highway 89, toward Cedar City.

Muddy Creek Village with bed & breakfast home.

Orderville Gem and rock shops, B & B home, gas, store, motels, cafe.

Private RV Park with tenting sites, 2 miles north of Orderville. Basic sites.

Glendale Country store, gas, old hotel.

Picnic Area at mile 95. Closed during the snowy season.

Private Campground (KOA) One mile north of the picnic area.

Road to Alton Leads northeast (2 miles).

Summit Elevation 7,513 feet.

Long Valley Junction Junction with **Utah Route 14.** Turn west onto Highway 14, toward Cedar Breaks National Monument and Cedar City. There is a store and a motel with restaurant at the junction. 41 miles from Cedar City.

This road climbs to over 10,000 feet and may see closures during the winter.

Swains Creek Pulloff for views and snow recreation parking. We're now in the **Dixie National Forest**.

Uinta Flat and Strawberry Point (north and south off the highway via backroads) This is prime snow-mobiling country.

Cedar Mountain Village Lodging to the south of the highway.

Duck Creek Loop road to the village (north of the highway). Cabins, store and other services.

Junction–Utah Route 143 Leads north through **Cedar Breaks National Monument** (camping, trails, views, forest recreation).

Cedar Breaks National Monument
The federal park features a great natural amphitheater, more than 600 feet deep and 3 miles in diameter, with startling rock formations. The top of the plateau above the amphitheater is at an elevation of 10,000 feet. Highway 143 travels the length of the monument. The visitor center is toward the south end of the par‚k with two spectacular viewpoints (**Spectra Point** and **Point Supreme**) located between the south gate and the visitor center, only a few minutes' drive from Highway 14. Spectra Point is reached via the **Wasatch Rampart Trail. Amphitheater Campground** is also located near the south end of the monument. Hwy. 143 through Cedar Breaks is closed during the winter

months. Hwy. 143 meets Interstate 15 near Parowan. The north entrance to Cedar Breaks is also reached via the scenic drive to Panguitch (see next page).

Back on Highway 143
We're now 18 miles from Cedar City.

Viewpoint Just west of the junction is a scenic overlook with spectacular vistas.

Leaving Dixie National Forest

Scenic Backroad Leads south to Kolob Reservoir and part of Zion National Park (Lava Point). It becomes the Kolob Terrace Road, leading south to Utah Route 9, near Springdale and the main entrance to Zion National Park. Restaurant near the junction.

Cedar City A major agricultural center, college town, and trading community for this region, and site of the summer Shakespeare Festival. Turn right for Interstate 15 and Parowan.

Iron Mission State Park A pioneer museum with mining artifacts.

RV Park and BLM information office—both at the north end of town.

Junction–Interstate 15 Take the northbound ramp, toward Parowan.

Interstate Exit 75 Take this exit toward State Highway 143 and the towns of Parowan and Brian Head.

119

Cedar Breaks (North) Drive

Parowan to Panguitch

This drive continues our near-circle route around Cedar Breaks National Monument, from Kanab to Panguitch via the Markagunt Plateau and Cedar City. For the first part of the trip, see the previous drive which begins on page 116. The Parowan Valley was occupied by the Anasazi from about 750 AD to 1250 AD, and pit houses and other relics are being found in the valley. Mormon pioneers arrived here on January 13, 1851, and then fanned out to found Cedar City and other nearby communities. The Rock Church standing in the middle of town is now a pioneer museum. Year-round trout fishing is available at Yankee Meadows Reservoir and the Red Creek/Paragonah Reservoir.

Along the Way

• Parowan Gap Petroglyphs

Before you leave the Parowan area, take a short drive to see this unusual site. The Indian rock paintings are located near the shore of an old (now dry) salt lake. They're located northwest of town on a sideroad. Drawn by several tribes, the paintings depict lizards, snakes, mountain sheep, bear claws, and the mysterious "mousemen" of Indian lore.

Follow Main Street north and take the last street in town that leads west. It turns to gravel for most of the drive. The petroglyphs are at the narrow cut in the mountains (the Gap). To take our drive to Cedar Breaks, return to Parowan and take Highway 143.

• Scenic Backroad

Just before the mile 10 milepost, make a left turn (west) off the highway onto this gravel backroad. It leads through a scenic area of the Dixie National Forest and then continues south to meet Highway 143, where you can turn east to reach the south entrance to Cedar Breaks National Monument.

• Brian Head

This is a sometimes rustic and sometimes modern resort town that began as a high-country ski resort and has branched out to provide

Utah

a full summer season of activity as well. You can drive to the top of Brian Head peak or take a ski lift up the mountain. There are several fine restaurants, as well as condo-type accommodations, several motels, and the Brian Head Hotel, which offers upscale resort living. There are campsites in town as well as in the Dixie National Forest.

The resort is well known for its powder skiing, with seven lifts, 43 runs on two hills and a network of groomed cross-country trails. Only 3 miles from Cedar Breaks National Monument, Brian Head is a fine place to stay while exploring the trails and other features of the park.

• Backroad to Rattlesnake Creek Trail

Halfway along this gravel road is the trailhead for the Rattlesnake Creek Trail, which offers a long and somewhat strenuous hike along the rim, past a primitive campground.

• Loop Road to North View

Just after passing the Cedar Breaks boundary, this short loop road takes you to a great view from the north rim.

• Cedar Breaks National Monument

Highway 143 leads south through the park, along the east rim of this huge amphitheater. The 5-mile road leads to the park's scenic attraction, including overlooks and trails. The visitor center is closer to the south entrance than the north boundary. The park campground and interpretation center are on a loop road near the main visitor center.

• Panguitch Lake

I once traveled this road on a sunny winter day and passed what seemed to be the whole population of the village of Panguitch Lake out on the frozen surface, drilling holes and ice fishing. This is also a great summer boating and canoeing lake. It's one of Utah's most scenic natural bodies of water and is reputed to be a great fishing hole, with rainbow, German brown, cutthroat, and brook trout in great supply.

Drives

Highway Log

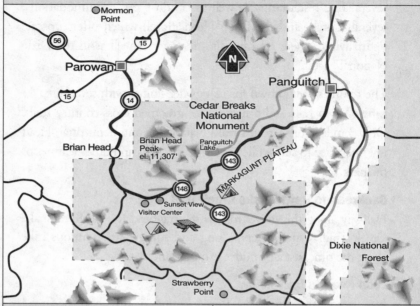

Parowan The drive begins at the junction of Interstate 15 and Utah Route 143. Parowan has motels, cafes, gas, and a grocery store. The **Parowan Gap Petroglyphs** are found approximately 12 miles northwest of town via Utah Route 127.

The highway climbs quickly toward Brian Head, with steep grades that are not suitable for long trailers. Beware! Chains are also necessary during much of the winter period.

Scenic Backroad To the right (west), to Dry Lakes (before milepost 10).

Brian Head (16 miles from Parowan) This is a favorite Utah ski resort and summer vacation town, next to the Dixie National Forest, with hotels, condos, restaurants from pizza to haute cuisine, camping, and stores.

Brian Head Peak (el. 11,307 feet) 4 miles north of the Cedar Breaks boundary, 9 miles past Brian Head town. There is a shelter atop the peak, offering great views of the town and cliffs rising from mountain meadows.

Entering Cedar Breaks N. M. The highway crosses a corner of this spectacular park. The monument is closed during the winter.

North View A loop drive to the rim of the plateau for your first view of Cedar Breaks.

Junction–Highway 148 This road leads south through Cedar Breaks.

Side Trip Through Cedar Breaks

The park is open from mid-May through late October, when snow closes the area (except for skiers).

Highway 148 runs along the rim of the Markagunt Plateau, above the huge natural amphitheater called Cedar Breaks. Along the way there are spectacular views of the rock formations below. The high spots along the rim drive are as follows:

Rattlesnake Creek Trail The trailhead is just north of the park boundary. This trail is for experienced hikers only, and advice from a park ranger is helpful in negotiating this steep path.

Alpine Pond Trail To access a series of hiking trails, start from the trailhead found next to a turnout about a mile south of the highway junction. There is a short, self-guiding trail leading to the pond's shore (wildflowers). A trail guide is available at the trailhead. Bristlecone pine trees grow near the **Chessman Ridge Overlook**, which can be reached by the trail or by car. A short road from the highway leads to the overlook.

Sunset View Another short loop road leads from the highway, overlooking the amphitheater.

Visitor Center The summer park headquarters is to the west of the highway, with Point Supreme nearby at the end of a short, easy trail.

Wasatch Ramparts Trail This is the longest trail (2 miles), starting at Point Supreme and leads along the rim through wildflower meadows to a small forest of ancient bristlecone pines near Spectra Point. It ends at a viewpoint with an elevation of 9,952 feet.

Amphitheater Campground The 30 sites are located south of the highway near the visitor center. It is generally open for use between early June and mid-September. The outdoor amphitheater is nearby, offering evening interpretive programs during the summer.

Picnic Area Near the campground, with water, tables and grills.

The south entrance is 2.5 miles from Utah Route 14.

Back on Highway 143
Hwy. 143 continues across the Markagunt Plateau.

Mammoth Creek Pulloff to a small parking area.

Campground Near milepost 32, to the north (Dixie National Forest).

Panguitch Lake Two lodges are located on a sideroad, and there is a small community here. This is a favorite ice-fishing place during the height of the winter.

The highway descends as it approaches the wide, oval-shaped valley.

Panguitch A small town with gas, motel, and restaurant.

Junction–U.S. Highway 89
For the route to Bryce Canyon, Escalante and Torrey, see the next scenic drive.

123

Bryce Canyon/Escalante Drive

Panguitch to Torrey

Sometimes I turn into a babbling idiot when I experience the awesome sights that lie along routes like this one. Put Bryce Canyon on the same drive as the Escalante Canyons area and you have a day (or several days) of scenic dynamite. To pursue a safe drive, it pays to keep your emotions under control.

Bryce Canyon in summer or winter is just about my favorite place in the whole world. For those with the esoteric spiritual passion for hoodoos, this is mecca. Nowhere else in the universe are there erosion pillars in such abundance or such a variety of hoodoo shapes.

During a recent mid-winter visit, a few hardy souls without care for personal safety or frostbite trekked through deep snow—descending into the powder a couple of feet with every step—struggling to reach the rim and the once-in-a-lifetime panorama of snowcapped spires glistening below. We later found that the Park Service plows paths to the rim, but not to the particular viewpoint we had strained to reach. After experiencing the wonders of the region, one can only sag into a night of contemplation about life and the meaning of it all. Hoodoos, canyons, basins, mesas, creeks, and rivers. They're all here!

Along the Way

- **Red Canyon**

    A BLM visitor center is open during the summer to explain the unique geology of the canyon. There's a campground beside the highway and Butch Cassidy's hideout is down the draw.

- **Bryce Canyon National Park**

    The pinnacle of Utah's scenic attractions! See above and Bryce Canyon details on page 139.

- **Kodachrome Basin State Park**

    Turn south off Highway 12 at Cannonville (there's a Kodachrome sign) and then continue on the paved road for 9 miles to the state park. Open year-round, this is indeed a photographer's delight, with high spires (more hoodoos), slickrock formations, and a desert

Utah

landscape. The park is particularly scenic in the late spring and early fall. You may hike, ride, or bike through the park. The arches are photogenic, as are the pillars that stretch to the sky. There is a pleasant campground with restrooms and showers. The Trail Head Station has camping supplies. The nearest motels are at Bryce Canyon, Tropic, and Escalante.

• Escalante Petrified Forest State Park

North of Escalante, a quiet town out of the Wild West, the park features deposits of colored mineralized wood and dinosaur bones.

Wide Hollow Reservoir, a 30-acre lake (more like a large pond), lies beside the park with boating and fishing in store. The park is just a mile from town, with a campground containing restrooms and showers, a dump station and a short interpretive trail.

• BLM Recreation Sites

This is one of three clusters of BLM recreation sites along the Escalante corridor. Primitive camping is allowed in the Escalante Resource Area and permits may be obtained at the two BLM visitor centers along the route—at Red Canyon and at the Dixie National Forest ranger station in Escalante.

The **Escalante Trail** trailhead is at Calf Creek. There's a parking lot next to the creek crossing. This 36.7-mile trail leads from the highway, offering an excellent 4- to 5-day backpacking trip. Shuttle services are available and must be booked in Escalante.

Farther east, North Creek Road leads to Barrier Reservoir. Phipps, Death Hollow, and Escalante Canyons recreation areas are found from the floor of the canyon beyond the Calf Creek crossing. The Calf Creek Falls Campground is the starting point for an easy 5.5-mile hike leading to the Lower Falls. The trailhead to the Upper Falls is located 5.5 miles north of the campground on the highway.

125

• Dixie National Forest Recreation Sites

As the highway crosses Boulder Mountain, there are two forest campgrounds beside the highway. This is a scenic place to stay while exploring the Escalante Canyons.

Drives

Highway Log

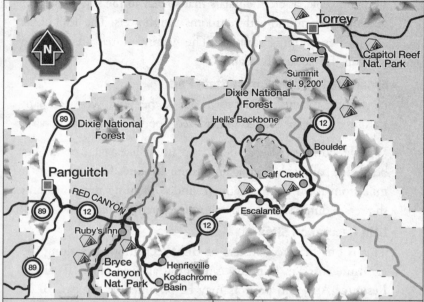

Panguitch Gas, motels, stores, restaurants. The drive begins by taking U.S. Highway 89 south for 7 miles.

Junction–Utah Route 12 Turn east (right). This road leads through the Red Canyon to Bryce Canyon National Park, Escalante, and Torrey.

Red Canyon This red rock canyon is worth stopping to see. A BLM visitor center is open during summer months.

Red Canyon Campground Just beyond the visitor center. There are trails and viewing opportunities.

Butch Cassidy Draw A backroad beyond the campground, after milepost 4.

Summit (el. 7,619 feet.)

Visitor Services Gas station, motel, campground, store—just east of the summit.

Junction–Highway 63 This is the road that runs south through Bryce Canyon National Park. The motel beside this road (Ruby's Inn) is a long-time favorite with travelers to the area, with a restaurant, laundry, gas station, and cross-country ski center.

Side Trip Through
Bryce Canyon National Park

Hwy. 63 leads south from U.S. Route 12, past Ruby's Inn to the park gate. An admission fee is charged. The 18-mile road runs along the canyon's rim. There are several viewpoints along the rim, plus other facilities:

Fairyland Point The first viewpoint, at the extreme north end of the canyon. A short sideroad leads to a turnaround and parking.

126

North Campground There are no hookups but a dump station is nearby. Showers are located at the nearby store, near Sunrise Point.

Visitor Center West of the road.

Sunrise Point This is a popular viewpoint, and the location of the Bryce Canyon Lodge.

Sunset Point and Campground No trailers are allowed on the highway south of the campground. This spot provides a truly spectacular view and access to trails into the canyon.

Inspiration and Bryce Points Both viewpoints are located off a road that leads east from the highway.

Paria View Another fine vista.

Viewpoints to the South Additional viewpoints are located at the south end of the park. **Rainbow** and **Yovimpa** viewpoints are at the far south end, with views of the plateau and canyon landscape.

Back on Highway 89

The highway leads east toward Escalante. The village of **Tropic** has two motels, a store and cafes.

Kodachrome Basin Scenic basin located 9 miles south of the highway on a backroad. Camping.

Henrieville A small town with few (if any) services.

The highway passes through a section of the **Dixie National Forest.**

Summit (el. 7,400 feet)

North Creek Road To Barrier Reservoir.

Escalante Petrified Forest State Park To the north with camping. The **Wide Hollow Reservoir** is located on this road.

BLM Information Center At the national forest ranger station.

Escalante A small town with gas, cafes, store, small old motels.

Posy Lake Road To BLM recreation sites to the north. There are campgrounds from 16 to 54 miles from the hwy.

BLM Recreation Site Hole in the Rock, 5 miles from Escalante.

Viewpoint On a high spot, looking across the valley with peaks in the distance. The road descends into an area known as the **Escalante Canyons**, with a variety of formations.

Escalante River Crossing

BLM Recreation Areas Calf Creek, Phipps, Death Hollow, and Escalante Canyons natural areas are accessed from the floor of the canyon.

Calf Creek Campground .One-half mile from the bridge. The road climbs from the canyon to the top of a mesa—very narrow at times but a thrilling drive through stunted pinyon pine & junipers. There are additional campgrounds along the remainder of the drive.

Boulder Small town with **Anasazi Indian Village State Park and Museum.** Picnic area at museum.

Summit (el. 9,200 feet)

Bicentennial Highway Drive

Torrey to Blanding

Although Capitol Reef National Park has a more subtle landscape than its neighbors, Bryce Canyon and Cedar Breaks, it has a majestic style of its own, made more meaningful by the signs of early pioneer settlement in the valley now occupied by part of the park. The landmarks in the park are the domes—a series of rounded peaks. The park name comes from the dome that somewhat resembles the top of the Capitol building in Washington, D.C. Other attractions in the park include the Waterpocket Fold (see below), hidden arches, and pinnacles. Orchards and remains of rural buildings along the highway provide glimpses into the lives of the families who farmed long ago along the Fremont River.

Along the 200 miles of this drive are several scenic backroads to explore, including a gravel road into the Valley of the Gods (the smaller cousin of nearby Monument Valley). Other backroads lead through remote sections of Capitol Reef National Park and into Cathedral Valley.

Ending the drive at Blanding places you in good position for exploring the Four Corners area, including the monument that stands at the Four Corners and the Hovenweep National Monument, an outstanding Anasazi ruin. Eighty miles south of Blanding is Monument Valley.

Along the Drive

• Capitol Reef National Park

The west entrance to the park is 4 miles from Torrey with the visitor center another 7 miles. It's adjacent to the old orchards of Fruita, the small Mormon settlement on the Fremont River which was occupied from the late 1800s. The **Capitol Reef Scenic Drive** begins at the visitor center and offers a 25-mile round trip in a portion of the park—through the Waterpocket Fold, a large wrinkle in the earth's crust that stretches for more than 100 miles. Other backroads from outside the park (see below) lead through other sections of Capitol Reef. The Fruita Campground is located near the visitor center, as is a picnic area. For details on the park attractions, see page 144.

Utah

• Side Trip through the Waterpocket Fold

This gravel route offers either a circle loop through Waterpocket Fold country, returning to Torrey, or a southerly drive all the way to Bullfrog Marina and Crossing on Lake Powell. Just east of the park's eastern boundary is a backroad that runs for a few miles south to the hamlet of Notom.

The Notom-Bullfrog Road then runs farther south through the Waterpocket Fold, across Cottonwood Wash, re-entering Capitol Reef National Park near the Cedar Mesa Campground. Drive for another few miles south and you'll reach the junction of the Burr Trail Road, which leads west, joining Utah Route 12 at Boulder.

There's a picnic area beside the Burr Trail Road, beyond the trailhead for the Strike Valley Overlook Trail. Highway 12 will take you north to Torrey, 11 miles from the park visitor center. Alternatively, turning south onto the Notom-Bullfrog Road will take you to Lake Powell.

• Backroad to Cathedral Valley

The hamlet of Caineville is the access point for the gravel backroad that runs north along the Caineville Wash, through the Waterpocket Fold area to Cathedral Valley, where great stone monoliths stand high over the desert. If you turn west and travel past Cathedral Valley Junction, you'll reach the monolith area and the Cathedral Valley Campground.

• Glen Canyon National Recreation Area

We touch this area which includes Lake Powell, as we cross the two rivers near Hite Marina. The recreation area stretches all the way south to Page, Arizona.

• Natural Bridges National Monument

To reach these impressive bridges carved by the White River, turn off Hwy. 95 onto Utah Route 275 and drive to the park entrance. There's a visitor center and campground near the gate. A loop road leads past the bridges with viewpoints and trails that lead into the river canyon, to the bridges, with a picnic area along the loop road.

Drives

Highway Log

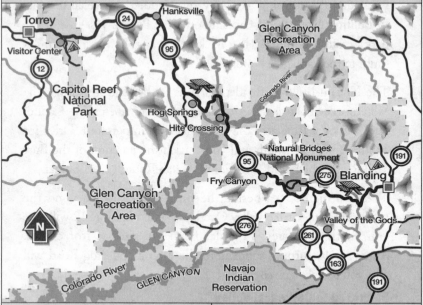

Torrey A small town with motels, gas, cafes, and store. We begin the drive by taking Utah Route 24 east from Torrey, toward Capitol Reef National Park. Just before entering the park, you'll find motels, a campground and restaurants.

Capitol Reef National Park

Yet another splendid example of southern Utah geology. The highway explores only a small part of the park, at the northern end of a long slim reserve. Entering the park at the north gate, a trail leads to Goosenecks—just inside the park. Then, there is the visitor center, beside the highway. Capitol Dome—the park standout—and other notable rock features can be seen to the left while driving through the park. The old orchards of Fruita are seen along the road. **Fruita Campground** is available to tenters and RVer, and is open throughout the year.

Capitol Reef Scenic Drive This road provides a 25-mile round trip through the park and has its start at the visitor center. It follows the west face of the Waterpocket Fold and into Grand Wash and Capitol Gorge. Along the drive are the impressive Egyptian Temple and Golden Throne formations. The northern spur (turn left) leads into Capitol Gorge. The southern spur leads to the banks of Pleasant Creek.

A sideroad to the left, near the start of the drive, leads along Grand Wash.

The main highway (Utah # 24) leaves the park, heading to Hanksville.

Scenic Backroad This road (at milepost 89) south from the highway runs to Notom and farther south into the lower section of Capitol Reef National Park—along the Waterpocket Fold. There is a primitive campground at Cedar Mesa (shortly after re-entering the park) and a picnic area farther south near the Strike Valley Overlook Trail.

Burr Trail Road leads west from the Strike Valley Overlook, to Boulder, with a return north along Highway 12 to Torrey. These roads provide a wonderful circle route through various sections of the park—a day trip from and to Torrey.

Back on Highway 24

The highway runs eastward past the Sleepy Hollow Campground (store next door at mile 95).

Caineville Wash Road Leads north from Caineville to Gypsum Sinkhole (26 miles), Cathedral Valley (26 miles), and Thousand Lake Mountain. This is another amazing backroad drive, one of many in and near the national park.

Hanksville Gas, store, cafe, motels. Mount Ellen is to the south of town.

Junction–Highway 95, the Bicentennial Highway. Take Hwy. 95 South toward Hite Crossing.

Junction–Utah Route 276 (at milepost 26) This road leads south to Lake Powell at Bullfrog Marina.

Hog Springs Picnic Area Cross the creek on the suspension bridge (milepost 33).

Viewpoint-Hite Overlook The northern end of Lake Powell is visible from the sideroad.

Colorado River Crossing (an arch bridge) A road (right) leads to **Hite Marina**. The marina has full visitor services including accommodation, a store, and gas.

Farley Canyon Access Road Three miles to Lake Powell (at milepost 53).

White Canyon Road To Lake Powell (no boat launch).

Junction-Utah Route 276 Leads west to Lake Powell, the Hall's Crossing Marina and ferry.

Junction-Utah Route 275 To **Natural Bridges National Monument** and Elk Ridge access road. There is a campground and picnic area in the monument (see page 154).

Junction-Utah Route 261 This winding, scenic road is a short cut to the town of Mexican Hat and Monument Valley (not recommended for long RVs and cars with trailers). The **Valley of the Gods** is accessed via a backroad.

Junction-U.S. Hwy. 191 Drive north on Hwy. 191 to **Blanding** (several motels, gas, stores, cafes) and **Edge of the Cedars State Park**.

Canyonlands & Monuments Drive

Moab to Page Arizona

This is another of those drives that offers a wealth of scenic splendor—so much so that the mind is boggled by the overwhelming beauty of it all. The secret to mind-control is to take more than one day. In fact, to see this area properly will take at least a day in and around Moab, a second day exploring the southern reaches of the Canyonlands, a day or two exploring Monument Valley and the nearby Valley of the Gods, and then a final day spent crossing the Navajo Reservation to Page and Lake Powell. That adds up to six days well spent in the northeastern corner of Utah and the north-central part of Arizona. Treating this drive as a full vacation experience leaves you with your senses duly heightened but without visual overload. Before leaving the Moab area on your way south, be sure to take in both the northern portion of Canyonlands National Park and Arches National Park.

The Valley of the Gods is a smaller but just as spectacular landscape as that in Monument Valley. The tours that leave from Goulding's Lodge in the Navajo Reservation will take you through both valleys, or you can drive through most of these scenic areas yourself.

South of Monument Valley, we reach the Navajo town of Kayenta and take U.S. Highway 160 south to either Arizona Route 564, which loops past the Betatakin Ruin and through the Indian village of Shonto, or Arizona Route 96, which leads west to Page and Lake Powell. Tuning to Navajo radio (AM 660) allows you to catch a feel for reservation life. The talk is in English and Navajo, and the music is a mix of Nashville and northern Arizona Navajo.

Along the Drive

• Canyonlands National Park

The northern section of the park—Islands in the Sky—is accessed north of Moab by taking Utah Route 313 west from U.S. Hwy. 191. The "island" is a wide mesa, connected to the "mainland" by a narrow strip of land. A visitor center is close to the park entrance, and a road leads south to three viewpoints from which there are

Utah

fine views of the canyons and the Green River far below. The **White Rim Trail** is a 100-mile 4WD roadway that follows a bench 1,000 feet below the rim. There are primitive campgrounds along this route. The views from the three viewpoints are spectacular at any time of day but are particularly fine at sunrise and just before sunset. There is a developed campground near the visitor center.

• Needles Overlook

For views of the midsection of Canyonlands National Park, turn west off U.S. 191, 14 miles south of Moab. The sideroad leads past a campground to the overlook, with panoramic views of the canyons and spires to the south and west.

• Newspaper Rock State Park & Canyonlands National Park

You do enter Canyonlands National Park on this sideroad 14 miles north of Monticello (19 miles south of Moab).

The road first passes Newspaper Rock State Park, an historic site with an ancient mural of Indian rock art carved by at least three different Indian cultures. The 50-acre park includes a campground, picnic area, and hiking trails. Drive farther west to the end of the road and the Needles section of Canyonlands National Park

Foot trails and 4WD roads lead to archeological features including the Confluence Overlook, Elephant Hill and Angel Arch. There is a visitor center and campground. The Needles Outpost sells camping supplies.

• Edge of the Cedars State Park

An historic site in the town of Blanding—the remains of an Anasazi pueblo.

• Goosenecks State Park

The San Juan River loops back and forth in a series of "goosenecks." Take Utah Route 316 and the state park road.

• Monument Valley

Turn west at the crossroads for Goulding's Lodge, and east to enter the Tribal Park. A fee is charged at the park entrance.

Drives

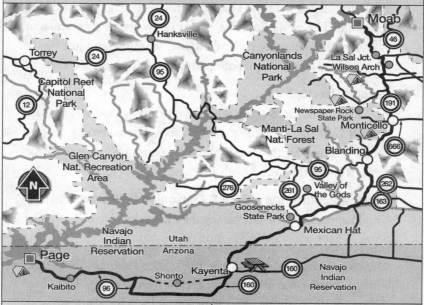

Moab (el. 4,000 feet) This small city has a full range of visitor services, and is close to both **Arches and Canyonlands National Parks**. The drive begins in downtown Moab, heading south on U.S. Highway 191. Several sideroads south of town lead into Canyonlands viewpoints.

La Sal Mountains Loop Road Leads west (see previous pages).

Junction–Utah Route 46 Leads west, toward La Sal and Naturita (CO).

Viewpoint–Wilson Arch East of the highway, on a short sideroad.

Needles Overlook Road (at milepost 93) This backroad leads to the BLM overlook of Canyonlands National Park. **Wind Whistle Campground.**

Junction–Utah Route 211 Leading west to the Needles section of **Canyonlands National Park** and **Newspaper Rock State Park**. Camping is available in both parks.

Backroad to Campgrounds Leads west into the **Manti-La Sal National Forest** (3 campgrounds).

Monticello (50 miles south of Moab, el. 7,050 feet) Small city with gas, motels, cafes, stores.

Junction–U.S. Hwy. 666 Leads west to Cortez and Durango.

A paved sideroad leads west into the national forest, with access to the three campgrounds mentioned above.

Devil's Canyon Campground South of town on the highway (# 191) in a scenic gorge.

Blanding A town with gas, motels, store, cafes. **Edge of the Cedars State Park** is an historic site in Blanding.

Forest Backroad First paved and then gravel, this road leads northwest from Blanding into the national forest, leading to the Dark Canyon Wilderness area (to the west) and north into the Needles section of Canyonlands National Park.

Junction–Utah Route 95 Leads northwest to Hanksville, toward **Capitol Reef National Park.**

Junction–Utah Route 262 Leads east toward the **Four Corners Monument & Hovenweep National Monument** (Anasazi ruin).

Bluff Small town with gas, motel, cafe, store.

Junction–U.S. Hwy. 163 Leads east to Aneth and the Four Corners.

We continue this drive via **Hwy. 163,** toward Mexican Hat (20 miles).

Valley of the Gods This fine collection of bluffs and hoodoos is accessed via an unpaved backroad. The road loops around to meet Hwy. 261, north of Mexican Hat.

Junction–Utah Route 261 To Fry Canyon and Hanksville, and access to **Goosenecks State Park** (four miles).

We continue on Hwy. 163 (south). The Mexican Hat rock is to the left before entering the town. A dirt road leads to the rock.

Mexican Hat Small town with gas, motels, trading posts and river rafting.

Entering Navajo Indian Reservation

Viewpoint–Redlands (milepost 9)

The road passes across Monument Pass (el. 5,209 feet) and enters Monument Valley.

Road through Monument Valley. Turn right (west) for Goulding's Lodge and the trading post. Turn left (east) for the Tribal Park (fee charged). There is a jumble of jewelry, Indian taco, fry bread and other Navajo stands at the junction.

Entering Arizona

Picnic Table (milepost 403) Beside a high rock monument.

Kayenta A major community for the Navajo Nation, with gas, motels, stores and cafes.

Junction–U.S. Highway 180–Take this route, which leads in a southwest direction and joins Hwy. 89 south of Page. The road climbs to above 6,000 feet.

Tsegi Gas, motel, store, cafes.

Junction–Arizona Route 264 This sideroad leads to the Betatakin Ruin (historic site and camping, 9 miles).

Junction–Arizona Route 98

Take this road (turn right) for the route to Page and Lake Powell. The BM & LP Railroad hauls coal to the Navajo Generating Station.

135

Road to Shonto Leads 4 miles to a Navajo village.

Road to Kaibito Gas available.

Page Town at the southern end of Lake Powell and the Glen Canyon National Recreation Area. The visitor center is on Lake Powell Blvd.

Other Utah Drives

• To Hovenweep National Monument & the Four Corners

Located in the southeast corner of Utah are two monuments of different types which annually attract hundreds of thousands of visitors. Take Utah Route 262 East, south of Blanding, and follow signs to Hovenweep, an outstanding example of the communities established by the prehistoric Anasazi civilization.

For the Four Corners Monument, take U.S. Highway 191 from the village of Bluff and then turn east onto U.S. Highway 160 to the monument. This is the one place in the lower 48 states where one can be in four states at the same time—if you're very careful to straddle the point. These gymnastics are not advised, but the panoramic views of the four states are outstanding and well worth the hour-long drive.

• Side Trip to Valley of the Gods

Leading off the southern section of the Bicentennial Highway (Utah Route 95), Utah Route 261 leads south, providing a shortcut to Monument Valley. Near the south end of this 33-mile switch-backed road is the gravel backroad that leads into the Valley of the Gods where you'll find impressive rock cliffs and monuments—a smaller version of Monument Valley.

• Side Trip through Cathedral Valley

East of Capitol Reef National Park, via Highway 24, you come upon a gravel backroad that leads north along the Cainville Wash and into Cathedral Valley. Past the campground the road continues, looping to the south through Fishlake National Forest, ending at the town of Torrey (a forest campground is at this junction) or continuing for a mile or so east to Utah Route 672. The road is closed during winter months, but at other times of the year it provides an excellent day-trip from the Capitol Reef park visitor center and campground.

Cathedral Valley is noted for the large stone monoliths that dominate the desert landscape.

Utah

Arches National Park

Arches National Park Near the Colorado border and south of Interstate 70, this national park contains the greatest density of natural stone arches in the world. Located in Utah's red rock country, the park connects with the Colorado River for a short stretch, and a bridge on U.S. Highway 91 leads from the park to the city of Moab. The nearby remains of a small part of the old **Spanish Trail** provide some historical perspective, as does the **Wolfe Ranch**, which lies inside the park.

We'll see many examples of natural arches in the national parks and monuments of southern Utah (see the following pages), but Arches has more in a smaller space than all the others. Sandstone is very vulnerable to erosion, and what was once flat land has been sculpted by wind and water, removing the soft sandstone to reveal stronger rock underneath. The shifting of salt beds under the park also contributed to the exposure of arches. Salt beds liquefied and buckled under the weight of heavier rock that lay above, causing faults, which resulted in earth layers being turned on edge. One such displacement is the **Moab Fault**—seen from the park visitor center.

There are more than 1,500 arches in the park, ranging in size from 3 feet to the huge **Landscape Arch**, which is 306 feet from base to base and 105 feet high. Pinnacles are also a feature of the park, and are good places to see these spires are at **Delicate Arch** viewpoint (in the extreme mid-eastern section) and along the Great Wall Road, which is the main north/south route through the park.

The park visitor center is at the southern entrance, 5 miles north of Moab. Here, you can watch a slide show that will orient you to the park attractions and walk through a geology and history display. Commercial tours are available, and a self-guiding booklet will lead you through the park. Naturalists lead walks through the **Fiery Furnace** area in the north-central part of the park. This 2-hour tour is given during the prime season—not summer, when it's too hot and exhausting to spend much time outdoors!

Park Attractions

At the extreme north end of the park road is **Devil's Garden**. A trail through the area provides views of a fine collection of arches, including the Tunnel, Pine Tree Arch and Landscape Arch, and leads past the Partition, Navajo and Wall arches, and ending after a 2.5-mile (one-way) walk at the Dark Angel Arch. People who don't wish to walk the full loop, which is primitive in places, should turn around at the Landscape Arch (1 mile) or Double-O Arch (2 miles). The starting point is the Devil's Garden Trailhead. This trail also offers wonderful views of the Salt Valley and the La Sal Mountains. This is an easy walk, as far as Landscape Arch.

The **Desert Nature Trail** begins at the front of the visitor center. This is a short, self-guided walk following a series of numbered posts that correspond to the features listed on an excellent brochure available inside. The trail is only 2/10 of a mile long (0.3 KM), but it offers a wealth of diversity in desert plants, including cacti, small shrubs, and desert grasses. A juniper hangs onto a rocky crevice and, in the fall, the squawbush (a sumac) turns bright red. You may see desert animals such as spiny lizards, cottontails, and squirrels.

Delicate Arch Trail provides a moderately strenuous hike for 1.5 miles (one way), crossing a suspension bridge over Salt Wash and climbing along the rock ending at the arch. The trail is off a sideroad, with the trailhead at Wolfe Ranch. The ranch is a national historic site, containing the remains of a rustic homestead settled by John Wesley Wolfe, a civil war veteran, and his family.

Another major area is the **Fiery Furnace**, which is located in the middle of the park. There are two viewpoints in this area, providing overlooks of the Salt Valley and the Fiery Furnace—a display of exposed sandstone fins. The viewpoint is at the head of the 2-mile guided walk. You'll see several arches, including Skyline, Broken, and Sand Dune.

Utah

Located along the highway north of the visitor center is the **Windows** area. From the highway you can see four of the most impressive arches: North and South Windows, Double Arch, and Turret Arch. The two Window arches—as seen from Turret Arch—are also called the Spectacles.

The most remote part of the park is **Klondike Bluffs**, situated at the end of a sideroad that departs from the main road just south of the Devil's Garden area. This is a vast area with panoramic views of many formations, including the awesome Tower Arch. It is also a popular cross-country hiking area. Backpackers should get advice at the visitor center on hikes in the area and be sure to inform the rangers of their intentions.

Camping

There is one campground in the park, operated on a first come, first served basis. It's located near the north end of the park in the Devil's Garden area, with 50 sites. The campground is suitable for tents, trailers, and RVs. There are two walk-in tent sites for group camping, and reservations may be made for groups of 10 or more. The Devil's Garden Campground is open from spring through early fall, at an on-site amphitheater where rangers give interpretive talks during evening hours. Overnight accommodations and restaurants are available in the Mormon pioneer town of Moab. For Moab motels and B & Bs, see the Places to Stay pages of this Utah section.

Bryce Canyon National Park

Unlike in most of the other parks in southern Utah, Bryce Canyon activity doesn't come to a halt during the summer months. Most of the attractions are at or above 8,000 feet, and temperatures are moderate if not slightly chilly.

The prime season for visiting this amazing hoodoo repository is from late April to mid-October. This isn't to say that the park is closed in winter. Far from it! Winter brings cross-country skiing, snowshoeing, and even overnight camping, so depending on your preferences, a visit is worthwhile any time of year.

Bryce Canyon's rangers have just about the simplest and best description of hoodoos that I've heard: "A hoodoo is a pinnacle or odd-shaped rock left standing by the forces of erosion." You'll know what a hoodoo is when you step inside the park. Although this is just one of the many scenic sections of Utah's Canyonlands, there is no finer display of pinnacles and castellated cliff tops anywhere. The canyon is situated in a series of twelve bowls that dip nearly 1,000 feet into the earth, revealing myriad layers of colored sandstone.

The park is situated in a region that includes several other national parks and monuments, including Cedar Breaks National Monument (to the west), Capitol Reef National Park (northeast), and the Glen Canyon National Recreation Area (along the Colorado River, to the southeast). Canyonlands, Arches, and Zion National Parks are a half-day's drive from Bryce Canyon. All in all, there are 10 other units of the national parks system within a five-hour drive. A vacation in this area should include several of these superb preserves.

To get there from the west, drive on U.S. 89 7 miles south of the town of Panguitch. Turn east at the junction and drive along Utah Highway 12 for 14 miles. Turn right on Utah Highway 63 and head 3 miles south to the park entrance. This road leads 18 miles through the park, and four major sideroads run to 13 overlooks. The visitor center is located just inside the park entrance.

Bryce Canyon is a hiker's paradise, attracting people from around the world. There are 23 marked hiking trails and all are self-guided.

It's also a special place for drivers, who can travel the rim of the canyon for almost the entire length of the park, with almost everything there is to see along the route. The canyon itself can be explored by foot or by horseback.

Bryce Canyon Lodge offers overnight accommodations inside the park. The lodge features motel-style rooms and western cabins, and there is a a dining room (801-586-7686). The complex is closed during the winter period. **Ruby's Inn**, a motel complex with a restaurant and store, is just outside the park and is open year-round.

Park Attractions

• Park Road

An extension of Highway 12, the road runs 18 miles to the south end of the preserve. The most popular places to stop for gazing at the canyon and pinnacles are Fairyland, Sunrise, Sunset, Inspiration, and Bryce viewpoints. In addition, Rainbow and Yovimpa viewpoints (at the south end of the road) provide fine panoramic views of the plateau and adjacent canyons. Trailers are not permitted on the park road south of the Sunset Campground (near the north end and the visitor center). A parking lot is available for trailer parking, for those who are not unhooking at the campground. You can explore the park on horseback; morning and afternoon trips are organized by wranglers from the concession based at the corral near the lodge, (801) 679-8665.

The park is popular with cross-country skiers, who come to ski on the Paria and Fairyland sideroads that are closed to car traffic during winter months and also to ski the Rim Trail. Snowshoes are available at the visitor center when there is enough snow to use them. The visitor center provides a trail brochure as well. Cross-country ski rentals are available outside the park, as are groomed trails. The Dixie National Forest, next to the park, is accessed by Highway 12 and also by Highway 143.

• Hiking Trails

Two backcountry trails are open during summer months. The **Under the Rim Trail** leads from several points along the rim, providing a walk of up to 22 miles along the canyon. The **Riggs Spring Loop** departs from Rainbow Point, is 7.7 miles in length and takes between 1 and 2 days.

Both trails are considered strenuous. The majority of the trails in the park are suitable for day hikes and most, including the following are considered easy-to-moderate:

• **Rim Trail**—Traverses the rim and is accessible at several points. The total round-trip distance is 11 miles, taking 4 to 5 hours.

Destinations

- **Bristlecone Loop**—Begins at Rainbow Point and leads 1 mile, climbing only 100 feet; an easy, short walk of about 1 hour.

- **Queen's Garden**—Trailhead at Sunrise Point; a 1.8-mile (one-way) walk, climbing 320 feet. The round trip takes about 2 hours.

- **Queen's Garden/Navajo Loop**—A combined trail beginning at Sunrise Point or Sunset Point, 1.3 miles climbing 521 feet and taking between 1 and 2 hours to walk.

The following hikes are considered strenuous:

- **Peekaboo Loop**—Access at Bryce, Sunrise, or Sunset Points; length between 4.8 and 6.8 miles with a climb between 500 and 800 feet. This walk takes between three and four hours.

- **Tower Bridge Trail**—Access north of Sunrise Point, with a length of 3 miles and a climb of 800 feet. The walk takes about 2.5 hours.

- **Fairyland Loop**—Begins at Sunrise Point, climbing 900 feet in 8 miles. The trail takes 5 hours to walk.

- **Trail to the Hat Shop**—This linear trail begins at Bryce Point and leads for 3.8 miles, climbing 900 feet; 4 hours.

Park Camping

There are two campgrounds in the park, and all of the 215 sites are available on a first come, first served basis. **North Campground** is just inside the park gate. Loop A of this campground is open year-round, providing winter camping possibilities. There is a dump station near the campground. **Sunset Campground** is located south of the visitor center. Campers should be aware of the crush to get into the campgrounds between mid-May and mid-September, when the two campgrounds are generally full every night.

It is best to arrive at the park early in the day to secure a site. A store, laundry, and showers are located near Sunrise Point (between the campgrounds). These are open between mid-April and mid-October. There are stores, motels, and cafes located on Highway 12, outside the park.

Utah

Canyonlands National Park

Canyonlands is an immense desert of rock, divided by two great rivers: the Green and Colorado. The rivers separate the national park into three distinctive sections that have their own, separate attractions: Island in the Sky, the Needles, and the Maze. The park is just southwest of the old Mormon pioneer town of Moab, with the park headquarters in town. The three sections are not connected by road, and you drive from different directions to get to each attraction. For more on this area, see Moab and the Canyonlands, page 150.

• Island in the Sky

This is a high, flat mesa that lies between the two rivers. For those with little time to spend, this is the easiest part of the park to see, and to walk. With several overlooks at an elevation of 6,000 feet, you can peer down into the White Rim and get fine views of the Needles and the Maze. The La Sal, Abajo, and Henry ranges are seen in the distance. To get there, drive from Moab north along Hwy. 191 and take Utah Hwy. 313 for 22 miles (southwest). The roads on top of the mesa are paved. Several trails lead to wonderful vista points, and to Upheaval Dome. The visitor center is open daily. There is a primitive campground and picnic area (no water). There are campgrounds, as well, in Arches National Park, just north of Moab.

• The Needles

Pinnacles and more pinnacles are the features here, in this more southerly section of the park. To get there, drive south from Moab or north from Monticello on U.S. Hwy. 191 and then drive west on Utah Route 211—passing **Newspaper Rock State Historic Park**—to reach the park entrance. The Needles Visitor Center is just inside the boundary with nearby trailheads to the Colorado River Overlook and the Cave Spring Trail.

There is a campground at Squaw Flat (a short drive from the visitor center) with tables and water (spring through fall); a fee is charged. There is also a campground in Newspaper Rock State Park (on Hwy. 211).

143

Destinations

• The Maze

This is a remote area of the park, accessible by 4WD or high-clearance vehicles, on the western edge of the park territory. To get there, drive south from Interstate 70 (near Green River) or north from Hanksville, on **Utah Hwy. 24**. Twenty Four miles south of I-70, there is a dirt road which leads 46 miles east to the **Hans Flat Ranger Station**. This road is suitable for two-wheel-drive vehicles. Another backroad (for 4WD vehicles only) leads north from Utah 95 near Hite. The **Horseshoe Canyon** section of the park is reached by a two-wheel-drive backroad, an hour's drive north of the Hans Flat Ranger Station.

Four-wheel-drive roads and foot trails lead to several scenic areas including the Land of Standing Rocks, the Doll House, and Ernie's Country. The Maze itself is a jumbled collection of canyons reached via a long trail with a descent of 600 feet. There are Indian pictographs on the walls of Horseshoe Canyon that are said to be more than 2,000 years old. This area is reached by a separate backroad. The life-size pictures on the Great Gallery are among the finest examples of prehistoric art to be found in America.

There are primitive campsites (no water, no fee) in the Land of Standing Rocks area and at the Doll House.

Capitol Reef National Park

Encompassing nearly a quarter-million acres of towering landscape, this lesser-known national park is named after Capitol Dome, a rock outcropping atop a high cliff which is capped with white sandstone. The rock resembles the Capitol building in Washington.

The rock formations in the park are part of the Waterpocket Fold, an eroded bulge which runs for 100 miles. The huge cliffs and pinnacles offer colorful views. A unique feature of this park is the old pioneer Mormon community of Fruita, which lies within the park. Orchards (apple, pear, apricot, cherry & peach) are maintained by the parks service at Fruita and picking is permitted in season. Guided tours of the orchards and historic buildings are given by park staff during summer months.

Highway 24 is the main route through the park. Hanksville is to the east and Torrey to the west. Highway 12 approaches Torrey from the south, providing a scenic route from such towns as Boulder and Escalante. While most of the park's hiking trails and other attractions are accessible from Highway 24, backcountry roads fan out to the more remote sections of the park. The visitor center is located along the highway, and interpretation programs are given during the prime season.

The peak season runs from mid-April through October. Summer temperatures range up to 90 degrees, but nights are comfortably cool. There are no commercial accommodations within the park, and people usually stay in motels in Torrey, Hanksville, Bicknell, and Loa.

• Trails

There are five easy-to-moderate trails:

- **Goosenecks Trail**—Start from the Goosenecks parking lot. This 1-hour walk is over 2 miles, with good views of Sulphur Creek Canyon and beyond.

- **Capitol Gorge Trail**—Start at the Capitol Gorge parking lot. The trail leads 2 miles to petroglyphs and the park's unique waterpockets, or "tanks."

- **Grand Wash Trail**—From a parking lot, this trail runs 4.5 miles (a 2.5-hour walk) along the bottom of the wash.

- **Fremont River Trail**—From the campground this trail leads 2.5 miles through twisted canyons near the river, for a 2-hour walk that is moderately strenuous after the first 1/2 mile .

- **Hickman Bridge Trail**—This 2-mile trail is self-guiding & a moderate walk.

Other trails in the park are considered strenuous. These include the **Rim Overlook Trail**, a spur off the Hickman Trail, which leads 4.5 miles and ends on top of 1,000-foot cliffs. The **Chimney Rock Trail** is a fairly hard climb with switchbacks and an easier hike on the upper loop. The 3.5-mile hike takes about 2.5 hours. The trail to **Cassidy Arch** (named after Butch, who hid here) leaves from Grand Wash and takes about 3 hours (3.5 miles). The trail climbs up high cliffs. The longest trail in the park is the **Frying Pan Trail**, with trailheads at Cassidy Arch or Cohab Canyon. It takes about 6 hours to hike and leads through much slickrock. This is for experienced and fit hikers only.

Camping

There are three year-round campgrounds in the park. **Fruita Campground** has water, restrooms, tables, and grills.

Cedar Breaks National Monument

If you appreciate the colorful landscape of Bryce Canyon National Park, you'll love Cedar Breaks National Monument, located a half-hour's drive east of Cedar City. Inside a deep sunken amphitheater are stone pinnacles, arches, and columns with canyon walls bearing shades of yellow, red and purple. Surrounding the park is the Dixie National Forest. Pines and aspens contrast with the colored canyons, and in the summer months meadows are rich with wildflowers. The spring scenes with frostings of snow on the tops of the ridges provide more magnificent vistas.

To get there, drive from Cedar City on Utah Highway 14. The visitor center is north of the southern park gate. The north entrance to the monument is reached by taking Utah Hwy. 143 south from the town of Parowan. From Panguitch, drive southwest via Highway 143.

The main season at Cedar Breaks runs from late May to mid-September. A visitor center is open from June 1 to October 15 (with changes depending on the weather). The elevation is high, and daytime temperatures sit between 60 and 70 degrees during July and August. Popular activities in the monument include hiking, walking, photography, nature study, picnicking, and camping. Park rangers hold morning interpretive walks and afternoon geology talks all during the summer season. Snow closes the park road during the winter, but access to the monument is available from Brian Head Resort (the nearby ski center, 2 miles north in the national forest) as well as Duck Creek Village and Panguitch Lake. Winter activity centers on cross-country skiing and snowmobiling.

• Trails

There are two hiking trails in the monument. Each is considered to be an easy walk. Seniors and those with mobility problems are cautioned that because of the high elevation (10,000 feet, 3,048 meters), more time may be needed to walk the trails than in the lower elevations.

- **Alpine Pond Trail**—The trailhead is at the Chessmen Ridge Overlook. It leads 2 miles through a forest to a beautiful little meadow and a pool.

- **Wasatch Rampart Trail**—Leading from the visitor center, this easy trail passes along the rim of the plateau with fine views along the way. The trail's length is 4 miles and it takes about 3 hours to walk it. Spectra Point is halfway along the trail, and many turn around at that point.

Camping

The only campground in the monument is open from June 15 to September 15 and has water, restrooms, tables, and grills. There is an outdoor amphitheater for evening interpretation programs.

Overnight accommodation is available at nearby Brian Head, as well as in Cedar City, Parowan, and Panguitch. No motel services are available inside the monument.

Cedar City

Cedar City, the home of the **Utah Shakespearean Festival**, is conveniently located between Zion National Park and Cedar Breaks National Monument. It is in Iron County, which also includes the communities of Brian Head and Parowan (the county seat—see page 156). Brian Head is 2 miles north of Cedar Breaks, N.M., and offers accommodations, food, and shopping. Parowan is north of Brian Head, close to Interstate 15, as is Cedar City.

The Dixie National Forest lies to the west and east of Cedar City, providing many recreational opportunities as well as camping. The highly regarded Shakespeare festival is staged each summer from the last week in

June through the Labor Day weekend. Not only the plays of William Shakespeare are put on in the Adams Shakespearean Theater and the Randall Jones Theater, but other playwrights' works are featured as well; plays by Edmund Rostand and Noel Coward were recently staged. The **Royal Feaste** is a saucy Tuesday and Friday entertainment with a medieval dinner and bawdy celebration in the King's Pavilion. For information on all festival events, phone (801) 586-7800 (Mon.–Fri., 8 AM to 5 PM) or (801) 586-4300.

Cedar City is also the home of **Southern Utah University**. Art fans should not miss visiting the Braithwaite Fine Arts Gallery, on the university campus at 351 W. Center. The Cedar Ridge Golf Course is located at 100 E. 800 North. Winter brings snow to the area, and there are groomed cross-country ski trails located at Duck Creek Village, 30 miles east of Cedar City. **Iron Mission State Park** preserves the early Mormon foundry established in 1851.

The downhill ski resort is located at **Brian Head**. This is a scenic resort town nestled in the Dixie National Forest north of Cedar Breaks. There are cross-country ski trails throughout the area, including those that provide access to scenery along the Cedar Breaks rim.

Summer brings people who stay at Brian Head while visiting Cedar Breaks and commuting to the Shakespearean festival. The resort stages its own summer cultural events including a jazz festival each July Fourth and the Children's International Folk Festival at the end of July. August brings a country dancing event, and people flock to the area to view the fall colors around Cedar Breaks. This is also a popular mountain biking area.

Where to Eat

There's a lot of fast food served in Cedar City, but people interested in something more substantial may like to visit **Escobar's**, which serves good Mexican food at 155 N. Main, or **Pancho & Lefty's** (also Mexican) at 2107 N. Main. Both restaurants are in the $$ range. The **Black Swan** (164 S. 100 W.) is done up in Olde Englishe decor and serves standard American cuisine ($$ to $$$). In Brian Head, the **Summit Dining Room** is a family restaurant located in the Brian Head Hotel ($$ to $$$).

Utah

Glen Canyon National Recreation Area

A place of stunning beauty and stark contrasts, Lake Powell and the recreation area surrounding it were created in 1972 with the damming of the Colorado River at Glen Canyon Dam. The huge reservoir stretches for 186 miles from Canyonlands National Park to the Arizona border. The area is a photographer's heaven with its combination of water and rock, providing unlimited opportunities for artful shooting, particularly if you have a boat to get out onto the lake, where rock islands and steeply walled inlets abound. It is also a very popular area for boating, including the very popular houseboating, plus fishing for bass, walleye (pickerel), catfish, and black crappie.

• Getting There

Three highways intersect Glen Canyon. At the extreme south end of the recreation area, U.S. Highway 89 leads east from Kanab to Page (Arizona), site of the Glen Canyon Dam. The northern route is the Bicentennial Highway (Utah Hwy. 95), which crosses the lake at Hite Crossing. In the middle area, Utah Highway 276 runs to the water with the John Atlantic Burr Ferry crossing the reservoir, cutting 130 miles off the route from Hall's Crossing to Bullfrog Marina. The latter route is the most popular, and there are visitor services on both sides of the ferry crossing. The ferry is capable of holding cars with trailers and motorhomes. It operates year-round, with enhanced service during the prime season.

• On the Water

Boating is the big activity at the reservoir, and there are five large marinas located along the waterway. Bullfrog Marina is 70 miles south of Hanksville. Wahweap Marina is 7 miles north of Page. There are lodges with overnight accommodations at both marinas. Other marinas are located at Hite, Halls Crossing (across the lake from Bullfrog), and Bullfrog (the largest marina in Utah). There is no charge for entering the recreation area, and the prime season runs from late March to late October. There are seven information centers in the area. The only year-round visitor center is at the Glen Canyon Dam near Page, but the visitor center at the Bullfrog

Destinations

Marina is open most of the year. Interpretation programs are given during the summer months at campgrounds in the Bullfrog and Wahweap areas.

• Trails

Those who prefer to use their legs instead of a motorboat have three good trails to hike. **Escalante Canyon** offers several trails leading from the Highway 12 turnoff. **Grand Gulch Trail** begins at the Kane Gulch Ranger Station and leads into a deep canyon that has been the site of archeological digs. **Dark Canyon** is located off Highway 95. The hiking opportunities here are many, with 55 miles of trails leading from trailheads off dirt roads.

Camping

Campgrounds are operated by the National Parks Service at Bullfrog, Halls Crossing, Hite, and Wahweap. There's a charge for camping.

Moab & the Canyonlands

Located near the Colorado border, south of Arches National Park and just south of the Colorado River, Moab has a rich history dating back at least 10,000 years, when native Indians lived in and roamed throughout the Canyonlands, painting pictures on the rocks that are now seen along several fascinating backcountry byways. Much later, the Old Spanish Trail crossed the area.

The town was permanently settled in 1880, receiving its name from the Bible. Following mineral discoveries, the town boomed during the 1950s and is now devoted to both mining and tourism. The town's location in the midst of several national parks and monuments makes it a popular

place to stay for vacationers who are visiting the area's attractions.

In addition to the major national parks and monuments covered on other pages, there are several points of interest around Moab that add to the pleasure of a stay in the Canyonlands region:

• Dead Horse Point State Park

From an overlook at the 6,000-foot level, the Colorado River (2,000 feet below) winds through the Canyonlands on its way to the Grand Canyon and on to the Gulf of California. One can see a series of formations on the canyons dating back 150 million years. This state park is named for the wild mustang herds that ran free on the mesas near Dead Horse Point. The cliffs provided a convenient corral for pioneer cowboys who herded the horses, which were then roped and broken. Legend has it that a band of horses were left corralled at the point. A gate was left open, but, for some unknown reason, the horses stayed there and perished of thirst, within sight of the Colorado River.

To get to this 7,000-acre park, take Utah Highway 313 south from U.S. Hwy. 191, north of Moab. The visitor center is just off Hwy. 313, on the way south to the point. There's a picnic area with shaded tables and grills near the point.

The **Kayenta Campground** is nearby. There are 21 campsites, modern restrooms, covered picnic tables, electrical hookups, and dump stations. Water is hauled to the campground from Moab. Reservations may be made in advance by phoning (801) 259-6511. Although the park is open year-round, the campground is open only from April through October. Because of the elevation, summer temperatures reach a low of 40 degrees and can climb to over 90 degrees during the day. There is a self-guiding nature trail, and the Shafer Trail winds along the top of the escarpment with fine views of the river far below.

• Canyon Rims Recreation Area

The Bureau of Land Management (BLM) operates this superb canyon area located south of Moab and north of the town of Monticello. It can be reached by taking U.S. Highway 191. The area includes much of the public land along the eastern and southern boundaries of Canyonlands National Park.

Access through the area is by a series of paved and gravel roads leading west from Hwy. 191. The Canyon Rims Backcountry Byway leads to the Needles Overlook. Utah Hwy. 211 is another scenic byway that leads west, to Needles Outpost, following the flow of Indian Creek. This road continues into Canyonlands

Destinations

National Park, where there is a Parks Service visitor center and campground.

There are several campgrounds within the Recreation Area, including three developed facilities. One is the Wind Whistle Campground, which has 17 sites and is off the road to Needles Overlook, about 6 miles from Hwy. 161. Another campground at Hatch Point has 9 sites, off the road to Anticline Overlook (24 miles from the highway via the Needles Overlook Byway and a dirt road leading north). There are several campsites in Newspaper Rock State Park (see below). There are picnic tables and pit toilets at the primitive campsites near Indian Creek, near the road to Needles Outpost (Utah Hwy. 211). Backcountry camping permits are available at the Needles Visitor Center in Canyonlands National Park.

• Newspaper Rock State Historic Monument

Located off Utah Hwy. 211 (in the Canyon Rims Recreation Area), this park features an outstanding panel of rock art, along with interpretive exhibits. Prehistoric Indians of the Anasazi culture occupied the lands along Indian Creek for a short period before the 1200s AD. Remnants of their rock dwellings and art exist throughout this area. Ute Indians later hunted in the region, but these nomadic natives did not establish permanent settlements here.

• River Recreation

The Colorado River and the Green River to the south offer river adventures, including white water canoeing and kayaking. Motorized rafts and jet boats are also used on the Colorado from Moab, with organized trips taking from a half-day to several days. For information, contact the Moab Information Center (800-635-6622) or Adrift Adventures (800-874-4483).

• Forest and City Camping

The **Manti-La Sal National Forest** is located in the La Sal Mountains, southeast of Moab. There are several forest backroads in the area, and two lead to forest campgrounds. To reach these rustic campsites, take Highway 191 south from Moab and turn east onto the **La Sal Mountain Loop Road**, which leads through the mountains to Castle Valley and ends at Utah Hwy. 128. Backroads lead off this loop route to **Oowah Lake** Campground and **Warner Lake** Campground. Farther south, past Monticello, another section of the same national forest is located in the Abajo Mountains. There is camping in this area as well. Several private campgrounds and RV parks can be found in and around Moab (see the Places to Stay pages).

Monument Valley

Monument Valley is Navajo territory. This vast area—with its magnificent red buttes beloved of Hollywood's western movies—is **Monument Valley Tribal Park**. It is reached by driving southwest on U.S. Highway 163 from the small settlement of Mexican Hat, in the "goosenecks" area of southeastern Utah (see the scenic drive that begins on page 132).

Aside from the memorable buttes, much of the attraction of Monument Valley is the Navajo culture. The huge Navajo Indian Reservation covers 25,000 square miles in three states. The Utah section alone covers one million acres. Several cultural attractions are found in the valley. **Goulding's Trading Post** re-creates valley life in the 1920s. The **Tribal Park Museum** features Navajo archeology, and the Indian relics are remarkable. The museum is open each day from 8 AM to 6 PM. **Oljedo Trading Post and Museum** in Monument Valley is a state historic site.

The road into Monument Valley is paved as far as the visitor center and museum. The rest of the routes in the valley are dirt sideroads, which are regularly maintained. Drivers have the choice of taking a self-guiding loop road that shows some of the attractions or taking a guided tour of the park. Guided tours are available from park headquarters, at Goulding's Lodge and—from outside the park—in the towns of Bluff, Monticello, Blanding, and Moab, as well as from the nearby community of Mexican Hat. Highway 163 continues south toward the Grand Canyon, which is 143 miles from the Utah/Arizona border.

Other nearby scenic wonders include the **Valley of the Gods**, with a series of sculpted rock formations, 10 miles north of Mexican Hat on a loop road off Hwy. 261. For the most spectacular scene of them all, with panoramic views of Monument Valley, the Goosenecks of the San Juan River and the Four Corners, drive farther north on 261 to the **Moki Dugway Lookout**.

Mexican Hat is a launching point for rafting trips on the San Juan River.

Camping & Accommodations

A campground is operated by the tribal park. There is a private RV park in Mexican Hat, the nearest town. Goosenecks State Park—4 miles northwest of Mexican Hat—has a public campground as well as fine views of the 1,000-foot chasm of the San Juan River.

The only overnight accommodations in the valley are at Goulding's Lodge. Tours are available here, as well as 64 rooms, a restaurant, and a swimming pool. For information, phone (801) 727-3231.

The nearest accommodation outside the valley is in Mexican Hat. There are three trading posts here, as well as two motels, an RV park, and two cafes. The community is 22 miles north of the Utah/Arizona border, across the San Juan River from the Navajo Reservation.

Natural Bridges National Monument

Located just off the Bicentennial Highway, the three perforated rock walls in the monument are spectacular examples of the forces of nature at work. To get there, see the drive on page 128, which will take you from Torrey and Blanding.

Geologically speaking, bridges are not arches. Bridges are created by the force of water carving holes in the rock. Natural arches are made by other forces of erosion. Stream erosion is a key to the formation of the three bridges in this park.

Two of the bridges are considered to be in a mature stage. **Owachomo Bridge** and **Sipapu Bridge** are no longer being eroded by streams, although wind and rain continue to shape their form.

Kachina Bridge is the youngest of the three, looking bulky and not as delicate as the older formations. It is located in White Canyon and still faces floodwaters each year. And—some distant day—they all will inevitably break up and disappear due to future erosion. In the meantime, these wonderful bridges are here to explore.

Although all of the stone bridges can be seen (more or less) from viewpoints along the one-way loop road, short trails will take you to the bridges for the kind of view you really should get if you've driven all the way to see them. Although it is the largest, Sipapu Bridge is hard to spot as you park along the road. Experienced hikers will wish to take the 8-mile (13 KM) trail linking the bridges, which are located in two separate canyons. There is some climbing to do on the longer loop trail.

The loop road and the park's visitor center are located atop the plateau, on the canyon rim. There's a difference in ecosystems between the top and bottom landscapes. On the plateau, pinyon pine and juniper prevail. The canyon bottoms exhibit desert plant life: shrubs and grasses. Where there is water, cottonwoods and willows grow. A walk into the canyons from the three access points provides a good look at the transition zone, which features Douglas firs, oaks, and maples.

The visitor center features an orientation slide show that tells of the history of the natural bridges area and has information on park wildlife. There is a picnic area along the one-way loop road, before you reach the first bridge (Sipapu). Upon entering the monument, you'll see a large photovoltaic power system, which was completed and turned on in 1980. Until recently, it supplied all of the power requirements of the monument. The park is open year-round but the prime season for viewing and hiking is from April through October. The fall season, when the aspens turn a bright yellow color, is particularly beautiful. During the winter, some trails may be closed because of snow and ice.

Camping

There is one campground in the park, located just west of the visitor center. This is a primitive campground with 13 sites and no water, a 21-foot limit, but no fee. Interpretation programs are held here during summer months. Water is available at the visitor center.

Destinations

Outside Accommodations

The nearest overnight places to stay are in **Fry Canyon**, which is 26 miles west on Utah Hwy. 95, and have very limited accommodations. The town of **Blanding** is 68 miles from the park and has more in the way of motels and restaurants, as well as RV parks. There is a campground/RV park at **Hite Marina**, 50 miles west in the Glen Canyon National Recreation Area.

Parowan and Brian Head

Parowan calls itself the Mother Town of Southern Utah. It was the first Mormon settlement in the area (1851), established to foster mining, and provided a base for development of other communities in the region. It's located north of Cedar City, just off Interstate 15 in southwestern Utah.

In recent years, the people of Parowan have established a Heritage Foundation to focus on the town's history, and one of its projects is the **Parowan Heritage Park**, now being planned and constructed with historic buildings brought to the site. There are a number of beautiful historic homes in the town, as well. For Parowan accommodations, see page 169.

The **Rock Church** stands in the middle of the Parowan town square. Completed in 1867, this building has been a church, town council hall, school, and social hall. In the 1940s, the church was restored by the Daughters of Utah Pioneers, who now operate a historical museum in the building. The **Jesse N. Smith Home** is located across the square from the church. It was built out of red adobe in 1857–58, and the Smith family lived here until 1880. It remained empty for many years and was restored to become another museum. Tours through the mansion can be arranged by phoning (801) 477-8728.

The **Parowan Gap**, a natural pass, is located 12 miles northwest of Parowan. Indians passing through the Gap left messages on the boulders here, and the petroglyphs feature drawings of snakes, lizards, mouse-men, mountain sheep, and bear claws. There's an information display at the Gap with the story of the Indian migrations.

Brian Head is both a mountain and a resort town. From the 11,207-foot peak, you can see the red rock pinnacles of Cedar Breaks National Monument and the surrounding Dixie National Forest. Brian Head is a powder skiing favorite, and the small town has become a destination resort that also operates as a recreation and cultural center during summer months. It's the northern gateway to Cedar Breaks, providing lodge and B & B accommodations, plus several good places to eat. There's fishing nearby at Panguitch Lake, Navajo Lake, and the Yankee Meadow Reservoir. For accommodations, see page 164.

Between the two towns lies **Parowan Canyon**. Highway 143 leads south from Parowan, passing through this scenic canyon. Five miles up the canyon is the **Vermillion Castle** picnic area and campground (called Five-Mile by locals). Here one sees high, red cliff formations. Beyond the castle area is the **Yankee Meadow Reservoir** mentioned above. An alternate (4WD) route to the reservoir is through **Second Left-Hand Canyon**, which leaves the highway just beyond the Vermillion Castle turnoff. Beyond the reservoir is **Paragonah Canyon** and the nearby **Reed Creek Reservoir**. A stand of ancient bristlecone pines can be seen by taking forest backroads along the north rim of Cedar Breaks, starting at Brian Head.

St. George & Kanab

Zion National Park lies between these two towns, and either could serve as a stopping place before driving to the spectacular park. Located 75 miles apart, they are linked by Utah Highway 9.

St. George is the home of Dixie College, a 2-year institution established in 1911. The town was the winter residence of the Mormon founder, and his home is now a museum. The **Brigham Young Winter Home** is located at 200 N. 100 West (using the unique Mormon street designation system) and is open year-round from 9 AM until dusk. Erected in 1877, the white **Mormon Temple** in St. George was the first temple to be completed in Utah. The temple grounds and visitor center are open every day. While Cedar City has its Shakespearean Festival, St. George has classical comedies and melodramas, which are staged each summer by the Pioneer Players in the Arena Theater at Dixie College. For information, phone (801) 628-3121. There are four golf courses in the area and there are two ghost towns to explore. Both **Old Frisco** and **Silver Reef** are located just north of town.

Kanab is another historic town and, like St. George, has an imposing early courthouse. Kanab has been a movie-making town for many years, nicknamed Little Hollywood because so many westerns have been shot around here over the past 40 years. **Frontier Movie Town** is a popular attraction, as are several of the movie sets that still sit near the community. The **Heritage House** (100 S. Main Street) is an important restored historic house that is open daily and contains memorabilia from the town's pioneer days.

• A Day-Trip

One of the best preserved of Utah's ghost towns is located on the **Smithsonian Butte Backcountry Byway**. Back in 1880, Captain Clarence Dutton and his expedition got their first view of the towers of Zion from atop what he called Smithsonian Butte (after the museum in Washington, D.C.). The byway can be reached from either Utah Highway 59 or Utah Hwy. 9. Both roads lead west from the St. George area.

To retrace Captain Dutton's original path, take Highway 59 8 miles west of Hildale and turn onto the byway at Big Plain Junction. **Caanan Mountain** lies to the east, with the **Vermillion Cliffs** in front of the mountain. **Smithsonian Butte** towers to the northeast. The gravel road veers east around the Butte with splendid views of the Virgin River Valley. This river has sculpted the canyons of Zion National Park and created the other deep canyons in this area.

At the river crossing is the old site of **Grafton** (2 miles west of Rockville). Settled here in 1862 after a flood destroyed the first town, Grafton was abandoned in the early 1900s. There are five buildings still standing, and the Grafton cemetery (just south of the townsite) is worth a visit. The famous bicycle scene in the movie *Butch Cassidy & the Sundance Kid* was shot here.

Zion National Park

Zion provides a wonderful diversity of landscape and ecosystems. From the forests of the surrounding plateaus (up to 9,000 feet elevation) to the deep sandstone canyons and desert riverbottoms, Zion National Park is a fine testament to the geological forces of nature. In the case of this park, it is the Virgin River that has done most of the sculpting, as it cut its way through layer after layer of stone. It still flows through the park, relentlessly cutting through Zion Canyon.

This was once a desert of huge, blowing sand dunes. In dinosaur times, a shallow sea covered the dunes, and lime from sea animals and other sources seeped into the sand, cementing the sand and creating sandstone. There was an uplifting of land and the sea drained away, leaving the rivers to carve the sandstone into the dramatic canyons now found throughout southern Utah. Zion Canyon is certainly one of the most dramatic and beautiful of these sandstone gorges.

The Paiute name for the canyon was *Mukuntuweap*, and in 1909 President Taft gave the Paiute name to what was then a national monument. Local Mormon pioneers called the area Zion and lobbied for a change in name when the monument was enlarged in 1918. The next year, it became a national park, and it has since been enlarged by the addition of the Kolob Canyons area.

The park now covers about 147,000 acres. Zion, as a "heavenly place," had been home to the ancient Anasazi culture, and then the nomadic Paiute Indians roamed the region. The early Mormon pioneers found it no less attractive than its former inhabitants, and it is now preserved for us all to enjoy.

Getting There

Utah Highway 9 runs east and west through the southern reaches of the park, which contain the major attractions. The town of Kanab is 41 miles to the east and St. George, 36 miles to the west. Cedar City is 55 miles northwest of the park headquarters, via Highways 9 and I-15. The Kolob Canyons area is accessed from Interstate 15, south of Cedar City. The park headquarters is 309 miles south of Salt Lake City.

Destinations

Park Attractions

About 2.5 million people visit Zion each year, which makes for a lot of people in the busier months. Sightseeing, walking the park trails, bicycling, camping, staying in the lodge, and riding are the major activities. During the summer months, there is a Junior Ranger program in the park for children 6–12 years of age. Zion is not just a few canyons to see, although the canyons are its most impressive feature. There is also a huge backcountry area north and west of the Virgin River canyons, and many visitors take off with a backpack to camp in the wilderness. Some of the longer trails lead through the backcountry, and camping is permitted along these routes (see next page).

The main visitor center is located near the south entrance to the park, on Highway 9. There are a variety of services in this area. There is a smaller visitor center at the entrance to the Kolob Canyons area of the park, off Interstate 15. There is no internal road connection between the two sections of the park.

• Four Scenic Drives

Four roads lead through various parts of the park, providing access to the major trails and camping sites. From the visitor center, the **Zion Canyon Scenic Drive** leads north along the rim of the canyon, with the Virgin River far below. There are two footbridges along the first section of the drive, between the turnoff and Zion Lodge. Both bridges lead to the Sand Bench Trail (see below). The **Emerald Pools Trail** leads down the canyon from opposite Zion Lodge. This is an easy walk (1.2 miles, about an hour's walk), ending at the Lower Pool with three waterfalls and fine views of cliffs that drop more than 600 feet.

The road continues past the lodge to the **Grotto** (with another footbridge) and a picnic area. Here are the trailheads for the **West Rim Trail** and the **Angels Landing Trail**. Passing beside the Great White Throne (a peak to the east) and Angels Landing (west of the highway) the road curves around another peak (the Organ), with a turnaround at the **Temple of Sinewava**, which is the trailhead for the **Gateway to the Narrows Trail**. This is an easy

Utah

trail, following the Virgin River past hanging gardens of wild-flowers in the spring and early summer period. There are several trailside exhibits. All along this drive—across the river and canyon—are spectacular rock formations including the Court of the Patriarchs, Cathedral Mountain, and the Pulpit.

Highway 9 (now called the **Zion–Mt. Carmel Highway**), leads east from the visitor center area passing through tunnels before reaching the east entrance to the park. There is a 1-mile trail to the Great Arch, with the Canyon Overlook at the halfway point.

Kolob Canyons Road is a short drive from the Kolob entrance to the park. At Lee Pass is the **Kolob Arch Trail**, a strenuous, 14-mile hike with a side-trail leading to the arch.

Kolob Terrace Road (open summer only) is accessed from Highway 9 at the village of Virgin, west of the south entrance. It leads through BLM lands before entering the park, running across the Lower Kolob Plateau and providing access to the Wildcat Canyon Trail and the remote Lava Point Campground. The northern trailhead for the West Rim Trail is at the campground.

Park Camping

The Watchman and South Campgrounds, located near the south entrance, are available on a first come, first served basis, and a fee is charged. One of these campgrounds is open year-round. Both campgrounds have water, picnic tables, fire grates, and dump stations. There are no hookups or showers. The Lava Point Campground is open from May to October. Here there are tables, fire grates, and toilets. There is no water provided here and no fee is charged.

Park Accommodations

Zion Lodge has cabins and motel rooms, as well as a restaurant, snack bar, and gift shop. Advance reservations are recommended, particularly during the busy summer season. For rates and reservations, phone (801) 586-7686. Tram tours on open-air busses are operated by the park concessionaire during the summer months. Reservations are made in the lodge. The Zion Canyon road was closed by an avalanche during the stormy winter of 1995. It may be wise to check lodge availabilities.

Destinations

Outside Accommodations

There are several private campgrounds within 25 miles of the park. The small town of Springdale has a full-service RV park. There are RV parks and motels in Kanab, St. George, Mt. Carmel, Hurricane, and Cedar City. See the Utah Accommodations pages that follow for motels and campgrounds.

ARCHES NATIONAL PARK

The Devil's Garden Campground is the one campground in the park—at the north end. It has 50 tent and trailer sites, plus two group sites for tents. The campground has running water and flush toilets from spring until fall and a fee is charged; in winter there are chemical toilets and no water nor fee. For park information, write to the Superintendent, Arches National Park, P.O. Box 907, Moab UT 84532. Or call (801) 259-8161.

BLANDING

Old Hotel Bed and Breakfast
118 E. 300 South
P.O. Box 86-6
Blanding UT 84512
(801) 678-2388

This 1911 home has been in the family of the owners (two sisters named Ora and Bernice) since 1913. The home was converted to a bed and breakfast facility in 1989. There are three bedrooms upstairs and four on the ground floor, all with private bath. The home has original period furnishings mingled with newer pieces. A full country breakfast is served, which may include a breakfast casserole plus home-made granola, hot breads, fruit, juice and coffee. It's open from April 1 through October 31 ($).

Gateway Motel
88 E. Center
Blanding UT 84511
(801) 678-2278

With 59 units, two with two bedrooms, this is Blanding's largest motel (it is part of the Best Western group). It has a swimming pool and playground as well as cable TV and movies ($).

Comfort Inn of Blanding
711 S. Hwy. 191
Blanding UT 84511
(801) 678-3271
or 800-221-2222

This inn boasts a sauna and hot tub as well as a pool. It also has a restaurant attached. There are 52 rooms available with cable TV and movies. Some rooms have kitchens. It's a local operation with friendly staff ($ to $$).

Blanding Area Camping

Kampark (801-678-2270) is open all year and has 52 RV sites with full hookups and 20 tent sites with toilets, showers, laundry, drinking water. There are also picnic tables, dump station, fishing and boating. **Devil's Canyon Campground** (801-587-2042) has pit toilets and no showers, with 33 RV and tent sites.

BRIAN HEAD

Brian Head Hotel
223 Hunter Ridge Rd.
P.O. Box 190008
Brian Head UT 84719
(801) 677-3000
or 800-468-4898

This large hotel (170 rooms) has many amenities, including a sauna, two outdoor whirlpools, a swimming pool, TV, movies, and kitchens. Non-smoking rooms are available. It also has the Columbine Cafe for breakfast and lunch, the Summit Dining room for fine dining, and a lounge (**$ to $$**).

Copper Chase Condominium Hotel
150 Ridge Road
P.O. Box 190218
Brian Head UT 84719
(801) 677-2890
or 800-468-4898

The Copper Chase is one of several facilities in town with condominium units; this one has 65 available of varying sizes, all with kitchens (fully furnished with appliances and utensils) and some with hot tubs. Also available to guests are a covered heated pool, whirlpool, and weight room (**$$**).

BRYCE CANYON NATIONAL PARK

Bryce Canyon Lodge and Cabins
P.O. Box 400

Cedar City UT 84721
(801) 586-7686

What a wonderful setting for a lodge and cabins, on the rim of the spectacular canyon, at 8,000 feet! The lodge is now a National Historic Landmark and was completely renovated in 1989. There are 4 suites available in the lodge, 106 double rooms in the motel and 40 cabins—all with gas fireplace and private bath. Facilities also include a restaurant, bar, gift shop, and general store. There are many activities available here, including bus tours, horseback riding, and hiking the many trails that descend into the canyon. Open late April to mid-October (**$$ to $$$+**).

Best Western Ruby's Inn
Bryce Canyon UT 84764
(801) 834-5341
or 800-528-1234

Ruby's is a huge complex with 216 rooms and lots of amenities. Among them are an indoor swimming pool and spa, a dining room with a seasonal buffet and deli, a gas station, and an enormous general store that alone can provide hours of entertainment: it's loaded with minerals, jewelry, and books, among other things such as groceries. There are other activities available as well: in summer there are trail rides, helicopter flights, and chuckwagon dinner rides; in winter there is snowmobiling and cross-country skiing. And best of all, it's located just minutes away from the amazing Bryce Canyon National Park ($ to $$).

Bryce Canyon Pines
Scenic Rte. 12, Box 43
Bryce UT 84764
(801) 834-5441

Also located minutes away from the national park, this motel has 50 units, some with fire places, plus an indoor heated pool, restaurant, cocktails, coffee shop, and laundromat ($).

Bryce Canyon Camping

Bryce Village Resort (801-834-5351) is open year-round for RV and trailer camping, with 26 full-service sites plus a dump station, laundry, and showers. **Ruby's Inn Campground and Trailer Park** (801-834-5301) has 200 sites (100 hookups for trailers and 100 tent sites); it is open from early April until late October.

CEDAR CITY

Meaudeau View Lodge
P.O. Box 356
Cedar City UT 84720
(801) 682-2495

This small lodge is well located, only an hour's drive from both Bryce and Zion National Parks, and offers a lovely setting of aspen, lakes, and meadows (the site of several movies, in fact). The lodge building itself is made of pine and has a striking circular fireplace in the sitting room. There are nine rooms as well as three 2-bedroom cottages with kitchens. Each room has a private bath. There is a full breakfast too, with egg dishes, home-baked breads, and fruit ($).

165

Places to Stay

Woodbury Guest House
237 South 300 West
Cedar City UT 84720
(801) 586-6696

This delightful Victorian home was built near the turn of the century for a prominent early citizen and mayor of Cedar City. It's now a superior bed and breakfast inn. There are four rooms available with private bath, each with its own distinctive charm. There is a delicious breakfast served as well. The location is especially convenient to the Shakespeare festival ($$).

Holiday Inn
1575 West 200 North
Cedar City UT 84720
(801) 586-8888
or 800-586-1010

If a standard motel is more to your liking, or if the B & Bs are full, this motor inn offers 100 units in addition to a heated pool, sauna, whirlpool, and exercise room. There is also a dining room and a coffee shop. To get there, take the central exit off I-15 ($ to $$).

Cedar City Camping

The **Cedar City KOA** (801-586-9872) is open all year with 200 sites, including 70 for tents. It has a pool, laundry, grocery store, and dump station. The **Country Aire RV Park** (801-586-2550) is also open year-round with 70 sites (30 for tents) as well as a pool, laundry, and playground.

GLEN CANYON NATIONAL RECREATION AREA

Defiance House
P.O. Box 4055
Bullfrog UT 84533
(801) 684-2233

This attractive resort lodge is perched on a bluff overlooking Lake Powell and the marina. There are 48 rooms available, plus a coin laundry, restaurant, and lounge. And of course, activities here focus on water sports: swimming, fishing, boating (rentals are available, including houseboats), and water skiing ($ to $$).

Glen Canyon Camping

There are two campgrounds in the area, both open year-round. **Bullfrog Basin Campground** (801-684-2243) has 86 sites but no dump station or showers. It does offer swimming, boat rentals, and a boat ramp. **Halls Crossing Campground** (801-684-2249) has 65 sites with hookups, dump station, and toilets, but no showers.

Utah

KANAB

**Best Western
Red Hills**
P.O. Box 758
Kanab UT 84741
(801) 644-2675

A motel with 72 units, it has a heated pool, a whirlpool, cable TV, and movies. There is a restaurant opposite the facility which is located at 125 West Center Street (**$ to $$**).

Aikens Lodge
79 W. Center Street
Kanab UT 84741
(801) 644-2625

A smaller motel with a more modest price tag has in its 25 units some with two and three bedrooms and some with kitchens. There is also a heated pool (**$**).

**Kanab Area
Camping**

Coral Pink Sand Dunes State Park is open all year with 22 pull-through sites and a dump station (801-874-2408). The **Ponderosa** is smaller with 10 trailer sites, pit toilets, and no showers or fee (801-586-2401).

MEXICAN HAT

San Juan Inn
P.O. Box 310276
Mexican Hat UT 84531
(801) 683-2220

This is a small, reasonably priced motel located on the banks of the San Juan River. Among the 23 units available are 2 two-bedroom units with whirlpool. River trips and summer cookouts are also available here (**$**).

**Mexican Hat
Camping**

There are a couple of smallish campgrounds in the area: **Burches Trading Post** (801-683-2221) has 15 full-service RV sites, showers, toilets, picnic tables, swimming, and boating; and **Valle's Trailer Park** (801-683-2226) with 31 sites (25 full-service) has amenities similar to those of Burches plus handicapped facilities.

167

MOAB

Landmark Motel
168 Main Street
Moab UT 84532
(801) 259-6147

This motel has 36 units (king and queen), laundry facilities, whirlpool and heated swimming pool, cable TV, and movies (**$ to $$**).

Places to Stay

Castle Valley Inn

P.O. Box 2602
Moab UT 84532
(801) 259-6012

This B & B inn has a magnificent setting at 4,500 feet, with 360° views of the mountains and the red formations surrounding it. There are six double rooms, four with private bath, plus two cottages with private bath and kitchen and a hot tub. A full breakfast is included; picnic lunches and dinners are available (**$ to $$**).

Pack Creek Ranch

P.O. Box 1270
Moab UT 84532
(801) 259-5505

An assortment of log cabins is available here, having one to four bedrooms, private baths and kitchens, some with living rooms and fireplaces. Both breakfast and dinner are included in the rates, as is the spectacular scenery of the La Sal Mountains. Trail rides and river rafting are among the outdoor activities available here (**$$$ to $$$+**).

Moab Camping

There are several camping facilities in the Moab area: **Canyonlands Campark** has 130 sites including some tent sites and many with full hookups (801-259-6848); another large one is the **Slickrock Campground**, also open year-round with about 180 sites (85 with full hookups, 30 for tents) plus drinking water, showers, laundry, swimming, and boating. Call (801) 259-7660.

MONTICELLO

Wayside Inn

P.O. Box 669
Monticello UT 84535
(801) 587-2261

This is a moderately priced Best Western motel with 35 units, cable and movies, heated pool and whirlpool. It's on U.S. 666, 2 blocks east of U.S. 191 (**$ to $$**).

Monticello Camping

KOA Monticello has 40 tent sites and 36 RV and trailer sites (7 with full hookup); call (801) 587-2884. It's open May through October. **Rowley's Trailer Park** (801-587-2355) has 17 full-service RV sites plus 45 tent sites and is open from April 1, through October 31.

MONUMENT VALLEY

Monument Valley spans the Utah/Arizona border. Goulding's Lodge is in the Utah section.

Utah

Goulding's Trading Post and Lodge

P.O. Box 36001
Monument Valley UT
84536
(801) 727-3231

Goulding's has a wonderful setting, tucked up against a hillside with great views of the fabulous red rock monuments. It has 62 units, some with balconies or patios ($$). The original trading post, still in operation, was established in 1923 and the rooms were added later. Many films have been shot here, and in fact the dining room, which serves Southwest cuisine, was originally built as a film set. Also in the complex are a gas station and a campground with 80 sites.

PANGUITCH

New Western Motel

P.O. Box 73
Panguitch UT 84759
(801) 676-8876

This motel is part of the Best Western chain and is open all year with 37 units (3 with two bedrooms). It has a coin laundry, heated pool and winter plug-ins ($).

Marianna Inn Motel

P.O. Box 179
Panguitch UT 84759
(801) 676-8844

Located at 669 N. Main Street, this inn is open April through October. There are 24 units and some are large enough for six to eight people. There is a whirlpool, and a family restaurant is nearby ($).

Panguitch Camping

Panguitch Big Fish KOA is the largest in the area, with 80 sites (45 RV and 35 tent). It has a dump station, laundry, and pool; call (801) 676-2225. It's open from April 1 to October 31.

PAROWAN

Swiss Village Inn

P.O. Box 967
Parowan UT 84761
(801) 477-3391

Swiss decor marks this Best Western motel. It has 28 units, a heated pool, and in winter, an enclosed whirlpool. There is also a restaurant here ($).

169

Jedediah's Inn and Restaurant

625 W. 200 South
Parowan UT 84761
(801) 477-3326

As the name implies, this motor inn has a restaurant attached, and there is also a lounge. There are 40 units available, with cable TV, movies, and phones. It is open year-round ($).

Places to Stay

Parowan Camping

Foothills RV Park is open all year and has 79 RV sites with full hookups, as well as 40 tent sites, water, showers, toilets, laundry, and dump station (801-477-3535). **Pit Stop Campground** has 20 RV and 34 tent sites, year-round (801-477-9990).

ST. GEORGE

Greene Gate Village
76 West Tabernacle St.
St. George UT 84770
(801) 628-6999

This B & B is certainly unique in that it comprises several authentic pioneer buildings of the area, offering 16 guest rooms, all with private bath. All are furnished in period style, and there is a pool and hot tub as well. A full breakfast is included and dinner is available (**$ to $$**).

Seven Wives Inn
217 North 100 West
St. George UT 84770
(801) 628-3737

The colorful history of this house is reflected in its name; it harks back to the local custom of polygamy in bygone days. The house dates to 1873 and is furnished accordingly. There are 13 rooms, all with private bath and some with fireplaces. There's a swimming pool. Full breakfast is served and picnic lunches are available (**$ to $$**).

Coral Hills Motel
125 E St. George Blvd.
St. George UT 84770
(801) 673-4844 or
800-542-7733

This Best Western motel has 98 units. It has a fitness center with year-round indoor and outdoor pools, 2 whirlpools, and an exercise room. There's a putting green, games room, and restaurant (**$ to $$**).

St. George Camping

Settlers RV Park has 160 RV sites and 50 tent sites and is open all year (801-628-1624). **Temple View RV Resort** is also open year-round with 252 RV sites and 40 for tents. Both have full hookups, water, showers, laundry, and swimming.

ZION NATIONAL PARK & AREA

Cliffrose Lodge and Gardens
281 Zion Park Blvd.
Springdale UT 84767
(801) 772-3234

This lodge sits on river frontage with 5 acres of lawns, trees, and flowers. There are 36 units with wonderful views of the surrounding cliffs of Zion National Park. There is a swimming pool The lodge is a 2-minute drive from the park (**$$**).

Utah

Under the Eaves Guest House
P.O. Box 29
Springdale UT 84767
(801) 772-3457

Not only does this B & B offer views of the canyon, it's actually constructed from stone blocks cut from there to form a cozy Tudor-style cottage. There are five rooms, three with private bath. A generous breakfast is served and picnic lunches are available ($ to $$).

Zion Park Lodge
Zion National Park
Springdale UT 84767
(801) 772-3213

One of the few lodges located in national parks, this one is set in the valley surrounded by wonderfully high cliffs. There are suites and cabins, all with private baths. There is a dining room and coffee shop, gift shop, and guided walks as well as tram and trail rides. It is located in the middle of Zion Canyon, across the road from the Virgin River ($$ to $$$).

Zion Area Camping

Zion Canyon Campground in Springdale (801-772-3237) has 75 full-service RV sites and 75 sites for tents. Rental cabins are also available, and there's a recreation room and restaurant on the property. **Zion RV Park** has 75 full hookups plus tent sites, laundry, swimming pool, gas station, and dump station (801-635-4272).

Inside Zion National Park, you'll find the **South Campground** and **Watchman Campground** near the entrance, with 141 and 228 sites respectively. Both can be reached by calling (801) 772-3256.

Places to Stay

Arizona

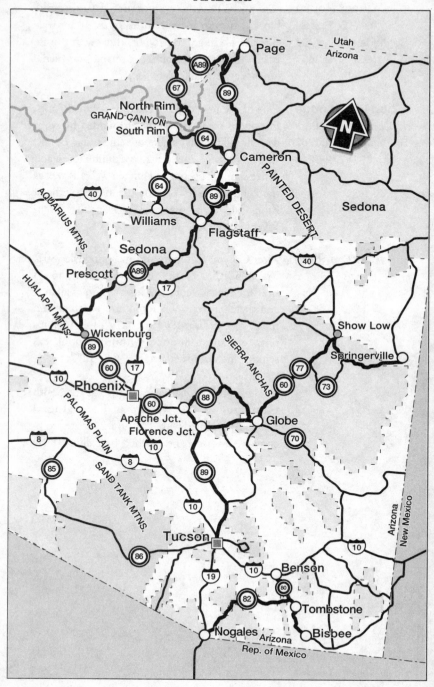

From high desert to low desert; saguaro to pinyon pine; rustic mountain lodges to Scottsdale's deluxe golf resorts—Arizona is a land of extreme contrasts. On a fall weekend, I began driving south from the pine-clad heights of the White Mountains near Springerville, passing through the deep chasm of the Salt River canyon, landing near midday in the scrub desert east of Globe. I drove west toward Phoenix, turning south at Florence Junction and driving along the Pinal Pioneer Parkway, a scenic route through a dry wash landscape decorated with groves of jumping cholla cactus and palo verde trees. Arriving in Tucson—the ultimate desert city—we visited Saguaro National Monument, which celebrates America's largest cactus in two giant preserves.

The journey then continued east and south through two of Arizona's pioneer Wild West towns, Benson and Tombstone, ending in the old mining town of Bisbee—a few miles from the Mexican border. To my astonishment, the approach to Bisbee featured green oak-covered foothills similar to the Sierra foothills in California. One could not ask for a more diverse series of ecosystems and landforms—all in one day's drive.

This is what makes Arizona so special for the traveler.

And then there are the geological wonders. The Grand Canyon is Arizona's best-known natural creation, and nearby Sunset Crater offers a backward glimpse into the earth's volcanic geology.

Sedona and its red rocks take one into another world, one of pillars, cliffs, canyons, and convergence. The nine scenic drives that follow lead through this incredible visual saga—from the Wild West to New Age funkiness—and a full measure of vacation adventure.

Grand Canyon—North Rim Drive

Page to North Rim

This short drive can be accomplished in less than half a day, giving travelers plenty of time to settle on the North Rim. There are several points of interest that add to the journey along the Kaibab monocline, then across the top of the plateau and on the forest drive between Jacob's Lake and the rim of the granddaddy of all canyons.

The route begins just east of the town of Page, created when the high Glen Canyon Dam was built to harness the waters of the Colorado River. Starting on U.S. Highway 89, driving south from Page, we encounter the Echo Cliffs a few miles south of town as the highway cuts through the cliffs and descends into the Cornfield Valley. Turning off the highway at Bitter Springs onto Alternate Route 89, the route leads eastward across the valley. Here are Navajo homes, some with hogans—the traditional Indian dwelling in these parts—as part of the family compound. Crossing the Colorado River on the Navajo Bridge, we enter the community of Marble Canyon. The Lee's Ferry historic site and river access point is located just north of the community via a paved sideroad.

At Jacob Lake, we turn south onto Arizona Route 67 to complete the drive to the North Rim. This is the Kaibab Plateau, a high area of aspen trees, pine forests, mountain lions, and bears and, during winter months, deep snow. Route 67 is closed during the snowy period each year. The road crosses the plateau, passing meadows and small lakes, ending at the parking lot for the Grand Canyon Lodge. From this spot, the South Rim is 18 miles as the crow flies. By road, the journey is more than 200 miles.

Along the Way

• Echo Cliffs

This 69-mile ridge of sandstone cliffs got its name from John Wesley Powell's second expedition through the area, when one of the party shot a gun at the river from a high point and the sound echoed 24 seconds later. There are two gaps in the cliffs—one blasted, which the highway runs through, and the other a natural break at the community called (naturally) The Gap.

Arizona

• Marble Canyon—Lee's Ferry Landing

467 feet above the rushing water, the Navajo Bridge crosses the Colorado over what is the first stage of the Grand Canyon. Six miles north of this community is Lee's Ferry, where John Doyle Lee operated a ferry across the Colorado from 1871, on what was then the main route connecting Arizona and Utah. The bridge replaced the ferry in 1928. Several pioneer buildings remain at Lee's Ferry Landing, part of the Glen Canyon Recreation Area. There's a campground near the site, plus a boat launch at the head of the Grand Canyon with a trail to the original ferry landing location. A walking tour map is available.

• Vermilion Cliffs

These red sandstone cliffs provide a fascinating 30-mile drive as the road winds along the base of the formation. **Cliff Dwellers** is an old pioneer community, where unusual stone buildings built under large rocks used to be the Trading Post. The store is now in a more ordinary building.

• House Rock Valley & Buffalo Ranch

The route passes across House Rock Valley, a high valley offering stupendous views across to the Echo Cliffs. The high, dark mesa in the middle of the area is called Shinumo Altar. The Colorado River is more than 1,500 feet below. The valley was named for two large boulders called Rock House Hotel by one of the first ranchers in the valley. The Buffalo Ranch covers 60,000 acres in the national forest. To see the ranch and buffalo, take Forest Road 445 south for 20 miles.

• Jacob Lake & the Kaibab Plateau

The lake (actually a small sinkhole) is not evident at the junction of Alternate 89 and State Route 67.

• Grand Canyon National Park—The North Rim

The park entrance is 45 miles south of Jacob Lake, with another 11 miles to drive to the rim. At the end of the road is Grand Canyon Lodge and other facilities, including a campground. For North Rim details, see page 230.

Drives

Highway Log

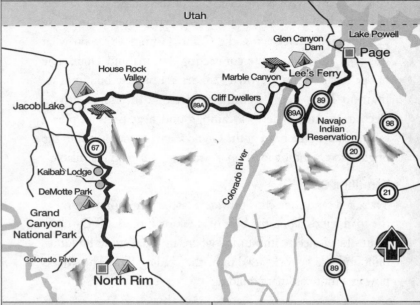

Page This town at the southern edge of Lake Powell and the Glen Canyon Recreation Area has full visitor services. **Glen Canyon Dam** is just north of town on U.S. Highway 89. The town's visitor information center is in Page Plaza on Lake Powell Blvd. Our drive leads south from Page via U.S. Route 89 South.

Viewpoint Just south of town, via a very bumpy road. Overlook of Lake Powell.

Junction–Hwy. 89 Curves back into Page. A shopping center is situated at the corner.

The highway enters the **Navajo Indian Reservation**, crosses the plateau and runs through a narrow cut in the Echo Cliffs before descending into the Colorado River Valley.

Junction–U.S. Hwy. 89A At Bitter Springs. **Take this highway**—leading northwest to Marble Canyon and then to Jacob Lake and the Grand Canyon North Rim.

Navajo Bridge Over the Colorado River. The bridge replaced Lee's Ferry in 1928. Picnic tables near the bridge.

Marble Canyon Small community with motel, cafe, and store. The road to the right leads to the **Lee's Ferry historic site and campground** in the Glen Canyon National Recreation Area. This is the northern end of the Grand Canyon (visitor center, fishing, boat launch, float trips, picnicking).

Balanced Boulders On the road to Lee's Ferry you'll see a mass of jumbled and balanced rocks standing on softer rock pillars.

Vermilion Cliffs Restaurant, quaint motel, & fly shop. The red cliffs to the west are of the same formation as the Echo Cliffs (other side of the river).

Cliff Dwellers Restaurant, modern motel, and store. The buildings built partially under large rocks used to be the Cliff Dwellers Trading Post.

House Rock Valley The Vermilion Cliffs are to the north as the road climbs to reach the top of the Kaibab Plateau. There are spectacular views along this part of the drive, with a panoramic view of the Colorado River and the series of cliffs.

Kaibab Monocline Overlook Views of the Cornfield Valley, Echo & Vermilion Cliffs, and Shinumo Altar.

Marker–San Bartolome To the north of the highway, with information on Spanish exploration of the area, including the Kaibab Plateau.

Road to House Rock Ranch (Forest Rd. 445) The national forest is home to wild bison, which graze on more than 50,000 acres here. The animals were introduced in the early 1900s, and the herd is now controlled to 100 animals. House Rock Ranch is 20 miles south of the highway and is open year-round.

Viewpoint–Kaibab Monocline An overlook with views of the formation.

Jacob Lake Gas, motels, cafe, and RV park. There is a Forest Service campground and a regional visitor center for the North Kaibab area.

Junction–Arizona Route 67 Take this road (the North Rim Parkway) south to reach the North Rim of the Grand Canyon and Grand Canyon National Park. This road is closed during winter months. It leads along the top of the Kaibab Plateau, at altitudes between 8,000 and 9,000 feet.

Crane Lake This is more of a large pond, beside the highway.

DeMotte Park This waystation lies just north of the entrance to Grand Canyon National Park. Services include a gas station, store, the Kaibab Lodge with overnight accommodations, and a Forest Service campground.

Grand Canyon National Park

North Entrance (fee gate)–The road continues southward on the plateau, with Kaibab deer frequently seen.

Cape Royal Road This sideroad leads east to several overlooks. Point Imperial Overlook is 8 miles. Cape Royal Overlook is 23 miles. There is a picnic area on the way to Cape Royal.

North Rim The road ends at the Grand Canyon Lodge parking lot. Services in the park include a campground, laundry, showers, cafes and medical clinic.

Grand Canyon—South Rim Loop

Flagstaff to South Rim & Williams

Because of its accessible location by car or train, the South Rim of the Grand Canyon is by far the more visited of the two sections of Grand Canyon National Park. By road, the South Rim is 109 miles from Flagstaff via Highways 89 and 64, and 58 miles from Williams via Highways 64 and 180; it is 210 miles from the North Rim. The highway log, which runs in a counter-clockwise direction from Flagstaff to the Grand Canyon and Williams, may also be read backwards to get you from Williams to the Grand Canyon.

An alternative to using the road is to take the scenic train from Williams. It runs regularly during summer months and on a much-reduced schedule during the winter. For information, phone 800-THE TRAIN. Once you're in the park you must use either your car or the park's shuttle service to see all of the canyon's sights. During winter it is possible to drive your vehicle on all park roads, including the West Rim Drive, which is closed to private vehicles during the busy summer months. Then you either walk the Rim Trail or use the shuttle bus.

While the total drive is only 167 miles, and it is possible to do the complete route in 1 day, this is really not the way to see the Grand Canyon. On a day-trip you'll find yourself constantly hurrying from one viewpoint to the other, looking at your watch and becoming frustrated with the shortness of time. It's far better to spend a day or two in the park—staying in one of the hotels or camping at one of two campgrounds located along the rim road: one in the village (with hookups) and the other near Desert View (no hookups, first come, first served).

Along the Way

• Sunset Crater National Monument

Ten miles north of Interstate 40 (north of Flagstaff), a loop road leads east to this cinder cone that is brightly colored around the rim. The volcano erupted first during the winter of AD 1064/65 and then occasionally for the next 200 years, making major changes in the landscape surrounding the vent, including the cre-

Arizona

ation of a prominent lava flow to the west and north of the crater in 1180. There is a visitor center at the site and a picnic area next to the Bonito Lava Flow.

• Wupatki National Monument

Near the end of the same loop road that joins Hwy. 89 (10 miles north of the Sunset Crater junction) is this outstanding series of Indian ruins, some of which have been unearthed and preserved. The visitor center is located beside the Wupatki Ruin which was inhabited by the Sinagua, Cohonina, and Anasazi people for about 400 years, beginning in the early twelfth century. The three prehistoric cultures lived here together for some of that time. They disbanded about 1225, scattering in different directions. In addition to the main ruin, there are other sites including the Wukoki, Citadel, Lomaki, and Nalakihu ruins. There is no campground at Wupatki, but there is a scenic picnic area at the base of Doney Mountain.

• Cameron

This historic little community lies along the Little Colorado River at the junction of Highways 89 and 64. Cameron was one of the earliest settlements in northern Arizona and lies within the Navajo Reservation. It was founded in 1916 by Hubert Richardson, who built the trading post here beside a suspension bridge. The bridge is still here but no longer carries traffic. There are several interesting red sandstone buildings in the village. The trading post (Richardson retired in 1966) offers a wide variety of Navajo crafts and supplies for the rural Indian residents who live in the area.

• Little Colorado Overlook

A short sideroad leads to a potholed overlook that offers fine views of the Little Colorado Canyon (1,200 feet deep) and the desert beyond. You'll have to fight your way past the Navajo jewelry stands for the full view. Across the canyon is Shadow Mountain, a black volcanic cone. Past the overlook, the road enters a pinyon pine forest before reaching the park gate.

Drives

Highway Log

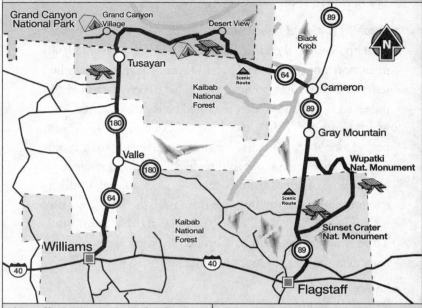

Flagstaff The city is the hub of north-central Arizona and has full visitor services. Our drive to the South Rim begins by taking U.S. Highway 89 north from the Flagstaff city limits. To get to U.S. 89 from downtown, take Business 40 (the business loop for Interstate 40) and veer left to get onto U.S. 89.

Elden Pueblo Ruins This historic site is just off the highway, at the city limits. A forest ranger station is nearby.

Side Trip to Wupatki Ruins & Sunset Crater

10 miles north of the Flagstaff city limits, this road offers a fascinating side trip to two outstanding parks. **Sunset Crater** is a volcano that erupted in the winter of 1064/65 and later vented lava from its base, creating two flows.

Around the base are a picnic area, a lava flow trail, and a visitor center. **The Wupatki Pueblo** is one of five excavated Sinagua Indian ruins in the Wupatki National Monument (farther north on the loop road). There is a visitor center at the Wupatki ruin, where a self-guiding tour will lead you through the multistoried pueblo and to the amphitheater and ball court. There's a picnic area at the base of Mt. Doney, with a trail ascending 689 feet to the hilltop.

Back on Highway 89

The loop road comes back to Highway 89, 10 miles north of the southern intersection.

Gray Mountain A small community with gas, motels, store, and cafe.

The mountain of the same name is to the east (el. 6,305 feet).

Cameron This town has some interesting historical artifacts (look behind the motel for a distinctive garden which dates back almost to the town's founding in 1916). Gas, store, motels, cafe, trading post.

Junction–Arizona Route 64
This is the road that leads west to the Grand Canyon's South Rim. Turn left (west) at the junction and drive toward the park gate.

Viewpoint The **Little Colorado River Canyon** is seen from this overlook, complete with Navajo jewelry stands. The highway climbs to a mesa called **Cedar Mountain**, covered with junipers (not cedars).

Leaving Navajo Reservation This area is called the Upper Basin, offering spectacular views, including Little Colorado Gorge.

East Entrance to the National Park
Desert View The first viewpoint on the way to Grand Canyon Village. The **Watchtower** provides views of the canyon, the Colorado River, and the Painted Desert to the far east.

Tusayan Museum & Ruin The remains of a small pueblo village may be toured, and the museum provides displays on life at the canyon more than 800 years ago.

Lipan Point A great panorama with a fine view of the river (far below) and the North Rim.

Picnic Area To the north.
Moran Point View to the west.
Picnic Area
Grandview Point At a high altitude, looking down on Horseshoe Mesa. Grandview Trail leads down the canyon to the remains of the Last Chance Mine.
Picnic Area To the north.
Yaki Point & Kaibab Trailhead The left fork of this sideroad ends at the South Kaibab Trailhead. Yaki Point (straight ahead) has views of the Kaibab Plateau.
Mather Point This is probably the best overall view of the canyon. The Tonto Platform lies directly below.
Yavapai Museum At this point there are several view platforms and a geological museum. The **Rim Trail** leads from the museum through the village to Hermit's Rest (paved for 3.5 miles to Mariposa Point).
Grand Canyon Village There is lodging, restaurants, gas, a store, medical clinic, and the visitor center.
South Entrance Station (fee gate)
Tusayan Full visitor services are available here, just 1 mile south of the park gate.
Valle Village with gas, motel and small theme park at the junction with U.S. Hwy. 180.
Williams On Interstate 40, 59 miles south of the park entrance.

Red Rock Drive

Flagstaff to Prescott

The red rock of the Sedona area is the scenic standout on this marvelous drive, which avoids freeways and other main highways. Our drive begins in Flagstaff by taking **Alternate U.S. Route 89** south. This road is found branching off U.S. Route 89, south of the downtown area or via Lake Mary Road. Alternate 89 continues through the Coconino National Forest, past Sedona and then through the Peeple's Valley to Prescott. If you're taking this scenic route on the way to Phoenix (and there is no more scenic way to travel between Flagstaff and Phoenix) you have two choices of route south of Prescott (see next page).

Along the Way

• Oak Creek Canyon Recreation Area

Driving south from Flagstaff, the route passes through high pine forest and then descends into Oak Creek Canyon for the rest of the drive to Sedona. Much of the shoreline is designed as public land (the recreation area). The Forest Service operates six campgrounds in the canyon (173 sites in all), and most are open from Memorial Day through Labor Day. These are basic sites with no hookups or showers. At Cave Creek Campground, 11 sites are available for reservation (call 800-283 CAMP).

• Slide Rock State Park

Located 8 miles north of Sedona in Oak Creek Canyon; young people of all ages get a thrill out of sliding down this natural waterslide (entrance fee).

• Indian Gardens

About 1876, settler Jim Thompson, built a log cabin in Oak Creek Canyon and began cultivating the old Indian gardens where natives had grown corn and squash for hundreds of years. Thompson remained at the ranch until his death in 1917.

• Sedona

A modern town, best known for its wonderful red rock scenery and seemingly bizarre convergence zones. The visitor center is located

182

Arizona

in the chamber of commerce office at the corner of 89A and Forest Road, at the north end of town. Both sides of Hwy. 89A are lined with boutiques, galleries, jewelry stores, and restaurants. For details, see page 253.

• Red Rock Loop Road—To Red Rock State Park

This road (upper and lower) loops into the prime red rock area, past Cathedral Rock, and leads to Red Rock State Park. The park has trails, and the visitor center doubles as an educational facility. There are two picnic areas near the park entrance. The northern half of the loop road is "primitive" (as the sign says) but takes you closer to Cathedral Rock. For a more comfortable ride to the state park (where the views are just fine) take the south loop entrance.

• Cottonwood & Clarkdale

These smaller towns are located just south of Sedona. Both have their charms. Clarkdale is the departure point for the Verde River Canyon Excursion Train, which runs through the scenic canyon past deep red cliffs.

• Jerome

Founded during the gold rush of 1876, this town hugs a mountainside on several levels as Hwy. 89A climbs through a series of switchbacks past stores, cafes, and an historic park.

• Prescott

The community is named for famous historian William Hickling Prescott and was founded in 1864. Situated on Granite Creek, an early source of placer gold, the town is the home of Frontier Days, the world's oldest rodeo. The town information center is at 117 West Goodwin.

Beyond Prescott

There are alternate routes connecting Prescott and Phoenix. If you want the more scenic mountain drive (avoiding the interstate), take U.S. 89 from Prescott (see the log that follows). The shorter drive is via State Route 69 east from town, connecting with I-17.

Drives

Highway Log

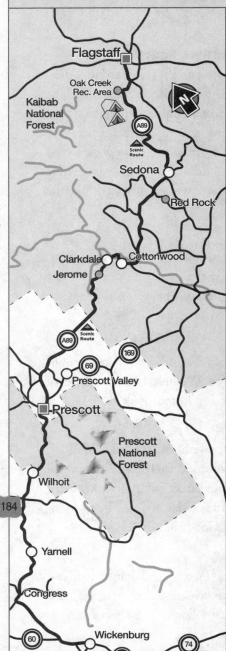

Flagstaff From downtown Flagstaff, drive south along U.S. Route 180 past Northern Arizona University and then keep to the left and take Alternate U.S. Route 89, passing through typical pine forests of this region in the **Coconino National Forest**, before the descent into Oak Creek Canyon.

Viewpoint View of the canyon.

Oak Creek Canyon Rec. Area Stretches along the highway for 12 miles to Sedona; 3 campgrounds.

Slide Rock State Park Day-use area.

Encinoso Picnic Area West of the highway, at mile 379.

Historical Marker–Indian Canyons

Sedona The town of Sedona offers a wide range of motels, inns, and restaurants. The Coconino National Forest ranger station and the town visitor center are both at the north end of town, near the junction of Hwy. 89A and **Arizona Route 179**. The latter road leads south to join Interstate 17 north of McGuireville. **Lake Montezuma forest campground** is southeast of I-17—about 20 miles from Sedona.

Upper Red Rock Loop Road See below for the better entrance to this scenic loop drive.

Lower Red Rock Loop Road A scenic drive to **Red Rock State Park** and back to the highway, passing impressive red rock cliffs and peaks.

Junction–Page Springs Road To Page Springs and McGuireville, plus access to national forest campground.

87 miles—2 hours

Junction–Arizona Route 260 East To Phoenix (via Interstate 17).

Cottonwood (take the loop road into town) Gas station, mini-mart, motel, and lounge, near the junction.

Clarkdale Small town with visitor services. The scenic train leaves from the Verde Canyon Train Depot. Beyond Clarkdale are two historic sites: Tuzigot National Monument and Dead Horse Ranch State Park.

The road ascends to the old mining town of **Jerome**, which is perched on the side of the mountain—on several levels (el. 5,246 ft.). Inn, saloon, cafe, craft and antique shops and **Jerome State Historic Park.**

Summit (el. 7,023 ft.) A road leads to the east, to the Mingus Recreation Area (3 miles) and Mingus Spring Camp (6 miles).

Junction–Arizona Route 169 Leads east to Dewey.

Lava Flow Cinder cones are seen from the highway, with a lava flow at the north end of the valley.

Prescott Valley A new community that is mainly on Hwy. 69 but is accessed via a sideroad.

Junction–Highway 89 Hwy. 89A ends here. Take Hwy. 89 for Prescott and beyond.

Granite Dells Road Leads southeast.

Matson Lake Recreation Area East of the highway via a backroad.

Prescott (el. 5,300 ft.) A college town and the former territorial capital of Arizona, with full visitor services. The visitor center is located in the downtown area. The huge high-rise building standing atop the hill north of the downtown area is the Sheraton Hotel.

Beyond Prescott

Hwy. 89 climbs into the **Juniper Mountains**, through the **Prescott National Forest**, with healthy stands of ponderosa pine.

White Spar Creek Campground Just inside the forest boundary.

Indian Creek Road To Ponderosa Park (2 miles) and other recreation sites in the Prescott National Forest.

Wilhoit A village with store and bar, just beyond the national forest boundary.

Yarnell (el. 4,783 ft.) Town with gas, motels, restaurants, store. The smaller town of Peeple's Valley is 3 miles ahead.

Congress (43 miles from Prescott) Congress is a small town sitting in the valley with mining activity seen on the hills. Gas, restaurant, store.

Wickenburg Another (larger) historic mining town with full visitor services. To drive to **Phoenix**, take U.S. Highway 89 southeast from Wickenburg. The road is is divided and then becomes U.S. Highway 60 which leads past Sun City and into the city of Phoenix.

Apache Trail Loop Drive

Apache Junction to Globe & Return

Not for the fainthearted, this circle drive takes up only 85 miles of driving but is an experience you will never forget. A handy day-trip from the Phoenix area, the drive is launched from Apache Junction about 25 miles east of downtown Phoenix (17 miles east of Tempe) and begins with Arizona Route 88 (Idaho Road), heading northeast.

The 46 miles between Apache Junction and Roosevelt Lake provides not only the most scenic part of the trip but also the most thrilling (some say heart-pounding) driving. The route is paved and relatively easy until just past Tortilla Flat—at the 18-mile mark—passing several points of interest including Lost Dutchman State Park and Goldfield, a commercial ghost town across the road from the park. You pass by Saguaro Lake (part of the Salt River system) and drive through the Canyon Lake Recreation Area, with camping and picnicking available.

After arriving at the Theodore Roosevelt Dam site, the rest of the drive is easy. Paved highway greets you, and you drive eastward near the lake, past the entrance to the Tonto National Monument (picnicking and a trail to the cliff dwellings). Twenty-nine miles past the dam and you're in Globe, the center of mining in the state.

The return drive to Apache Junction is along U.S. Highway 60, through the Tonto National Forest.

Along the Way

- **Lost Dutchman State Park**

  East of Apache Junction, this park has 35 campsites, water and a dump station. A good place to stay before and after "doing" the Apache Trail.

- **Goldfield Ghost Town**

  A commercial attraction, a minuscule theme park, with saloons, cafes, and mining displays.

- **Needle Vista Point**

  Views of the valleys and the cactus-dominated landscape.

• Canyon Lake Recreation Area

There are several recreation sites with boat ramps, marinas, viewpoints, and camping. Tortilla Flat is a funky little village with false-fronted buildings set beside the lake.

• Apache Lake

The highway (only because of its altitude) is set high above this lake. The road makes its way down to the bottom. Apache Lake Marina is reached by taking Forest Road 79.

• Roosevelt Lake & Dam

The Theodore Roosevelt Dam is an impressive work of construction that seems to be continually upgraded, with periodic holdups on the road before you join the main highway (Route 88). Arizona Route 188 leads north along the lake with access to five Forest Service campsites.

• Tonto National Monument

The Sinagua Indian cliff dwelling looks down on Lake Roosevelt. There is a visitor center and picnic area with lake views. A trail leads to the ruins.

• Picket Post Mountain

A landmark and lookout point during Indian wars, site of the Camp Pinal Outpost at the end of Stoneman Grade to the east. Soldiers protected Pinal City and the Silver King Mine from Apache Raiders. It was the home of Col. William Boyce Thompson, a mining magnate who founded the Southwestern Arboretum at the foot of the mountain.

• Boyce Thompson Southwestern Arboretum

This outstanding garden is a state park. In addition to southwestern American trees, shrubs, and flowers, the park features collections of cacti and other plants from around the world. There is a plant shop at the arboretum entrance, with many varieties of palms and cacti available for purchase. Plant lovers should not miss this attraction, and a full day can be well spent picnicking and walking the paths of this impressive park.

Drives

Highway Log

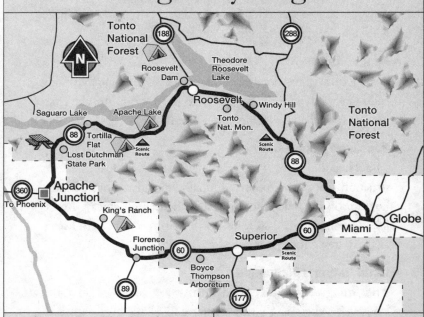

Apache Junction The drive begins in this community at the junction of U.S. Hwy. 60 and Arizona Route 88. Take Route 88 (Idaho Road) for the first leg of the drive: The Apache Trail Scenic Byway. The road is paved until just past Tortilla Flat.

Lost Dutchman State Park (camping and picnicking) Just south of the highway. The **Goldfield Ghost Town** is to the north of the road.

188 Entering Tonto National Forest Viewpoint–Needle Vista To the south (milepost 203).

The landscape is that of a desert garden with palo verde trees and saguaro and other cacti, including prickly pear, cholla and ocotillo.

Canyon Lake Recreation Area Viewpoint, picnic areas, marina, boat ramps. The road crosses Boulder Creek without a bridge.

Boulder Canyon Trailhead A national forest trail to the south.

Picnic Area At Laguna Boating Site.

Tortilla Campground Across the road from the main drag of Tortilla Flat.

Tortilla Flat A rustic little main street with cafes and picnicking and marina nearby. The road climbs quickly to high ridges with fine stands of cacti.

End of Pavement For the next 22 miles (to Roosevelt Lake), the road is unpaved with a steep descent that challenges your driving abilities and requires steady nerves.

Tortilla Trailhead To the right, 1 mile beyond the pavement.

The road descends into a deep canyon, with fine views. Hold on!

One-lane bridge over Fish Creek
Reavis Ranch Trailhead One mile off the road.
Viewpoint Apache Lake.
The road rides high above the lake, then descends to cross Pine Creek, and ascends toward Roosevelt Lake.
Roosevelt Lake Dam and Spillway There may be construction work near the dam, bringing some slight delays. The lake is just ahead.
Junction–Arizona Route 188 This highway leads north toward Strawberry and Hwy. 87. There is a campground beside the lake, north of the junction. We continue east on Hwy. 88, toward Globe.
Roosevelt There is gas, a cafe, motel accommodations, and a ranger station in this community.
Tonto National Monument Located south of the highway (now paved!). This is an outstanding Sinagua cliff dwelling along a trail that departs from the visitor center. A scenic picnic area overlooks the lake.
Windy Hill Boat Ramp (north)
Schoolhouse Point Campground–4 miles north; 23 miles from Globe.
Junction–Arizona Route 288 Leads north to Sierra Ancha Experimental Forest and a campground, then on to Young (mostly unpaved).
Globe The center of mining in Arizona; there are huge mountains of tailings beside the highway. There is an historic main street, and the area

has full visitor services, in Globe and the neighboring town of Miami.
We now head west on U.S. Highway 60, driving toward Phoenix.
Miami The huge mining operations dominate the town. Gas, stores, motels, restaurants. There's a picnic area beside the highway.
The highway climbs into the **Tonto National Forest**. The Magma Copper operation is seen to the north.
Picnic Area Near the hilltop.
Hoodoos Just past the summit, many of the pillars have "hats."
Oak Flat Campground To the south, via Magma Mine Road.
Devil's Canyon More erosion pillars, a tunnel and an arched bridge over Queen Creek.
Junction–Arizona Route 177 To Winkelman (south).
Superior Gas, store and cafe.
Historical Marker About Picket Post Mountain (south of the highway).
Boyce Thompson Arboretum (State Park) This outstanding desert garden displays native and imported species of trees, cacti, and other plants. Fee charged.
Saguaro Cacti From here to Apache Junction are fine stands of the cactus. To reach Phoenix, continue west on U.S. Highway 60.

189

Salt Canyon Drive

Globe to Springerville

The Salt Canyon is often called Arizona's Little Grand Canyon. It's not as wide and not nearly as long as its cousin to the northwest, but it's an impressive gorge that offers a real benefit for travelers in that the highway descends to river level. The canyon is within the San Carlos Apache Indian Reservation, about 30 miles north of Globe via U.S. Route 60. As the highway enters the reservation, the traveler descends through several switchbacks until reaching the canyon floor and crosses a bridge over the Salt River. The road then begins to climb up the side of the cliffs to a high overlook that offers fine views of the canyon and Becker's Butte—a prominent formation on the other side of the gorge.

Climbing over the final rise, the highway leaves the Salt Canyon only to descend into the smaller Cedar Creek Canyon before reaching the small Indian community of Carrizo.

While our drive—logged on the following pages—follows U.S. 60 to the town of Show Low and then takes takes Arizona Route 260 through the White Mountain forests to Springerville, there is an alternate route that leads through the Fort Apache Indian Reservation to the historic Fort Apache site, passing the Kinishba Ruins (see below).

Along the Way

- **Tonto National Forest**

  Just north of Globe, Route 60 enters the southern portion of this national forest. The Jones Water forest campground is beside the highway, 20 miles north of Globe.

- **San Carlos Apache Reservation**

  This reservation is part of the larger reserve also occupied by the Fort Apache peoples. The highway begins its descent into the Salt Canyon after entering the reserve. There are picnic areas on both sides of the road about half-way down the descent.

- **Salt River Canyon**

  One of the chief natural attractions of this part of Arizona, the Salt

River has carved a great gorge, which is intersected by the highway. The trip down to the canyon floor features about 5 miles of winding roadway. After crossing the bridge, look for the scenic picnic area located on two levels, overlooking the river and along the length of the gorge.

• Road to Kinishba Ruins and Fort Apache

An alternate route to Springerville and the resort areas in the White Mountains (Greer and Sunrise Ski Area among others), Arizona Route 73 leads east from Route 60 near the village of Carrizo. North off Route 73 is the Kinishba Ruins, the remains of an early Indian settlement. Farther along the road is the site of Fort Apache, the U.S. Army fort which was built to protect pioneers and other travelers from Indian attacks during the 1900s. Ironically, Fort Apache is now an Indian town and the partially preserved fort is on display. Highway 73 leads north from Fort Apache to connect with Highway 260 at the Indian village of Hon Dah, east of Show Low and Pinetop-Lakeside. Springerville is 28 miles east of the junction.

• Apache-Sitgreaves National Forest

This large national forest completely surrounds the community of Show Low and extends southward to the edge of the Mogollon Rim and the Apache Indian Reservation. There are forest campgrounds east and west of Show Low.

• Mogollon Rim Overlook

A street leading south off Route 260 leads to a viewpoint looking down from the Mogollon Rim, a high escarpment stretching for more than 200 miles in a general east/west direction. The overlook provides fine views of the White Mountains, which lie to the southeast.

• Sunrise Ski Area & Greer

The Apache Nation operates this popular ski area which is located south of the highway. Greer is the nearby resort town offering accommodations, including B & B inns, and restaurants for skiers and summer travelers.

Drives

Highway Log

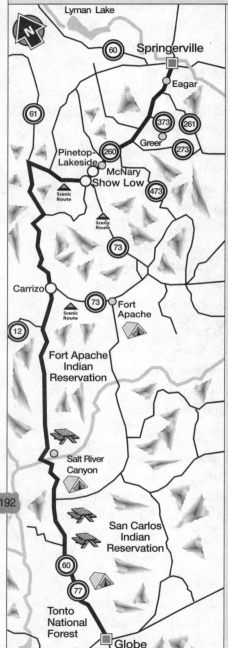

Globe Arizona Route 77/U.S. 60 leads north from the junction with U.S. 70. Hwy. 60 also runs east from Phoenix.

Entering Tonto National Forest (milepost 258).

Picnic Table and Historical Marker (just north of milepost 265)

Jones Water Campground For tents and trailers (milepost 268).

Picnic Area (past milepost 272) with restrooms.

Picnic Table with barbecue stand, east of road at milepost 282.

Entering San Carlos Apache Indian Reservation

Large Pullout Before descent into canyon (milepost 288).

Salt River Canyon The road descends for 5 miles into this deep canyon before crossing the river.

Picnic Area Overlooks the canyon about halfway down.

Salt River Crossing A new bridge has replaced the original narrow span.

Salt River Trading Post Indian art and crafts, store.

Picnic Area Just beyond the trading post, with several sheltered tables on two levels. A fine view of the canyon.

Viewpoint–Becker's Butte (past milepost 297) Historical marker and picnic table with shelter. The highway ascends to the plateau above the canyon. Atop the canyon is a juniper & pinyon pine forest typical for this elevation.

Carrizo Creek Bridge The small village of Carrizo is just off the highway.

Junction–Arizona Route 73 Leads south toward Kinishba Ruins, Fort Apache and Bonito Campground, and then runs northward to Whiteriver, Sunrise Ski Area and Pinetop-Lakeside. This is an historic alternate route to Show Low and the White Mountains region.

Cedar Canyon The highway enters another canyon, with Cedar Creek flowing at the bottom of the gorge.

Forestdale Indian Trading Post Eight miles south of Show Low.

Entering Sitgreaves National Forest Show Low (el. 6,331 ft.)–This town is surrounded by the national forest and is a major trading center with full visitor services including several motels.

Junction–Arizona Route 260–We turn right (southeast) onto Route 260 for Pinetop-Lakeside and the White Mountains region.

Mogollon Rim Overlook Off the highway to the south. An impressive view from the rim.

Pinetop-Lakeside This is a resort community just east of Show Low, offering a variety of visitor services. Visitor info. at west end of town, ranger station north of the highway.

Junction–Arizona Route 73 At the village of Hon Dah. The road runs south to Whiteriver and Fort Apache. This is the other end of the scenic drive through the White Mountains (see above).

McNary Grocery store.

Forest Road To Big Bear Lake & Little Bear Lake (to the north).

Junction–Arizona Route 473 To Hawley Lake (recreation site, cabins, fishing). Apache permits are required.

Junction–Horseshoe/Cienega Lake Road Leads south to recreation facilities (cabins, fishing with permit).

Junction–Arizona Route 273 To **Sunrise Ski Area** (south 10 miles). There is accommodation and food available at the ski resort, operated by the Apache. The road also leads to Greer and provides access to Big Lake.

Forest Road Leads north to two recreation sites.

Greer Junction (Route 373)–This short road leads south to the small mountain resort community of Greer.

Junction–Arizona Route 261 Big Lake is 20 miles south of the junction, with several forest roads through the Sitgreaves National Forest (Big Lake Campground).

Eagar The smaller cousin to Springerville. Drive 2 miles north for more services

Springerville A sizeable mountain town with gas, motels, restaurants, and stores. U.S. Hwy. 666 leads south through the rugged White Mountains, providing an extremely scenic drive to Safford.

Pinal Pioneer Parkway

Florence Junction to Tucson

The parkway itself stretches for some 40 miles from Florence, at the north end, to Oracle Junction, 27 miles north of Tucson. It offers a more scenic and wandering route between Phoenix and Tucson than the usual and faster drive along Interstate 10. The title "parkway" is a little overstated; it is a two-lane highway that passes through a fascinating desert environment, and the "park" is totally natural: desert washes, wild gardens of cholla cactus and saguaro, and several picnic areas, with roadside trees and other flora identified by signs posted along the parkway.

For the sake of convenience, we begin our scenic drive east of Phoenix, at a four-corners called Florence Junction. To get there from the big city, drive east on U.S. Route 60 or the Arizona Route 360 freeway. You'll find Florence Junction 16 miles east of Apache Junction. Turn south onto U.S. Route 89 to begin the drive to Tucson, which is shown on the following highway log.

Along the Way

- **Salt-Gila Aqueduct**

  South of Florence Junction, the highway crosses the Salt-Gila Aqueduct. The Salt River disappears into this large aqueduct system, which provides water for agricultural purposes, making thousands of acres of desert green.

- **Poston's Butte**

  An historical marker notes the contributions made to the state by Charles Debrille Poston (1825–1902), called the Father of Arizona. Poston promoted territorial status for Arizona and served local silver mining interests by lobbying for federal legislation to create the Territory of Arizona in 1863. He was Arizona's first congressional delegate. He planned but never built a temple to the sun, 2 miles west of the highway on Primrose Hill, and was buried on the hill, now called Poston's Butte.

- **Florence**

  This medium-sized town is mainly an agricultural center with a prison to assist the economy. McFarland State Historic Park is located off U.S. 89 and State Route 187. There is a sign on the highway giving directions to the park.

• Pinal Pioneer Parkway

South of Florence, Highway 89 becomes the parkway. The Pinal Mountains lie to the northeast. Watch for signs posted near trees and other plants of interest along the 40 miles of the parkway. There are several picnic areas along the drive.

• Tom Mix Monument

The statue and historical marker note the death—on this spot—of Tom Mix, the famous western movie star on October 12, 1940. Tom Mix, who played himself in his movies, is portrayed in an equestrian sculpture mounted on a pedestal. There is a picnic area here with grills. A stile to the rear of the pulloff leads to a natural garden of several varieties of cactus plus desert bushes. This is a pleasant area for a short walk into the open desert. You'll find the cacti (particularly cholla) in great abundance.

• Road to Biosphere 2

Oracle Junction is a strip of gas stations and cafes near the junction of Routes 89 and 77. For a short side-trip to Biosphere 2, drive north on Highway 77. It has its own hotel, dining room, and guided tour (a fee is charged). While the scientific value of this project seems to be dubious, Biosphere 2 will stay as an interesting theme park. Think of it as a giant aquarium with people inside instead of fish.

• Road to Tucson Mountain Park
& Saguaro National Monument

Take Speedway Blvd. west across the hills to Tucson Mountain Park, a large tract of desert landscape. The central attraction here is the Arizona-Sonora Desert Museum. To the north of the park is the western portion of Saguaro National Monument—an outstanding natural area with one of the finest stands of the giant cactus in the state.

Drives

Highway Log

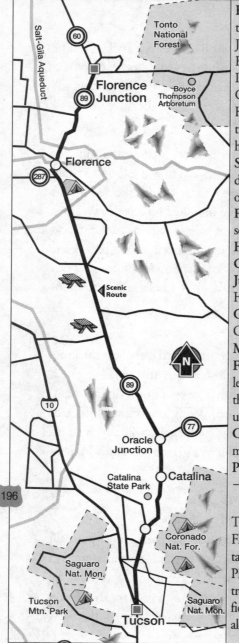

Florence Junction A desert intersection, 16 miles southeast of Apache Junction and 33 miles east of Phoenix. From Phoenix, take U.S. Highway 60. If you're coming from the east (from Globe), get here by taking U.S. Highway 70. We begin the drive by turning south onto U.S. Highway 89, heading for Florence.

Salt-Gila Aqueduct The Salt River is diverted into a series of aqueducts, one of which leads through this area.

Florence This town has a full range of services, an RV park and golfing.

Historical Marker–Poston's Butte Gila River Crossing

Junction–Arizona Routes 287/89B Hwy. 287 leads west to the **Casa Grande Ruins National Monument**. One-half mile from Hwy. 70 is **McFarland State Historic Park**.

Florence/Kelvin Highway This road leads east across the desert flatlands to the small town of Kelvin, which is situated across the mountain range.

Cactus Forest Road Leads west 11 miles. There is a fine display of cholla.

Picnic Tables Two areas, to the east.

Pinal Pioneer Parkway

The stretch of Highway 70 between Florence and Oracle Junction (a distance of 40 miles) is named the Pinal Pioneer Parkway. Along the highway, trees and other plant species are identified and there are several historic sites along the route. The landscape is distinguished by frequent lavish displays of several forms of cacti.

Tom Mix Monument (past milepost 116) A memorial to the early western movie actor who died on this spot.

Picnic Area At the Tom Mix Monument. Behind the picnic area is a fence with stile. Go through the stile and you'll wander through the desert with saguaro, large cholla bushes, and other desert plants.

Tom Mix Wash The highway crosses the wash just south of the marker. This area has several such washes draining the desert.

Roadside Tables The first is by an old verde tree to the west of the highway. The second is one-half mile south.

Roadside Table 1/2 mile south.

Park Link Drive Leads west across the desert to Red Rock (20 miles).

Ruth's Rainbow Trading Post A stop, near milepost 100.

Picnic Area Two covered tables.

Junction–Arizona Route 77 This is the end of the Pioneer Parkway. Route 77 leads west to Oracle (11 miles) and then north to Mammoth and Winkelman. A short distance north of Oracle Junction is the site of **Biosphere 2**, which offers tours of the scientific experiment and theme park. The Biosphere complex includes a hotel and restaurant.

Oracle Junction Motels, store, cafe. We continue south toward Tucson on Highway 89.

Catalina (4 miles south of Oracle Junction) Gas, motel.

Oro Valley A new Sun City development.

Catalina State Park Day-use, east of the highway. The road becomes divided at this point. The highway is called Oracle Road and continues into downtown Tucson (including the historic Spanish settlement) as the Miracle Mile.

Intersection–Speedway Blvd. To Tucson Mountain Park. Oracle Road continues southward into downtown Tucson.

Tucson Mountain Park

Speedway Blvd. leads west across the hills into Tucson Mountain Park, where the **Arizona-Sonora Desert Museum** is located. The museum is one of the most outstanding nature exhibits in America, focusing on desert animals and plants. The main park road also leads to the western section of the **Saguaro National Monument** which protects one of the nation's out-standing forests of saguaro cactus. There is a visitor center at the monument with a short self-guided trail winding around the visitor center. **Bajada Loop Drive** leads scross the desert hills for six miles, through outstanding "groves" of stately aguaro.

197

Tombstone Drive

Benson to Bisbee

This very short drive leads from Interstate 10 to a few miles from the Mexican border in the extreme southeast corner of the state. Benson, our starting point, is 45 miles east of Tucson and 63 miles west of Lordsburg, New Mexico. Benson is a pioneer transportation hub that has contented itself with becoming a stopping point for tourists who come to search out the history, ruins, and artifacts of this Wild West country, once ruled by Geronimo and Cochise. The Indians were defeated by the army, and white outlaws soon prevailed.

Located on the San Pedro River, a Butterfield Stage station was built beside the river, with mail and passengers from St. Louis and San Francisco arriving twice weekly from the late 1850s. The railroad came to Benson in 1880, serving the many silver and copper mines in the region.

Tombstone is 22 miles from the Interstate 10 junction. Benson has a few remaining traces of the Wild West days, but Tombstone is the epitome of that age—a short period of time when drifters passed through the area, desperados dominated the social scene, and, as a result, the towns were tough little places where the rule of law was not highly regarded. Bisbee, 24 miles south of Tombstone, is the best preserved pioneer mining town in the entire Southwest.

Along the Way and Beyond

• Benson

There are several good motels in Benson, and the Horseshoe Restaurant and Lounge provides a bit of western atmosphere while you dine. There are campgrounds with RV hookups and grassy tent sites north of Interstate 10 on Ocotillo Road and another on Highway 80. The San Pedro Valley Arts and Historical Museum is a local museum and gallery at 180 San Pedro Street. The local festival, Butterfield Days, is held every second weekend in October. The town information center is at 363 West 4th Street.

• Amerind Foundation

This outstanding museum of Indian life is also a research center, located 12 miles east of Benson via Interstate 10 (take the Dragoon exit, #318). The museum contains artifacts of southwestern Indian life and antique Spanish furnishings, which complement the Spanish colonial–style buildings. This arts center also includes paintings and sculptures on early western themes by such artists as Frederic Remington, Oscar Borg, and William Leigh.

• Road to Patagonia & Nogales

Arizona Route 82 joins Highway 80 3 miles north of Tombstone, leading to a scenic area that includes the San Pedro Riparian Conservation Area and the towns of Sierra Vista and Patagonia. For a description of this route, see the next scenic drive, on page 202.

• Tombstone

Sporting many of the town's original historic buildings, board-walks, and false fronts, the whole town of Tombstone has become a Wild West theme park, complete with saloons, old-style restaurants, the original Bird Cage Theater, an historical museum (in the old courthouse), and gift shops. A prime attraction is the OK Corral, where the Earp brothers and Doc Holliday faced the Clanton and McLaury brothers in October 1881 (see page 260). There are motels, three B & B homes and three campgrounds with hookups.

• Other Ghost Towns

While Tombstone is a living ghost town, there are several other sites where rowdy towns once flourished but are now merely shadows. These include Charleston (8 miles southeast of Tombstone, 1/2 mile from the San Pedro Bridge), Gleeson (16 miles east of town via a gravel backroad), and Convention City where only heaps of rubble can be seen.

199

• Bisbee

The drive through the Mule foothills features oak trees and a canyon with a tunnel. There are two original hotels in town (see page 210 for Bisbee details).

Drives

Highway Log

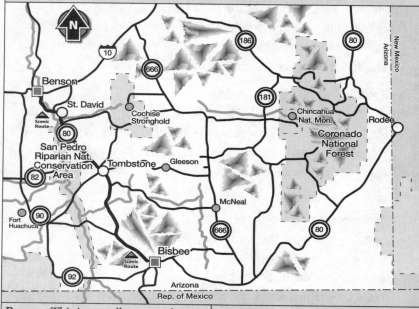

Benson This is a small town with visitor services including gas, motels, cafes and stores. The visitor information center (chamber of commerce) is on 4th Street.

The drive begins near downtown Benson, at the junction of Business 10 (4th Street) and Arizona Route 80.

Apache Powder Road Leads west.

Sibyl Road Leads east across the valley into the Dragoon Mountains and the **Coronado National Forest.**

St. David Village with cafe, store, and gas station.

Twin Lakes Recreational Ranch A trailer park—a home for sunbirds.

Junction–Arizona Route 82 This road leads west to Sonoita, Patagonia and Nogales (see next scenic drive, starting on page 202).

Middle Arch Rd. This is a backroad leading northeast into the Coronado National Forest and on to meet U.S. Route 666 near Sunizona.

Tombstone Gas, motels, cafes, saloons, shops, grocery store, museum. The old main street, Allen Street, is one block off the highway (which is Fremont Street). The Arizona Territorial Museum, the old courthouse and now a state park, is at Allen & Toughnut.

Road to Gleeson This 22-mile dirt backroad runs east from Tombstone, passing through tiny Gleeson, and joins U.S. Route 666 just north of Elfrida (another small village).

Road to McNeal Another backroad running east, meeting U.S. Route 666 and then curving south, leading to the border town of Douglas.

Junction-Arizona Route 90 The highway runs west to the town of **Sierra Vista**. The unpaved continuation of this road leads farther west to old **Fort Huachuca**, an historic site, and into the Coronado National Forest. There is a ranger station just inside the forest boundary, and the road provides access to other forest backroads and recreation sites, including campgrounds and picnic facilities. The road curves into the **Mule Mountains**, rising into gentle hills with oak trees providing a contrast to the desert landscape. This region receives more rain than the sur-rounding desert, creating scenery reminiscent of the Sierra Nevada foothills in California.

Mule Pass–The hwy. runs through a tunnel before entering Bisbee.

Bisbee This historic mining town is still very much alive, with full visitor services including two great old hotels (the Copper Queen and the Bisbee Inn), plus B & B inns and homes, motels, gas, restaurants, and stores. There are daily mine tours.

Beyond Bisbee

Bisbee offers fascinating drives through the old streets of downtown and up the hills where houses perch on narrow lanes. Several roads lead from Bisbee to further adventure:

Crossing the Sonoran Desert–U.S. Highway 80 leads east to Douglas and the Mexican border crossing. The town of **Agua Prieta** is just beyond the border stations.

From Agua Prieta, Highway 2 (Mexico) leads southwest for 100 miles to the small town of Imuris and then runs northeast for another 150 miles to Sonoita, Mexico, just south of the Arizona border.

It is possible to re-enter the United States at this point. **Organ Pipe Cactus National Monument** is just north of the border. If you stay on Highway 2, you'll wind up at another Mexico/Arizona border crossing, just south of Yuma. This is a vast expanse of Sonoran desert, with few communities or civilized amenities.

To Cochise's Stronghold–From Bisbee, drive to just west of Douglas and head north on U.S. Route 666, through McNeal and Elfrida and turn left (west) just north of the winter resort village of Sunsites. This unpaved road leads through part of the Coronado National Forest, ending at Cochise's Stronghold.

This is an outstanding historical site 201 where Cochise and his Indian followers held out before their final defeat. There is a campground here, in addition to several fine hiking trails and picnic areas.

Patagonia Drive

Tombstone to Nogales

Far from the fabled Patagonia of Bruce Chatwin's celebrated travel book *In Patagonia*, Patagonia, Arizona, is a small, former Wild West town in the midst of several mountain ranges, north of the Mexican border in the southeast section of the state. With Patagonia Lake nearby, a bird sanctuary on the doorstep, and a lingering pioneer atmosphere, this little town offers a different kind of place to stay and visit—quite apart in its semi-isolation from such obvious tourist towns as Tombstone and Nogales.

Most of the drive is within Santa Cruz County, which has an amazing range of landscapes, from flat desert to forested mountainside. The variety in altitude and exposure makes for pockets of agricultural activity including vineyards and market gardens.

At the end of the drive are the two Nogales, actually one urban area straddling the U.S./Mexico border. Mexican people cross the border to shop in Nogales, Arizona. Americans cross over to buy Mexican crafts, to eat Mexican food, or to play the horses and other sports at the off-track betting room.

We begin the drive 3 miles north of Tombstone, at the junction of Arizona Route 80 and Arizona Route 82. Turn onto Highway 82 which leads west. After 6 miles the road crosses the San Pedro River and continues for another 11 miles to the small town of Sonoita. Just before reaching Sonoita, a gravel road leads south from the highway to the farming community of Elgin—a community that is now in the grape-growing business. Sonoita Vineyards is one of Arizona's very few wineries.

202

Route 82 curves south in Sonoita, after the junction with Arizona Route 83. Patagonia comes into view after traveling through the foothills of the Patagonia Mountains, which loom behind the town. From Patagonia, a network of forest backroads leads through the Coronado National Forest.

Route 82 continues, leading in a southwest direction, with Nogales another 16 miles. The road ends at the border crossing in downtown Nogales, where you may walk or drive to the sister city.

Arizona

Along the Way

• San Pedro Riparian National Conservation Area

Considered one of the best birding spots in the United States, this protected area stretches for more than 40 miles on both sides of the San Pedro River, from St. David south to the Mexican border.

Our drive passes through the conservation area and there is an information center next to the railway crossing beside the river. Another access point is to the south, via Highway 90, west of Bisbee. Forty percent of the nesting gray hawks of the U.S. live in the sanctuary.

• Road to Sierra Vista

Highway 90 leads south to the largest town in this part of Arizona: Sierra Vista. A growing haven for "sunbirds," Sierra Vista sits at the foot of the Huachuca Mountains, next to the site of Old Fort Huachuca. In 1886, the fort was the advance headquarters for the campaign against Geronimo. The modern Sierra Vista is the "hummingbird capital of America."

• Sideroad to Coronado National Memorial

The Elgin sideroad not only takes you to a wine-tasting experience, but it continues in a winding fashion through the Coronado National Forest to Lake View Campground and on to the national memorial that celebrates the explorations of Francisco Coronado. The site can also be reached by driving south from Sierra Vista on Route 92.

• Patagonia

Crafts and art galleries have replaced the saloons and rowdy culture of early Patagonia. The Ovens of Patagonia is a fine bakery with restaurant. There's cowboy atmosphere at the Wagon Wheel Bar.

West of town is the Patagonia-Sonoita Creek Preserve, a bird sanctuary managed by The Nature Conservancy. The preserve is open Wednesday through Sunday from 7:30 AM to 3:30 PM. Turn west on 4th Avenue, turn south on Pennsylvania, then cross the creek; the entrance to the creekside area is not quite another mile.

Drives

Highway Log

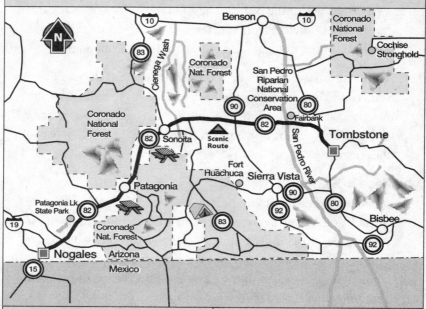

Tombstone The drive begins just north of Tombstone, which is south of Benson and north of Bisbee on Arizona Route 80. Drive north from Tombstone on Route 80, past the **Boot Hill** cemetery, and turn west toward the main drag (James Street).

Backroad This road leads east across the desert, into the Coronado National Forest and farther east to meet U.S. Highway 666. This is the road to take to see **Cochise's Stronghold**, a historic site on another forest backroad running west from Hwy. 666, just north of Sunsites (a small village).

Junction–Arizona Route 82
Turn left (west) onto Route 81 for Sonoita, Patagonia and Nogales.

San Pedro Riparian National Conservation Area This strip of land on both sides of the San Pedro River is managed by the BLM to protect the environment and wildlife along the floodplain. The conservation area office sits beside the river (before reaching the railway tracks).

San Pedro River Bridge

Sanders Road Leads south along the river through the conservation area, to Sierra Vista. The road is unpaved, at mile 57.5.

Truman Road Leads south.

The highway crosses the wide river valley. The **Whetstone Mountains** are seen to the north. The **Huachuca Range** is to the southwest.

Whetstone Mostly trailers with a few regular houses. Gas, cafe, RV park.

Junction-Arizona Route 90 This road leads south to the town of **Sierra Vista**, providing access to the **Fort Huachuca** historic site. Hwy. 90 runs north to meet Interstate 10 (27 miles). The road climbs through a notch in the southern Whetstone Mountains, to descend into the Cienega Wash.

Sands Ranch A rangeland conservation area. The Sands Ranch Road runs north, just west of the Route 90 junction.

Historic Marker–Mexican Land Grant: San Ignacia del Babocomari.

Cienega Wash This wash, crossed by the highway, drains a large section of the region. It is protected by the BLM, and much of the region is included in the Empire-Cienega Resource Conservation Area.

Sonoita (el. 4,970 feet) The Empire Mountains lie northwest of this small community. Gas and cafes.

Junction-Arizona Route 83 Highway 83 leads north to meet Interstate 10 (27 miles).

Side Trip to Parker Canyon Lake

Highway 83 leads south (partially paved) to Elgin, a wine-growing town, and then to **Parker Canyon Lake**. Lakeview Campground is at the south end of the lake. The drive from Sonoita to the campground is about 30 miles. The road then continues southward, passing through the Coronado National Monument, an historic site, ending at Arizona Route 92 south of Sierra Vista.

Back on Highway 82

We continue on Arizona Route 82 which now runs in a southwest direction toward Nogales.

Historic Marker Old Camp Crittendon.

Backroad–Coronado National Forest This mostly unpaved backroad leads south to Harshaw, San Raphael, and Lochiel, through the national forest along the eastern flank of the Patagonia Mountains.

Patagonia (18 miles from Nogales, el. 4,050 feet) This small, Old West town is situated in a picturesque valley at the foot of the Patagonia Mountains. The town has motels, several B & B homes, cafes, bars, gas, and stores. The historic train station stands out in the center of town. The outstanding attraction is the **Patagonia-Sonoita Preserve**, a renowned bird-watching area.

Roadside Table There's a picnic table on a short canyon loop.

Patagonia Lake State Park A sideroad leads to the day-use area.

Kino Springs Road To a golf course 205 with restaurant and lounge.

Winery This winery with tasting room looks like a Castilian fortress.

Nogales (el. 3,865 ft.) The city has a full range of visitor services and the Mexican border crossing, which leads to Nogales, Mexico.

Other Arizona Drives

• Dragoon Mountains & Cochise's Stronghold

The Dragoons run north and south, a few miles east of Benson. The Coronado Forest covers much of the range and is accessed from the south—via Highway 80 beyond Bisbee and Douglas, or by taking U.S. Route 666 from the junction of Interstate 10 at exit 331, east of Benson. Before leaving the Tombstone area, you might consider a side trip to the stronghold of the great Indian leader Cochise. It was here, in the Dragoon Mountains, that Cochise made his last stand against the forces of the U.S. Cavalry. It was a natural stronghold for Cochise and his followers, serving as a refuge. The site may be accessed directly from Tombstone by the gravel backroad that leads east across the desert from the town, through Gleeson (a ghost town) and then north to Sunsites and west to Cochise's Stronghold. There is a walking trail at the stronghold, in addition to a picnic area. A home site for earlier natives, there are rock carvings in a large cave.

• Chiricahua National Monument

This is an outstanding drive to a scene of extreme natural beauty. If a camping vacation is to your taste, drive to Douglas on Arizona Route 80 and then continue northeast on Hwy. 80, entering the Coronado National Forest via one of several backroads. The main recreation route through the forest leads west from Hwy. 80 just north of Rodeo (51 miles from Douglas). There's a forest ranger station at the community of Portal, beside the national forest boundary. A backroad leads through the forest, providing access to three campgrounds. It ends just south of the entrance to the Chiricahua National Monument.

Chiricahua features an amazing array of standing rock formations that are magical at any time of day but particularly so at sunrise and sunset. From the Chiricahua rocks it's possible to drive northwest to Interstate 10 (at Wilcox), a distance of about 36 miles. You can also return to Highway 80 and drive north from Rodeo to meet Interstate 10 in New Mexico.

Benson

Benson This crossroads town lies beside Interstate 10 which connects with U.S. 80 and State Route 90. Benson was established as a Butterfield Stage station in 1858, at a crossing of the San Pedro River. Then, in 1890, the Southern Pacific Railroad laid tracks through the area and Benson became a railroad center, where freight was transferred to the old Atlantic & Pacific Line (now the Santa Fe) to supply the silver and copper towns of southern Arizona. Today, it's a quiet town offering services to travelers who pass through, perhaps staying overnight, on their way to more romantic destinations such as Tombstone and Bisbee.

There are, however, several reasons to explore the immediate area around Benson—not the least of which is the **Amerind Foundation** in Texas Canyon, just 12 miles east of town. The foundation is an archeological museum and research center that preserves artifacts of the early Indian inhabitants of the region.

William Fulton put down roots here, purchasing the FF Ranch in the 1920s. His concept of an Indian museum developed over the next dozen years as he wrote scholarly articles on his field work in and around Texas Canyon. From 1937, the museum and its outbuildings took shape. The canyon itself is worth the short drive from Benson along I-10 to the Dragoon turnoff (# 318). The museum is 1 mile east of the junction. It is open daily from 10 AM to 4 PM and an entrance fee is charged (602-586-3666).

There is a local arts and history museum in Benson—at 180 S. San Pedro Street—containing displays of settlers and early cultures. The museum's gift shop stocks the work of local artists and craftspeople, including ceramic pieces and paintings. It is open Thursday through Saturday (602-586-3070).

Cochise's Stronghold, a historic site in the Coronado National Forest, provides a fascinating day-trip from Benson. This is the rocky fortress where the great chief and his followers held out against the U.S. Cavalry and the drive provides some fine scenery in addition to the historical experience. To get there, take I-10 east from town, exiting at the Dragoon exit (Texas Canyon). Drive east for 13 miles until you get to U.S. 666 and turn south (right), driving for another 6 miles. Turn west and drive into the national forest.

Where to Eat

Benson is not known for its fine dining, although the **Country Club** has a good restaurant. For Old West flavor, try the **Horseshoe Restaurant and Lounge**, a cafe on East 4th Street. **Ruiz' Mexican Restaurant** is on West 4th Street.

Bisbee

At an elevation of 5,300 feet in the Mule Mountains, Bisbee is an anomaly: situated at the far southeast corner of the state so as to be close to the Mexican border, yet hidden in the mountains with a moderate climate that makes rose growing a prime avocation in the town. There's a lot of Old West, mingled with brick Victorian buildings, and a sense of survival through a century in which copper mining has become only a memory of richer days past. Yet, the town is amazingly well preserved— with narrow, winding streets that climb the sides of canyons and seem best-suited for mountain goats. Two venerable hotels invoke the rich history of this place, as do such historical and formerly hysterical sections of Bisbee as Brewery Gulch and the town's curving Main Street. Bisbee is a must-see on your tour of southern Arizona. While Tombstone is mostly a museum-piece—a re-creation of the Wild West town where the Clantons met the Earps—Bisbee is for real, a living example of the early mining towns of Arizona, the rest of which grew quickly and then died just as fast.

The Mule Mountains were first a part of Apache country. Before the 1870s, only a few white prospectors dared to enter the area, now called Cochise County. But the discovery of major copper deposits changed all that, for both the Apache and the European settlers. The army drove the Apache to less valuable lands, and mining claims were staked in the mountains by 1877. Phelps Dodge invested in a large number of claims in 1881, and copper mining began in earnest. By the turn of the century it was a company town. Phelps Dodge built the Copper Queen Hotel, still a grand old hostelry with a wonderful period bar.

In 1908, most of Main Street was destroyed by fire, but the town was rebuilt. The new, sturdier construction of 1910 is still on show today. Mining continued until 1975, when the town turned its attentions to tourism and retirement living.

Old miners' hostels became refined bed and breakfast inns. Saloons have been turned into antique shops and art galleries. Two mines (long closed to mining) have become tourist attractions with an underground mine tour and open-pit viewing. The charm of a lost era still remains in this fascinating little city.

Things to See and Do

A visit to Bisbee is, necessarily, a trip back in time and the best way to gain an understanding of the fascinating history of the area is to visit the several historical museums that chart the development of mining in the Mule Mountains. The **Bisbee Mining and Historical Museum** is located in the former Phelps Dodge General Office, at 5 Copper Queen Plaza. This is one of Old Bisbee's most impressive buildings (602-432-7071). The **Historical Society Museum**, at 37 Main Street (with free admission) has displays and artifacts on the pioneer history of the city. **Mulheim House** (207 Youngblood) is perhaps the finest example of nineteenth-century Victorian architecture in Bisbee (602-432-4461).

Most of the town's antique stores are located along Main Street, as is the famed **One Book Bookstore** (38 Main St.). This is the writing and sales office of Walter Swan, who wrote *Me 'n Henry*, a nostalgic book about a young boy and his older brother growing up on an Arizona homestead. Swan opened his store to sell the book and his unique storefront operation quickly became a national institution. He wrote more books and opened the store next door to sell them—The Other Book Bookstore. Swan is in his store on most days to swap stories and autograph copies of

Destinations

Me 'n Henry. His other books include *The Old Timer's Cookbook* and a book of stories for children.

Two of Bisbee's former mines should be on your list of things to see. The Lavender Mine is a large open pit. The main attraction is the **Queen Mine,** the former Phelps Dodge operation, which now has a guided tour of an underground slope at 118 Arizona Street (602-432-2071). The tour office is located south of the Old Town, off the U.S. 80 interchange. Tours start daily at 9 and 10:30 AM, at noon, and at 2 and 3:30 PM. A van tour leaves the Queen Mine site for a tour of surface mines and the historic district at 10:30 AM, noon, and 3:30 PM.

Then, take a walking tour of Brewery Gulch and the rest of the historic district, following a map which is available at the office of the chamber of commerce.

Gardeners will enjoy the displays of desert plants at **Arizona Cactus & Succulent Research Inc.**, located 6 miles south of town (8 Mulberry Lane, at Bisbee Junction). The botanical garden contains more than 750 varieties of cacti and other plants of the high desert. The nonprofit center has an extensive library with photographs and research materials on cacti and succulents. There is a series of greenhouses, and classes on landscaping with desert plants are given on a frequent basis. For information, phone (602) 432-7040.

There are two old hotels that offer a great glimpse of the 1900–1910 period and, even if you're not staying in one of them, I recommend at least a visit. The **Bisbee Grand Hotel** was built in 1906, promptly burned to the ground, and was immediately rebuilt. Located on Main Street, it was restored to its original Victorian style in 1986. There is a saloon, theater, and Ladies Parlor on the ground floor, with rooms upstairs (nine rooms and two suites). It operates as a B & B. The **Copper Queen Hotel,** which overlooks Main Street from its perch around the corner from Brewery Gulch, was the mining company hotel, built in 1902. The saloon is just the place for a glass of Bisbee's fine hometown beer (Dave's Electric Beer) or stronger libations. Fine dining is offered in the Dining Room. Rooms start at about $65 (for two). For details on these and other Bisbee accommodations, see the Arizona Places to Stay pages, starting on page 274.

The town is filled with fine bed and breakfast homes and inns, several of them former miners' boarding houses. There are several conventional motels and four RV parks—one with its own golf course.

• Near Bisbee

Douglas, a border town, is just a half-hour's drive southeast of Bisbee, via U.S. Highway 80. **Agua Prieta**, the Mexican town, is just across the boundary, offering a popular market area with curio shops, restaurants, and plazas. The town is small enough that you can just walk across the border for an easy morning or afternoon of sightseeing. There's a golf course just north of Douglas on U.S. Highway 80.

A national historical landmark, the old **Gadsden Hotel** (in Douglas) is an elegant building that was built in 1907 and—like many other original buildings in this region—was destroyed by fire and rebuilt in 1927. There's a marble staircase off the lobby, chandeliers, two Tiffany skylights, and a stained glass mural. The hotel is open daily, (602) 364-4481.

The **San Bernardino Ranch** (also called the Slaughter Ranch) is found east of Douglas via a gravel road. This 300-acre site became the 1884 home of John Slaughter, a former Texas Ranger who became the sheriff of Cochise County. He farmed the cattle ranch for 30 years. Today it's a museum, restored to its Victorian charm, and tours are given daily between 10 AM and 3 PM. For infor-mation, phone (602) 364-4481.

Northeast of Douglas on U.S. 80 is the Douglas Wild Animal Park, with exotic birds, animals, and a petting zoo. For information, call (602) 364-2515.

• A Day-Trip from Bisbee and Douglas

Farther distant from both Bisbee and Douglas is Portal, a small community close to the New Mexico border, 7 miles west of Route 80 (turn west just north of Rodeo, NM). Sixty-two miles from Douglas, Portal is the gateway to several points of interest, including recreation sites in the Coronado National Forest.

Cave Creek Canyon is the site of the Southwestern Research Station of the American Museum of Natural History. The center has a wonderful collection of plants and animals and is a renowned birding area with hiking trails.

Farther down the gravel road, deep in the national forest, is the **Chiricahua National Monument**. Features of the monument include Bonita Canyon, the historic Faraway Ranch, and several interpretive trails, together with camping and day-use areas. For information, phone (602) 824-3560. There are several national forest campgrounds that can be accessed from the road to the monument, and the ranger station in Portal has information on these and other recreation areas.

The gravel road leads across the summit of the Chiricahua Mountains, ending just west of the national monument. To make the trip a circle route, take the paved road leading west from the monument and turn south onto Arizona Route 181. Then turn south on U.S. 666 to return to Douglas.

The shorter but less scenic route to the Chiricahua National Monument is by this paved route (take U.S. 666 north from Douglas and turn east on Arizona Route 181).

Canyon de Chelly National Monument

From its rim, Canyon de Chelly (pronounced de SHAY) drops a thousand feet. At the bottom, Navajo hogans and nearby fields and orchards are seen—a vision of present-day life that continues a theme which is 2,000 years old. The first people in the canyon were the Basketmakers.

Canyon de Chelly is a Hispanicized version of the Navajo term *Tseyi*, meaning "among the rocks" or "canyon." This canyon and its tributary Canyon del Muerto have seen permanent residents since about AD 300, when pithouses were built and farming began. The Basketmaker II people hunted game in the area and practiced a primitive form of horticulture. They founded several communities including Tse Yaa Tsoh, located in a huge Canyon del Muerto niche.

Arizona

Between AD 1050 and 1300, Anasazi Indians lived in the canyons, building the cliff dwellings that are the major attraction for visitors today. These villages (some of them large towns) include White House, Sliding Rock Ruins, Mummy Cave, Junction Ruins, and Standing Cow Ruins. The Anasazi were the first to paint drawings on the canyon walls, followed by the Navajo, who added more art works.

The Rio de Chelly flows through the canyon, providing water for farming and the Navajo residents. Like Chaco Canyon—to the east in New Mexico—it is a place of serene beauty and awesome silence.

The Pueblo period began during the Anasazi period, between AD 700 and 1150. After this initial period, the Anasazi left the plateaus above the canyons to move into the cliff dwellings, supposedly to provide fortification against hostile forces. Some archeologists believe that the Anasazi moved to the cliffs to escape the ravages of the floodplain and the heavy rains of winter.

Later, in the twelfth and thirteenth centuries, other Indians from Chaco Canyon and Tsegi Canyon moved here but didn't stay for long. By AD 1284, the last of the Anasazi had left, and, as in Chaco Canyon and other sites, their flight is still a mystery. Could they have departed because of drought? Perhaps enemies appeared, causing a swift departure. Nobody knows for sure.

Hopi Indians seem to have come here around 1300, a theory borne out by remains of ceramic art in the canyons. The Navajo, a nomadic Apache tribe, came from the Great Plains in the fifteenth and sixteenth centuries, and the area became a Navajo stronghold with the colonization of most of the Southwest by Spaniards. It was a staging point for raids on the Spanish and later the U.S. Army.

In the early 1800s, an all-day battle was fought between the Navajo and the Spanish, ending with the Indians being trapped in Massacre Cave. In 1864, Col. Kit Carson led his cavalry detachment into the canyon, burning Navajo homes and fields. The army forced more than 8,000 Navajo to walk to Fort Sumner, New Mexico, where they were held captive before being returned—an event known as the Long Walk.

Today, about 300 Navajo live in and work the fields of Canyon de Chelly during the summer months. Out of the way, apart from the large cities of the Southwest, this unique collection of former Anasazi and Navajo communities remains one of the most significant reminders of the first settlers of the Four Corners region.

How to Get There

Canyon de Chelly National Monument is located close to Arizona Highway 63, at the town of Chinle. The site is 95 miles from Gallup, New Mexico, via Highways 666, 264, and 191. If you're arriving from the north, take U.S. Highway 191 south from its intersection with U.S. 160 and drive south for 62 miles to Chinle. From the south, drive north on U.S. Highway 191 from the junction of Interstate 40.

What to See & Do

The best way (and the easiest) to see the ruins and canyons is to drive along the two scenic routes—the South Rim Drive (36 miles round trip) and the North Rim Drive (34 miles round trip). The South Rim Drive provides access roads to eight overlook viewpoints. There are four overlooks on the North Rim Drive. The most popular overlooks are on the South Drive: Junction Overlook, with views of First Ruin and Junction Ruin, and the White House Overlook.

Travel by foot into the canyon is allowed only in the presence of a park ranger or guide. The one exception is the White House Trail. This 2.5-mile round-trip walk leads to the best-known Anasazi ruin in the canyon. It is named after a long wall in the upper ruin that is covered with white plaster. The trail begins at the White House Overlook, 6 miles from the park headquarters and information center. The village was home to about 100 Anasazi between AD 1060 and 1275. The descent is 500 feet and the trail takes you across the river. Set aside 2 hours for the round trip.

The best way to see the other ruins in the canyon is to take the guided tour by vehicle offered by Thunderbird Lodge, the hotel inside the monument, near the visitor center (write Chinle, AZ 86503). The lodge uses vehicles that can negotiate the sandy terrain (with some quicksand) and mud following flash floods. Other visitors use their own 4WD vehicles, hiring a Navajo guide through the Park Service. Horseback trips into the canyons are also available.

Other visitor services include picnic sites. The Cottonwood Campground is located near the monument headquarters, with fireplaces, drinking water, and restrooms. Gasoline, propane, food, and other camping supplies are available in Chinle.

Coronado National Forest

Situated on several mountain ranges in southeastern Arizona, the Coronado National Forest offers three major historical sites and more than twenty recreation areas. The four forest areas in the extreme southeast section of the state are all within reach of several centers: Benson and Bisbee—at the south end of the state—are close to forest tracts that straddle the Chiricahua Mountains and the large section of the forest lying just north of the Mexican border, between Nogales and Sierra Vista; and Safford, which is close to the large northern tract in the Pinaleno Mountains. Rose Canyon Lake and other nearby recreation sites are near Tucson.

• Chiricahua National Monument

This scenic park is located in the national forest east of Benson and north of Douglas. It is accessed from either the east or west side of the Chiricahua mountain range. From the east, drive west from Benson to either U.S. Route 666 or Arizona Route 186, and drive south to Arizona Route 181.

From Douglas or New Mexico, take U.S. Highway 80 south from Interstate 10 or north from Douglas, and then turn west onto the sideroad that leads through the village of Portal (ranger station) and the mountains.

215

Historic sites include the Faraway Ranch and Bonito Canyon. There is a campground in the monument, as well as along the gravel road leading westward from Highway 80 past Portal. There are interpretive trails and guided tours of monument sites. For information, phone (602) 824-3560.

Destinations

• Fort Bowie

Just outside the national forest boundary, Fort Bowie is located at the northern edge of the Chiricahua Mountains, northwest of the Chiricahua National Monument. Visitors can stroll through the ruins of the fort, which was constructed in 1862. It was a stop on the Butterfield Stage route. The site is accessed via a self-guided foot trail. To get there, drive south from Interstate 10 from the junction just east of Bowie, or northeast from Arizona Route 186 (9 miles north of Hwy. 181).

• Cochise's Stronghold

The refuge of the great chief Cochise and his Apache followers, who were chased into the high granite reaches of the Dragoon Mountains, the stronghold provides a fascinating glimpse of the days when Indian wars dominated the scene in the Old West. The site is operated by the National Forest Service (602-826-3593) and includes a campground, picnic area, and hiking trails. There are several other prominent historic sites in Cochise County that commemorate the struggles between the cavalry and the Apache, but Cochise's Stronghold provides the best overview of those turbulent times.

U.S. Route 666 leads south from Interstate 10 and runs north from Douglas, on the Mexican border. Just north of the community of Sunsites is a gravel road that leads west to the stronghold. If you're driving east from Benson, another scenic route leads from Interstate 10, at the Dragoon exit. Drive east along this sideroad to meet Highway 666 and drive south for another 8 miles to the gravel road.

• Coronado National Memorial

Located just north of the Mexico boundary, south of Sierra Vista, the memorial commemorates the explorations of Francisco Coronado and other Spanish conquistadors in 1540. Operated by the National Park Service, the memorial is open daily with a visitor center, museum, and hiking trails. Montezuma Pass is a spectacular scenic attraction. For information, phone (602) 366-5515.

• Recreation Sites South of Safford

Riggs Lake is at the end of a partially graveled forest road which leads east from U.S. Route 666, 9 miles south of Safford. Along this road are three forest campgrounds: Arcadia, Shannon, and Riggs Lake. The Riggs Flat Campground is farther to the west. Mt. Graham (el. 10,717 feet) dominates the scene here. There is a ranger station at Riggs Lake, 10 miles down the road.

• Rose Canyon Lake

Mt. Lemmon rises more than 9,000 feet from the desert floor, northeast of the city of Tucson. At the end of a winding road is the area's prime downhill ski center. Along the road are several forest recreation sites. Sabino Canyon, close to the city at the edge of the mountain's slopes, is a favorite haunt of birders, photographers, and hikers, who often wade into the river to see wildlife. Farther along the road are forest campgrounds: Mound Basin, Rose Canyon, and Spencer Canyon. Rose Canyon Lake is situated near the end of the road, before you reach the ski area.

• Nearby Places of Interest

The **Rex Allen Arizona Cowboy Museum** is in Wilcox, a town situated on Interstate 10, east of Benson. The museum displays memorabilia of the cowboy movie star, one of the famous singing cowboy entertainers—in a league with the other major stars of the genre, Roy Rogers and Gene Autry.

Fort Huachuca, in the town of Sierra Vista, is a restored fort and museum of southwestern military history. It's one of the few remaining active army posts of the Old West. For information, phone (602) 533-5736.

217

Flagstaff

For many years, Flagstaff and the town of Williams (30 miles west) have been fighting it out for the honor of being the place from which tourists should stage their visits to the Grand Canyon. Williams is closer to the South Rim and offers the train ride to the national park. Flagstaff is a bigger city—a university town—and is close to a number of additional attractions to capture the visitor's interest. Take your choice. However, you should think twice before rejecting Flagstaff as your base for an exploration of northern Arizona.

With an elevation of 7,000 feet, Flagstaff provides pleasantly warm days and refreshing nights during the summer months. Late afternoon showers are customary during the summer and fall period, clearing the air for that refreshing pine scent that infuses the atmosphere throughout this region.

Things to See & Do
• Local Festivals
Several annual festivals showcase the arts in Flagstaff, including the Zuni Artists Exhibition at the Museum of Northern Arizona (May); the Festival of Native American Arts, held at the Coconino Centre for the Arts (June); the annual Hopi Artists Exhibition (at the museum in June); the Navajo Artists Exhibition (same venue in July); the Festival in the Pines (August); and the city's Festival of the Arts, held annually in July, with symphonic and pops concerts, chamber music, theater, and classic film showings.

• Mountain Recreation
Because the city lies at the base of Mt. Wheeler, the highest peak in Arizona, Flagstaff is noted for its winter activity. The Snow Bowl attracts skiers from across the country. With 35 trails, it's the most extensive ski area in the state. The Nordic Ski Center north of town offers groomed cross-country ski trails, as does the Mormon Lake nordic ski area. Summer sporting attractions include a championship 18-hole golf course and fishing in Mormon Lake and Lake Mary, both less than a half-hour's drive from town. Oak Creek, just south of town, is a trout angler's haunt. The city has an Urban Trails System with biking and hiking trails.

• To the Grand Canyon
There are two highways you can take to reach the South Rim of the Grand Canyon from Flagstaff. Our preferred route is covered in the scenic drive beginning on page 178. This route follows U.S.

Highway 89, past Sunset Crater and the Wupatki National Monument to Cameron, and then follows the path of the Little Colorado River to the national park's western edge. The shorter route is the drive out of Flagstaff on U.S. Highway 180, through the San Francisco Mountains to the crossroads community of Valle and then completing the trip north (still on Hwy. 180) to the south gate to the park.

• Native Culture—Ancient & Contemporary

The history and culture of Arizona's native Indians attracts thousands of visitors annually to the city and environs. Wupatki National Monument, the Sinagua ruins, is located 20 miles north of Flagstaff, just off Highway 89 (on our suggested route to the Grand Canyon; see the log on page 180). As well, the city is within a day's drive of the Zuni and Hopi reservations. Descendants of the Anasazi, the Hopi, settled towns northeast of Flagstaff.

• In Flagstaff

Fort Valley Road (Highway 180) leads to several points of interest. The **Coconino Center for the Arts** features galleries displaying regional artists and traveling national exhibitions. The Center stages an annual "Trappings of the American West" show. For information, phone (602) 779-6921. Next door to the arts center is the **Arizona Historical Society/Pioneer Museum**. The museum includes pioneer buildings and historical displays of Arizona settlement (602-774-6272).

The **Arboretum at Flagstaff** is one of two fine arboreta I visited during my recent tour of the state (the other is the Boyce Thompson Desert Arboretum near Phoenix). Flagstaff's arboretum is located in a wooded area on Woody Mountain Road, off old Route 66, west of town. Native Arizona plants and flowers are featured, as well as rare plants and flowers not naturally found in northern Arizona.

Visiting the two botanical gardens provides an insight into the incredibly diverse nature of Arizona ecology. For information, phone (602) 774-1441.

Destinations

The **Museum of Northern Arizona** (on Fort Valley Road) houses a large collection of southwestern native arts and crafts, in addition to displays on northern Arizona's geology and history. It is the location of several annual native art and crafts exhibitions (see previous page) and always has special museum attractions (602-774-5211).

The **Lowell Observatory**, named for pioneer astronomer Percival Lowell, is located atop Mars Hill just west of the downtown area. The observatory is open daily for guided tours, slide shows and lectures (phone 602-774-2096).

Two vastly different historic homes can be viewed in the city. **Walnut Canyon National Monument** is an example of ancient Sinagua Indian cliff dwellings. You can walk through the canyon on paved trails or you can follow the rim. It's located 5 miles east of town, off Interstate 40.

Riordan Mansion (a state park) was the home of one of Flagstaff's first families and has been restored as a testament to the pioneering spirit of Arizona's founders. The mansion is found off Milton Road, near Northern Arizona University.

• Scenic Route to Sedona

South of Flagstaff, Alternate Route 89 leads down into Oak Creek Canyon and to the red rock country surrounding Sedona. This drive is featured on page 182. The short drive to Sedona makes a fine day-trip from Flagstaff, providing lots of time to visit picnic parks along the creek, the old Indian Gardens, and then Sedona with its clusters of chic boutiques, new-age crystal shops, and superb resorts. Before descending into the Oak Creek Canyon, the route passes through pine forest, with access to several small lakes that also provide recreation areas with picnicking and fishing.

The Red Rock Loop Drive just south of Sedona provides great views of the natural red rock architecture. If you're spending only a day visiting the Sedona area before returning to Flagstaff, this short but spectacular tour is a *must*. For the full treatment, follow the scenic drive which begins on page 182.

Grand Canyon—South Rim

Having seen the Grand Canyon from three sides (South Rim, North Rim and at Lee's Ferry, the start of the canyon) one can only marvel at the strange geological occurrences that created this most impressive of nature's wonders. We know that the huge Colorado Plateau started to uplift a few million years ago, just as the Colorado River began to cut a channel through the earth on its way to the Sea of Cortez. The uplifting action served to keep the river on its course as it continued to grind through the rock, resulting in a gorge more than 200 miles long, with hundreds of side canyons and dozens of buttes rising from the valley floor. Eighteen miles wide in places, the canyon is America's most visited natural destination—a mecca for travelers from around the world.

A caution: if there is one time of the year NOT to visit the South Rim if at all possible, it's the summer. July and August find so many people at the South Rim that quiet enjoyment of the spectacle is rarely possible. May and June and September and October provide the ideal periods for visiting. The North Rim is less crowded during summer months. Winter on the South Rim should also be considered. While the weather can be harsh, the canyon takes on a special, relaxed quality during the winter with snow on the plateau and butte tops.

Although Spanish explorers were the first non-Americans to see the Grand Canyon, it was virtually unknown until John Wesley Powell and his intrepid band of geographers explored the canyon by boat in 1869. Miners followed before the first tourists arrived, and the remains of mines are found below the rim. Teddy Roosevelt was instrumental in providing national monument status for the canyon in 1908, and the area received national park designation in 1919. Today, more than three million visitors tour the park (most on the South Rim) and most of those arrive during July and August.

Two thousand square miles of plateau and canyon now lie in the park. The geological features are of different ages—inner gorges date back two billion years while buttes closer to the rims are merely 200 million years old. The canyon itself is a youngster, created only a few million years ago.

Destinations

Doing both rims should take a week, with a day's drive (210 miles) between the two national park locations. This is—for most—a once-in-a-lifetime opportunity and it behooves one to spend enough time in the park to truly catch the many wonders of the canyon, particularly if there are children involved. There are short and long hikes into the canyon available, plus the famous mule rides led by rangers—as far as the river and Phantom Ranch, or part-way down to a mid-way shelf. Air tours of the canyon provide an easy way to see the full glory of the region. Raft trips—starting from Lee's Ferry just south of the Glen Canyon Dam at Page, Arizona—take as long as a week to float down the full length of the canyon. Any way you do it, this probably will be your most remembered vacation experience.

How to Get There

The most popular driving route to the South Rim leads to Grand Canyon Village via U.S. Highway 180. It is accessible from either Williams or Flagstaff, by driving north from Interstate 40. From Williams, drive north on Arizona Route 64 and then continue on Hwy. 180 through the village of Tusayan to the south gate to the park.

Our preferred route from Flagstaff is via Sunset Crater and the Wupatki National Monument (Indian ruins) to Cameron (via U.S. 89) and then west to the Desert View gate on Arizona Route 64. This scenic drive is covered on page 178.

The shorter drive from Flagstaff to the south gate is via U.S. Highway 180, which leads northwest from Interstate 40. This is a scenic drive through the San Francisco Mountains and the Kaibab National Forest.

It's also a thrill to take the scenic train trip from Williams to Grand Canyon Village. The train runs daily through the busy summer season and less frequently during winter months. Call 800-THE TRAIN (800-843-8724) for information on this revival of the long-time steam-train journey that captivated visitors as far back as the turn of the century. The train pulls into the South Rim village close to the El Tovar Hotel. Taking the train means that you don't have a car to drive along the rim to the various overlook locations. However, the park operates a bus shuttle along the South Rim and it's possible to enjoy an even more relaxed vacation if you don't feel compelled to dash all over the place in your car. During summer months, the Rim Drive is closed to cars.

Things to See and Do
• Information Services
The main park visitor center is in the cluster of services in Grand Canyon Village, near the hotels. It is open daily from 8 AM to 5 PM and there are displays in the adjacent exhibit hall. There is also a summer information center at Desert View (near the west gate). Copies of the park newspaper, *The Guide*, are given to motorists at the park gates. For advance information, write to Grand Canyon National Park, P.O. Box 129, Grand Canyon, AZ 86023, or phone (602) 638-7888.

• Mather Point
For most visitors, this is the first good view of the Grand Canyon, as it is the first overlook on the drive from the south gate to the Village facilities. What becomes apparent later, after seeing the canyon from other overlooks, is that from Mather you can only see a very small part of the Grand Canyon. Below the point is the Tonto Platform, a flat ledge on which you can see several trails. With binoculars you might see a mule train traversing the Platform. It is so far away that most of its features are blurred, and it's not as flat as it looks.

• East Rim Drive
The drive from the Village to Desert View is about 23 miles (37 KM). The drive takes you past several short roads that lead to overlook locations. Each view is different, and only by traveling the length of the rim (as far as a car will take you) can you truly get the effect of the greatest canyon on earth! From west to east, following are the viewpoints and other places of interest.

223

• Yaki Viewpoint and Kaibab Trailhead
The first sideroad leads to the Yaki Viewpoint (keep to the right). From Yaki Point, the high slope of the Kaibab Plateau is seen across the canyon. Also in view are the many side canyons, cut by water draining into the main canyon. The South Kaibab Trailhead is

reached by taking the left fork in the road. The trail descends from the parking area to a geological feature called Cedar Ridge (actually populated by juniper trees). This trail is the preferred route up the canyon for those who have taken this or the Bright Angel Trail down to the Tonto Platform or the river. It's a little longer but much easier to climb than the very steep Bright Angel Trail. It's 3 miles to Cedar Ridge, and this walk provides the best short route with canyon views.

• Grandview Point & Trail

Located 600 feet above Grand Canyon Village, Grandview is just that. Horseshoe Mesa is directly below the viewpoint—the site of the old Last Chance copper mine. The trail leads down the side of the canyon. The mine, owned by Pete Berry and his partners, Niles and Ralph Cameron, operated from 1890 to 1907.

• Moran Point

This viewpoint was (supposedly) named for famed painter Thomas Moran, who is known for his watercolors of both the Grand Canyon and Yellowstone. The Sinking Ship, a rock formation with approximations of a ship's structure, masts, and bridge can be seen from this point. In addition, two portions of the river can be seen from Moran Point. The upstream view provides a look at the Colorado wandering lazily through the red sandstone. The deep walls of the Inner Gorge are seen downstream.

• Tusayan Ruin & Museum

The ruins are what remains of a small pueblo that has been partially excavated. The museum holds displays of life in the village when it was inhabited about 800 years ago. The 30 people who lived here farmed corn, squash, and beans. They made beautiful pottery, some of which has been excavated and is on display. It is thought that the Tusayan were the ancestors of the modern-day Hopi Indians.

The museum, 3 miles from Desert View, is open daily from 9 AM to 5 PM and is usually closed in January. A self-guiding trail leads through the ruin.

Arizona

• Lipan Point

Perhaps the most impressive view of the canyon is seen from Lipan Point. The river turns west at the canyon bottom, past the Palisades and into the Inner Gorge. There is also a fine view of the Kaibab Monocline and the North Rim. In the distance, Cape Royal is seen about 6 miles to the north, beyond the river. From the viewpoint, the river is 3 miles distant.

• Desert View

There are fine canyon vistas from this viewpoint, but it has been named for the eastward view of the Arizona Painted Desert, which shows its pink colors in the far distance. Services here include a campground, summer information center, store, cafe, and service station. The service station and campground are closed during winter months. The **Desert View Watchtower** was designed by architect Mary Coulter and constructed in the 1930s. Coulter took her inspiration from similar structures in Anasazi communities at Mesa Verde and Canyon de Chelly.

The tower is 70 feet high, and a staircase takes you to the top for fine views in all directions. The levels of the tower are decorated in native motifs, and the souvenir shop is built somewhat like a ceremonial kiva. Look for the river flowing through Marble Canyon (to the north of the tower). Not marble, the rock formation is actually limestone. Just beyond Desert View is the east gate to the park. Cameron is 32 miles to the east via Highway 64.

• West Rim Drive

This 8-mile drive begins in Grand Canyon Village and ends at Hermit's Rest, passing several viewpoints. The road is closed to private cars during the busy summer period (another reason to come in the off-season), and a shuttle bus takes you to the various viewpoints along the rim.

The drive begins just west of Bright Angel Lodge. The overlook at this point is at the top of the Bright Angel Fault, through which the Bright Angel Trail descends toward the canyon floor. The West Rim Drive was originally constructed by the Santa Fe Railroad and

Destinations

opened in 1912 as a tour route. West of the Bright Angel Trailhead are several overlooks:

• Bright Angel Trailhead—Overlooks I & II

As the road climbs, there is a good view of the Bright Angel Trail from two overlooks connected by a walkway. Originally an Indian route to the gardens on the Tonto Platform, the path was used by miners to transport supplies by pack mule. It was operated as a toll road for nearly 290 years. You can see the trail from the lower viewpoint, with switchbacks snaking down the side of the cliffs. This is a nine-mile journey to the riverside. The Rim Trail, which begins in front of the Yavapai Museum and passes beside the El Tovar Hotel, leads along the West Rim as far as Pima Point.

• Maricopa Point

Under this overlook is Horn Canyon with the river and Inner Gorge far below. The river is obscured. The Battleship is the name of the prominent formation to the right as you look over the canyon.

• Powell Point

There is a monument commemorating John Wesley Powell at the viewpoint. There is no view of the river from this spot. Years after his explorations of this region in 1869 and 1871/72, he was made director of the U.S. Geological Survey.

• Hopi Point

The most impressive views from the canyon's West Rim are available here. The Palisades of the Desert are seen far to the east. The river is also seen from this point. The Alligator is the formation just to the west—a long red jutting point of rock capped with shale. The Tonto Platform is also seen below, as is the Tonto Trail, which crosses the platform.

• Mohave Point

Hard beside the Alligator, Mohave Point provides a good look at the Hermit Rapid, seen to the west. Semihidden behind the Alligator is Granite Rapid. Past Mohave Point is the Abyss, where

Arizona

the road curves around a cliff almost 3,000 feet deep. This is a good point to get out of the car and walk along the West Rim Trail. There are good views of Monument Creek as it carves its way down the cliffsides. The creek gets its name from the stone towers seen in the creekbed.

• Pima Point

This overlook provides a grand vista with views of the Inner Gorge, the Powell Plateau (far to the west), and Cape Royal (also part of the North Rim—15 miles east).

• Hermit's Rest

The end of the drive is dedicated to Louis Boucher, a French Canadian prospector and miner who came to the Grand Canyon about 1890. He lived alone and built a home beside the remote Dripping Springs, near the end of what has come to be known as Hermit Canyon. He mined copper to the west of that canyon and had a well-known fruit orchard that attracted tourists. He moved to Utah in 1912. Shortly after, the Santa Fe Railroad, which exploited the Grand Canyon for tourism purposes, built a tour road following Boucher's trail to the Tonto Platform, where a tent/cabin campground was established. The road ends here but the canyon continues as the river flows toward Lake Mead.

• Towers and Temples

The high monuments—pinnacles and buttes—rising from the canyon have mystical names provided by early mapmakers. They include Shiva Temple, Wotan's Throne, the Tower of Ra, and Zoroaster Temple. Even without fancy names, these buttes would be impressive. The towers are seen from most of the South Rim viewpoints and are identified on the national park map/brochure.

227

Park Services

Rental cars are available at the Grand Canyon Airport rental desks. The regular **shuttle service** between Grand Canyon Village, the town of Tusayan, and the Grand Canyon Airport operates on an hourly schedule. **Air tours** of the Grand Canyon can be booked at any of the Grand Canyon lodges (at the transportation desks). A list of tour operators is

Destinations

available at the Visitor Information Center. Several fixed-wing and helicopter tours depart from the Grand Canyon Airport.

Bus tours within the park operate daily, taking visitors to Desert View and Hermit's Rest from the Village. The **Railroad Express** provides bus service for those wishing to take a one-way trip on the scenic steam train (from and to Williams).

Medical services are available at the Grand Canyon Health Clinic, located on Clinic Road (off Center Road). The **Park Pharmacy** is open Monday through Friday from 8:30 AM to 12:30 PM and from 1:30 PM to 5 PM (602-638-2460). There's a **dentist** available Monday through Wednesday from 8 AM to 3 PM—call (602) 638-2395. **Gasoline** is available in the Village and (during summer months) at Desert View. There is a **laundry with showers** at Camper Services, near Mather Campground. The park even has a **Beauty and Barber Shop**, located in Bright Angel Lodge. **Pet kennels** are available, open daily from 7:30 AM to 5 PM, call (602) 638-2631.

Where to Eat in the Park

No need to go hungry while visiting the South Rim. The **El Tovar Hotel**'s dining room is open for breakfast, lunch, and dinner. The **Arizona Steakhouse** is beside the Rim Trail, west of the El Tovar, with cafeteria-style service. The **Bright Angel Restaurant** is located in the lodge of the same name and is open daily from 6:30 AM to 10 PM. The lounge here is open from 11 AM to midnight. The **Maswik Cafeteria** is located across the road from the visitor center. It's closed during winter months.

Meals are available at **Phantom Ranch**, with breakfast, lunch, and a stew dinner served daily. Reserve your meals at the Bright Angel Transportation Desk.

Where to Stay

There are motels in Tusayan, the community outside the south entrance to the national park. In addition, there are two respectable motels in Cameron, located east of the park at the junction of Highways 89 and 64. Several of these motels are listed in the Arizona Places to Stay pages.

Arizona

Inside the park, visitors will find several places to stay, including campgrounds and an RV park. The **El Tovar Hotel** is the historic lodge built in 1905 and, since then, the prime place to stay within the park. Constructed of pine logs and fieldstone, the El Tovar offers rusticity with gentility, at prices in the high to deluxe range. Nearby motel-type accommodations include the **Kachina Lodge,** the **Thunderbird Lodge,** the **Yavapai Lodge** (open seasonally), **Bright Angel Lodge,** and **Maswik Lodge. Moqui Lodge** is closed during January and February.

For information on all these park accommodations, write to Grand Canyon National Park Lodges, P.O. Box 699, Grand Canyon, AZ 86023. For advance reservations, call (602) 638-2401. For same-day reservations, call (602) 638-2631.

Phantom Ranch, on the canyon floor beyond the north side of the river, has overnight dormitory and cabin space. Advance reservations are necessary. Call (602) 638-2401 or contact the Bright Angel Lodge transportation desk while in the park. This desk also handles reservations for mule trips into the canyon.

Camp sites are available in the **Mather Campground** (open year-round, no hookups). For advance reservations, call MYSTIX at 800-365-2267.

Trailer Village, with hookups, is located next to Mather Campground(call 602-638-2401).

Desert View Campground (no hookups, self-reservation) is closed during the winter months. There is a commercial campground with hookups 7 miles south of the Village, outside the park in the town of Tusayan. For reservations, call (602) 638-2887. A national forest campground is located just outside the south gate in the Kaibab National Forest. Call (602) 638-2443 for information.

A strong caution: I can't emphasize enough the need to plan your trip several months in advance to secure accommodations in Grand Canyon Village and Phantom Ranch. If you're contemplating a vacation here, you'll need to make your bookings about 6 months in advance for weekend and holiday stays. Because the South Rim is so busy during the summer, serious vacation planning should begin a year before your visit.

Destinations

Grand Canyon—North Rim

How to Get There

As the crow flies, the South and North Rims are about 12 miles apart. By car, it's a drive of 210 miles—leaving the park by driving beside the South Rim to Desert View and taking **Arizona Route 64**, then turning onto **U.S. Highway 89** at Cameron. You drive north for 59 miles and turn west onto **Alternate Route 89** at Bitter Springs (a few miles south of the town of Page). The final leg of the journey is via **Arizona Route 67**, the North Rim Parkway that runs south from Jacob Lake and continues through the park, ending near the North Rim at the courtyard of the Grand Canyon Lodge. The northern part of this drive (via Alt. Route 89 and Route 67) is covered in the scenic drive on page 174.

• Lee's Ferry Landing

The drive between Bitter Springs and Jacob Lake is a fascinating one, as the road passes through the Cornfield Valley and then climbs up to the Kaibab Plateau—past the Vermilion Cliffs and through House Rock Valley. Eighteen miles beyond Bitter Springs, Alt. Route 89 crosses the Colorado River over the Navajo Bridge, at Marble Canyon. It is here that a short side trip of about 30 minutes will provide a whole new dimension to your enjoyment of the Grand Canyon.

Lee's Ferry was the only crossing of the Colorado River in this entire region between 1871 and the early 1900s. The ferry boat was operated first by John Doyle Lee, a Mormon settler who moved here with his wife and family, operating a farm that was irrigated by water from the Paria River. Lee was put on trial and executed in 1877 for his part in the Mountain Meadows Massacre, when 140 California-bound pioneers were killed by Mormon settlers who resented the presence of U.S. troops in the region.

Emma Lee continued to operate the ferry until she sold it to the Mormon Church in 1879. The ferry sank and was replaced by the Navajo Bridge in 1928. There is a campground at the recreation site that provides picnic tables overlooking the river.

The historical background of Lee's Ferry is fascinating, but there is another important reason to visit here; Lee's Ferry Landing marks the beginning of the Grand Canyon and is the only spot along the canyon where one can drive to the beach at the water's edge and see the Colorado River racing its way into nature's most impressive gorge. The Navajo sandstone, seen on the opposite side of the river, is what forms the South and North Rims.

The Landing is a favorite spot for anglers, who put their boats into the water here, and this is the location for the start of the 1- and 2-week rafting trips through the canyon.

The road to the historic site takes you through a scenic part of the **Glen Canyon National Recreation Area.** The "balanced rocks" to the west of the road are the result of boulders tumbling from the rim of the cliffs and coming to rest on softer rock, leaving the boulders resting on protected pillars. There's a campground near the old Lee homestead, and a trail leads across the Paria River to the original ferry crossing.

To think that about 280 miles downstream, the river ends its journey through the Grand Canyon by flowing quietly into Lake Mead, brings a sense of awe and wonder. When I left Lee's Ferry, I hoped that the next time I visited this place, I could start a 2-week expedition on the full 280-mile canyon journey However, the North Rim beckons and we're on our way—back to Marble Canyon and the red cliffs.

• The Kaibab Plateau

For 30 miles beyond Marble Canyon, Alternate Route 89 leads along the base of the Vermilion Cliffs. Along the way are several small communities that have been here since pioneer days. **Cliff Dwellers Lodge** has two unique stone structures that housed the original trading post. Above House Rock Valley, the summit offers a wonderful view over the river to the Echo Cliffs. To the south is the dark mesa called Shinumo Altar. The Colorado River is more than 1,500 feet below the summit.

If time permits, drive from the highway to visit **House Rock Buffalo Ranch**. The animals' range covers some 60,000 acres of national forest land. The first buffalo were brought here in the early 1900s by Buffalo Jones, a former buffalo hunter who drove his herd across the plains to the Kaibab Plateau. The herd is now owned by the state, which allows the buffalo to roam free, with the deer and other animals.

The route to the rim turns south at the small community of Jacob Lake and then crosses the plateau. This is a pristine area of aspens and pines, filled with more wildlife including deer, bears, mountain lions, and coyotes. The plateau was called Buckskin Mountain by white settlers. Long before, the Indians named it *kaiuw a-vwi* ("mountain lying down"). The route passes Crane Lake before reaching Demotte Park, a community with visitor services including Kaibab Lodge and the North Rim Country Store—just outside the national park gate.

At the North Rim

It's a 7-mile drive from the north entrance station to the end of the road beside the Grand Canyon Lodge. The North Rim Parkway travels beside Little Park Lake, passes a picnic area near Lindberg Hill and meets Cape Royal Road. Beyond the junction is the trailhead to the Widforss Trail and the mule paddock. There's another picnic area closer to the North Rim Village.

As you proceed down the Parkway toward Grand Canyon Village, you'll see a series of open meadows—grassland parks in the midst of the Kaibab forest. One of the wild creatures inhabiting the forest is the Kaibab squirrel, with white tail and ear tips, living in the large ponderosa pine trees.

When you reach the end of the road, it's only a short stroll to see the canyon—either from Bright Angel Point or through the hotel to the stone terraces. On a good day, when not too much smog is drifting over the canyon from the Navajo Generating Station, you can see all the way to the San Francisco Peaks far to the south.

Ten miles distant, you can see the Bright Angel Trail dropping down from the South Rim to the Indian Gardens on the Tonto Platform. You can also see (maybe with some difficulty) the South Kaibab Trail.

Things to See and Do

The North Rim park is smaller and has a more human dimension than the sprawling South Rim section. There's only one lodging place here, and because of its more remote location, fewer people visit this section of the park. Without thousands of other visitors roaring around, one feels more relaxed strolling along the rim and sampling the trails. There are three trails that offer thrilling views:

- **Bright Angel Point Trail**

  This short trail should be an essential part of your visit to the North Rim. It's only 1/4 mile long, a paved path leading along a narrow ridge between two gorges. It ends at Bright Angel Point—a narrow rock that provides an overview of Transept Canyon (on the right) and Roaring Springs Canyon (to the left). The long chasm stretching toward the river is Bright Angel Canyon.

  Roaring Springs Canyon gets its name from the noisy spring that delivers water into a stream tumbling down the rock wall. Some of the water is pumped to the rim facilities, while a second pipe carries water from the spring all the way to Indian Gardens far below and then is pumped again to the South Rim. The elevation at Bright Angel Point is 8,145 feet.

- **North Kaibab Trail**

  Leading down the face of the cliffs to the river, the trail originally led to a camp at the mouth of Bright Angel Creek (in 1905). This camp is now Phantom Ranch. The complete trail system across the canyon—from North to South Rims—was completed in 1922. The trail descends for 14.2 miles, from 8,200 to 2,400 feet. For a good day hike, walk down to Roaring Springs. This is a 4.7-mile round trip, and the descent (and subsequent ascent) is 3,200 feet. The trailhead is beside the paddock, north of the Village. Those who make the trip to Phantom Ranch usually ride on a mule.

Destinations

• Widforss Trail

There's a gravel road leading to the west from the North Rim Parkway, ending at the Widforss Trailhead. This 5-mile (one way) hike follows the rim of Transept Canyon to Widforss Point. The first half of the walk is easy and self-guiding—with a trail guide available at the trailhead.

The trail was named after Gunnar Widforss, an artist from Sweden who painted the Grand Canyon for several years and was buried at the South Rim following his death in 1914.

• Cape Royal Road Drive

This 23-mile road is found north of the Village and it is advisable to plan for a full day's trip. The road leads to several viewpoints through forests of Douglas fir, Englemann's and blue spruce, white fir, and ponderosa pine.

A sideroad wanders beside Bright Angel Creek to **Point Imperial**, where one can see Marble Canyon (9 miles distant). This is the highest viewpoint on either rim, at an elevation of 8,803 feet. Both the view and elevation are enough to take your breath away.

The Walhalla Plateau reaches out into the canyon, and the road descends into a completely different ecosystem. By the time we've reached the end of the road, we lose the pine and aspen forest. However, the forest is still in evidence at **Greenland Lake**. There's an interpretive exhibit at this point, focusing on the eroded limestone that caused the formation of ponds and sinkholes in this area. Greenland Lake is one such sinkhole.

Vista Encantadora is farther along the main Cape Royal Road, past the turnoff to Point Imperial and Greenland Lake. This viewpoint is set in the mixed northern forest.

The view at the **Indian Country** pulloff is across the Marble Platform to the Echo Cliffs and beyond—to the Navajo and Hopi Indian reservations.

The Walhalla Glades Ruin is at the end of a short trail leading from the side of the road. There's a box at the pulloff containing guides to the trail and ruin. The ruin is what is left of a small Indian village, occupied for about 100 years from AD 1050.

Angel's Window is a remarkable opening in a large rock formation. It's seen at the bottom of a steep hill, and there's a pulloff for those who wish to have a longer view. There is a trailhead across the road from the pulloff, leading to Cliff Spring (1-mile round trip). The trail passes a small Indian ruin that includes a storehouse, thought to have been a granary for the few residents. The top of the Angel's Window rock can also be reached from a trail that departs from the Cape Royal parking lot.

Cape Royal—at the end of the road—is an extremely popular overlook. The trail features interpretive signage on the various plants and animals of the forest, a pinyon/juniper woodland. Here is the path to Angel's Window, which then proceeds to Cape Royal. The elevation of the Cape Royal viewpoint is 7,863 feet.

North Rim Park Services

Grand Canyon Lodge, which overlooks the canyon, provides the only lodging in the North Rim section of the national park. There are modern motel rooms in the pine forest in addition to cabins and fairly new cottage accommodations. There is a dining room, gift shop, and lounge inside the lodge, and other services may be arranged here, including horseback riding and mule trips into the canyon (if they're not fully booked). The lodge is open from early May to late October, when snow shuts down the park road. For information and reservations, write TW Services, Box 400, Cedar City, UT 84720, or call (801) 586-7686.

The **North Rim Campground** is located north of the Village, with showers, a campers' store, and nearby gas pumps. Reservations may be made by calling MYSTIX (800-365-2267) or writing to P.O. Box 85705, San Diego, CA 92138-5705. There are no hookups in this campground. Other campsites are located outside the park gate, in Demotte village and in the Kaibab National Forest.

Mule trips can be arranged inside the park or by phoning Grand Canyon

235

Destinations

Scenic Rides at (602) 638-2292. The mule ride to **Phantom Ranch** takes a full day. Overnight accommodation is available at Phantom Ranch, in a dormitory or in cabins. Although there is no road to this rustic overnight stopping place—only a hiking or mule path—it's usually booked months in advance. For reservations, call (602) 638-2401or 638-2631 or check at the lodge in case there have been cancellations. Mule trips should also be booked well in advance of your visit to the North Rim.

The park staff have an ongoing summer interpretation program that includes guided walks and lectures. For the daily schedule, see the park newspaper or inquire at the Parks Service information desk in the Grand Canyon Lodge.

There is a medical clinic, staffed by a nurse practitioner. Please check the park newspaper for the clinic open hours or call 638-2611.

Kingman & Bullhead City

These two towns are located in northwestern Arizona, south of Las Vegas. Kingman is a stopping-point along Interstate 40, whereas Bullhead City is on the Colorado River to the west of Kingman. Both are within easy reach of several Colorado River recreation areas including Lake Mohave, a widening of the river just north of Bullhead City, and the Topock Gorge, a prime rafting area. To the south is Lake Havasu and more river-based recreation.

Kingman, a 30-minute drive from Bullhead City and Laughlin, has the usual complement of chain motels, most clustered near the I-40 exits. The local visitor information center is on Andy Devine Avenue—a tribute to the late gravelly voiced actor, the town's foremost former celebrity. Kingman is one of the few places from which to take a nostalgic trip over part of the former Main Street of America.

Bullhead City is a project town, built for the construction of the Davis Dam, which holds back the Colorado River, creating Lake Mohave. Its main claim to fame today is that it lies just across the river from Laughlin, Nevada—a gambling and resort center spread along the bank of the Colorado. There are several motels and a campground in Bullhead City,

Arizona

and ferries cross the river almost on a minute-by-minute basis, taking visitors to the casinos in Laughlin. A bridge and a road over the dam provide routes joining the two riverside towns. Of course, you can also stay in the gleaming casino hotels, which range in price from dirt cheap (Edgewater) and medium-priced (Flamingo Hilton) to deluxe (Harrah's). There's a large RV parking lot across the street from the casino strip.

Things to See and Do

• In Kingman

For a good overview of the history of this part of Arizona and Mohave County in particular, we suggest that you pay a visit to the Mohave Museum of History and Arts, at 400 West Beale Street. You'll discover that while the pony express and Butterfield Stage Company did not deliver mail in what is now Mohave County, camels did the job—at least for a while. The Camel Corps (with 28 beasts) was organized in 1857 by Lt. Edward Beale, who had charted the wagon road from New Mexico to California. Beale's drivers hated the smelly, foul-tempered camels, and the experiment was quickly concluded. Most of the mail was then carried by local horse riders and riverboats.

• Hualapai Mountain Park

Fourteen miles from Kingman, the park has a campground, cabins, trails, and picnic areas and is a good place to stay while in the area. The trail system is extensive, leading through the slopes of Aspen and Hayden peaks. Although the trails do not climb the side of Hualapai Peak, the 8,417-foot landmark dominates the scene from many of the viewpoint locations. For more information and reservations, call (602) 753-0739.

• On the River

Canoeing on the Colorado is popular in this area. Even through the Topock Gorge, the river flows quietly, providing a relaxed downriver experience. Canoe rentals are available at Jerkwater Canoe Co. at Topock, and a free boat-launch ramp is available in Jack Smith Park in Needles, California (another I-40 town, 42 miles southwest of Kingman). Topock Gorge starts at the I-40

Destinations

bridge (in Needles) and ends at Lake Havasu. It's situated in the Lake Havasu Wildlife Refuge, where the river meanders through sloughs, wetlands, and—below the gorge—flat desert terrain.

• Lake Mohave

Lake Mohave and its environs offer recreation and overnight camping. **Davis Camp** is on the Colorado, just below the Davis Dam. Once, construction crews building the dam stayed here. Now there are campsites with showers, a picnic area, and a boat ramp. **Katherine Landing** is a resort center, located behind the dam. There are launch and dock facilities, an RV park, campgrounds, a store, plus a modern motel with a restaurant.

• Near Bullhead City

Across the river, in Nevada, is a scenic area called **Christmas Tree Pass.** Lying in the Newberry Mountains, the pass gets its name from the pinyon and juniper trees that have been decorated with cans, bulbs, and other "ornaments" over the years. This collection of what some would call trash is not as scenic as **Grapevine Canyon,** which is accessed by a trail which leaves from near the Christmas Tree Pass parking lot. Water flows year-round through this small canyon, keeping grape vines alive. At the mouth of the canyon, you'll find petroglyphs on the rock walls. National Park staff provide guided tours of the canyon, with the schedule available at the Katherine Landing ranger station.

The remains of the old **Katherine Mine** lie close to the Davis Dam, just north of Bullhead City. It's found off the main entrance to Katherine Landing, above the Park Service ranger station. Gold was discovered here in 1904, and the mine operated until 1942, by which time 12 million dollars or so in gold had been removed from the deep shafts—one more than 900 feet deep. A set of concrete pillars marks the location of the mine workings. The tailings piles are clearly seen, near the rusting hulks of old mine equipment.

To visit nearby **Chloride,** a ghost town in slightly better shape, drive east from Bullhead City on Route 68 to U.S. Hwy. 93. Turn north for 10 miles and then turn east into the old mining town.

• Route 66 Reminders

Arizona Route 66 is still here—a short piece of two-lane road that curves northward from Kingman, passing through Hackberry and Peach Springs, ending a few miles east of Seligman on Interstate 40. Route 66 also leads south from Kingman to the Colorado River at Topock, passing through the ghost town of Oatman. Together, these stretches of Route 66 provide 157.8 miles of nostalgic touring. A few original buildings remain on Route 66 (25 miles from Kingman) in Oatman, born as a gold rush town in 1906, with a motel, three cafes, three saloons, and a flea market.

Lake Havasu City

An hour's drive south of Bullhead City and Kingman is the resort and retirement town of Lake Havasu. The town received notoriety when developer Robert McCulloch bought and imported the London Bridge from England and then rebuilt the structure across a piece of sand next to the Colorado River. A dredge carved out the channel, creating an island, and water now runs under the bridge. This is flat desert country, with dark mountains flanking the Colorado. The Parker Dam has widened the river to form Lake Havasu.

Things to See & Do

Twenty-five thousand people live here, many of them retired, and the town is a prime wintering spot for sunbirds. Desert walks and golf form the major avocation of the locals, and of many visitors. Canoeing and boating on the lake and river to the north are also popular. Rental canoes are available in town from Bob's Canoe Trips, (602) 855-4406. Topoc Gorge stretches south for 15 miles from the I-40 bridge near Needles, California, providing the launchng point for a fascinating canoe journey.

Lake Havasu State Park covers 11,000 acres of lakeside lands, including 45 miles of shoreline. The park is accessible only by water. You'll find 225 boat camps and sandy beaches along the lake. Lake Havasu Marina at Windsor Beach State Park is reached by car. There are four golf courses including the championship London Bridge course and the Nautical Inn's 18-hole executive course.

Destinations

English Village, the tourist development beneath the London Bridge, features boutiques, English-style eating and drinking places, and even a hot dog stand. The town is becoming *the* place to be for young people during spring break—so beware if you're coming to Lake Havasu in March wanting to have a quiet time. Otherwise, this desert community is a restful, relaxed resort town.

The Lords and Ladies Club of Lake Havasu (yes, everyone here is an artificial Brit) sponsors desert walks every other Saturday morning, throughout the year. During summer months, the walks are held from 7 AM to 10 AM, and during the winter season from 9 AM to 2 PM. The walks are interpreted by geologists and botanists. The chamber of commerce information center has current schedules. The Visitor and Convention Center is located at 1930 Mesquite Ave., Suite 3. For advance information, call (602) 855-4115 or 800-242-8278.

Where to Eat

Every type of food from yogurt to continental cuisine is available in Lake Havasu. For good dining with a view, the **Captain's Table** at the Nautical Inn serves three meals a day, with seafood and prime rib the house specialties for dinner. **Jerry's**, on McCulloch Blvd., has 24-hour breakfasts and moderate prices. You can bring your boat to park in a slip and dine beside the lake at **Black Meadow Landing** (at the Parker Dam). **Casa de Miguel** (N. Palo Verde Blvd) and **Taco Hacienda** (Mesquite Ave.) serve tasty Mexican cuisine.

Nogales

For about 120 years, Nogales has been a trading center based at the junction of two railroad lines connecting with Mexico, just across the border from town. Nogales, Arizona, is the smaller town of the two border communities. Nogales (Sonora), Mexico, has 200,000 people—ten times the number who live on the U.S. side. The Mexican town is a popular destination for visitors, who drive or stroll across the boundary to shop and to eat in the many fine Mexican restaurants. Several prosperous mining camps were located just east of Nogales, including Washington Camp and Duquesne (only 2 of the 233 mines that once operated in the re-

Arizona

gion). The railroads followed the mines across Arizona and the Santa Fe arrived in the early 1880s, joining the Arizona & New Mexico R.R. which came to the border from Benson.

Things to See & Do

One of the more interesting historical sites in the area is the former **Pete Kitchen Ranch**, now a museum north of Nogales. Kitchen was a fierce and independent settler who built a fortress on his ranch, refusing to be moved during the Indian wars, which ended with the surrender of Geronimo in 1886. The **Pimeria Alta Historical Museum**, at 136 Grand Avenue, provides displays on the Pimeria Alta Indians, who inhabited the area long before white settlers arrived, as well as artifacts of the European settlement.

All around Nogales is the **Coronado National Forest**, providing recreational sites and hiking trails. West of town, the Pajarita Wilderness borders on Mexico and extends into the mountains. Arizona Route 289 (Ruby Road) leads through the wilderness to Lake Pena Blanca and beyond. There are several campgrounds along this route. Beyond the lake, the road is suitable only for 4WD vehicles as it runs through Sycamore Canyon and further west to arrive in Arivaca in Pima County. This was a favorite area for the Yaqui Indians, and many visitors travel the forest routes by horse. There were several mines in the region.

• Day-Trips from Nogales

The best scenic route in the area is the Patagonia Scenic Drive which is covered beginning on page 202. It leads to the old frontier town of **Patagonia** (19 miles northeast of Nogales), where you will find the bird sanctuary managed by The Nature Conservancy. This is a magnet for bird-watchers, who have identified more than 300 varieties of birds in this protected habitat flanked by cottonwood trees. The sanctuary is located on Sonoita Creek.

North of Nogales near Interstate 19 is the old **Presidio of San Ignacio du Tubac**. Although Spanish explorations began in the early 1500s, the presidio dates back only to around 1752 and was attacked by Apaches for the next 100 years. Juan de Anza, later the founder of San Francisco, revived the colony in 1764, and St. Ann's

Church was built in 1796. Nearby is the **Tumacacori National Monument**, the historic Mission San Jose de Tumacacori, an adobe church built in the early 1800s. Tubac is probably the best place to catch a full glimpse of the early Mexican settlement of what is now Arizona.

Organ Pipe Cactus National Monument

A prime piece of Sonoran desert is the major attraction of this reserve comprising mountains and flatlands touching the Mexican border southwest of Phoenix. It may be out of the way but is worth visiting for the variety of desert plants that thrive here—including the namesake cactus, which is common in Mexico but not found in the United States outside of this region. The prime flowering time for the large cacti is May and June.

How to Get There

From Phoenix, take Interstate 10 west for about 25 miles (past the urban area) and turn south onto Arizona Route 85. This highway passes through the town of Gila Bend (37 miles from the interstate) and continues south through Ajo and Why. Just south of Why, the road enters the national monument. The total distance from Phoenix to the park boundary is just over 115 miles.

From Tucson, drive west on Arizona Route 86. This highway leads directly to the village of Why, with most of the drive spent in the large Tohono O'Odham (formerly Papago) Indian reservation, passing through several small communities. From Tucson to Why, the distance is 119 miles. Turn south at Why onto Arizona Route 85 and you'll be inside the monument within a few minutes.

Things to See & Do

In addition to the organ pipe cactus, the monument has stands of saguaro, prickly pear, cholla, hedgehog, and barrel cacti (26 species of cacti), as well as ocotillo and several varieties of trees including palo verde and ironwood. Organ Pipe is unusual in that it contains two Sonoran desert zones: Lower Colorado (hot and dry) and Arizona Upland (where most of the large cacti are found). Each area contains plants and harbors animals of its regions. In addition, the park has a few additional plant species that have migrated from Mexico and are not found elsewhere in either of the U.S. desert regions. This unusual confluence of desert ecosystems makes the monument a special place indeed, and several days are required to fully explore the area.

• Park Services and Trails

The visitor center and other park services are located near the southern edge of the park. Several of the shorter trails are in this area, with trailheads at the visitor center and at the campground. There are picnic areas on several of the park sideroads, two of which offer extensive loop drives.

The campground located a few minutes' drive south of the visitor center is open year-round. It has water, restrooms, grills and a dump station. The park amphitheater is a short walk from the camp sites. The short trails within this vicinity offer good desert walks with views of the nearby Ajo and Sonoyta mountain ranges.

The **Palo Verde Trail** leads between the campground and visitor center, a 1.3-mile (one way) walk. The **Visitor Center Trail** is a 1-mile round-trip trail that is wheelchair-accessible and is a self-guiding introduction to the desert scene. The **Perimeter Trail** circles the campground (1 mile, round trip).

The **Desert View Trail** is another loop trail leading from the campground, heading west with views of the Sonoyta Valley and the Cubabi Mountains across the Mexican border.

Another trail offers a 4-mile round-trip walk to and from the **Victoria Mine**, one of several gold and silver mines that operated within the monument area in the early 1900s. This trail heads south from the Campground Perimeter Trail.

The longest trail in the park (**Estes Canyon–Bull Pasture Trail**—4.1 miles, round trip) is found off the Ajo Mountain Drive, climbing to a high plateau where ranchers once kept cattle during winter months.

• Driving through the Monument

The two maintained loop roads provide your best opportunity for fully exploring the variety of plant and animal life in the park, as well as catching some fine desert and foothills scenery.

The **Ajo Mountain Drive** skirts the foothills of this range of 4,000-foot-high mountains on the eastern side of the monument. This is where the best stands of organ pipe cactus are found, along with other plant varieties. After turning onto the sideroad, the drive leads around a one-way loop. There are three picnic areas along the drive. The first, in the hills, provides a view of Tillotson Peak (el. 3,374 feet). The second is located at Angel Canyon, the farthest point along the loop road. Next is the trailhead for the Estes Canyon–Bull Pasture Trail, with the third picnic area located across the road from the trailhead. The Ajo range is to the east, with the Diablo Mountains directly to the west of the picnic area. The road then leads across the Sonoyta Valley, returning to Highway 85.

The **Puerto Blanco Drive** leads around the Puerto Blanco Mountains, providing a wide range of scenery along the 53-mile route. Plan for at least a half-day for this drive, which should include a stop at a desert oasis (Quitobaquito Springs). This is a one-way gravel route beginning at the visitor center. After passing along the northern foothills of the mountain range, the road reaches the site of the former Golden Bell Mine. There's a picnic area at Bonito Well and the oasis is virtually on the Mexican border. Puerto Blanco Drive continues east from the springs, running beside the border to Highway 85.

Where to Stay

Aside from the campground, there is no place to stay inside Organ Pipe. There are minimal lodgings in Lukeville (at the border crossing) or in Why and Ajo. Gila Bend, 75 miles from the park visitor center, is your best place to stay, with several motels and restaurants in this town.

For more park information, write the Superintendent, Organ Pipe Cactus National Monument, Rt. 1, Box 100, Ajo, AZ 85321, or call (602) 387-6849.

Arizona

Page & Lake Powell

Because Page was founded in 1957—a project city built for the construction of the Glen Canyon Dam—it's a prosaic community lacking historical mileposts. However, the scenery on all sides of Page is spectacular, and this modern community of 7,000 people serves as a base for explorations of scenic and geological wonders including the Grand Canyon, Rainbow Bridge, and the shores of Lake Powell, plus several historical treasures: the nearby Hopi and Navajo reservations and the Lee's Ferry Landing site.

The town sits on a mesa overlooking the dam and Wahweap Bay. Lake Powell and the surrounding land make up the Glen Canyon National Recreation Area, managed by the National Park Service. The main visitor center for the recreation area is at the Bullfrog Marina, halfway up the lake. The Park Service also operates a self-guided tour of the Glen Canyon Dam, just outside Page, and several smaller seasonal information offices at Lee's Ferry (south of Page near Marble Canyon), Dangling Rope, Hall's Crossing, and Hite Marina.

There are modern lodgings operated by the park concessionaire, ARA Leisure Services—Wahweap Lodge (6 miles north of Page), Bullfrog Resort and Marina, Hall's Crossing Marina, and Hite Marina (at the north end of Lake Powell). The same company rents houseboats and powerboats, conducts raft trips through Glen Canyon from the dam to Lee's Ferry, and offers an all-day cruise to Rainbow Bridge National Monument. For information and reservations, call 800-528-6154.

Several campgrounds are operated by the National Park Service, and there are commercial RV parks at Wahweap, Bullfrog, and Hall's Crossing. There's a campground at Lee's Ferry, south of town (see day-trip below). Camping is permitted along the shoreline of Lake Powell, with a 14-day limit; there are also several primitive campgrounds accessible by car, including one at Hite Marina.

Scenic Drives from Page
• To the North Rim of the Grand Canyon

The most scenic drive of all is the half-day (one way) trip to the North Rim. For a description of this route, see the scenic drive

Destinations

starting on page 174. The route passes the Lee's Ferry historic site, where you can see from water level the Colorado River flowing into the Grand Canyon, as well as have an opportunity to tour the former Lee homestead. This should not be considered as a day-trip, however. Once you're on the North Rim, you'll want to stay to walk the several trails and camp or stay overnight at the Grand Canyon Lodge.

• Day-Trip to Lee's Ferry

If the North Rim is too far away for comfort, the shorter trip to Lee's Ferry is highly recommended. This can easily be done in a half-day round trip from Page—by taking Highway 89 south as far as Bitter Springs (25 miles) and then turning west on Alternate Route 89. Drive across the Cornfield Valley for another 14 miles until you cross the Colorado River on the Navajo Bridge. This is Marble Canyon (the village and the canyon). Turn right onto a sideroad that leads to the Lee's Ferry site. The historic homestead is on view at the end of the road.

At Paria Beach you may stop and dip your toes in the Colorado River as it enters the beginning of the Grand Canyon. You may launch your boat and fish in the river. There's a campground here, operated by the Parks Service as part of the Glen Canyon National Recreation Area. The campground provides picnic tables with a view of the river, and the road into the site features several interesting rock formations, notably the collection of balanced rocks.

• Hopi Reservation Day-Trip

The Hopi mesas lie to the east of Page, providing a 181-mile day-trip with a cultural focus. To travel to the Hopi Reservation, take Highway 89 south to The Gap and turn east onto U.S. Route 160, and then drive to Tuba City (10 miles) and turn right on Arizona Route 264. Near the intersection is Moenkopi, a small village. Another 14 miles takes you to the Coal Canyon Overlook, and the road continues through several Hopi villages including Hotevilla, Old Oraibi, and Shongopovi. Old Oraibi is considered to be the oldest continually inhabited settlement on the continent.

Arizona

Continue on the same road to **Second Mesa**. This village has an intriguing Cultural Center along with eating places and shops selling silver and other Hopi products. Drive north on Navajo Road 43 to Pinion. Part of this section of the drive is over gravel road. The Pinion Trading Post is a popular store.

Then take Navajo Road 41 from Pinion to Highway 160, passing the coal mines of Peabody Coal—with the world's longest conveyor belt taking coal to a railhead for transport to the Navajo Generating Station. The Black Mesa and Lake Powell Railroad operates the efficient, electrified train system.

From the Hwy. 160 intersection, drive 9 miles to the **Navajo National Monument**. There's a visitor center near the Betatakin Ruin, the ancient home of an Anasazi community. Returning to Highway 160, drive 12 miles southwest to Highway 98, turn right and drive the last 66 miles to Page. Along the way there are several overlooks with views of Navajo Mountain and Bryce Canyon in the distance.

Phoenix & the Valley of the Sun

Phoenix is a huge city. But then, Phoenix is more than Phoenix—it's also Tempe, Scottsdale, Glendale, Peoria, and Chandler, among the 22 sprawling suburbs and other cities that surround Phoenix. The urban area is so vast and interrelated that it's called The Valley of the Sun, a touristy term that refers to the 300 or so days of sunlight the area receives each year and ties the whole region together as one destination.

You know this is a city made for visitors when you see golf courses everywhere—more than 100 in the Phoenix area and many with their own deluxe resort hotels. Add to golf the prospect of desert Jeep rides or balloon flights and endless shopping places, and you have the basis for a vacation of a different kind. Of course, Phoenix and its suburbs do not have the Old West feeling of a place like Tucson, or the cultural and gustatory focus of Santa Fe. Phoenix makes up for this lack of history and ethnic diversity with a bustling atmosphere tempered with relaxed resort life.

Destinations

First let's get the various major urban areas figured out. Phoenix is the southcentral portion of the Valley of the Sun. Scottsdale stretches along the immediate east side of Phoenix, with Tempe south of Scottsdale. Fountain Hills and Mesa are yet farther east. Glendale is due west of Phoenix with Sun City, El Mirage, and Sun City West beyond Glendale.

The rustic mountain towns called Carefree and Cave Creek are just north of Scottsdale and Phoenix. The Boulders, a fine resort with unusual architecture in a spectacular setting, is set in these hills. To the south of the larger cities is a welter of smaller communities including Chandler, Guadalupe, Tolleson, Goodyear, Avondale, and another score of little towns all jumbled together in the wide desert valley.

Think of Phoenix as the downtown for the Valley of the Sun. Scottsdale is the ritzy neighbor with most of the deluxe resorts and sprawling mansion communities. Tempe is the seat of learning (Arizona State University is here). The two Sun Cities are where retirees have come to roost, taking advantage of the year-round warmth of the valley. Carefree (a modern planned community) is next door to Cave Creek. The two towns are as different as night from day, for Cave Creek is a rustic old pioneer town.

In 1860, Phoenix was a village on the banks of the Salt River, the site of ancient settlements of the Hohokam Indians. The Hohokam, thought to be ancestors to the Pima Indians, lived in the area from about AD 300 until AD 1450. There is no record of them after that, and only a few ruins remain to remind modern-day Phoenicians of their existence. There are now about 2.2 million people in the valley, and the area is still growing.

In the next few pages, we'll cover a few of the highlights of the Phoenix area. For more details and help in planning your visit to the Valley of the Sun, contact the Phoenix and Valley of the Sun Convention & Visitors Bureau—call 800-528-0483. The main information center is located at One Arizona Center, 400 E. Van Buren, Suite 600, Phoenix, AZ 85004-2292. The center is open Monday through Friday from 8 AM to 5 PM.

Another information center is at the northeast corner of Adams and Second Streets, in the Hyatt Regency Block, open from 8:30 AM to 5 PM. For general information on current activities, call (602) 254-6500.

• City Parks

There are two distinctive parks in the area that offer quiet walks and other things to do—both situated in the desert environment. **South Mountain Park** is the largest municipal park in the world. It is located south of the Salt River, off Interstate 10. A second entrance, an extension of Central Avenue, leads through a large portion of the park, offering a drive to the Summit Lookout.

Papago Park is a desert area shared by the cities of Phoenix and Tempe. In addition to the picnic areas and hiking trails, the park houses the Phoenix Zoo, an 18-hole golf course, and the Desert Botanical Garden. You could easily spend a complete day exploring the attractions of Papago Park. The botanical garden has indoor and outdoor displays of every desert plant imaginable, including a 3-acre exhibit that has displays of the historic uses of Sonoran Desert plants. Sixty-fourth Street runs through the park (north/south), and either McDowell or Van Buren Street will take you west to the park from downtown Phoenix.

• Museums, Galleries, & Gardens

The **Heard Museum** features an outstanding range of exhibits on the art and culture of southwestern native peoples. Indian artists demonstrate their craft skills daily in the galleries. The museum is located at 22 East Monte Vista Road, (602) 252-8848. The **Phoenix Art Museum** is the Southwest's largest art gallery—featuring paintings, photography, sculpture, and fashion from the Renaissance to modern times, plus a children's gallery. The museum is at 1625 N. Central Avenue, (602) 257-1222.

The **Arizona State Capitol Museum** (1700 West Washington St.) celebrates the history of the state capitol building—built in 1900 and restored to its 1912 appearance. The museum is open weekdays from 8 AM to 5 PM, (602) 542-4675.

There are two notable Indian cultural centers in the area portraying the cultural history of the tribes that settled the area before the European settlement. The **Hoo-hoogam Ki Museum** is located on the Salt River Indian Reservation, a few minutes' drive east of

Destinations

Scottsdale. The museum features displays with artifacts from the Pima and Maricopa tribes. For information, phone (602) 941-7379. Pima and Maricopa culture is also on display at the **Gila River Indian Arts and Crafts Center**, which is found 30 miles south of Phoenix via Interstate 10 (exit 175), at Sacaton. There is a botanical park and a gift shop, with accommodations available. Call (602) 963-3981.

Pueblo Grande Museum and Cultural Park (4919 E. Washington St., Phoenix) is the site of Hohokam ruins that were occupied from AD 1 through AD 1450. Some exhibits show excavated material and some highlight other aspects of Native American culture. Call (602) 495-0901.

Desert Center at Pinnacle Peak is a desert garden open daily for self-guided tours. It is in Scottsdale, at 8711 E. Pinnacle Peak Road. Call (602) 585-5743 for a recorded message. Those interested in impressionist art will enjoy a visit to the **Fleisher Museum**, in the Perimeter Center at 17207 N. Perimeter Dr., Scottsdale. The museum is dedicated to showing the work of the California School of American impressionist artists. More than 200 works are on display. The gallery is open daily from 10 AM to 4 PM but is closed on holidays, (602) 585-3108.

The **Pioneer Arizona Living History Museum** is located north of the city, via Interstate 17. Here, a complex of restored pioneer buildings displays early life in the state. People in period costumes populate the old buildings, which include a bank, opera house, miners' camp, and a Victorian home.

• Other Things to See & Do

Apache Greyhound Park, the dog racing track, is in Apache Junction, 17 miles east of Phoenix. The track features racing Thursdays through Mondays from October to May. For information, call (602) 982-2371 or 244-2729.

Cave Creek and Carefree are neighboring mountain villages north of the city, offering shopping and dining. Cave Creek dates back to the 1800s and has much of its old mining town flavor. Carefree is a modern upscale residential community. There are several old-timey eating places (saloons) in Cave Creek, and this scenic area is a fine place to visit, particularly near the end of the day.

Set in the foothills of the McDowell Mountains, **Taliesin West** is a national historic landmark—the winter home, studio, and school founded by architect Frank Lloyd Wright. This outstanding example of Wright's style is open daily for guided tours: October–May, Mon.–Thurs. from 1 PM to 4 PM, Fri., Sat., and Sun. from 9 AM to 4 PM; June–September, 8 AM to 11 AM.

Phoenix Area Resorts

There are two five-star resorts here: **Marriott's Camelback Inn Resort, Golf Club and Spa** (602-948-1700) and the **The Wigwam Resort** (602-935-3811). Both are famed for their deluxe lodgings, super-attentive service, wonderful locations, and fine food. If you need to know how much you'll spend at these resorts, you can't afford to stay. The Wigwam, with 229 adobe-style units and three golf courses, was founded in 1929 as the first ultra-deluxe resort in the area.

Then there are the top-level resorts, which offer recreation, beautiful views, fine food, and mingling with the beautiful people. All are in the deluxe price range, with rates from $115 to $250 per day (for two). These include **The Boulders**, with perhaps the finest desert setting in the area—at Carefree, north of the main urban area. There are jogging and hiking trails, several pools, and visitors stay in 136 adobe-style casitas (602-488-9009).

The **Sheraton San Marcos** is a Spanish-style complex with a golf course, tennis center, and fountain courtyards (602-963-6655). The **Scottsdale Princess** (800-223-1818) is next to the Phoenix Tournament Players Golf Course, the home of the annual Phoenix Open. The resort has three pools, a spa, and tennis courts, with a 400-acre horse park next door.

Mountain Shadows, in Scottsdale, is yet another superb golfing resort, with two 18-hole courses and a tennis complex (602-948-7111). Hilton has three **Pointe Hilton** resorts—Squaw Peak (602-997-2626), Tapatio

Cliffs (602-866-7500) and South Mountain (602-438-9000). All three have scenic mountainside locations.

This listing only touches the surface of the resort industry in the Phoenix area. The Convention and Visitors Bureau has information on them all. Many hotels in Phoenix, Tempe, Mesa, and Scottsdale have slightly more modest accommodation, including excellent bargains at some very fine hotels. These finds include the **Red Lion Posada Resort** (Scottsdale, 800-547-8010), the **Scottsdale Plaza** (602-948-5000), the **Sheraton Mission Palms Hotel** (Tempe, near the university, 602-894-1400), and the **Camelhead Embassy Suites** (Phoenix, 800-447-8483).

Scenic Drives from Phoenix
• Apache Trail

At the eastern edge of the greater Phoenix area, the Superstition Mountains provide a backdrop for great sunrises. The best scenic drive in the area leads behind this range, over the old **Apache Trail**. For a description of this drive to Roosevelt Lake (one of several lakes along the Salt River route), see pages 186 to 189. The log for this drive begins in Apache Junction, 17 miles east of the city via Highway 60/89.

• Pinal Pioneer Parkway

Another scenic drive featured earlier in this Arizona section (page 194) provides the scenic way to get to Tucson. To get to Florence Junction (the start of the southbound drive), take the same route (60/89) east from Phoenix and continue for 16 miles past Apache Junction. Turn south toward Florence and you'll soon be at the start of the Pioneer Parkway.

One point of interest along the way is the Tom Mix Memorial, at the spot where the venerated western movie star left this mortal coil. It is truly a touching experience for movie fans, made most interesting because of the adjacent desert plants. There is a picnic spot at the memorial site.

There are several additional picnic areas. Trees and shrubs along the route are marked with botanical information.

Arizona

Sedona & the Verde Valley

Sedona is admired by some and derided by others for its New Age consciousness. Completely surrounded by the Coconino National Forest, the ethereal quality of the red landscape and the southwestern light has brought together a population of laid-back souls who seem to operate more crystal shops and New Age establishments here than anywhere else on the continent. Maybe some of the off-the-wall local atmosphere comes as a result of Zane Grey's writings and surrealist artist Max Ernst living and painting here.

To be serious about Sedona, the red rock landscape here fills one with wonder, and Sedona has taken advantage of this superb natural setting to become a resort community of some stature. It's a new town— incorporated in 1988—with a full range of amenities, including plush resorts such as Enchantment and Poco Diablo, plus many motels, more than a dozen bed and breakfasts, and shop-till-you-drop boutique plazas in different parts of town. The golfing is challenging and scenic, and there are restaurants of every kind, including two superb Mexican establishments. Above all, the scenery is staggering—particularly on the Red Rock Loop Road, just south of town.

At the northern edge of the Verde Valley, Sedona has developed as one of the most remarkable resort towns in the West. The epitome of enlightenment, with harmonic convergence around every corner, this town owes its popularity more to the beautiful red rock environment than to any spiritual awakening that might be achieved here. Call me cynical if you wish, because thousands of visitors come to Sedona each year to seek out something special happening here—I just haven't yet discovered what it is. However, the natural beauty of the area more than makes up for any psychic disappointment one might suffer while fruitlessly searching for a charge from purported energy vortexes.

Adventurers came into this remote area as early as the mid-1800s and a post office was established in 1902, but because of the difficulties in transporting food and other materials into the area, Sedona remained a small village until the 1950s. Earlier, during the '20s and '30s,

Hollywood discovered the huge red rock amphitheater in which the town of Sedona now sits. First Zane Grey's *Call of the Canyon* was turned into a film here, and then other westerns were shot in the region through the next two decades.

After World War II, the area became a retirement haven, and artists led by Max Ernst came to the valley to paint the surrealistic scenery. The Sedona Arts Center was founded in 1968. In 1984 the population was 7,500; it was not until 1988 that the city was incorporated.

Thus, one of the newest cities in the U.S. has become one of the most popular vacation centers for Arizonans, as well as attracting thousands of annual visitors from afar. Tourism caused a jump in population, and now about 15,000 people live in this city, which is like almost any other small western town, except for its magnificent geological scenery. The older towns of the area are to the south: Clarkdale, Jerome and Prescott. Jerome is a near ghost town while Sedona flourishes in the light of the New Age.

The **Chamber of Commerce Information Center** is located on the corner of Highway 89A and Forest Road, at the north end of town. This is the area known as Uptown Sedona—filled with both chic and rustic boutiques, restaurants, and creek-side motels.

How to Get There

Located south of Flagstaff, the **Oak Creek Canyon** is a fine introduction to the area, with forest camping, historic sites, and joyful children sliding down the natural chute at Slide Rock State Park. Highway 89A leads into the canyon, through the Coconino National Forest. This short drive (27 miles) offers a full day of interesting things to see and do. The whole drive is a changing spectacle of steep canyonsides and wooded valley.

From Phoenix, the shortest way to travel to Sedona is via **Interstate 17** and then north into the Verde Valley on **Arizona Route 179**. If you have a day to spare, the more scenic route from Phoenix is via U.S. Highway 60 through Wickenburg and Prescott, entering the valley by taking Highway 89A across Mingus Mountain.

For details on this route, see the scenic drive that begins on page 182 and read the highway log in reverse.

Things to See and Do

• Red Rock Splendor

Psychic energy vortexes aside, this is what we come to Sedona to see: the magnificent ridges, cliffs, peaks, and pinnacles formed of dark red rock. There are several conglomerations of rocks to admire. Stretching behind the town is the longest display, with the **Cockscomb** at the left (to the south), **Chimney Rock** slightly to the right and in front, **Capitol Butte** (with a rounded top looking as if it should be the Capitol dome in Washington), **Sugar Loaf** in the center, **Coffee Pot Rock** sticking out from Sugar Loaf, and then to the right the **Mt. Wilson** area, with **Steamboat Rock** at the extreme right side.

A tour of Schnerby Hill Drive (off Hwy. 179 at the north end of town) leads past **Elephant Rock** and **Snoopy Rock**. Snoopy looks, from certain angles, like the cartoon dog, lying on his back with feet and nose in the air. Farther down Hwy. 179 is **Submarine Rock**. The Chapel of the Holy Cross (see below) is atop another rock beside the **Two Nuns**. Take Chapel Road to see this formation and the church. Farther south are **Bell Rock** and **Courthouse Butte**.

Cathedral Rock, considered by most the finest formation of them all, is best viewed from the Red Rock Loop Road (see below).

The **Chapel of the Holy Cross** sits on the rocks—a startlingly modern chapel that contrasts with its natural environment. The chapel is located three miles south of the intersection of Highways 179 and 89A (call 602-282-4069).

• Outdoor Recreation

If you haven't driven through **Oak Creek Canyon** on your way to Sedona, you should head north of town—to picnic at a forest table; to sun on and slide down the rocks at Slide Rock State Park; to see the Indian Gardens, the site of an abandoned farm of the Yavapai tribe, later made into a ranch by settler John Thompson (in 1876); to hike on one or more of the 10 national forest trails which climb up to and along the rim of the canyon; to camp in a choice of six

Destinations

campgrounds—the largest being Cave Springs with 78 sites, 11 of which are available by reservation (call 800-283-2267); to hook your trailer or RV to services in a shady RV park; to fish for trout in the creek—it's stocked regularly during the summer months and fish are guaranteed every day at the Rainbow Trout Farm; and to shop in one of a steady line of boutiques as the highway enters the built-up Sedona area. There are several motels plus bed and break-fast homes in this same area north of town.

The **Sedona Ranger Station**, located on Brewer Road (call 602-282-4119) is open weekdays and is a good place to obtain information on Forest Service facilities including trails and campgrounds in the area.

The prime red rock views are best seen by taking the **Red Rock Loop Road**, off Hwy. 89A, just south of town. You can access the area by taking either the upper or lower road. Lower Red Rock Road is the paved portion, leading to **Red Rock State Park**. The park sits in the midst of the red rock peaks, with the creek flowing below the park information center, which doubles as an environmental education facility. There are picnic areas and trails, open during daylight hours.

Golfers will find four courses within a short drive of town. **Oak Creek Country Club** and **Sedona Golf Resort** are 18-hole championship courses, both open to the public. **Poco Diablo Resort** and the **Canyon Mesa Country Club** have 9-hole executive courses.

• In Sedona

Art shows are held at almost any time during the year. The **Sedona Arts Center** holds a changing schedule of shows, including exhibitions by members of the Artists & Craftsmen Guild in the center's Upper Gallery. The **Hopi Artists Gathering** is an annual event, showcasing Hopi Indian art and crafts. There's a theater wing in this same building, staging performances during the summer months and from October through April. For Arts Center information, call (602) 282-3809. There are 40 commercial galleries; most are geared to western and contemporary tastes.

There are several popular music festivals, including Jazz on the Rocks, held each September, and two classical festivals: Symphony in the Park, with performances by the Flagstaff Symphony, and the Sedona Chamber Music Festival. **Tlaquepaque** is a Spanish/Mexican-inspired shopping and eating complex, at the north end of Sedona. It is also the scene of theatrical shows and several annual festivals including the Fiesta del Tlaquepaque, a Mexican festival (October) and Festival of Lights (December).

• Jeep Tours

Jeeping has become *the* thing to do while visiting Sedona. More than a dozen tour operators will rent you a 4WD vehicle or take you on a trip through the red rock canyons and high country. Some of the most popular tours are arranged by Pink Jeeps—call 800-8-SEDONA or (602) 262-5000.

Sedona Adventures (800-888-9494 or 602-282-3500) also has Jeep tours of the area, including their Vortex Quest trips through the Coconino National Forest and a Sedona night-life tour.

Other tours are available—by horseback, in hot air balloons, and also on fixed-wing airplane and helicopter flights.

• In the Verde Valley

Fort Verde State Historic Park is southwest of Sedona in Camp Verde. It's located off Interstate 17, via Arizona Route 260. This fort was occupied by General George Crook and his troops during the Indian campaigns in the 1870s. Now restored, it provides a look into the military history of the area. For information call (602) 567-3275.

257

There are two Indian ruins open to the public and in the same general area, 35 miles south of Sedona. **Montezuma Castle National Monument** is one of the best preserved Indian cliff dwellings in the Southwest. For information, call (602) 567-3322. **Tuzigoot National Monument** is a prehistoric ruin, occupied by the Sinagua Indians in the 1200s. Its location is between Cottonwood and Clarkdale, south of Sedona via Highway 89A (602-634-5564).

Destinations

• Verde River Canyon Excursion Train

While the canyons near Sedona are accessible by car, the Verde River Canyon is not. However, a scenic railroad pulled by diesel locomotives makes the trip through the canyon from the depot at Clarkdale. The line runs past the red cliffs, over high bridges to Perkinsville. It was originally built to transport ore between the mines at Jerome and the Chino Valley. The train leaves Clarkdale at 1 PM and returns around 5 PM. During the summer, it departs at 10 AM, returning at 2 PM. During April, May, and October, there are two trips per day: at 9 AM and 2:30 PM. For details and reservations, call (602) 639-0010. The depot is 25 miles from downtown Sedona via Highway 89A.

• Jerome

Perched halfway up Cleopatra Hill (part of Mingus Mountain), Jerome is an old mining town that has survived as an artists' colony. The town seems destined to fall down the slope but it hangs on for dear life, in more ways than one. Founded in 1876, the town sits above what was the largest copper mine in Arizona. Fifteen thousand people lived here in 1929 (far more than in Sedona) and the town prospered until the mines and the mining economy began petering out during the Great Depression. The last mine folded in 1953. Artists discovered the decaying community during the mid-1960s, and painters and craftspeople moved into the cliffside houses and established shops selling southwestern art and crafts, including trinkets and gewgaws fashioned from copper, silver, and gold. There are several places with character in which to eat but, alas, only one place to stay—the **Miners Roost Hotel**. The hotel has several Victorian rooms with shared baths, and a restaurant and saloon downstairs. Other accommodations are located in nearby Clarkdale and Cottonwood.

Jerome State Historic Park is just off Highway 89A, on a ridge. The mansion here was built in 1917 by James "Rawhide Jimmy" Douglas, for a short time the owner of the Little Daisy Mine. The house holds displays of local mining history, and a walk through the grounds offers several views of the town and the Verde Valley below. Major landmarks are identified on placards at the viewpoints. More local history is told in the **Jerome Historical Society Mine Museum**. This building from the turn of the century has exhibits on the town's growth and industry when it was the booming copper camp, plus a book and gift shop.

Where to Eat

• In Sedona

Except for Santa Fe, Sedona has the Southwest's best eating. There are fine restaurants in the resorts including **Enchantment**, **L'Auberge de Sedona**, and the **Willow Room** at Poco Diablo Resort. Some of the most adventuresome places to eat in the entire West are in and around Sedona. **Oaxaca** is a very good Mexican restaurant on Hwy. 89A, at the north end of town ($$). The breakfasts here are particularly enticing. Tlaquepaque, the Spanish colonial shopping complex, has two excellent restaurants: **Rene** and **Rincon del Tlaquepaque**. The former serves French and American cuisine. Rincon serves Arizona variations of standard Mexican cuisine; the patio is wonderfully shaded by sycamores. Both restaurants are in the $$ to $$$ range.

Orchards Grill, uptown on Hwy. 89A, serves an array of "southwestern" dishes, ranging from duck sausage pizza to Cajun seafood. From the treed entrance to the crisp tablecloths and attentive service, this grill does it as it is supposed to be done ($$ to $$$). **Bell Rock Inn**, 7 miles south of town at 6246 Hwy. 179, serves American cuisine in a setting offering fine red rock views. A patio and lounge complement the main indoor restaurant ($$). **Page Springs Bar and Restaurant** is a casual steak, soup and salad place, beside Oak Creek, via Hwy. 89A and Page Springs Road ($ to $$).

259

• In Jerome

You can dine at **Betty's Ore House Cafe** (a coffee shop) and at **The Hacienda** (Mexican). Barbecue is served at the **Jerome Palace**, which has a quaint bar. **Mary's European Coffeehouse and Bakery** is a real find—serving pastry, muffins, Danish, and croissants with coffee and tea.

Destinations

Tombstone

The Town Too Tough to Die was without doubt one of the most lawless mining camps in the American West. From this one-time city of 10,000 (miners, merchants, floozies, cowboys and rustlers, itinerant thugs, saloon keepers, and—in general—a lot of just plain unsavory people), the controversial legend of the shootout at the O.K. Corral and tales of numerous other deaths by misadventure have developed (some apocryphal) over the past 110 years.

It all began rather calmly when, in 1877, silver was discovered in large quantities by prospector Ed Schiefflin. By 1879 it had become a town and was named by Schiefflin when a friend commented that "the only thing you'll find out there will be your own tombstone." Millions of dollars worth of silver were extracted each year, but within a decade it was all over—at least the mining was finished. Cattle ranching kept the town going but the population dwindled and most of the buildings decayed. But in the mid-1900s, tourists discovered the one-time home of the Earps and Clantons. Historic buildings were repaired and restored. Boot Hill, the first cemetery to be so named, became a top attraction and the famed shootout was re-enacted to thrill visitors.

It's now a prime attraction on anybody's tour of southeastern Arizona, with saloons and distinctive restaurants. The old courthouse has become a museum of Wild West history and the whole town has been designated a national historic landmark.

How to Get There

Tombstone is 70 miles southeast of Tucson, and is easily reached via Interstate 10 to Benson and then south from Benson on Arizona Route 80. The town lies on the scenic drive described on page 198.

Things to See and Do

The Boot Hill Graveyard is a must. The cemetery holds the graves of many of Tombstone's bad men, as well as most of the early settlers of the mining camp. Most of the historic buildings are along the boardwalks that line **Allen Street,** one block west of the highway. Gunfights and barroom brawls are staged along Allen Street on several Sundays each month. The **Bird Cage Theater**, from 1881 the home of bawdy entertainment—a dance hall, saloon, theater, brothel and gambling house—has no performances today but is open for tours. Bullet holes score the theater's old walls.

The **Crystal Palace Saloon** is an 1879 watering hole and gambling den that has been faithfully restored; the long back-bar is not the original but a fine replica. The saloon is open daily for drinking and eating, with entertainment on weekends.

The **O.K. Corral and Historama** provides a 30-minute presentation which re-creates Tombstone's early years with films and animated figures on a revolving stage. Next door to the Historama is the corral where it is said the legendary gunfight between the Earp and Clanton brothers and Doc Holliday took place (it didn't). The fight actually took place on what is now a vacant lot near the corral on Fremont St. There are life-sized figures that portray the five men (three dead and two wounded) during the gunfight. Nearby there are several other historic buildings including the photographic studio of C. S. Fly, which has a showing of historic photos. An admission fee is charged for these attractions.

An old 1880s home is now the **Rose Tree Inn Museum**. In the courtyard is a rose tree more than 100 years old—reputed to be the world's largest. Covering a huge arbor (8,000 square feet) the old rose plant blooms each April.

A large brick structure at the corner of Toughnut and Third Streets, the **Tombstone Courthouse** was built in 1882. It's now a state historic park and museum filled with artifacts and photographs of the 1880s. The town gallows is on display in the courtyard, and the gift shop is the best place in town to buy books on the history of the town and region. You can visit the old offices of the *Tombstone Epitaph* to see how pioneer newspapers were produced and purchase a souvenir copy of the second-oldest continuously published paper in Arizona.

The **Silver Nugget Museum** is another commercial museum, commemorating a gambling den and brothel that has been restored and is replete with authentic Victorian furnishings.

In addition to these attractions, there are period restaurants, souvenir stores, and a tour of the **Good Enough Silver Mine** under Tombstone's streets, entered through a mining museum and gift shop.

There are several small motels close to the historic area, plus a Best Western on the highway. Three B & B homes also offer accommodation (see the Places to Stay pages). There are three campgrounds: a KOA and two RV parks.

Where to Eat

Among the dozen or so eating places in town are several saloons on Allen Street. Perhaps the most intriguing of Tombstone's eating places is the **Bella Union**, an 1881 opera house and saloon that serves lunch and features live dinner shows with singers in period costumes. There's also a Sunday buffet. The Bella Union serves draft beer, like most of the eating places here. For reservations, call (602) 457-3543 or 457-3656. The **Lucky Cuss Restaurant** specializes in mesquite-grilled barbecued ribs and other western food. **Vogan's Alley Bar** (on Allen, two doors west of 5th) serves good burgers and beer, with "breakfast" served on Friday and Saturday nights from midnight until 2 AM.

The **Longhorn**, on the corner of Allen and 5th, is a popular place with locals, serving normal American food in a slightly rustic setting. **Don Teodoro's** serves Mexican dishes for lunch and dinner, with brunch on weekends.

Tucson

Renowned for its ample supply of sunshine (350 days each year) and moderately warm climate during winter months, Tucson is not the sleepy desert town imagined by most people who haven't been there. It is a fast-growing city of nearly 700,000 people, and yet it has maintained the small-town atmosphere that endeared the community to the Spanish, then Mexican settlers, and in 1846 the Americans. Of course Europeans weren't the first people to live here; this portion of the Sonoran Desert was originally home to the Hohokam Indians, who farmed the area during the first century AD, and then was the homeland of the Pima and

Arizona

Sobaipuri tribes. For a short time, during the Civil War, the Confederate flag flew over Tucson—before Arizona gained territorial status in 1863. Three historic districts—all in the downtown area—offer different viewpoints of the city's heritage.

Popular day-trips from Tucson include drives to the Tombstone/Bisbee area southeast of the city in Cochise County and south via I-19 to Nogales and the Mexican border.

How to Get There

From Phoenix: The city is 111 miles southeast of Phoenix via Interstate 10. A slightly longer but more scenic route involves driving east from Phoenix on U.S. Highway 60 and then turning south onto U.S. Hwy. 89 at Florence Junction. From Florence, the route is known as the Pinal Pioneer Parkway. This tour is featured in our scenic drives (page 194).

From Southern California and Yuma: Tucson is 184 miles southeast of Yuma (at the California border), via Interstate 8 and then Interstate 10. There is an alternate route that has the benefit of providing a tour of Organ Pipe Cactus National Monument. For this drive, leave Interstate 8 at Gila Bend (exit 118) and head south on Arizona Route 85. This road continues south from the village of Why into Organ Pipe Cactus. Route 86 leads east from Why through the large Tohono O'Odham Indian reservation.

From El Paso: Head west on Interstate 10.

What to See & Do
• Historic Districts

Within a ten-square-block area are three historic districts that provide fine walking tours. The best place to start is the **Convention and Visitors Bureau,** at 130 S. Scott Ave. There are maps of the historic districts here, as well as material on other Tucson-area attractions. The information center is located in a 1928 building, originally the Thomas-Davis Clinic. Bordered by Pennington, Granada, and Speedway, the **El Presidio District** includes several original buildings from the Spanish colonial period, in addition to buildings constructed by the earliest European leaders of Tucson

Destinations

society. **El Presidio Park** was the site selected by Lt. Col. Hugo Oconor (actually Hugh O'Connor, an Irishman working for the Spanish Army) for the new frontier presidio, called Plaza de las Armas. The Vietnam Veterans Memorial is in this park. North of the park is **La Casa Cordova**, one of the oldest buildings in the city. It has been restored as a Mexican heritage museum.

The exhibits in the **Tucson Museum of Art** include pre-Columbian artifacts, Spanish colonial art and furniture, and modern works. Around the corner on Main Street is the Janos Restaurant. This building, called the **Stevens Home**, and the **Fish House** (the El Presidio Gallery) at 120 N. Main are two more early homes. The **Steinfeld House**, at 300 N. Main, is a brick/stucco Spanish mission–style home and a fine example of a Tucson mansion from the turn of the century.

The **Barrio Historic District**, south of Cushing St. and the Tucson Convention Center, includes the Cushing Street Bar and Restaurant, named for Army hero Howard Cushing. The building combines the original Joseph Ferrin home and country store, built in the 1880s. The shrine at the corner of Simpson and Main Streets is listed in the National Register of Historic Places.

There are two art centers located in the adjacent **Armory Park Historic District**. The **Temple of Music and Art** was built in 1927 as a stage and movie theater and is now the home of the Arizona Theater Company. It includes a main theater, cabaret, gallery, and restaurant. It's located at 330 S. Scott St.

The **Tucson Children's Museum** (200 S. Sixth Ave.) is a 1901 structure that was the Andrew Carnegie Library. As with several other buildings in the area (including the Steinfeld House), it was designed by architect Henry Trost. **El Fronterizo**, at 471 S. Stone Ave., was the printing plant for the Spanish language newspaper founded in 1878 by Carlos Y. Velasco.

There are two buildings lying outside the official historic districts that nonetheless are fascinating to history buffs. The old **Southern**

264

Pacific Railway Depot (419 Congress St.) is now a Carlos Murphy's restaurant. The **State Building** is across the street at 416 Congress, a striking pink adobe building with an inlaid tile mosaic.

Parks and Gardens

For a city lying on the flat southern desert, Tucson has an amazing variety of natural places that offer superb outdoor rambles. Nearby mountain ranges and hills provide scenic beauty and a habitat for cacti and other desert plants. Man-made gardens in the city range from commercial cactus farms to the city's botanical garden.

• Saguaro National Monument—East

The finest stands of the saguaro cactus in Arizona are found in the two sections of the Saguaro National Monument, lying beyond the eastern and western edges of the city. The larger (and older) portion is located east of town at the end of Old Spanish Trail in the Rincon Mountains. Cactus Forest Drive, an 8-mile loop road, winds through an extensive saguaro forest. The loop begins near the park visitor center and leads in a clockwise direction. A sideroad leads off the loop route to a picnic area at Mica View.

For those who wish to have a walk through the saguaro, a trail leads from the north side of the loop (past the Mica View road) to the visitor center. Nearby, there is the shorter Desert Ecology Trail, which offers a self-guided introduction to desert life. A second picnic area is located on the Javalina sideroad.

The monument is perfect for longer hikes, with more than 75 miles of trails leading through the desert and mountain landscape. Several longer hiking trails climb into the mountains, where the landscape changes from desert scrub and grassland to oak and pine woodlands and—at the top—to a mixed evergreen forest.

265

Backcountry camping is permitted, but only at designated campsites, and permits must be obtained at the visitor center in advance of an overnight trip. Ranger-led programs are offered during winter months. There is a shop with books and park guides for sale, and a slide show about the saguaro, the Sonoran Desert and its wildlife.

Destinations

• Saguaro National Monument—West

This portion of the national monument is located next to Tucson Mountain Park on Kinney Road, in the vicinity of the Old Tucson Studios (theme park) and the Arizona-Sonora Desert Museum. The easiest way to get to Saguaro West is to take Speedway Blvd. from downtown Tucson. The road crosses the Tucson Mountains, after becoming Gates Pass Blvd. Turn right onto Kinney Blvd. and the park is two minutes' drive from the intersection. Another route into Tucson Mountain Park leads from southern Tucson via Ajo Way (Highway 86) and Kinney Road.

The Red Hills Information Center is open daily, offering guided walks during winter months, as well as books and brochures on the park attractions. The 6-mile Bajada Loop Drive passes through a magnificent forest of saguaro, interspersed with other cacti and desert bushes. This unpaved road begins 1/2 mile from the information center and leads in a counterclockwise direction (although portions of the road have two-way traffic). Near the beginning of the route is the Sus picnic area. The Valley View Trail provides a 3/4-mile (one way) walk to a viewpoint where the Avra Valley stretches before you. The loop road continues until it meets Golden Gate Road near Apache Peak. Turn left and you'll soon see a sign for the Signal Hill Picnic Area. This area was used by the prehistoric Hohokam people—probably the ancestors of the Papago Indians. Their petroglyphs are found on rocks near the picnic area. The loop drive continues via Kinney Road, returning to the starting point with the visitor center another two miles on.

Desert animals are often seen, even in the vicinity of the visitor center. Park wildlife includes the abundant kangaroo rat, gopher and coachwhip snakes, the diamondback, javalina (the collared peccary), and varieties of birds including quail, Gila woodpeckers, which live in the saguaro, and thrasher. There are two desert garden areas with interpretive trails close to the visitor center, and longer trails lead into the foothills, where there are several old mine sites, and higher up the mountainsides. Camping is not permitted in this section of the monument.

Arizona

• Sentinel Peak Park

The finest panoramic views of the city and surrounding mountains are seen from several viewpoints on top of the peak called A Mountain for the whitewashed "A" provided by students at the University of Arizona. To see the views (superb day or night), drive 2 miles west of the city on Congress Street and take Sentinel Peak Road. The road loops around the mountain.

• Tucson Mountain Park

Much of the Tucson Mountains is included in this county park, which features stands of saguaro and other desert plants. There are picnic areas, hiking and riding trails, and a campground. The park is 8 miles west of the downtown district via Speedway Blvd. There is no entrance fee. The park is reached by taking Speedway Blvd. west from Tucson, north of the downtown district. From the south end of the city, take State Route 86 west from Interstate 19 and turn north into the park.

Inside Tucson Mountain Park is one of the finest wildlife museums in the country, the **Arizona-Sonora Desert Museum**. More than 200 species of desert animals and birds are housed in realistic settings, and the museum includes pathways that connect botanical gardens filled with desert plants. There's a fine picnic area sheltered with ramadas, in addition to a snack bar and gift shop. For information, call (602) 883-2702.

Old Tucson, a Wild West theme park also used by many studios for filming movies, TV series and commercials, burned to the ground in a spectacular nighttime fire in April 1995. The false-fronted streets of Old Tucson had long been a favorite family attraction. Old Tucson officials were planning to rebuild the attraction when this book went to press.

• Coronado National Forest

This superb area of forest-clad mountains sits northeast of the city, offering several recreation areas that include campgrounds. Narrow **Sabino Canyon** has a marvelous display of desert vegetation beside a creek that cascades down the hills of the Catalina Mountains.

Destinations

A day can easily be spent in the canyon; to get there, take Tanque Verde Road from the city and turn onto Sabino Canyon Road. Visitors park next to the visitor center. From here, you walk, cycle, or ride a horse into the canyon, or take the shuttle train, for which a fee is charged. There are picnic areas and swimming places along the 4-mile paved roadway. There's also a trail that leads for about 12 miles to the top of Mount Lemmon.

There's an exciting driving tour available in this same area, leading to and through the **Mt. Lemmon Recreation Area.** A paved road climbs the Catalina Mountains to the 9,000-foot level, through a range of ecological regions—from cactus scrubland to mixed conifer forest. There are turnouts near the top that offer fine views of the basin and city. There are picnic areas, campgrounds, and hiking trails along the route, and skiing during winter months. This is said to be the most southerly ski area in the U.S., although the folks at Cloudcroft may object. To get there, drive east from the city on Broadway Blvd. and take Catalina Highway.

• Tohono Chul Park
Nine miles north of the city, at Ina and Oracle Roads, the park has displays of several hundred varieties of desert plants, with nature trails winding through the demonstration gardens. There are galleries, a cafe, and a gift shop. For information, call (602) 742-6455.

• Tucson Botanical Gardens
Located at 2150 North Alvernon Way, the botanical park features a Tucson-area garden, tropical greenhouse, and displays of iris, herbs, and wildflowers, as well as North American vegetables. There's an admission fee and the gardens are open daily from 8:30 AM to 4 PM (602-326-9255).

• Museums
Fort Lowell Museum features the reconstructed commanding officers' quarters, with artifacts and pioneer furnishings showing life in a frontier western army post. The museum is located at 1900 North Craycroft Road (602-885-3832).

Arizona

John C. Fremont House (151 S. Granada Ave.) is in the Convention Center complex in downtown Tucson. This restored 1880 adobe home was the residence of Arizona Territorial Governor John Fremont. The house contains period furnishings and a fine collection of American antiques. It's open Wednesday through Sunday from 10 AM to 4 PM. For information, call (602) 622-0956.

The above restorations are managed by the Arizona Historical Society, which also has its main museum at 949 E. Second Street. The museum has a research library, as well as a Mining Hall, Transportation Hall, and a collection of nineteenth-century music boxes and phonographs. It is open Monday–Saturday from 10 AM to 4 PM. For information, call (602) 628-5774.

Old Pueblo Museum is in the Foothills Mall at Ina and La Cholla (602-742-2355). This museum features permanent and changing exhibits on southwestern history, culture, and natural science. For directions to the Tucson Children's Museum and the Tucson Museum of Art, see the Historic Districts section (on page 263).

Tucson Resorts

As is the case with Phoenix, Tucson is home to several deluxe resorts, in addition to a half-dozen fine guest ranches. Most of the resorts are built around golfing. These golf resorts and spas are located outside the main built-up area in the foothills overlooking the desert landscape.

Lowe's Ventana Canyon Resort is one of the premier resorts in the area—13 miles northeast of town at 7000 N. Resort Drive. The resort has adobe-style architecture with 400 units and several dining rooms featuring southwestern cuisine. The sprawling complex overlooks an 80-foot waterfall and has two large pools and 17 holes of golf plus tennis, an exercise center, and 2 miles of fitness trails. Prices here range from $200 to $500 (for two).

The **Westin La Paloma** is in the super-deluxe category, located at 3800 Sunrise Drive, 11 miles northeast of the city. With Spanish colonial architecture, the resort has almost 500 units and is set in the foothills of the

Catalina Mountains. Room rates run from just over $200 to more than $520 (800-222-1252). The **Westward Look Resort** is also on a high point overlooking the Tucson Basin. Each room has a private balcony, and there are tennis courts, whirlpools, and a fine restaurant.

Canyon Ranch Spa (8600 Rockcliff Rd.) is a renowned fitness resort, also in the Catalina Mountains. Expect to take part in a spa program if you stay here, with swimming, tennis, racquetball, cycling, hiking and a choice of optional health and beauty treatments, with a minimum 4-day stay (800-742-9000).

The newest deluxe vacation destination in the area is the **Sheraton Tucson El Conquistador**, north of Tucson at 10000 Oracle Road. With 45 holes of golf, 31 tennis courts, and 434 rooms, this resort rates among the top places to play and relax in Arizona. For information, call 800-325-7832.

Guest ranches include the **White Stallion Ranch**, 20 miles northwest of town via Interstate 10 at 9251 W. Twin Peaks Road. With the Tucson Mountains nearby, the ranch features horseback riding, a swimming pool and whirlpool, tennis, a dining room, and lounge. Rooms are in cottages and in the main lodge. The ranch operates on the American plan (three meals with lodging). As with other guest ranches, the White Stallion schedules cookouts, hayrides, dances, and entertainment. For information, call (602) 297-0252.

The historic **Tanque Verde Ranch** dates back more than 100 years and has a cottage complex plus indoor and outdoor pools, tennis courts, a sauna and horseback riding. The restaurant here is open to the public by reservation (602-296-6275). To get there take Speedway Blvd. and drive east for 18 miles.

The **Lazy K Bar Guest Ranch** (8401 N. Scenic Drive) is also hard against the Tucson Mountains, 17 miles northwest of the city via Interstate 10 and Ina Road. The ranch is set in a saguaro forest with desert all around and features riding, an outdoor pool, whirlpool, tennis courts, and nature trails. The ranch operates by the American plan (all meals included)and is closed during July and August.

Williams

Set in the midst of the Kaibab National Forest, Williams is the closest community of any size to the Grand Canyon. By road or scenic train ride, the South Rim of America's foremost natural spectacle is only 60 miles from this community.

This is not a large town (only 2,550 people live here) but it offers accommodation in motels and RV parks and has a few restaurants in which to eat before making the trip to the Grand Canyon. At an elevation of 6,280 feet, Williams' chief asset is the pine forest, which offers camping, hiking and scenic drives. The adjacent mountain was named by surveyors for William Sherley "ol' Bill" Williams, a beaver trapper who roamed through this area in the early 1800s.

Several recreational sites and picnic areas are close to town, offering forest camping and fishing. The **Cataract Lake Campground** is reached by taking 7th Street north and then turning onto First Road (west) which becomes Cataract Lake Road. There are 18 camp sites here.

Kaibab Lake Campground is 2 miles north of Interstate 40, via Bill Williams Ave. (Route 64 N). With 60 sites, this area is open May 15 to Oct. 31. A hiking trail circles the lake. White Horse Lake is about 20 miles south of town via 4th Street and then left on Forest Road 110. After seven miles, turn onto Forest Road 109 and the campground is three miles from this intersection. There are 85 sites. The campground is open from May 15 to October 31, and the road is plowed during winter months for ice fishing.

Fishing spots with no camping include the **Santa Fe Dam** (4th Street, south of town). **Buckskinner Park** (Third Dam) is south of town via 6th Street. There are picnic tables in this city park. **McLellan Dam** is off I-40, west of Williams via exit 157 at Devil Dog Road, and a 4-mile drive from there.

Farther away is the **JD Dam** (19.5 miles) via 4th Street, Forest Road 110, and then Forest Road 105. Turn right on Rd. 105 and drive 1/2 mile to the lake. All of these lakeside locations offer fine recreation opportunities.

Destinations

• Day-Trips from Williams

Wildlife viewing is a popular activity in the area. Perhaps the best route to take for birding and viewing other wildlife is the **Bill Williams Mountain Loop Road** (Forest Rd. 108) which provides access to Coleman Lake and the Bixler Mountain area. To take this trip, drive south from town on 4th Street (Perkinsville Road) and turn west on Forest Rd. 108. Coleman Lake is a few minutes' drive from this intersection. Road 108 continues circling around Bill Williams Mountain, with a sideroad leading west to the Bixler Mtn. recreation area. The road meets Interstate 40 two exits west of Williams.

Of course, the ultimate day-trip is the drive northward to the Grand Canyon. We strongly recommend that you budget more than one day for your visit to the South Rim (see page 221).

Arizona

The Guest House Inn
3 Guest House Road
Ajo AZ 85321
(602) 387-6133

This highly recommended B & B inn is one of several places to stay in this little town north of Organ Pipe Cactus National Monument. The four guest rooms are in the middle of this charming house built in 1925 to house guests of the Phelps Dodge mining company. There are combination or shower baths. The Walker family provides fine hospitality. There's a patio with picnic table, and shops and restaurants are nearby. A full breakfast and afternoon tea are served ($).

Mine Manager's House
1 Greenway Drive
Ajo AZ 85321
(602) 387-6505

Another home from the Ajo copper mining days, the B & B inn has five units, all with unique decor and names (the Maid's Room, the Cornelia Suite). Hosts are Faith and Martin Jeffries. A full breakfast is served and afternoon refreshments are available. You may also reserve a place for dinner. ($ to $$).

Marine Motel
P.O. Box 446
Ajo AZ 85321
(602) 387-7626

This standard motel on U.S. Highway 85 has 20 units. Refrigerators are available and some units have showers. The motel is one mile north of the town center ($).

Ajo Camping

The **Shadow Ridge RV Resort** is located 1/2 mile north of town at 431 N. 2nd Avenue. All 46 sites have RV hookups. Laundry & rec. room. (602) 387-5055

BENSON

Quail Hollow Inn
P.O. Box 2107
Benson AZ 85602
(602) 586-3646

This Best Western operation offers good accommodations with reasonable prices. The motel has a heated pool, whirlpool and laundry. There's a restaurant nearby. Some rooms have showers and refrigerators ($).

ARIZONA • Places to Stay

Benson Camping

Chief Four Feathers KOA campground has 87 sites; most with hookups, with a few sites set aside for tenting. There are many pull-through sites. Cabins are available, plus dump station, laundry, store, pool, recreation room, playground, and propane. It's located 1 mile north of I-10, take the Ocotillo Road exit (#304).

The **Red Barn Campground** is also north of I-10 on Ocotillo Road. With grassy tent sites and RV spaces, the park also has a store, laundry, and propane.

BISBEE

Copper Queen Hotel
Drawer CQ
Bisbee AZ 85603
(602) 432-2216
or 800-247-5829

The old Copper Queen is a major historic landmark, built just after the turn of the century during Bisbee's greatest mining years. Around the corner is famous Brewery Gulch and the town's Main Street is just a half-block away. The hotel is well preserved with a fine dining room and atmospheric saloon. There are 45 rooms decorated in the Victorian style of these original hotels of the pioneer West. The place reeks of history and makes a great base for a vacation in southeastern Arizona ($$).

Bisbee Grand Hotel
61 Main Street
Bisbee AZ 85603
(602) 432-5900

Dating back to 1906, when it was constructed, burned to the ground, and quickly rebuilt, the hotel benefits from its 1986 restoration. There are nine rooms and two suites upstairs, all with Victorian furnishings and decor. On the ground floor, you'll find the Saloon, a small theater, and the old Ladies' Parlor—now a civilized extension of the Saloon. Melodramas are presented in the Bisbee Grand Theater. Continental breakfast is served to overnight guests on the veranda or in the guest rooms ($$).

Bisbee Inn
45 OK Street
Bisbee AZ 85603
(602) 432-5131

This intimate B & B inn has 18 rooms which share five shower rooms and seven restrooms. All rooms have a washbasin. It was called the LaMore Hotel when it opened in 1917. Breakfast is served

Arizona

(all-you-can-eat!). Hosts are Joy and John Timbers. There is a TV room and laundry, and an evening social hour features refreshments ($).

The Inn at Castle Rock
112 Tombstone Canyon Rd.
Bisbee AZ 85603
(602) 432-7195

The long-standing B & B inn was closed for a while but reopened with new management in 1993. It's an oddly shaped building under the shadow of Castle Rock, which rises from across the road. The hillside behind the inn features thick plantings of trees, pampas grass, roses and other foliage. There are twelve rooms and two suites, all with private bath. A continental breakfast is served. This inn has its own mine shaft and several porches, and is a great place to take children for an overnight stay ($).

Bisbee Camping

Bisbee is a great place to camp, with several RV parks, including the **Turquoise Valley Golf & RV Park** on Newell Road. There are full hookups, showers, and laundry but no tent camping (602- 432-3091).

The **Queen Mine RV Park** has 25 spaces, including tent sites, with showers and laundry facilities. It's on Highway 80, next to the Mine Tour office, near the downtown area (602-432-5006). **Shady Dell RV Park** has 16 sites under the trees, at 1 Douglas Roa (602-432-7305).

BULLHEAD CITY

Grand Vista Hotel
1817 Arcadia Plaza
Bullhead City AZ
86442
(602) 783-3300

This is a high-quality Best Western operation, located 2 miles south of the Bullhead City town center on State Route 95. There are 80 rooms, a swimming pool, and whirlpool. Weekly rates are available ($$).

Lake Mohave Resort
Katherine Landing
Bullhead City AZ
86430
(602) 754-3245

Katherine Landing is just north of Bullhead City—part of the Lake Mead National Recreation Area. This resort has a combination of rooms and efficiency units, a lounge, beach at hand, laundry, rental boats, marina, boat ramp,

275

Places to Stay

and waterskiing or fishing on the lake. Rental houseboats are also available, and you are advised to reserve your boat months in advance. There's a restaurant, open each day at 8 AM, Fridays and Saturdays at 7 AM ($$).

Bullhead City Camping

Riverview RV Resort is nearly 3 miles south of town on SR 95 and then 1.25 miles east on Ramar Road. The park covers 105 acres and accepts self-contained vehicles only. Coin laundry, store, whirlpools, putting green, tennis courts, exercise room, par-3 golf (extra fee). **Davis Camp**, a campground, is operated by Mohave County Parks. It's 1 mile south of town below the Davis Dam on SR 95. There are 124 sites beside or near the Colorado River, laundry, boat ramp, dock, and a visitor center. **Katherine Campground** is just 5 miles north of town in the Lake Mead National Recreation Area (Lake Mojave Resort).

CHINLE

Canyon de Chelly Motel
P.O. Box 295
Chinle AZ 86503
(602) 674-5875

With 68 units, an indoor pool, and a restaurant that opens at 6:30 AM, this motel is 3 miles west of Canyon de Chelly National Monument. It's a quarter-mile east of U.S. Hwy. 191. Rates depend on the season; they're higher in the summer months ($ to $$).

Holiday Inn Chinle
P.O. Box 1889
Chinle AZ 86053
(602) 674-5000

This large new Holiday Inn has a complex rate structure, with four different rate periods. As with the above, the rates are higher in midsummer and lowest from January through April. The hotel is located at the entrance to Canyon de Chelly National Monument, on Indian Road 7, 2.5 miles east of U.S. 191. There's a heated pool, and laundry, and the restaurant opens at 6 AM ($$ to $$$).

Chinle Camping

Cottonwood Campground, inside Canyon de Chelly National Monument, has 75 sites and is open year-round. RVs are limited to 32 feet.

Dump station but no showers. Extras include a visitor center, nature trails, and museum.

For information on camping within the national monument, call the park office at (602) 674-5436. For more detailed information on Canyon de Chelly, see page 212.

EAGAR See listings for Springerville/Eagar

FLAGSTAFF

Woodlands Plaza Hotel
1175 West Route 66
Flagstaff AZ 86001
(602) 773-8888
or 800-972-8886

This fine Best Western hotel is really a resort in itself, complete with 125 rooms, heated pool, sauna, whirlpools (indoor and outdoor), steam room, and exercise room. The Sakura Restaurant is on the site, with another dining room serving Southwest cuisine. It's near Northern Arizona University, 1 mile west of downtown on the I-40 business loop, exit 191 (**$$ to $$$**).

Birch Tree Inn
824 Birch Avenue
Flagstaff AZ 86001
(602) 774-1042

This delightful B & B inn has five rooms, three with private bath. The inn has a game room, pool table, piano, and organ for guest entertainment. There are bicycles for riding, and tennis courts are nearby (there are tennis racquets for borrowing). The hosts serve afternoon beverages and a full breakfast (**$ to $$**).

Country Club Condos
5700 E. Oakmont
Flagstaff AZ 86004
(602) 526-4287

For those who prefer a condo environment, this complex has 18 units for rent, with check-in at 4 PM. One-, two-, and three-bedroom units with kitchens and a heated pool. Weekly and monthly rates are available (**$$ to $$$**).

Flagstaff Camping

Flagstaff KOA is located at 5803 N. Hwy. 89, 1 mile north of I-40. All 200 sites—open and shaded—have hookups. Laundry, dump station, store and propane, bike rentals, playground, rec. room. (602) 526-9926. There are several National Forest campgrounds near Flagstaff where one can get closer to nature. These include

277

Places to Stay

the **Bonito Campground**, in Sunset Crater National Monument (north via Hwy. 89). No showers. Nature program, trails, volcano (602-526-0866). **Ashurst Lake Campground** is southeast of town via Lake Mary Road and Hwy. 82 E. Pit toilets, no showers (602-527-7474).

GILA BEND

Space Age Lodge
P.O. Box C
Gila Bend AZ 85337
(602) 683-2273

This is a Best Western motor lodge, 1/4 mile east of the town center at 401 East Pima (take Business Loop 8). There's a pool and whirlpool, and the coffee shop is open 24 hours ($).

GLOBE/MIAMI

Copper Hills Inn
Globe Miami Highway
Box 506, Miami AZ
85539
(602) 425-7151

This Best Western motel is located across the road from the huge mining operations, in Miami, just west of Globe. There's a pool here; the dining room and coffee shop open at 5 AM. There are two 2-bedroom units and one efficiency unit ($).

Cloud Nine Motel
P.O. Box 1043
Globe AZ 85502
(602) 425-5741

With 71 units, this motel is at 1649 East Ash Street, east of downtown on U.S. 60. Heated pool and whirlpool, and ten rooms have a whirlpool tub. Some rooms have king beds ($$).

**Pinal Mountain
Bed and Breakfast**
360 Jess Hayes Road
Globe AZ 85501
(602) 425-2562

This small B & B inn has cable TV and a kitchen available. Rates are reasonable and this is a chance to get away from the busy mining environment or the noise of the highway for a quiet stay ($).

Globe Camping

Several national forest sites are located around the Globe/Miami area. **Jones Water Campground** is 17 miles north of Globe on U.S. 60 (the road to Salt River Canyon). Pit toilets, no showers, 14-day limit. **Pinal Campground** is located southwest of town via Forest Roads 112 and 55 and then to the campground on FR 651. No showers or drinking water. Hiking trails. Limit—14 days. **Pioneer Pass**

Campground is 8.5 miles south of Globe via Forest Road 112. There are hiking trails but no showers. Limit—14 days.

GRAND CANYON NATIONAL PARK

For indoor accommodations and campgrounds in the South Rim and North Rim sections of the park, see the Grand Canyon pages beginning on page 221.

JEROME

The Miner's Roost Inn
309 Main Street
Jerome AZ 86331
(602) 634-5094

Set on top of the Ore House Restaurant in this old mountainside former mining camp, the rooms are decorated with Victorian furnishings and artifacts. The restaurant below serves fine home-style cookin' at a very low price—a perfect combination ($).

KINGMAN

Wayfarer's Inn
2815 E. Andy Devine Ave.
Kingman AZ 86401
(602) 753-6271

This extensive Best Western operation has large rooms with several two-bedroom units, a laundry, heated pool, and indoor whirlpool. A coffee shop is across the road. All rooms in this motel have a refrigerator and microwave oven ($).

The Sunny Inn
3275 E. Andy Devine Ave.
Kingman AZ 86401
(602) 757-1188

This budget motel has more than the usual features for such an inexpensive place to stay. Pool, indoor whirlpool, laundry, queen beds ($).

Kingman Camping

There are eight privately operated campgrounds and RV parks in the Kingman area including **Hualapai Mountain Park Campground** at the county park about 13 miles from I-40. There are no showers, but cabins can be rented. There is a network of nature trails through the park.

Kingman KOA is located at 3820 N. Roosevelt Ave., via State Route 66 (the old Route 66) and

Places to Stay

Airway Ave. Laundry, dump station, store, propane, pool, recreation room, miniature golf.

There are two BLM campgrounds in the area: **Windy Point Campground**, 23 miles northwest of town via Hwy. 93 and then on the Chloride/Big Wash Rd. Pit toilets, no drinking water, no showers; **Wild Cow Campground**, located 20 miles south of town on Hualapai Mt. Road. Pit toilets, no showers, no drinking water. RV limit—20 feet.

LAKE HAVASU CITY

Island Inn Hotel
1300 W. McCulloch Blvd.
Lake Havasu City AZ 86403
(602) 680-0606

This is one of the newest of the resort hotels in this lakeside tourist town. A four-storey red brick building, it's close to almost everything, including the London Bridge and downtown shopping. The hotel has a swimming pool and whirlpool, a lounge, and a restaurant which opens at 6 AM. Rates vary with the seasons. Summer brings discounts in this and other hotels in Lake Havasu City (**$ to $$**).

Ramada London Bridge Resort
1477 Queen's Bay Road
Lake Havasu City AZ 86403
(602) 855-0888

If you insist that you have to lodge right beside the London Bridge, then these are your digs. This Ramada is veddy veddy British (well, it tries), with its almost-Tudor flourishes and the English Village shops. King's Retreat is the restaurant which serves a variety of English and American dishes. Kokomo's is the lakeside lounge. Also: golf course, tennis, two pools, whirlpool, courtesy bus to Laughlin casinos (**$ to $$$**).

Nautical Inn Resort
1000 McCulloch Blvd.
Lake Havasu City, AZ 86403
(602) 855-2141

This long-established lakeside complex has all of its rooms overlooking the water. There are standard rooms and suites, with 30 two-bedroom townhouses, a golf course, tennis courts, shops, and water sports on the lake which is just outside your door. This resort was here before most of the London Bridge hubbub arose and offers a calm, relaxing place to stay (**$$ to $$$**).

Arizona

Lake Havasu Camping

Havasu Springs Resort has a large RV park and motel units, with a marina, large swimming pool, restaurant, and lounge. You can rent houseboats here and/or play golf on the 9-hole, par-3 course. It's 22 miles south of town off Hwy. 95—1/2 mile north of the Parker Dam (602-667-3361).

Sandpoint Marina and RV Park is located 12 miles south of the city on Hwy. 95. There are shaded sites with cabanas, dump station, laundry, store, propane, restaurant, beach, boat ramp, and rental boats including houseboats.

Lake Havasu State Park has two campgrounds. The **Cattail Cove** site accommodates RVs up to 30 feet and has tenting sites. There's a dump station, flush and pit toilets, laundry, store, propane, beach boat ramp and rental boats. It's 17 miles south of town on Hwy. 95. The **Windsor Beach** site is on London Bridge Rd., west of Hwy. 95. This smaller campground has sites without hookups, a beach, and boat ramp.

MESA

Dobson Ranch Inn
1666 S. Dobson
Mesa AZ 85202
(602) 831-7000
or 800-528-1365

This is a large Best Western resort that has 212 units, including suites, a golf course, pool, fitness center. The resort offers a full complimentary breakfast. Heated pool, whirlpool, exercise room. The Other Place is the hotel's southwestern restaurant which serves up-to-date chile-flavored cuisine (\$\$ to \$\$\$).

Arizona Golf Resort
425 S. Power Road
Mesa AZ 85206
(602) 832-3202

You may want to stay here if you're a serious golfer or tennis player. This is a resort motor inn and conference center, with an 18-hole golf course, four tennis courts, pool, whirlpool, laundry, and any combination room or suite you could ask for. The restaurant opens at 7 AM. Rates vary with the seasons (\$\$ to \$\$\$).

Places to Stay

Best Western Mesa Inn
1625 E. Main Street
Mesa AZ 85203
(602) 964-8000

This standard motel offers less expensive accommodation than the above two resort operations. There are 99 units, a heated pool & whirlpool, with a restaurant next door. Rates vary with the seasons; mid-April through December months bring the prices to rock bottom ($ to $$).

PAGE

Wahweap Lodge
P.O. Box 1597
Page AZ 86040
(602) 645-2433

This resort complex is in the national recreation area, overlooking Lake Powell. Rooms have patios and balconies. There are two heated pools, a whirlpool, rental boats, a marina, and a variety of other options including houseboat rentals, rafting and boat trips. There's a dining room, lounge, restaurant, and coffee shop ($$ to $$$).

PHOENIX & AREA

Phoenix—as a tourist city—is a contradiction. The main city is a frenetic jumble of high-speed freeway traffic, sprawling tract-house suburbs, a downtown just beginning to mature—all the personality of a pubescent city-state.

On the other hand, the hills at the north and east sides of the metro area provide secluded locations for hundreds of fine resorts and lodges, many tied into golfing. The best of these are listed in the Phoenix section starting on page 251. For full information on accommodations (and golf) in the area, write the Phoenix & Valley of the Sun Convention and Visitors Bureau, 400 E. Van Buren St., Suite 600, Phoenix, AZ 85004-2290, or phone (602) 254-6500. Below is a selected list of unique places that found our interest.

282

Camelback Inn
5402 E. Lincoln Dr.
Scottsdale AZ 85253
(602) 948-1700

With 36 holes of golf plus a fine spa resort operation, the Camelback has won a five-star reputation as one of the top resort hotels in the country. The Chapparal Room is renowned for fine dining. The pool and pool deck are places to relax and be seen. Expensive and worth it! ($$$).

Arizona

The Boulders
34631 N. Tom
Darlington Rd.
Box 2090
Carefree AZ 85377
(602) 488-9009

The same can be said for The Boulders. The site and the buildings, which disappear into the rocks and hills, make up one of the most startlingly beautiful resorts in the desert Southwest. Adobe-style buildings have spacious rooms with fireplaces and patios. There are two heated pools, whirlpools, 36 holes of golf, tennis courts, rental bikes, and an exercise room. Units include 1- and 2-bedroom homes. The location of this superb resort is north of Phoenix, 1.5 miles south of Cave Creek Road. The Boulders is just the place for that special occasion ($$$+).

The Buttes
2000 Westcourt Way
Tempe AZ 85283
(602) 225-9000

Much less expensive (by about 100 to 200 dollars) than the aforementioned resorts, the Buttes is a hillside resort hotel overlooking Phoenix from this east-side suburban city. Two heated pools, whirlpools, sauna, water slide, volleyball, health club, tennis (extra fee), Top of the Rock Restaur-ant, dining room, coffee shop, lounge, enter-tainment ($$ to $$$).

Maricopa Manor
Box 7186
Phoenix AZ 85001
(602) 274-6302

There are five grandly done suites in this uptown Phoenix bed and breakfast inn. It's close to restaurants and shopping, with an intimate European ambience. You can avoid the hustle and bustle of downtown Phoenix by staying at this distinctive inn ($ to $$).

Phoenix Camping

Green Acres RV Park III is in Tempe, close to almost everything in the Phoenix area at 1890 E. Apache Blvd. There are 60 RV spaces with showers and laundry. (602) 829-0106.

283

Desert Edge RV Park is located 17 miles north of the city, next to I-17. Take the Deer Valley Rd. W. exit. It's 1/2 mile north by the Frontage Rd. to 22623 N. Black Canyon Hwy. The 250 sites all have hookups. Laundry, propane, dump station, pool, whirlpool, recreation room. (602) 869-7021.

Two national forest campgrounds are situated near Cave Creek and Carefree, in the northern part of the Phoenix metro area. **CCC Campground** is 20.5 miles north of Carefree on Forest Road 24. This is a primitive campground with no drinking water. **Seven Springs Campground** is 20 miles northeast of Carefree on FR 24. There is water but no showers. Several nature trails are nearby.

PINETOP–LAKESIDE

Bartram's White Mountain Inn
Route 1, Box 1014
Lakeside AZ 85929
(602) 367-1408

This quiet country B & B inn offers three units (one with private bath), in addition to a 2-room cottage with bath and kitchen. It's in the Lakeside half of these contiguous resort communities near Show Low. To get there, take State Route 260 and turn onto Woodland Rd. and then Woodland Lake Rd. Woodland Lake Park is nearby. Weekly rates are available (**$ to $$**).

Buck Springs Resort
P.O. Box 130
Pinetop AZ 85935
(602) 369-3554

This cabin resort is spread over several pine-shaded acres, 3 miles' drive from Pinetop via SR 260 and Buck Springs Rd. The housekeeping cottages have one or three bedrooms. Included are 2-storey units. The rates vary with the seasons and with the days of the week (**$ to $$**).

Lakeside Inn
Box 1130-D
Pinetop AZ 85935
(602) 368-6600

This motel is conveniently situated on the highway (State Route 260, 1637 West White Mountain Blvd.). With large rooms and indoor whirlpool, the motel also has twelve rooms with wood-burning fireplaces (**$ to $$**).

Pinetop–Lakeside Camping

Rainbow Forest RV Park offers 36 sites—30 with hookups. It's reached by taking SR 260 for 1.25 miles from Lakeside and then driving 1/4 mile south on Rainbow Lake Drive. There are open and shaded sites and laundry facilities (602-368-5286). **Rimcrest RV Resort** is 4 miles northwest of Lakeside via SR 260 and then 1 mile southwest via

284

Arizona

Webb Dr. and Lower Ridge Road. The pine forest shades the RV sites. Laundry, dump station (602) 537-4660. **Lakeside Campground** is a national forest recreation site on SR 260. There are pit toilets, no showers. A store and laundry are nearby with boat rentals and a park visitor center (602-368-5111).

PRESCOTT

Hassayampa Inn
122 East Gurley Street
Prescott AZ 86310
(602) 778-9434

This venerable hotel is a real find. It's in downtown Prescott at the corner of Marina and Gurley. Built in 1927, it's still an elegant building decorated with ceiling frescos and wonderful sofas and rugs in the lobby sitting areas. The restaurant, the Peacock Room, has ornate decor touches as well as fine food. Many of the rooms have the original Spanish furniture, imported for its opening (**$ to $$**).

Prescott Country Inn
503 S. Montezuma St.
Prescott AZ 86303
(602) 445-7991

This is a former motel, nicely converted into a B & B inn. It has 12 units clustered around the parking area—each with its own little patio. Ten of the units have kitchens. Three have gas fireplaces. There are several good restaurants in the immediate area, and a continental breakfast is served (**$ to $$**).

Prescott Pines Inn
901 White Spar Rd.
Prescott AZ 86301
(602) 445-7270

With 13 units including a separate chalet, this B & B inn offers breakfast by reservation (extra cost but well worth it) and an uncommon level of service. The yard is brightly landscaped, with fountain, flower beds, and pine trees all around. Jean Wu and Michael Acton are hosts. From the town center, take Hwy. 89 south—which becomes White Spar Rd. (**$ to $$**).

Prescott Camping

Willow Lake RV Park is a large private operation with 199 sites, many of which have hookups. There are 27 tenting sites without services. Many of the sites are shaded. Laundry, dump station,

285

Places to Stay

store, propane gas, pool, and recreation room. Get to Willow Lake Rd. via SR 89 (602-445-6311). **Point of Rocks Campground** has 100 sites, 4 miles north of town on State Route 89. This well-treed area includes a dump station, laundry, store, propane & recreation room (602-445-9018).

There are also four campgrounds near Prescott (among others) in the national forest. These include **Indian Creek**, 4 miles southwest via Hwy 89 and FR 63; **Lower Wolf Creek**, 7.5 miles south via County Rd. 52 and FR 97; **White Spar**, 2.5 miles south on U.S. 89; and **Granite Basin**, 9 miles northwest via Iron Springs Rd. All are primitive camping areas (except for water at White Spar), all with pit toilets and not a shower in sight.

SEDONA

Enchantment Resort
525 Boynton Canyon Rd.
Sedona AZ 86336
(602) 282-2900
or 800-826-4180

Sedona's deluxe resort is set in a red rock canyon. Enchantment offers standard hotel rooms, as well as one-and two-bedroom suites in individual casitas and 45 efficiency units. This is a place for relaxing and looking at the striking geology and (for the more adventurous) swimming—there are four heated pools—playing croquet or using the putting green, bashing tennis balls, bicycling or taking the fitness program offered by the resort. There's also a pitch & putt golf course. The dining room opens at 7 AM and closes at 9 PM. Sunday brunch is served from 11:30 until 2:20 ($$$).

286

Canyon Villa Bed & Breakfast Inn
125 Canyon Circle Dr.
Sedona AZ 86336
(602) 284-1226
or 800-453-1166

This is a recently built (1992) mission-style inn, designed to blend into the ambience of the Sedona rock canyons. There are eleven rooms, all of which have whirlpool baths, and some have fireplaces. There is also a swimming pool, and the inn's famous cinnamon rolls have become its signature at breakfast time. There is a two-night minimum stay for weekends and you are advised to reserve well in advance ($$ to $$$).

Arroyo Roble Hotel
400 N. Hwy. 89A
(Box NN)
Sedona AZ 86336
(602) 282-4001

This large Best Western hotel occupies a scenic spot along Oak Creek in the center of "uptown" Sedona, close to shopping and restaurants. The rooms have a private patio or balcony. The hotel's Resort Villas, at creekside, are two-bedroom units. A heated pool offers indoor and outdoor swimming. Whirlpools, laundry, sauna, exercise room. Extra fee for tennis, racquetball, massage ($$ to $$$).

Bed and Breakfast at Saddle Rock Ranch
255 Rock Ridge Dr.
Box 10095
Sedona AZ 86336
(602) 282-7640

The owners call this B & B inn an "Old West movie estate." It is a hillside ranch home, built in 1926 with three units, a pool, and whirlpool. The rooms have fieldstone fireplaces, beds with canopies, and private baths. Afternoon snacks are served, plus breakfast. The flower gardens are beautifully landscaped. This is a special place with a wonderful red rock view ($$ to $$$).

Sky Ranch Lodge
P.O. Box 2579
Sedona AZ 86336
(602) 282-6400

Located 1 mile north of Sedona on Highway 89A (the road to Flagstaff), this motel has 94 units on a mesa overlooking the town and Oak Creek Canyon. Many of the rooms have fireplaces. Included are 20 efficiencies and 2 housekeeping cottages. Heated pool, laundry, whirlpool ($ to $$).

Railroad Inn at Sedona
2545 W. Hwy. 89A
Sedona AZ 86336
(602) 639-0010

The people who own the Verde Canyon Scenic Railroad also run this motel at the south end of Sedona. It's a standard motel with some efficiency units, and the inn offers a combo package that includes the train ride and meal. A restaurant is on the premises. For value received, this motel has about the best rates in town ($ to $$).

287

Sedona Camping

The **Sedona RV Resort** is located on Hwy. 89A, 7 miles south of the Hwy. 179 junction (6701 W SR 89A). Most of the 174 sites have pull-throughs and almost all have hookups. Pool, whirlpool, store, propane, dump station, miniature golf, playground.

Places to Stay

There are three national forest campgrounds within 12 miles of Sedona via U.S. 89A (north of town). All are within the Oak Creek Canyon Recreation Area.

SPRINGERVILLE and EAGAR

Sunrise Inn
125 N. Main Street
Eagar AZ 85925
(602) 333-2540

This is a Best Western motel, new in 1993, with 40 units. There's an indoor whirlpool, laundry, and exercise room. Ten of the rooms have microwave ovens and refrigerators. The motel serves a complimentary continental breakfast to guests and it's a good thing—the nearest restaurants are a mile away, in Springerville ($).

Springerville/Eagar Camping

There are a number of camping places in the area including **Jones RV Park** in Eagar (602-333-4650) and the **Casa Malpais Campground** in Springerville—on Hwy. 60 West (602-333-4632). **Lyman Lake State Park**, 18 miles north of Springerville via U.S. Hwy. 180/666, has 25 campsites with hookups and cabana shelters, plus a tenting area. The park has picnic areas, a boat dock and ramp, fishing, dump station, & ranger station.

TOMBSTONE

Lookout Lodge
Hwy. 80, P.O. Box 787
Tombstone AZ 85638
(602) 457-2223

Most local accommodations are older, small motels. Overlooking the Dragoon Mountains to the east, this Best Western operation is the most modern place to stay in Tombstone. It has been recently renovated and has a heated pool. Complimentary continental breakfast is served   ($ to $$).

Tombstone Motel
9th Street at Fremont
Tombstone AZ 85638
(602) 457-3478

An older and smaller motel, close to the historic downtown area, this veteran of many years of visitors to this amazing town offers comfortable, clean accommodations. Restaurants, saloons, and souvenir shops are only a block away ($).

Arizona

TUCSON

Lowe's Ventana Canyon Resort
7000 N. Resort Drive
Tucson AZ 85715
(602) 299-2020

At the top of the luxury list is this fabulous hotel. With 398 units, this golf and tennis resort at the foot of the Catalina Mountains has everything: two pools, whirlpool, saunas, bicycles, steam room, tennis (10 courts), two dining rooms, restaurant, and lounge ($$ to $$$+).

Tanque Verde Ranch
14301 East Speedway
Tucson AZ 85748
(602) 296-6275

It's a country inn with a focus on riding. The rooms and suites are luxurious—many with fireplaces; all with private patios. The ranch has a hundred or so horses, to be ridden over the desert hills. Breakfast, lunch, and dinner are served. The Dog House is the ranch barroom. You bring your own poison and they provide a locker for it. Indoor and outdoor pools, tennis, riding, health spa, and program for children ($$$).

Lodge on the Desert
306 North Alvernon Way
Tucson AZ 85733
(602) 325-3366

Behind the adobe walls of the compound is an old ranch house that used to be out in the desert but is now right in Tucson. The ranch house is the main lodge for this B & B inn, a grouping of Spanish buildings (casas), many with fireplaces and patios. There is a restaurant and American plan is available for the full treatment. Several notable restaurants are nearby ($ to $$).

Westward Look Resort
245 Ina Road
Tucson AZ 85704
(602) 297-1151
or 800-722-2500

One of the earlier resorts in Tucson, Westward Look has undergone renovations and offers rooms, dining and recreation at a reasonable price. With 244 units, 3 pools, whirlpools, tennis, dining room, and coffee shop, it's north of town on State Route 77 ($$).

Tucson Camping

There are several deluxe RV parks near Tucson, including the **Cactus Country RV Resort**, 16 miles southeast of town via I-10 and Houghton Rd (exit 275). The resort has 260 sites with full hookups, a dump station, laundry, propane, pool, and whirlpool.

Places to Stay

New Mexico

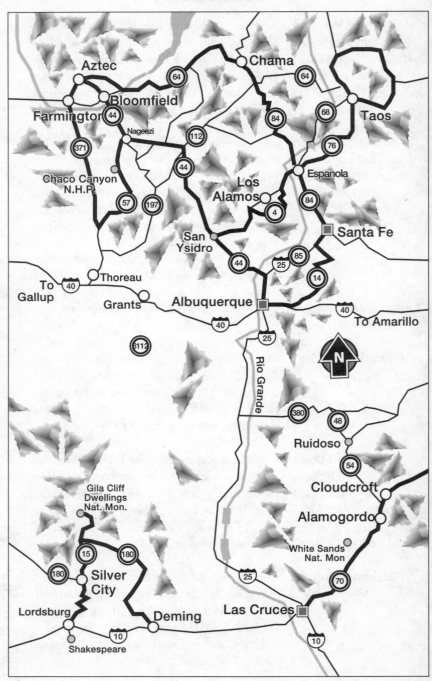

S et on the high desert, this state beggars description, for only hyperbole comes to mind. With its pervasive native Indian and Mexican heritage and influences, modern New Mexico is—to me—the quintessential New World state: people anchored in the cultured past of the Pueblo peoples and the early Spanish settlers, translating these historical treasures into a lifestyle that works in these otherwise unsettling times. And the food. Oh, the food!

In a survey of favorite American cities to visit, *Conde Nast Traveler's* readers came out for Santa Fe as their preferred American city to visit. And in this book, most of our New Mexico scenic drives take you to Santa Fe or lead from this multicultured city into nearby mountains or to fascinating old towns and villages that, unlike Santa Fe, have not been modernized. Taos, only a short drive from Santa Fe, also provides an ambit for art and culture, particularly the preservation of Indian traditions in the Taos Pueblo—more than 1,000 years old and occupied during all that time.

This isn't to say that scenery is overshadowed by history. Far from it. These drives, singly or in combination, will take you through some of the most dramatic desert and mountain scenery in the nation. The Rockies are here: the Sangre de Cristo range. The peaks of the Sandias look down on bustling Albuquerque. The Jemez Mountains provide a backdrop for several Indian pueblos, as well as ruins of peoples long departed, and the laboratories of Los Alamos. The Sacramento Mountains offer one of America's most perfect historic inns, only a few miles from the magnificent gypsum dunes of the White Sands National Monument—an other-worldly spectre of shifting space and shadows.

And the food! The Destinations pages tell you where to find it.

Chama Drive

Santa Fe to Chama & Aztec

When famed artist Georgia O'Keeffe came to New Mexico, she stayed at the Ghost Ranch, located about halfway between Santa Fe and Chama, in a valley through which flows the Rio Chama. O'Keeffe was entranced by the magical light of the northern New Mexico sky and the unique rock formations of the region. She found cattle skulls and painted them, explored the desert of the area, and painted wildflowers in sumptuous colors and sensuous shapes, establishing herself as the most prominent southwestern artist of the century. She spent her later years in her now-historic home in Abiquiu, a few miles south of the Ghost Ranch. The ranch was once a thriving dude ranch for the rich and famous and is now owned by the Presbyterian Church. Just north of the ranch, beside the highway, is the **Ghost Ranch Living Museum**, operated by the National Forest Service.

Highway 84 is our main route to the northern attractions. By traveling this 200-mile route, you'll see the vast expanse of country that excited Georgia O'Keeffe and the many artists who followed her to the Santa Fe area. The communities featured on this drive couldn't be more diverse. **Santa Fe** is a sophisticated center of the arts and crafts, containing the heritage from three major cultural influences: the Spanish, the Pueblo Indians, and the later European settlers. **Chama** is a rustic, frontier mountain town, best known today as the southern station for the **Cumbres & Toltec Scenic Railroad**. The third town is **Aztec**, the site of the **Aztec Ruins**—an ancient Anasazi pueblo that contains a reconstructed Great Kiva.

Along the Way

• Indian Pueblos

Before reaching Espanola, we pass the **Tusuque**, **Santa Clara**, and **Pojoaque** pueblos, three of the more prominent pueblo communities in the area that have Indian art and crafts for sale.

The **San Ildefonso Pueblo**, west off the main route—via Route 50—offers an outstanding example of early pueblo culture.

New Mexico

• Abiquiu

Twenty-two miles northwest of Espanola, this quiet little town has seen many changes of civilization over the past several thousand years. Prehistoric nomads roamed the Chama River Valley before the Anasazi arrived about 1,000 years ago, fleeing from the drought that decimated the populations of Mesa Verde and Chaco Canyon to the west. The Abiquiu Pueblo occupied a prominent hilltop overlooking the valley.

The Anasazi flourished here until about AD 1550, and another two centuries elapsed before the Spanish arrived to settle the area. The town was the home of thousands of Indians who were taken into slavery by the Spanish. The Hispanicized Indians were called *genizaros*. In 1830, the settlement became one of the stops on the Spanish Trail, which linked Santa Fe with Los Angeles. The **Abiquiu Inn**, found along the highway, is a delightful place to stay and eat.

• Recreation Sites

North of Abiquiu, the Forest Service operates one of the most scenic recreation areas in the state. The **Amphitheater Campground** is situated in a splendid natural bowl. The sites are suitable for trailers, RVs, and tents. There's a picnic area as well. Farther north, about 32 miles south of Chama, Route 115 and then Forest Road 559 lead northeast to the **Canjilon Lakes,** a recreation area in the Carson National Forest. The lakeside campgrounds are about 10 miles from Highway 84.

There are two state parks that feature camping; both lie west of the highway on sideroads. The **El Vado Reservoir and State Park** are reached by taking Route 531 just north of Tierra Amarilla. **Heron Lake State Park** is on County Rd. 95. This road also leads west to the **Rio Chama Trail**, which runs along the Continental Divide.

The Divide runs through the Jicarilla Apache Indian Reservation, and this is just one of several recreational encounters you may have with this large reservation between Tierra Amarilla and Aztec.

Drives

Highway Log

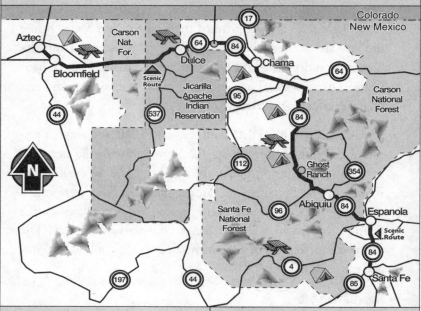

Santa Fe The drive begins at the corner of Cerrillos Road and St. Francis Drive. Take St. Francis Dr. (U.S. 84/185) north toward Espanola.

Junction–Paseo de Peralta This road leads to the Santa Fe Ski Basin.

We continue north on Hwy. 894, passing the National Cemetery, climbing on the divided highway.

Santa Fe Opera The outdoor opera house is 7 miles from downtown.

Tesuque Indian Pueblo There's an RV park operated by the pueblo, close to the highway. The pueblo site is several miles north of the RV park.

Pojoaque Pueblo Shopping for Indian crafts and restaurants.

Junction–Highway 502 This road leads west to Los Alamos and Bandelier National Monument.

Junction–Rd. to Nambe Lake Falls Recreation Area East to camping.

Espanola Town with gas, motels, cafes, stores. We continue north to the Hwy. 84 turnoff.

Junction–Hwys. 84/68 Take Highway 84 northwest toward Abiquiu & Chama.

Junction–Hwy. 554 Leads north to El Rito. Two bars at intersection & country store 2 miles north of junction.

Abiquiu Village, 46 miles from Santa Fe, with gas, RV parking, country inn.

Picnic Area With views of valley.

Junction–Rd. to Abiquiu Dam—#96 Leads west to reservoir—1 mile. Camping. Also to Coyote and Galina.

Picnic Table (Carson National Forest)

Historic Ghost Ranch To east. Now owned by Presbyterian Church.

Ghost Ranch Living Museum Operated by national forest. Open daily 8:30 AM to 4:30 PM.

Echo Canyon Amphitheater Campground To the west of highway. Picnic area and camping in beautiful natural bowl. 21 trailer and tent sites.

Junction–Hwy 115 32 miles south of Chama. Leads east to **Canjilon Lakes** (10 miles to campgrounds).

Picnic Area One table to west of hwy.

Forest Road 125–To east. Leads (via Rd 124) to vista point.

Picnic Table To west, with shelter.

Junction–Highway 162 Loop road to town of **Tierra Amarilla.**, el. 7860 feet. Gas, cafe, store.

Junction-Highway 64. Leads southwest to Tres Piedras & Taos.

Junction–Hwy. 112 Leads to dam & **El Vado Lake State Park** (14 miles).

Junction-County Road 95 To **Heron Lake State Park** and Rio Chama Trailhead (on the Continental Divide), **Heron Dam** 10 miles, camping.

Backroad to Hwy 532 Through Jicarilla Apache Reservation.

Junction–Sideroad 334 To Los Brazes. Cafe at junction.

Picnic Table To west of the highway.

Chama El. 7,860 feet. Town with motels, B & Bs, ranch resort, cafes, stores. Station for **Cumbres & Toltec Scenic Railroad.**

Junction–Hwy. 176 Leads east over Cumbres Pass to Antonito. The road parallels the railroad.

Junction–Hwys. 64/84 Take this route west to Jicarilla and Aztec. State Visitor Information.

Continental Divide El. 7,275 ft.

Junction–Hwy 84 Hwy. 84 turns north to Pagosa Springs (Colorado). Continue west on Hwy. 64 toward Aztec.

Monero Old mining village.

Lumberton Village with gas station, bar, cafe, small store.

Dulce Town with large motel, gas, cafes, store; on edge of Jicarilla Apache Indian reserve.

Picnic Area West of the town.

Junction–Hwy. 527 (Jicarilla Apache Centennial Hwy.) Leads west to Stone Lake and village of Cuba. Entering the Carson N.F., the highway now passes through the San Juan Basin Gas Field.

Sim's Mesa Campground–part of Navajo Lake State Park.

Ranger Station (Carson N. F.)

Junction–Hwy. 539 To **Navajo Dam and State Park** (camping). This is one of three park sites open for day use and camping.

Junction–Hwy. 511 To state park.

Bloomfield Town at Hwy. 544 295 junction. Gas, motels, cafes, stores. Take **Hwy. 544** to Aztec and Ruins.

Aztec Town on the Animus River with historic district and Aztec National Monument (Anasazi ruins including Great Kiva). Gas, RV park, motels, stores.

Chaco Canyon Loop Drive

Aztec to Chaco Canyon & Bloomfield

If there is one place in New Mexico I would recommend to gain an understanding of the incredible feats of the Anasazi and the mysteries surrounding the Anasazi culture, it would have to be Chaco Canyon. We camped in the canyon during a sunny late-September week, when the nights were cool, the skies were clear, and the moon was full. It was an unforgettable experience as the hundred or so campers communed with the spirits of prehistoric people who lived here more than a thousand years ago. The canyon is in an out-of-the-way location, some 60 miles southeast of Farmington in the northwest corner of the state (near the Four Corners), and 150 miles northeast of Gallup. The site is formally called Chaco Culture National Historic Park. For a more detailed description of the canyon and the sites, see page 341.

Along the Way

• Getting There

The shortest and easiest route is south from Bloomfield via State Route 44 with the turnoff at Nageezi. Highway 44 is also the main route north from the Albuquerque area. From Albuquerque, drive north and turn on U.S. Highway 25 to take Route 44 northwest from Bernalillo.

However, we are not ones to do things directly, and our preferred route begins in Aztec (see previous drive). First, exploring the Anasazi ruins at Aztec provides a good preview of what is to come at Chaco Canyon. Second, this drive leads southward beside the huge Navajo Indian Reservation (the Indians' impressive agricultural region), through the edge of the Bisti Badlands, and then by a series of backroads to the canyon. Anyone can drive to Chaco Canyon by state highways; it takes an adventurer to negotiate county roads in the cattle country of San Juan County which we are about to describe.

When I first drove this route, the county roads were only a rumor. There were no available maps along the way, and a bit of backtracking was necessary to discover the right road to take east from Highway 371. After seeing the Aztec ruins, head out of town toward Farmington on Highway 550, through strip development and past a shopping mall. There is an Anasazi site (the Salmon Ruins) off Highway 64 east of town (closer to Bloomfield). You'll discover State Route 371 leading south from its intersection with Highway 550 after passing through Farmington. The road climbs to a plateau on which are the large Navajo farms and the impressive irrigation system used by the farmers.

• Bisti Badlands

Thirty miles south of Farmington, the Bisti Badlands, a protected natural area, is seen to the east. There's a parking lot with information in the wide Gateway Wash that runs through the badlands, and there is a rough road (see the highway log), which leads east for six miles past the old Bisti Trading Post, providing access to the wilderness. You'll find shale, sandstone, and coal formations in unusual shapes. Primitive camping is allowed in the badlands. Take plenty of water along if you're planning a long hike or an overnight camping visit.

• On to Chaco Canyon

Ten miles south of the Badlands (40 miles south of Farmington), you'll find County Road 7650 leading east from Highway 371. This is the shortcut to Chaco Canyon that is described in the following log. The road (when dry) is suitable for pickups and other high-clearance vehicles; actually the roads are surprisingly good. You take this road for about 7 miles until you meet County Rd. 7870. Turn right and drive southeast until you meet State Route 57, passing a farm just before meeting Route 57.

You'll have to open and close a barbed-wire cattle gate along the county road. For those who have large RVs or long trailers, or are otherwise reluctant to trust these county roads, drive farther south along Highway 371, past the Chaya Trading Post until you meet Highway 197. Take this road until the junction with State Route 57. Turn right and you'll soon arrive at Chaco Canyon.

Drives

Highway Log

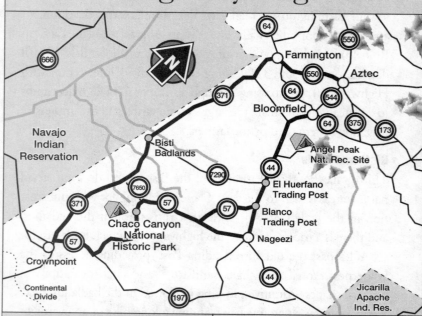

Aztec This small town features one of the most significant Anasazi ruins in the Four Corners area, including a restored Great Kiva. We leave Aztec via Highway 550, leading south toward Farmington.

Farmington A large agricultural town with gas, shopping mall, restaurants & motels. The highway leads through the length of this long community.

Junction–Highway 371 This intersection is hard to find, what with road construction in the area. Take Hwy. 371 south toward Crownpoint.

Dunes Recreation Area An offroad vehicle park.

The road climbs to the top of a mesa, passing through the farmlands of the huge Navajo Indian Reservation.

Historic Marker–Bisti Badlands

Junction-Backroad 7290 Leads east into the badlands. The main highway descends into the valley of the badlands, crossing Gateway Wash.

Junction–County Road 7500 - to the east, leading to the **De-Na-Zin Wilderness**.

Backroad Route To Chaco Canyon This series of county roads provides a fascinating (and short) route to Chaco Culture National Historic Park. The road is suitable for pickups, 4WD cars and other high-clearance vehicles. Those with large trailers and RVs are not advised to take this route.

Junction–County Road 7650 To east, 40 miles south of Farmington. Take this high desert road for approx. 18 miles to N.M. Highway 57 and turn south to Chaco Canyon. The shorter route is to take **Road 7650** for 7 miles east to the junction of **County Road 7870**, turn right, and drive southeast to join N.M. Hwy. 57 and turn right for Chaco Canyon. There's a cattle gate to open (and close) along the way.

Easier Highway Route
to Chaco Canyon

Continue south along Highway 371 toward Crownpoint.

Chaya Trading Post Seven miles south of short route turnoff (Rd. 7650).

Lake Valley Small community 3 miles off the highway to the east.

Junction–Highway 57 Turn northeast onto this highway toward Chaco Canyon and Nageezi.

Junction–Highway 197 This road leads north toward White Horse.

Continue on Hwy. 57 (which is now unpaved) to reach Chaco Canyon (20 miles from junction).

Chaco Culture National Historic Park This amazing Anasazi site, built by prehistoric Indians, was the focus of regional trading and cultural activity for hundreds of years.

To complete our loop drive, head north on N.M. Hwy. 57.

Junction–Road to Blanco Trading Post and Hwy. 44. At writing, the county was pondering closure of this road at Blanco. A more secure route is taken by driving on County Rd. 7800 (15 miles to Nageezi).

Nageezi Small community with gas and store at the junction of County Rd. 7800 and Hwy. 44. Highway 44 leads south to San Ysidro & Bernalillo. Our suggested loop drive continues north via Highway 44.

Blanco Trading Post 8 miles north of Nageezi. The old trading post is filled with Indian weaving and other crafts and is worth stopping to visit.

Junction–County Road 7290 At the Huerfano Trading Post.

The unpaved road leads west through the **Bisti Badlands**, a protected wilderness area. This road provides a scenic way to return to Farmington and Aztec.

Junction–Angel Peak Road Seventeen miles south of Bloomfield. The road leads east to the **Angel Peak National Recreation Site**. Trails and camping, 6 miles from the highway.

Bloomfield Town situated at the junction of Highways 64, 44 and 544 (the latter leads north to Aztec, while Hwy. 64 leads west to Farmington and Shiprock). **Navajo Lake State Park**, with several recreation sites offering lake activity and camping nearby—to the east and northeast.

Nacimento Mountains Drive

Bloomfield to Albuquerque

Bloomfield is in the midst of a popular recreation area, dominated by Navajo Lake, which is a widening of the San Juan River—stretching from Bloomfield to beyond the Colorado boundary. With more than 200 miles of shoreline, the lake is fed by two rivers and offers some of the best lake fishing in the Southwest. Bloomfield and the larger Farmington (to the west) are ideal places to begin a vacation in the Four Corners region, which is steeped in the history of the Anasazi people.

Bloomfield is 200 miles northwest of Albuquerque. Within a half-day's drive are Mesa Verde National Park, the enchanting city of Durango plus Silverton and Ouray (all three in southwestern Colorado), the Four Corners Monument, Chaco Culture National Historic Park (see previous drive), the Aztec Ruins (3 minutes away), and the outdoor attractions of Navajo Lake State Park.

Along the Way
• Early Attractions

The drive to Albuquerque offers a wide variety of scenic and cultural attractions, including Chaco Canyon, the Jemez Indian reservation, and the Coronado State Monument at Bernalillo. Heading south on State Route 44, the first major scenic site is the Angel Peak Recreation Area, located off a sideroad that leads east from the highway, 17 miles from Bloomfield. The peak itself is almost 7,000 feet high. The recreation area offers hiking trails, picnic areas, and campgrounds (no water). The mountain is considered a sacred place by the Navajo people.

• Jicarilla Apache Reservation

The reservation is a recreation region full of native culture, located 50 miles or so east of Bloomfield via Highway 64. The 850,000-acre reservation includes mountain ranges, deep canyons, and high desert mesas. Basic camping areas are set on four small lakes, with picnic tables, fireplaces, and firewood available (permits required), and there's a modern motor lodge located in the town of Dulce.

The Apache celebrate with the Little Beaver Roundup, held early in July, and the Stone Lake Fiesta (mid-September). There are a number of historical sites scattered throughout the reservation. The Tribal Arts and Crafts Shop is the place to shop for Apache handicrafts. Guides are available for hunting forays (mule deer, elk, bear, turkey, and waterfowl).

• Scenic Side Trips

One of the fine scenic sideroad drives in northwest New Mexico is found by taking State Route 96 for 7 miles and then continuing on Route 112 to **El Vado Lake State Park**. Much of this road is unpaved, but the scenery is impressive as it passes through the **Santa Fe National Forest**. If time is available on your vacation schedule, this is an excellent alternate route to Highway 64 and east to Taos. The state park has campsites, picnic areas and a mountain lake perfect for canoeing. Highway 126 is another worthwhile route to take for a side trip. The first major attraction is **Fenton Lake State Park**. The road passes Redondo Peak (el. 11,254 ft.) and meets Highway 4 (the main route to Los Alamos and **Bandelier National Monument**. This is also an alternative way to reach Santa Fe and then Albuquerque via Highways 502 and 84 (to Santa Fe) and then by Highway 25 (to Albuquerque).

• Near Albuquerque

We touch the edges of the Jemez Mountains. Beyond San Ysidro, the **Zia Pueblo** is a small and old community set in a farming valley. While the original pueblo is standing, it is mainly used for ceremonial occasions. The Zia residents live in modern houses across the valley. Bernalillo, on the old Camino Real, is the site of **Coronado State Monument**, a center for commemorating the winter stopping place of Francisco Vasquez de Coronado, the Spanish explorer who traveled with his party through the Southwest in 1640–1642. Bernalillo was established after the Spanish reconquest of New Mexico by Diego de Vargas in 1692. We reach Albuquerque (20 miles to the south) by taking the Highway 25 freeway.

Highway Log

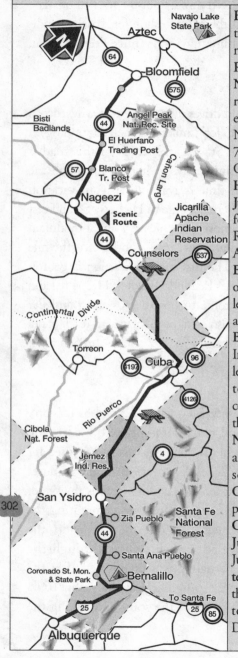

Bloomfield Crossroads town at junction of Highways 64, 44 & 544. Gas, motels, cafes, stores. The **Salmon Ruins** are just south of Hwy. 64. **Navajo Lake State Park** features several recreation sites around the lake, just east and northeast of town. The Aztec National Monument (Anasazi ruins) is 7 miles north of town.

Our drive heads southeast via **Highway 44**, toward Bernalillo.

Junction–Angel Peak Road Leads east for 6 miles to Angel Peak National Recreation Area. Hiking and camping. Angel Peak: el 6,988 feet.

El Huerfano Trading Post At junction of County Rd. 7290. This backroad leads west through the **Bisti Badlands**, a protected wilderness.

Blanco Trading Post A store with Indian rugs and other crafts. The road leading west may or may not be open to Chaco Canyon, depending on county whims. There's a better road to the south.

Nageezi Small community with store and gas. Take **County Rd. 7800** southwest to Hwy. 57 for **Chaco Canyon National Historic Park** (see previous drive).

Counselor Gas field community.

Junction–Highway 537 (Tancosa Junction) The **Jicarilla Apache Centennial Highway** leads north through the Jicarilla Apache Indian Reservation to join Highway 64 just south of Dulce.

Rest Area You'll see teepees over picnic tables with port-a-pottys nearby—all at the junction.

The junction is 86 miles north of Bernalillo. There's a rustic store here.

Continental Divide (el. 7,275 feet)

Junction–Highway 96 This mostly unpaved road leads north to Hwy. 96 and then north (as Hwy. 112) to El Vado Lake State Park.

Cuba Village with gas & store.

Junction–Hwy. 126 Leads southeast past **Fenton Lake State Park**, and on to join Hwy. 4 (for Los Alamos and Bandelier National Monument).

Junction–Hwy. 197 Leads southwest to Torreon & White Horse. This is a backroad route which can take you to Chaco Canyon. Again, a very scenic route across the Continental Divide.

Our drive via Highway 44 continues south, beside the Jemez Mountains.

Rest Area Picnic table beside highway.

Jemez Indian Reservation The highway passes through the reserve.

San Ysidro Small town with gas, cafe, store; at the junction with Highway 4. Hwy. 4 leads north into the Jemez Mountains (see drive, page 308).

Zia Pueblo The small Indian reservation is a pueblo town. The old pueblo is used for ceremonial occasions, with more modern homes in the valley.

Santa Ana Pueblo Another of the several Indian pueblos in the Jemez Mountains region. Two miles off the highway to the northeast.

Rio Rancho A town next to (the larger) Bernalillo.

Coronado State Monument and State Park Just off the highway to the north, the visitor center has displays on Francisco Coronado's stay in the area. There are picnic tables beside the river just below the visitor center parking lot. The state park features camping with RV sites and picnic shelters.

Junction–Highway 85 This main route connects Santa Fe and Albuquerque. Take the north ramp for Santa Fe and the south ramp to Albuquerque. Our drive takes Hwy. 85 south.

Junction–Tramway Road This road leads east toward the Sandia Mountains, to the aerial tramway station. The tram will take you to Sandia Peak, overlooking the Albuquerque basin. For the scenic drive to Sandia Peak, see page 304. The tram ascends the western flank, whereas the drive winds along the eastern side of the Sandia Range. There is a restaurant beside the tram station.

Albuquerque New Mexico's largest **303** city features a wonderfully historic Old Town, filled with restaurants, boutiques, a Spanish square, and mission church (see page 329). To get to Old Town, drive along Interstate 40 and turn south onto Rio Grande Avenue.

Turquoise Trail Drive

Albuquerque to Santa Fe

The normal fast route between the two major cities of New Mexico is Highway 25, a divided highway that will get you there in under an hour. Our recommended drive has the same cities as starting point and destination, but takes you through some nifty mountain scenery (with a scenic side-trip to Sandia Peak), several historic mining towns, and the incredible sights of Cerrillos, an old Spanish town that seems to have popped out of the pages of a 200-year-old picture book. The turquoise (in "Turquoise Trail") refers to the mineral found near Cerrillos and you can find it on sale there and in several of the other small towns along the way.

Along the Way

• Interstate 40 to Highway 14

The initial few miles of the trip are mundane, taking Interstate 40 east from downtown Albuquerque for about 17 miles to the Highway 14 junction. Turn north onto State Route 14 to really begin this scenic drive. We've risen in altitude, having ascended the southern flank of the Sandia Mountains, a small range extending north for 25 miles. We're 52 miles from our destination.

• Sandia Crest Scenic Byway

Cedar Crest is the first little town on this northward route. This is the junction point for the Sandia Crest Scenic Byway, a national forest route up the side of the mountains, passing several picnic areas, numerous hiking trails, and the Sandia Peak Chair Lift. In the summer, the lift is a scenic way to get to the top. In winter months, it services a downhill ski area. However, it is possible to drive to the summit and that's the way we are going.

The byway is one of a series of national forest byways, selected as extraordinary scenic drives. The byway passes through a mixed spruce and fir forest as the route approaches the top.

Sandia Crest is a restaurant, gift and souvenir shop, cross-country ski center, observation platform, hiking trail across the ridge, and forest of television towers.

New Mexico

The view across the valley above Albuquerque is splendid, and is at its best during the fall when the colors are at their finest.

• Small Towns

Just two miles north of Cedar Crest is the even smaller community of **Antonino**. The area north of here was settled by miners who came during the gold rush. Nearby **Madrid** was a coal mining town. Both towns are art and crafts centers, with studios and galleries selling local works. Madrid has a colorful main street, left from its coal mining heyday.

Cerrillos is a one-of-a-kind town. When traveling down the dusty streets of Cerrillos, one cannot believe that this is the United States. The effect is more of an early nineteenth-century Mexican village, with adobe-walled yards, tumble-down buildings, and decaying structures including what once was the famous Clear Light Opera House, a temple of culture in the pioneer southwest.

Cerrillos is the place to look for turquoise, particularly in the Trading Post, housed in a huge adobe building at the far end of town. North of Cerrillos, you'll see the **Garden of the Gods** beside the road, at an elevation of 6,500 feet: vertical beds of the Galisteo formation, dating back 70 million years.

• To Historic Santa Fe

To get to the center of all things in Santa Fe—the Plaza—you can choose among three routes to the historic downtown district.

- Interstate 25 will take you to the St. Francis Drive exit. Turn onto St. Francis and follow it until reaching Cerrillos Road. Turn right for the historic district.

- Take Interstate 25 farther north to the next exit, at Old Pecos Trail. Exit here and continue on Old Pecos Trail and then Old Santa Fe Trail. This street leads directly past the Plaza.

- Take Cerrillos Road all the way into downtown Santa Fe. It joins Galisteo Street three blocks before reaching San Francisco Street, which runs past the Plaza.

Drives

Highway Log

Albuquerque With its historic Old Town sitting near the Rio Grande, Albuquerque is a great place to visit, and to eat! Our scenic drive to Santa Fe begins by taking **Interstate 40** west from the downtown area for a short time until reaching exit 175, to Highway 14 north.

Junction–Highway 14 Take this highway north toward Golden. We're now at the southern edge of the Sandia Mountains, 52 miles from Santa Fe.

Cedar Crest A small town near the junction with the interstate. Gas, cafes, store, campground, RV parking.

Junction–Highway 536 Take this scenic drive to Sandia Peak.

Scenic Byway to Sandia Peak

Highway 536 leads west from the junction with Highway 14. A large sign tells you that this is the **Sandia Crest Scenic Byway**. The 16-mile road winds up the eastern flank of the Sandias, in **Cibola National Forest**.

Sandia Park A small community just north of Cedar Crest. The Tinkertown Museum is a popular family attraction.

Sulphur Canyon Picnic Area Picnic tables in the forest, to the south as you begin to ascend the mountain.

Doc Long Picnic Ground To the south of the highway, at milepost 2.

Tree Spring Trail– To the left of the road (above the 8,000-foot marker).

Dry Camp Picnic Ground To the right of the hwy., above the trailhead.

Sandia Peak Chair Lift To the left of

the highway 1/2 mile beyond the picnic tables. During winter months, this is a downhill ski area with restaurant in the day lodge (at mile 7).

Junction–Highway 165 To Placitas. Six miles to the crest.

Capulin Springs Picnic Ground To the right of the highway, also a Snow Play site (cross-country skiing).

Nine-Mile Picnic Ground To the left, at mile 9. The byway is now passing through a mixed spruce and fir forest as the route quickly ascends toward the crest.

Sandia Crest:–Pathways and stairs from the parking lots lead to an observation deck. There's a cafeteria-style restaurant and gift shop at the top. The metal forest to the north of the viewpoint features television and FM radio antennas serving the city of Albuquerque and the surrounding area.

Our drive continues by retracing the byway, descending to Hwy. 14.

Back on the Turquoise Trail

Drive north on Highway 14 from the junction.

San Antonito Gas, restaurant.

Junction–Highway 344 This road leads east to Cedar Grove and San Pedro.

Golden An old gold rush town, now just a village. Gas, store, crafts.

Madrid A former coal mining town, revived from its ghost town days, now an art and crafts center with a quaint main street and several original buildings. Mine Shaft Tavern and cafe in Madrid.

Junction–Highway 301 Leads west to Interstate 25.

Cerrillos An old Spanish town with much of its heritage preserved. This is more like Mexico than the United States. Much adobe construction, with sandy roads. Cerrillos is a center for turquoise mining. The old Clear Light Opera House is a decaying gem. Antique shops, Murphy's Saloon. The Trading Post is in a large adobe building. Petting zoo next to the store.

Galisteo Village to the west of the hwy. via a dirt road (9 miles). The road also leads to Hwy. 41.

Junction–Hwy. 586 Leads west to Interstate 25.

Junction–Camino Alto Gas station, just past the sprawling New Mexico State Penitentiary.

Junction–Interstate 25 and the edge of Santa Fe. Cerrillos Road leads through strip development (motels, restaurants, service stations) into downtown Santa Fe and the historic Old Town, two blocks from the town square.

The old Spanish square in the historic district is a haven for history buffs with the Governor's Palace and state museum.

Jemez Mountains Drive

Albuquerque to Espanola

This drive is a scenic roundabout route between Albuquerque and Santa Fe, or the basis of a longer stay in the Jemez Mountain region, or part of a two-day trip to Taos (the second half is featured in the next drive, page 312). The Jemez Mountains area is filled with attractions: Indian pueblo communities, the Anasazi ruins in Bandelier National Monument, Los Alamos with its science museum, plus a host of recreation areas, state parks, picnic areas, and the campgrounds and trails of the Santa Fe National Forest. Throughout the drive are the ever-present Jemez Mountains, offering great views and a number of scenic rivers that run beside or near the highways.

The mountains were formed from cataclysmic volcanic eruptions which occurred some one million years ago. They are part of the westernmost New Mexico Rockies, which cover the northern part of the state from Colorado (near Chama). Chicoma Peak (11,461 feet) is prominent on the western horizon along the early part of the drive.

Along the Way

The drive begins in downtown Albuquerque, on Interstate 25, heading north toward Santa Fe. After 15 miles, turn west onto State Route 44 at Bernalillo and drive for another 33 miles—to San Ysidro. Then, take Highway 4, which leads northeast to the town of Los Alamos.

- **Jemez Pueblo**

    The first community, 6 miles down the road, Jemez is a native village with dusty streets. Jemez is the sole surviving pueblo in the seven *provincia de las Hemes* noted by Spaniards in 1641 and is the last pueblo in the state where the Towa language is still spoken. Cameras and tape recorders are not permitted to be operated in the community, in keeping with pueblo custom. A crafts market is open daily.

- **Jemez Springs**

    Hot springs fans should stop for a while in the **Jemez Springs Bathhouse**, and there's a motel nearby for an overnight stay.

New Mexico

Just beyond the village is **Jemez State Monument**. Here, the village of Giusewa was occupied by ancestors of the Jemez Indians before the arrival of the Spanish in 1541. The ruins of this community stretch along the cliffs—close to the remains of the great stone mission church of San Jose de los Jemez, built by the Franciscans about 1622.

• Forest Recreation

The pleasures to be had in visiting this region include the wonderful outdoor experiences found in the forests. A short drive north of the forest ranger station is a soda dam, constructed naturally by soda springs and the river that flows through the buildup of soda. A picnic area is across the river, to the east. This is a good spot for fishing, as is the next picnic area—at milepost 25 in Dark Canyon. **Fenton Lake State Park**, off the highway to the west via Route 126, has campsites and a picnic area. Highway 126 provides a scenic route running over the mountains for 40 miles, to the town of Cuba, with more forest and state park recreation sites nearby.

Redondo Recreation Site has 59 family campsites just north of the highway, some suitable for trailers, with hiking trails as well. Then you'll see signs for recreation sites in the **Jemez Falls Recreation Area**. This is a great scenic park with nature trails, picnic areas (including a covered picnic shelter) and campgrounds. As the road wanders along the higher elevations, we come upon **Valle Grande**. Often called the world's largest crater, it is actually a giant caldera formed a million years ago when a series of volcanos collapsed and whole mountains were engulfed, forming the great valley. Today, cattle graze on the sloping hills.

309

• Bandelier National Monument

An outstanding example of Anasazi pueblo construction, the ruins attract many thousands of visitors yearly. There is camping available in the monument, and the visitor center includes a restaurant. For details on Bandelier, see page 336.

Highway 4 comes to an end near Los Alamos. Highway 30 leads to Espanola, where there are more visitor services.

Drives

Highway Log

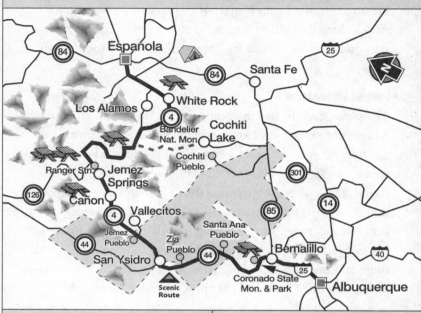

Albuquerque Our route leaves the city via Interstate 25 (the road to Santa Fe). Drive north on I-25 for 15 miles.

Bernalillo Gas, motels, cafes, stores. This town is the site of Francisco Coronado's stay in the area in 1640.

Junction–Highway 44 At the north end of Bernalillo. Take this exit and drive west on Hwy. 44, past the **Coronado State Monument and Park.**.

Santa Ana Pueblo Two miles off the highway—to the northeast.

Zia Pueblo Six miles past the Santa Ana turnoff. The pueblo and community are 1 mile off the highway.

San Ysidro A small town at the edge of the Jemez Indian Reservation.

Junction–Highway 4 Take this road, leading northeast toward Los Alamos through the Jemez Mountains.

Jemez Pueblo East of the highway at milepost 6. Driving through the pueblo is permitted, although photographs are not permitted to be taken. The pueblo crafts market is open daily.

Sideroad to Vallecitos Leads east for 4 miles.

Junction–Route 290 Leads east to Ponderosa and then, as a gravel road, takes a twisting backroad route through the mountains, past **Cochiti Pueblo** and **Cochiti Lake**, joining Highway 4 a few miles west of Bandelier National Monument. Camping.

Picnic Area Several covered tables east of the highway, near spectacular red rock outcroppings.

Canon Small village.

Junction–Route 485 Leads west toward Peggy Mesa, through the Santa

Fe National Forest. Camping along this road. Gas station and store 2 miles north of the junction (milepost 11).

Picnic Areas West of the highway, beside the river. These recreation sites are closed during late fall and winter.

Jemez Springs Small town spread out along the highway and river. Motels, store, gas, cafes, bar, mineral baths at the Jemez Springs Bathhouse.

Jemez State Monument To the east, with ruins behind the visitor center, along the cliffs.

Ranger Station With Santa Fe National Forest information, at the north end of Jemez Springs.

Scenic Marker–Soda Dam This unusual formation has been built by water from a mineral-rich spring.

Battleship Picnic Area Across the river, to the east. Fishing.

Indian Head Picnic Area East of the highway. Fishing.

Dark Canyon Picnic Area Fishing. At milepost 25.

La Cueva Picnic Area

Junction–Highway 126 To Fenton Lake State Park (8 miles). Gas, lodge, and store at the junction. The route continues over the mountains to join Hwy. 44 at Cuba.

Redondo Recreation Site Camping with trailer sites, picnicking, trail.

Overlook–Jemez Canyon South of highway. Parking lot with trail to the overlook site.

Jemez Falls Recreation Area (mile 31) Camping, trails, picnic area with shelter at end of road.

East Fork Recreation Area East Fork Trail (at milepost 32, beside highway).

Las Conchas Campground (1/2 mile beyond East Fork R. A.

Historic Marker–Valle Grande Notes the formation of giant caldera, now this wide valley.

Forest Road 289 Leads south through corner of Bandelier National Monument and on to Los Utes Spring and St. Peter's Dome Road. This is an exceptional drive (for 4WD and high-clearance vehicles). See forest rangers for advice and a map.

Junction–Highway 501 To Los Alamos. The town of **Los Alamos** is the site of the Los Alamos National Laboratories, with gas, motels, restaurants, stores, museum (see page 356).

Bandelier National Monument Anasazi ruins, information center, campgrounds, food service (see page 336).

White Rock Town with gas, cafes, stores, motels.

Junction–Highway 502 West to Los Alamos, east toward Espanola.

Take 502 briefly and then Highway 30 to reach **Espanola** (13 miles). To continue to **Taos**, see the next drive, which covers the High Road to Taos.

The High Road to Taos

Espanola to Taos

As a continuation of the previous drive from Albuquerque to Espanola, this is the perfect route to drive to Taos—if you like dramatic scenery and don't mind spending an extra hour on the road. The road, actually a combination of several highways (76, 75, and 518), winds across high mountain plateaus and passes through several communities which have seen little modernization since they were settled during the eighteenth and nineteenth centuries. At the end is Taos, the town of such diverse residents as Kit Carson and D. H. Lawrence. During the winter, the town is a ski center and—year-round—it's New Mexico's second shrine to New Mexico art and crafts. Like Santa Fe, Taos is built around its old Spanish plaza which is ringed with galleries, shops, and restaurants.

Along the Way

Our drive begins in Espanola, at the junction of Highways 84 and 76. For those approaching this drive from the south (Santa Fe), you may wish to start on Highway 503, which leads east toward Chimayo from Highway 84, a few miles south of Espanola (at the Pojoaque Pueblo).

• Chimayo

Chimayo is a pleasant old Spanish town, located at the junction of Highways 503 and 76. There are several fruit stands where, in the fall, you'll find ristras of red peppers hanging to dry in the sun. The Chimayo pepper is famed throughout the state. Indians occupied the Chimayo valley centuries before the arrival of the Spaniards. Founded in the early eighteenth century after the reconquest of New Mexico, Chimayo has been a center of the Spanish weaving tradition for over 250 years. There is also a plaza here, off Highway 503, and the Sanctuario, Chimayo's old church, is a historical delight, open daily for tourists to visit. There are several fine bed and breakfast homes in the town, as well as standard motels.

• Into the Mountains

Highway 78 climbs after leaving Chimayo, first passing through the small old town called Truchas. Truchas Peak dominates the skyline here, with an elevation of 13,101 feet. The town was founded during the early settlement of the state by the Spanish. In 1754, Governor Thomas Feles Cachupan granted land on the Rio Truchas to families of Santa Cruz and Chimayo. Nuestra Senora del Rosario des Truchas was on the northern frontier and was subject to attack by Plains Indians, so the governor stipulated that the houses should form a square with only one entrance—a method of "circling the wagons" with houses. Some of the old original buildings are still standing. Others are on their knees. The historic adobe church is fascinating, as an example of the early Spanish church architecture. There's a cafe across the road from the church. The next village of any size is Las Trampas, founded in 1751 by twelve pioneer Hispanic families from Santa Fe.

• A Forest Loop Drive

On the log that follows, we've included a fascinating loop drive through the national forest. The route leads east from the highway on Forest Road 439 and continues back to the highway on Forest Roads 439A and 440. We're in the Sangre de Cristos, and the scenery is not only woodsy but there are great views of the mountain peaks to the east.

• Back on the Highway

Highway 518 leads north and joins State Route 68, 4 miles south of Taos at the community of Ranchos de Taos. We complete the drive by taking Highway 68 north into the main Taos community.

Before reaching Ranchos de Taos, however, there is an interesting historical site at Pot Creek and a picnic area and fishing hole just north, at Tierra Azul. Taos is at an elevation of 6,983 feet, with a population of more than 3,000. It's a small town and easy to get around in by walking.

The Spanish community of Taos developed 2 miles southwest of Taos Pueblo. The community was a supply base for the mountain men of the area and was the home of Kit Carson, who is buried here. The town park bears his name. Taos is a gateway to forest country featured in the next scenic drive.

Drives

Highway Log

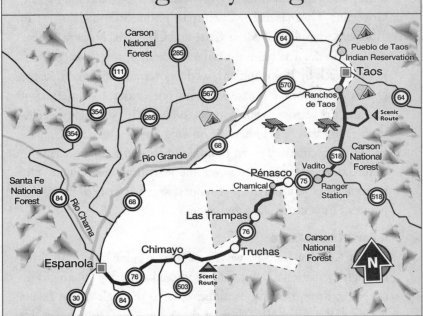

Espanola A town with services including gas, restaurants, motels, stores. It's located at the junction of Highway 68 (the direct route north to Taos), Highway 84 (north to Chama, south to Santa Fe), and Highway 76 (the High Road to Taos).

Our drive begins in Espanola, taking **Highway 76** east from the major junction, toward Chimayo.

Junction–State Route 520 Leads south as a short cutoff to Hwy. 503 and access to Hwy. 84/285).

Chimayo An historic old Spanish town with gas, motels, bed and breakfast inns, crafts stores and fruit stands. Visit the old mission church (the Sanctuario) and the old town square. The town is spread along both Highway 76 and route 503.

Junction-State Route 503 Leads south to the Santa Cruz Reservoir, Nambe Pueblo, Pojoaque Pueblo and Highway 84/285.

Junction–Sideroad to Cordova Leads into the valley to a small community.

Historic Marker-Truchas

Truchas Peak (el 13,101 feet)–In the Sangre de Cristo Range, with glaciers visible to the east.

Truchas An historic little town, settled in 1754. There are many decaying buildings along with occupied old structures. Gas, cafes.

Boundary–Carson National Forest

Ojo Sarco Village with no services.

Las Trampas Small town with historic adobe church. Cafe across from the church.

Forest Road 207 Leads south to small

village of El Valle and further to three campgrounds and the **Trampas Trail**.

Forest Road 160 Leads south. No camp sites.

Chamisal Small village in the Picuris Indian Reservation with store.

Junction–Highway 75 Leads left to Espanola. Take Highway 75 (right) toward Taos.

Penasco Village with gas and cafes.

Junction–Highway 73 Leads south to village of Rodarte and on to join Forest Road 116 (camping at Hodges Forest Site and Santa Barbara Site, both on Road 116).

Ranger Station Camino Real station for the Carson National Forest, beside the highway just beyond the junction.

Vadito Another small village.

Junction–Highway 518 The road leads right (south) to More and Las Vegas and then north toward Taos. Turn left for Taos (19 miles).

Trailhead To Amole Canyon (trail #4), at milepost 58.

Forest Road 442 To the right (east). This is prime snowmobiling country during winter months.

Vista Point-U.S. Hill Pulloff just beyond forest road junction.

Junction–Forest Road 439–To the east at mile 64.

Side Trip on Forest Loop

This side trip on forest roads provides an interesting hour's trip through the Carson National Forest, taking you back to the highway just a mile north of the turnoff. Forest Road 439 provides the start of the loop drive through the national forest leading through the Rancho Grande Grant. The route leads east and continues via Forest Roads 439A and 440. By the time you find Road 440, you're pointing west. This road leads west along Maestas Ridge, past Maestas Spring, joining Hwy. 75 at Pot Creek.

Back on Highway 75

Forest Road 440 To the east (2 miles north of Forest Road 439). The end of the loop drive described above.

Pot Creek Cultural Site In the national forest. Open during summer months.

Tierra Azul Picnic Ground To the west of the highway. Fishing.

Leaving Carson National Forest

Talpa Near junction with Highway 68. Gas, store, snack bar.

Ranchos de Taos This historic community is at the junction with Hwy. 68. There are several crafts shops, along with restaurants and stores.

Junction–Highway 68 Four miles from downtown Taos. There are services along the highway as the route enters the built-up area of Taos.

315

Enchanted Circle Loop Drive

Taos to Red River & Return

The Enchanted Circle Tour is one of two overlapping circle routes through the Carson National Forest, north and east of Taos. The longer Valle Vidal tour uses the same start and finish points but cuts a wider path through the Sangre de Cristo Mountains. We chose to feature the shorter tour as a half-day or day-long drive from Taos. We'll also point you in the proper direction if you choose to do the Valle Vidal Loop.

Roads on the Loop Tour

We begin at the Plaza in downtown Taos, heading north on **State Route 64/68**, driving past the town park named for frontiersman and guide Kit Carson. The park contains the graves of Carson and his family. There's a blinking light 4 miles north of the Plaza (past the sideroad to Taos Pueblo), from where you may wish to drive 7 miles to the east on N.M. 64 to see the spectacular views from the Rio Grande Gorge Bridge. Otherwise, we continue north (straight) taking **State Route 522**. Continue on the road for about 40 miles until you reach the small community of Questa. The longer Valle Vidal Loop takes State Route 522 (straight) while the Enchanted Circle Loop takes **N.M. 38**. This road leads past the Carson National Forest ranger station and the Molycorp molybdenum mine and mill (on hills, north of the highway).

Another 13 miles of driving and you're arriving in Red River, a rustic ski and summer resort town. Highway 38 continues in a southeasterly direction for another 18 miles to Eagle Nest, a small recreation-based town that sits at the junction of Highway 38 and U.S. 64. The lake here is a popular fishing spot. It's another 31 miles on the return drive to Taos via Highway 64 (turn left at the junction).

Along the Way

- **Millicent Rogers Museum**

  Five miles north of Taos, the museum features the art of northern New Mexico. Opened in 1956, the core of the museum's collection came from the estate of Millicent Rogers, a prodigious collector who did much to foster the art and crafts of the region. She

New Mexico

amassed many of these art works during the 1940s. Displays include Native American textiles, basketry, jewelry, and paintings. The building is built in a respectful adobe style and is open daily from 9 AM to 5 PM. If you have time to visit only one local art museum, this is it!

• D. H. Lawrence Shrine

The Kiowa Ranch, once owned by Mabel Dodge Luhan (a woman with a fascinating story of her own), was the home of novelist D. H. Lawrence and his wife, Freida, in 1924 and 1925—given to them by Mrs. Luhan. Frieda continued to live at the ranch after the author's death. She later married Angelo Ravagli. In 1934, they built a shrine for Lawrence's ashes. Aldous Huxley was one of the many literary and other artistic visitors to the ranch, which is now owned by the University of New Mexico. The shrine on San Cristobal Road is open daily.

• Red River Fish Hatchery

Two miles north of Questa on N.M. 515, the hatchery rears trout and is open daily. The visitor center features a display on the fish-rearing process, with a free self-guiding tour.

•Red River Resort

Set in the forests of the Red River Valley, this rustic and informal town provides a getaway for those who eschew the sophistication of the ritzier ski and summer resorts. This popular summer and winter playground offers excellent stream and lake fishing, guest ranches, hotels and tourist courts. The ski area is right in town. Wheeler Peak is to the southeast. Restaurants run to steak and barbecue cuisine, and there are several small cafes serving "down-home food." This is a great place to stay for a thorough exploration of the region.

• Eagle Nest Lake:

This popular fishing lake is leased for public fishing by the New Mexico Department of Game and Fish. The lake is also a mecca for windsurfers. If you wish to wander farther, the Wild West town of Cimmaron is located east of Eagle Nest, via Highway 64.

Drives

Highway Log

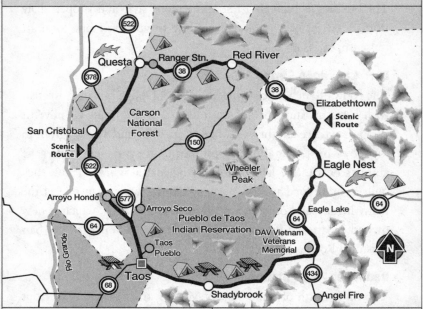

Taos We depart from Taos, taking Highway 68 from Taos Plaza in the downtown district.

Kit Carson Park Just north of the Plaza, offering picnicking, tennis, & ice skating. No camping.

Turnoff to Taos Pueblo The right fork leads to the pueblo. We continue on Hwy. 68, driving north.

While driving north, Taos Mountain is to the east. The Ski Valley is hidden behind the mountain.

Junction–Highways 64, 150 & 522 Hwy. 64 leads west to the Rio Grande Gorge and the high bridge. N.M. Hwy. 150 leads east to Taos Ski Valley,. To continue on the Enchanted Circle, take **Highway 522**.

Sideroad to Museum One mile to Millicent Rogers Museum, containing one of the finest collections of Indian art and artifacts of the American West.

Backroad to John Dunn Bridge (7 miles from the Hwy. 64 junction) Take the narrow gravel road (left) to the bridge, a popular spot for starting kayak and canoe trips.

Carson National Forest-Boundary

San Cristobal Road Leads to the **D. H. Lawrence Shrine**. This is the former ranch where the author wrote from 1922 to 1925. His ashes are buried here.

Cebolla Mesa Campground Take Forest Road 9 for 4 miles. Campsites look over the Rio Grande Gorge. Hiking trail to river. A bridge leads over the river to the **Rio Grande Wild River Recreation Area** (visitor center). Gas pump at junction.

84 miles—3 to 4 hours

Red River Fish Hatchery Beside the highway 2 miles north of Forest Rd. 9 junction.

Questa (el. 7,500 ft.) This old frontier town now houses employees of the nearby molybdenum mine. Gas, cafe, store, small motel, RV parking.

Junction–Highway 38 Another, longer, loop drive (the Valle Vidal Loop) leads along Hwy. 522.

Turn right onto **Hwy. 38** to continue the Enchanted Circle Route.

Ranger Station The Carson National Forest Questa ranger station is open daily (except Sunday).

Columbine Campground Forest sites by the creek in a picturesque canyon.

Goat Hill Campground

Molycorp Mine and Mill This is a major industrial enterprise, in the middle of the national forest.

Fawn Lakes Campground To the north of the highway.

Elephant Lakes Campground Close to the Fawn Lakes, a fishing area.

Junebug Campground Sites beside Columbine Creek.

Red River A ski and summer resort town, with motels, lodges, gas, RV parks, B & B inns, cafes and stores. This rustic town retains a Wild West flavor. Visitor center on the highway.

Junction–Highway 578 This road leads to the Tall Pine Museum and the Goose Lake Jeep Road (suitable for 4WD vehicles only, a wild but scenic ride). We continue on Highway 38 toward Eagle Nest Lake and the town of Eagle Nest.

Cross-Country Ski Area 3.3 miles east of the junction.

Bobcat Pass Elevation: 9,820 feet. This is the boundary of the Carson National Forest.

Elizabethtown (ghost town) Beside the highway and along the sideroad are ruins of several buildings, including the Mutz Hotel and a pioneer cemetery.

Eagle Nest This town is a tourist destination for fishing and lake sports including windsurfing. The town is 31 miles from Taos.

Junction–Highway 64 Take Highway 64 west toward Taos.

Wheeler Peak Wilderness This superb scenic recreation area is northwest of Eagle Nest. The peak (el. 13,161 feet) is the state's highest mountain. It is accessed mainly through Taos Ski Valley.

DAV Vietnam Veterans Memorial Just off the road, to the north, is an impressive chapel, now operated by the Disabled Vietnam Veterans. The memorial is open daily.

Junction–Highway 434 This road leads south to Angel Fire (3 miles), a ski and summer resort with downhill skiing and championship golf.

Palo Flechado Pass (el. 9,101 feet)

Capulin & Las Petacas Campgrounds

La Vinateria Picnic Area

Taos We're back where we began!

White Sands Drive

Las Cruces to Cloudcroft

This route is the first of two scenic drives set in southern New Mexico, both of which involve mountain travel. Within an hour's drive of the Mexico border, there are mountains high enough to make winter skiing possible. Cloudcroft is an example of several ski resorts in the area.

The drive between Las Cruces and Cloudcroft offers a startling contrast in terrain. It begins in one of the state's prime agricultural areas (home of the New Mexico green chile) in the university city of Las Cruces just 44 miles from El Paso, Texas. Taking U.S. Highway 70 northeast from Las Cruces, the route soon crosses over the San Andres Mountains into desert terrain. In the distance are glistening gypsum sands as we come down the eastern slope and pass through the White Sands Missile Range. Sideroads lead to recreation sites situated in the Organ Mountains, a small range at the southern end of the state. Sixty-eight miles from Las Cruces, the city of Alamogordo is a favorite with "sunbirds"—who bring their RVs and trailers to this community to take advantage of the winter sun.

The ascent of the Sacramento Mountains begins just east of Alamogordo, as we take U.S. Route 82 to Cloudcroft. This is also a convenient route to proceed on to Carlsbad and Carlsbad Caverns National Park and to the Ruidoso region which is north of Cloudcroft, also in the mountains.

Along the Way

• Pat Garrett Murder Site

Just east of Las Cruces on Highway 70 is the site of the final showdown between famed Lincoln County sheriff Pat Garrett and the last of the outlaws he battled over many years. Garrett had shot and killed William "Billy the Kid" Bonny at Fort Sumner in 1881. The circumstances surrounding Garrett's death, on February 29, 1908, by cowboy Wayne Brazel, are still a matter of conjecture.

• Aguirre Springs National Recreation Area

The BLM operates this scenic recreation area which is just south of Highway 70 in the Organ Mountains (fishing, camping, picnicking and riding).

320

New Mexico

• White Sands National Monument

High rolling dunes of fine gypsum sand lie in the Tularosa Basin, at the base of the San Andres Mountains, between Las Cruces and Alamogordo (on Hwy. 70). Picnicking between the dunes is an other-worldly experience with sheltered tables set by the sand. There are "trails" over the dunes, and the road through the shifting sands is regularly maintained with snowplows.

• Alamogordo

This city is home to those who work at the local air force base, and to many RV and trailer vacationers. This is a "space-age" community, and the International Space Hall of Fame is the leading attraction, with a planetarium and Omnimax screen for the showing of space- and science-related large-screen movies.

• Fresnal's Shelter

This prehistoric Indian campsite is located in the cliff face across the canyon from Highway 82 as the route climbs toward Cloudcroft. This site was an occasional shelter for a nomadic hunter/gatherer tribe (called the Archaic Culture) that inhabited the Sacramento Mountains between 6,000 and 500 BC. Stone tools and basket fragments have been found here.

• Trailhead for Osha Trail

This 2.5-mile loop of moderate difficulty passes through the Canadian Life Zone (osha, also called loveroot, is a native New Mexico plant). Stands of aspen and Douglas fir are crossed before reaching high mountain meadows. Fall is the best time of year to explore this area, when the gold aspen leaves are at their most colorful. There are good views of Cloudcroft and the White Sands from the trail.

• Cloudcroft

This ski and summer resort town offers rustic accommodation, B & B homes, and one of the most charming mountain lodges in the country (Cloudcroft Inn). At the western entrance to the town is a trestle used by the famous Cloud Climbing Railroad. The trestle is all that remains of an old rail line.

Drives

Highway Log

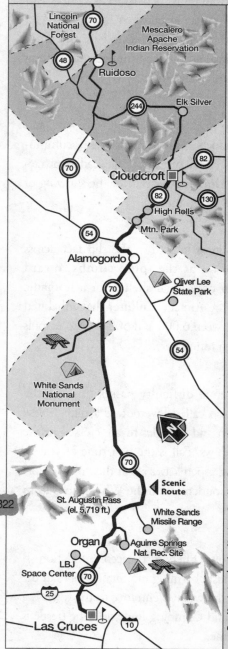

Las Cruces The drive begins in downtown Las Cruces, heading northeast on U.S. Route 70.

Junction–Interstate 25 Highway 70 crosses Interstate 25 before heading east toward White Sands and Alamogordo. The freeway leads north to Albuquerque and south to El Paso and the Mexican border. We continue east on U.S. Highway 70.

Lyndon B. Johnson Space Center located 6 miles north of the highway.

Organ Small town with gas and cafes. The highway climbs through a small range (the Organ Mountains).

San Augustin Pass (el: 5,719 ft.)

Organ Mountain Recreation Lands The San Augustin Interpretive Pavilion is located near the pass.

View Point A large pullout provides views of the Tularosa Valley and the glistening gypsum sands.

Aguirre Springs National Recreation Site Off the highway (5.5 miles) to the south (BLM).

White Sands Missile Range This military range (U.S. Army) takes up much of the valley, with several complexes seen along the route. There are infrequent closures of Highway 70 when missiles are being tested. Watch for signs. The highway descends to the valley floor, with yucca displays.

White Sands National Monument Enter the gates of this unusual landscape and you're in for a fantastic and eerie treat. The information center has displays and a gift shop. There are picnic areas at the end of the road that leads through the dunes, and several hikes are available through the dunescape.

Holloman Air Force Base

Alamogordo (el. 4,345 feet) This large desert community with many RV parks is a university town with a variety of services for tourists, including cafes, motels, parks, and stores. The **Space Hall of Fame** is a science center with a planetarium.

Junction–Highway 54 This road leads south to El Paso, passing **Oliver Lee State Park** (camping). We take **Hwy. 54/70 north** through Alamogordo. The town visitor center is beside the highway next to **Alameda Park** (RV parking).

Junction–Indian Wells Road This road leading east takes you to three major local attractions: the Space Hall of Fame, the Southwest Archeology Museum, and the University of Southern New Mexico.

Junction–Highway 82 This is the route to Cloudcroft. Turn east here.

Lincoln National Forest As the route enters a scenic canyon, we cross the national forest boundary. From here, the road continues to climb.

Vista Point Overlooks the canyon, just before entering a tunnel.

High Rolls (el. 6,750 feet) A rambling town in the high hills. Gas, cafe, and stores.

Mountain Park An adjoining community with fruit stands. This is apple-growing country.

Junction–Route 130 Leads southeast to Sunspot and Weed (22 miles) through the Sacramento Mountains. A scenic drive accessible to all vehicles.

Cloudcroft This summer and winter resort town lies atop the Sacramento Mountains and was originally a railroad center. There is a full range of services including motels, cafes, a downhill ski operation, tennis courts and the Lincoln National Forest all-around. The visitor center is a log building beside the town park.

A Scenic Side Trip to Ruidoso & Beyond

Highway 244 leads 14 miles northeast to the village of Elk Silver. It turns left and leads toward U.S. Highway 70 (another 15 miles). Turn right onto Hwy. 70 and drive for another 14 miles to **Ruidoso** with its famous racetrack, skiing, and visitor facilities. If you continue past Ruidoso on Hwy. 70, you'll meet U.S. Hwy. 380, which will take you northwest through the **Capitan Mountains**, passing **Lincoln State Monument**, to **Carrizozo**. This is a scenic route by which to drive to **Tularosa** and then return to **Alamogordo**, a drive of 155 miles.

323

Ghost Towns Loop Drive

Deming to Gila Cliff Dwellings & Lordsburg

Ghost towns of a different kind are featured along this loop tour beginning in Deming and ending in Lordsburg. Both cities are situated on Interstate 10, which runs north of the Mexico border in southwest New Mexico. Deming is 59 miles west of Las Cruces and 83 miles east of the Arizona boundary. There are shorter ways to reach the Gila Cliff Dwellings from the interstate (including Route 90 from Lordsburg), but this loop drive explores a fine scenic region featuring the southern ridges of the Mogollon Mountains, while passing by several prime recreation sites before returning to the interstate via the charming Victorian mining town of Silver City.

The drive begins on U.S. Highway 180, which leads in a northwesterly direction from Deming. This highway continues in a more or less direct fashion to Silver City, but we turn off the main road to take State Route 61 and then State Route 35. The latter is designated a **National Forest Scenic Byway**, as it follows the Inner Loop along the Mimbres River. Highway 35—now the Scenic Byway—provides access to Bear Canyon Lake and several scenic (4WD) backroads that lead through the mountains to the east of the river and highway.

Along the Way

• Butterfield Stage Stop

A picnic area and rest stop between Deming and the Highway 61 turnoff provides some historical interest. Stagecoaches of the Butterfield Overland Mail Co. began carrying passengers and mail in 1858, from St. Louis to San Francisco across southern New Mexico. The 2,795-mile journey took 21 to 22 days. In 1861, the service was rerouted through Salt Lake City. Other Butterfield stage stops can be found in Nevada, on the more northerly route.

• City of Rocks State Park

Twenty-eight miles northeast of Deming, beside Highway 61, is this unusual geological formation, now part of a state park that includes a campground, botanical garden, and visitor center. The

324

New Mexico

jumbled rock formations are seen from the highway and can be more closely examined inside the park boundaries.

• Lake Roberts

Forest recreational facilities are located beside and near this 71-acre lake. There are two campgrounds and several picnic areas. There's a grocery store in the tiny village of Lake Roberts. This is a good place to camp before visiting the Gila Cliff Dwellings, which are 25 miles to the northwest.

• Gila Cliff Dwellings National Monument

A valley trail leads to the prehistoric Mogollon Indian village, set within a series of caves in the Mogollon Mountains. The 42-room pueblo was inhabited in the late 1200s and is the only National Parks Service site protecting remains of the Mogollon culture. The monument is surrounded by the Gila National Forest and the spectacularly beautiful, 685-square-mile Gila Wilderness—the first designated wilderness area in the U.S. For details, see page 352.

• Ben Lilly Memorial

Three minutes' walk from Highway 15, a plaque at the top of some steps honors Ben V. Lilly, a famed mountain man who migrated to the Gila Wilderness from Mississippi and Texas. Climb to the rock ledge behind the plaque to get a prime view of the wilderness Ben Lilly loved so fervently.

• Pinos Altos

Seven miles north of Silver City, this pioneer mining town survived early Apache attacks to produce over 8 million dollars of gold, silver, copper, lead, and zinc before the mines played out in the early 1900s. Some of the original buildings remain.

• Silver City

Now a tourist town, Silver City was founded by prospectors and miners. There are many fine Victorian buildings, and the chamber of commerce has a fascinating self-guided tour of the historic buildings. For details on the walking and/or driving tour and other Silver City highlights, see page 368.

Drives

Highway Log

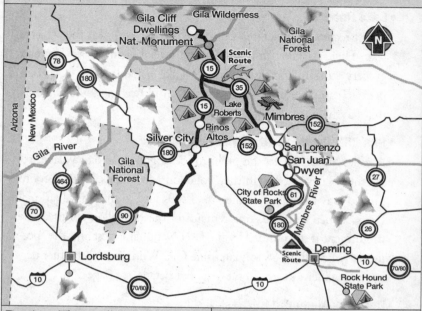

Deming This small town is close to several fine parks, including Pancho Villa State Park, on the Mexican border, and Rock Hound State Park. Both are reached by taking Highway 11 south. Our drive leads north via **U.S. Highway 180**, toward Silver City.

Junction–Highway 26 Leads east to Hatch, following the route of the Atchison, Topeka & Santa Fe Railway.

Rest Area Picnic tables at the site of an old Butterfield stage station.

Junction-Highway 61 We turn onto Hwy. 61 for our scenic route to the Gila Cliff Dwellings. Hwy. 180 continues northwest, to Silver City.

City of Rocks State Park Just off the highway (2 miles). The park is maintained in a natural state and is set in a fascinating boulder formation.

Faywood Small village, post office.

Junction–Highway 152/35 Highway 61 ends here. We continue northward (left) by taking Highway 35, toward Mimbres. This is the beginning of the National Forest Scenic Byway, following the "Inner Loop" along the Mimbres River.

Mimbres Small, spread-out town with gas, store, cafes, ranger station.

Junction–Bear Canyon Lake Road Fishing, camping, reservoir.

Junction-Route 61 A road for 4WD vehicles only, leading east for 120 miles. Wall Lake is 39 miles along this track. No food or gas. Scenic but difficult.

Forest Road 74 At the Continental Divide (el. 6,599 ft.). This is used as a camping spot.

Hiking Trail Trailhead to the right of the highway opposite a group campground. This is 4 miles south of Lake Roberts.

Trail (#96) Two miles north of previous trailhead.

Upper End Campground Part of the Lake Roberts Recreation Area.

Lake Roberts Picnic Ground

Mesa Campground A trail leads from the parking lot.

Viewpoint Overlooks the lake.

Lake Roberts Motel, store, wilderness outfitters, gas.

Junction–Highway 15 Leads north to Gila Cliff Dwellings and south to Silver City.

To Gila Cliff Dwellings

Take Highway 15 north for 19 miles.

Viewpoint–Gila Wilderness A fine view of the spectacular wilderness from an elevation of 7,440 feet.

Trail The trailhead for the Military Trail is to the east of the highway.

Trail Another trail on an old forest road track.

Alum Camp Trail To the left, as the road winds through the forest..

Gila River Recreation Area Camping area and Gila River Trail, both beside the river. There's a small community with a store, gas, and RV parking. The road continues to the valley floor. The visitor center for the **Gila Cliff Dwellings National Monument** is 4 miles from the store.

To Silver City & Lordsburg

Junction–Highways 15 & 35– We return from the cliff dwellings to the Lake Roberts area and drive south via Highway 15, toward Silver City (25 miles). This route is unsafe for large RVs and trailers over 20 feet because of hairpin turns and inclines.

Junction–Sideroad To Sheep Corral Canyon (7 miles).

Junction–Road 149 Leads east to Meadow Creek (3 miles).

Junction–Road to Signal Peak Trails To right and left (either side of cattle guard).

McMillen Campground

Cherry Creek Campground

Ben Lilly Memorial A short trail leads to scenic views and marker.

Pinos Altos Historic town (1803) just off the highway. Museum and opera house, re-created fort and Buckhorn Saloon buildings.

Silver City Gas, motels, cafes, stores. The old mining town has many remaining historic buildings, which are found on a walking tour.

Junction–Highway 90 Take this route south toward Lordsburg.

327

Lordsburg and Shakespeare– Shakespeare is a ghost town just south of the living town of Lordsburg. Gas, motels, cafes and stores in Lordsburg. Privately owned Shakespeare is open sporadically on weekends and generally on holiday weekends.

Other New Mexico Drives

• A Scenic Drive in the Carson National Forest

Off the High Road to Taos, there are two forest backroads that provide interesting side trips. Road #207 leads south to El Valle, a small mountain village, and then leads on to the Trampas Trail and three separate campgrounds. The next road (#160) has no recreation sites but offers a drive in the woods. At the junction with Highway 75, bear to the right—toward Taos.

Six miles on, turn onto Highway 518 and head north. (If you take 518 South, you'll be headed across the Sangre de Cristo Mountains, toward Las Vegas. This is an exciting route with several campgrounds and the Sipapu Ski Area, but it doesn't lead to Taos.) For the next few miles, there are excellent views of the mountains, and a trailhead (at milepost 58) points the way to hike to Amole Canyon. This is just one of 300 miles of trails in the national forest that often lead to stupendous mountain views.

• Cloudcroft to Sunspot Loop Drive

One of the prime attractions of the resort town of Cloudcroft is that it offers superb scenic drives leading to historic sites and nearby communities. One of the best of these is along the **Sunspot Logging Road** (a 50-mile trip). Drive south from town on N.M. Route 130 for 2 miles to the junction with Forest Road 64. Turn onto this paved road and you'll soon come to the **Nelson Canyon Vista Trail**, which provides wonderful views of the Tularosa Valley and the White Sands. The road ends at **Sunspot**, the site of the world's largest solar observatory. There are self-guided tours and guided tours on summer Saturdays. There are also great views from the observatory grounds. When returning, turn onto Forest Road 164. The three springs at **Bluff Springs** have created a waterfall. There is a picnic area here. To return to Cloudcroft, follow Road 164 to N.M. Route 130 and drive west through Cox Canyon and into town. Route 244 leads through the **Mescalero Indian Reservation** and connects with U.S. 70—to Ruidoso and **Lincoln State Monument**, where the Lincoln County War took place.

328

New Mexico

Alamogordo

Although it's a community without a long cultural and historical underpinning, Alamogordo is a neat, modern city within range of a wide selection of landscapes and recreational activity. On the east are the forested Sacramento Mountains, the highest range in southern New Mexico. To the west are the sand dunes of White Sands National Monument—one of the most unearthly sights on earth. Beyond the dunes is the White Sands Missile Range, in a desert valley where mere mortals are forbidden to enter. In recent years, the area has become a favorite place for "sunbirds" to spend their winters, baking in the hot sun of the southwestern desert. Alameda Park is easily seen beside U.S. 70. Picnics are a popular activity in the park, and the free zoo has a small collection of animals and birds from America and Africa. The destiny of the town has been tied to nearby Holloman Air Force Base, the largest employer in the area. There are several modern motels spaced along Route 70, the main road from Albuquerque and Las Cruces.

Things to See and Do

• Space Center

This is the chief man-made attraction in Alamogordo, a five-storey glass and concrete cube that is home to the International Space Hall of Fame. There are exhibits on the birth and progress of the space age—astronauts, scientists, and rockets. In a unique combination, the Clyde W. Thombaugh Space Theater includes both a planetarium and an Omnimax film system. The theater often features laser light shows, as well as star shows and films on the huge screen. Outside the dramatic building is a collection of spacecraft and launch vehicles. The Space Center is about three miles from downtown Alamogordo via U.S. Hwy. 70, Indian Wells Road and Scenic Drive (505-437-2840 or 800-545-4021).

• Oliver Lee State Park

This fascinating natural area is 12 miles south of town via U.S. Hwy. 54 and then a county road for 2 miles. Springs flow out of the desert year-round, creating comparatively lush vegetation.

This location was one of the final strongholds of Apache warriors and the site of several Indian/cavalry battles. There's a visitor center with exhibits on the human and natural history of this canyon which lies at the base of the Sacramento Mountains. There is a campground and an interpretive trail.

• Three Rivers National Recreation Site

Thirty-seven miles north of the city, a drive here proves an easy day-trip. This protected area includes more than 5,000 rock carvings made by Mogollon Indians who lived here between AD 900 and 1400. An interpretive trail leads to the site of a prehistoric Indian village. To get there, take Route 70 north for 13 miles and continue on U.S. Hwy. 54 to Three Rivers, where an 8-mile sideroad leads east to the preserve, managed by the BLM.

• White Sands National Monument

Situated 16 miles southwest of Alamogordo, this amazing place features more than 200 square miles of gleaming gypsum sand that shifts around—with some of the dunes as high as 60 feet. There's a visitor center at the park entrance, and there are sets of sheltered picnic tables in the midst of the vast whiteness.

• Cloudcroft and Ruidoso

Cloudcroft, a resort village, sits atop the Sacramento Mountains, 18 miles east of the city. The drive from Las Cruces to Alamogordo and Cloudcroft is described in the scenic drive beginning on page 320. Beyond Cloudcroft is Ruidoso, the famous horse racing town, which also features skiing (as does Cloudcroft). The All American Futurity, the richest horserace in the United States, is held at Ruidoso Downs each Labor Day.

The Lincoln State Monument (the scene of the Lincoln County War) is in the same mountain area. For directions, see page 323.

New Mexico

Albuquerque

This is a city made for drivers. Spread out over a wide area in the upper Rio Grande Valley, its attractions are numerous but require a car to fully explore. From the Sandia Peak Scenic Byway to the Coronado Monument, the region is defined first by the river and then by the nearby mountains.

Named after the Viceroy of New Spain, the Duke of Alburquerque—the first "r" was dropped in later years—the community sat beside a busy crossroads during the days of American settlement. In 1880, the Santa Fe Railroad pulled into what then was a small town and the city quickly took shape. It was the destination of cattle drivers from as far away as Texas. Today, Albuquerque is home to 500,000 people but the cultural heart of the city is still the Old Town and the Plaza where the first Spanish mission was established. The human history of the area is much older than the Spanish conquests. Several pueblos are in the area, most to the north of town, and the Pueblo Indian culture has been a continuing influence on life in the Rio Grande Valley as well as providing destinations for tourists.

Things to See and Do
• Old Town Albuquerque

Close to the city's newer "downtown," the Old Town area is bordered by Rio Grande Blvd. (on the west), Central Avenue (to the south), and Mountain Road (north). More than 100 restaurants and shops—many in historic adobe buildings—are located in the area. The centerpiece of Old Town is the Spanish Plaza, across from the Church of San Felipe de Neri. The church has been considerably rebuilt and enlarged since its founding in the 1700s, but the original thick walls are still intact within the structure. While homes were originally built around the Plaza, offering community security, these have given way to jewelry and crafts shops, galleries, and restaurants. The **Albuquerque Museum**, located at the northern edge of Old Town, has a multimedia show on the history of the city since 1875 as well as displays of artifacts and exhibits on the Spanish/American periods titled "Four Centuries—A History of

Destinations

Albuquerque." Across from this museum is the **New Mexico Museum of Natural History**, which opened in 1986 with displays on the development of the state's natural resources. The Dynamax Theater is part of the complex.

On Christmas eve, the Plaza is gently lit by thousands of "luminarias," candles set in paper bags with beds of sand, which have replaced the lighted pinyon pine logs carried by early Spanish settlers on their way to the church.

• Indian Pueblo Cultural Center

Before visiting one or more of the 19 existing Indian pueblos in this part of New Mexico, a trip to this horseshoe-shaped complex is recommended. The center is located one block north of Interstate 40 at 2401 Twelfth Street and features historical displays on the development of the Pueblo villages—now occupied by more than 40,000 people. The building has been designed as an homage to the landmark Bonito Pueblo in Chaco Canyon. During spring and summer, demonstrations in the performance area include retelling Indian rites with spectacular dances, in addition to potterymaking and silver crafts. There's a restaurant that serves traditional Indian foods, plus modern American dishes. The gift shop has kachina dolls and jewelry from the Zuni, Hopi, and Navajo peoples, as well as sand paintings. An admission fee is charged and the center is open daily from mid-April through early January and daily except Sunday during the winter months. For information, call (505) 843-7270.

• University of New Mexico

Located in the middle of the city, this is the state's largest university and it showcases pueblo architecture in several of its buildings. Free to visitors are the **Maxwell Museum of Anthropology**, which specializes in exhibits on the native cultures of the Southwest, the **Museum of Geology and Meteorites**, containing a multitude of old rocks in addition to exhibits on the flora and fauna of New Mexico, and the **Fine Arts Center** in the New Mexico Union Building. The latter includes a theater complex and is home to the

New Mexico

New Mexico Symphony and the University Art Museum. A campus map and an updated calendar of university events are available at the Visitors Bureau in the Fine Arts Center. For information on university happenings, call (505) 277-3729.

• Sandia Peak Aerial Tramway

Drive 19 miles north of the city on Interstate 25 (the direct route to Santa Fe) and turn east onto Tramway Blvd. The cable gondola will take you to the top of Sandia Peak, at the top of the Sandia Mountain range. The trip takes about 18 minutes, climbing from an elevation of 6,599 feet to the crest at 10,378 feet. There is a cactus garden and a restaurant at the base, with a Forest Service information station, hiking trails, and another restaurant at the top of the tram ride.

• International Balloon Fiesta

During early October, the Albuquerque sky becomes filled with dozens of colorful hot-air balloons. Inaugurated in 1972, this festival has grown to the point that now, almost 500 balloons take part over the ten-day period. Mass flights take place during morning hours and a highlight of each festival is the Balloon Glow when hundreds of balloons are inflated after sundown. The best source of information about the upcoming Balloon Fiesta is the Albuquerque Convention and Visitors Bureau, at 1-800-284-2282 or (505) 243-3696.

Where to Eat

Albuquerque food is a mix of traditional Mexican dishes, the newer Southwest cuisine and barbecue. A good place to start on your own research into the local food scene is Old Town, where several notable restored historic buildings surround the Spanish Plaza. These include **La Hacienda**, a rambling collection of rooms that features Mexican and other regional dishes plus many baked goods. It's located on a corner at 302 San Felipe Street N.W. ($$). **High Noon Restaurant and Saloon** (425 San Felipe) has a schizophrenic approach to dining. At lunch, American and Mexican dishes are served in this casual spot. For dinner, the menu switches to continental cuisine with a few American dishes

Destinations

added. There are three rooms in this old adobe building, each lit by sky-lights ($$ to $$$). A third choice in Old Town is **Restaurant Antiquity**, serving continental cuisine in yet another historic building. This is an extremely intimate place, at 112 Romero ($$$).

There are several restaurants with distinctive food at a lower price than the Old Town restaurants we have recommended. At the **M & J Sanitary Tortilla Factory Restaurant** (403 2nd St. S.E., downtown) the Mexican food is fresh and plentiful. Expect to taste such specialties as blue corn enchiladas and carne adovada ($). Central Avenue is the old Route 66 highway, and the **66 Diner** keeps up the tradition the famed old cross-country road inspired. You'll be able to order chicken fried steak, burgers, meat loaf, and other 50s comfort food in this spiffy chrome-finished restaurant—at this location since 1987 ($).

We can't mention Albuquerque food without telling you about the **Quarters Barbecue Restaurants**. They're not mentioned in the usual tourist handouts nor are you required to wear a tuxedo. Attracting patrons from the university as well as local families, both of these popular places are barn-like rooms with long tables and always have a hearty crowd chowing down on the fabulous food. Both places feature slow-smoked open-pit barbecue dishes (ribs, links, chicken, etc.) with beans and other fixings and plenty of beer on tap. One Quarters is located at 905 Yale Blvd. (southeast of the downtown area) and the other is at 4516 Wyoming Blvd. (on the east side near Interstate 40) ($ to $$).

Side Trips from Albuquerque

The drive featured in this book starting on page 304 leads from Interstate 40 east of town to the Sandia Peak Scenic Byway and farther north to several fascinating old towns including Madrid and Cerrillos. This is a great way to avoid the freeway when traveling to Santa Fe. Salinas National Monument preserves the ruins of three old Spanish mission communities (Quarai, Abo, and Gran Quivita) 60 miles southeast of Albuquerque. For a view of Indian and Spanish life of four centuries ago, drive east on I-40 to the Tijeras exit, then turn south on New Mexico Route 14 and continue to the village of Punta de Aqua. A paved road leads into the ruins area.

New Mexico

Aztec & Farmington

Aztec is a small community 14 miles north of Farmington in northwestern New Mexico, close to the Four Corners. Throughout this region, the ancient Indian peoples called the Anasazi built magnificent stone structures—whole communities with apartments, ceremonial kivas, and plazas—in which they based their culture and trade.

Aztec Ruins National Monument is one of the largest and best-restored ruins of the Anasazi culture, named by mistaken pioneers who believed that the former inhabitants were Aztec Indians from Mexico. A pueblo with several hundred rooms has been partially uncovered, and a portion is intact. The Great Kiva, a stupendous 48-foot-wide round chamber set into the ground, is the largest such structure excavated to date. It has been fully restored. There is a visitor center with a small museum at the park entrance. A self-guided tour leads from the visitor center through the pueblo ruin and into the Great Kiva. Aside from the normal park service brochure on the monument, the center has an excellent trail guide that will guide you through the two main structures. This small booklet, with color pictures and drawings of the stone construction techniques, is not only a good tool while visiting the park but also provides a brief history of the Anasazi. Picnic tables are located under the shelter of a grove of cottonwoods next to the ruins.

Other Things to See & Do

• Navajo Lake

This is the state's largest reservoir, backing up the waters of the San Juan River for more than 30 miles. A pinyon-juniper forest borders the lake. This is a popular spot for boating, fishing (for trout, catfish, and bass), and swimming. There is a marina with boat ramps, houseboat rentals, and camping supplies. There are three recreation sites located around the lake, all toward the southern end. Closest to Aztec is the San Juan River Recreation Area (via Route 511). The Pine River Recreation Area is also along Route 511, at the mouth of the Los Pinos River. Sima Mesa Recreation Area is farther to the east, via Highway 64 and then north to the lake on Route 527.

Destinations

• Aztec Museum

The museum features an exhibit of pioneer Americana that includes several old buildings—a general store, a pioneer cabin, the doctor's and sheriff's offices, a blacksmith's shop and foundry, and a church.

• Salmon Ruins & Farmington Museum

One of the region's larger prehistoric Indian sites, the ruin is located just south of Farmington, overlooking the San Juan River. It is thought to have been built by the Anasazi and occupied by later groups during the ninth and tenth centuries. There is an on-site museum and archeological research center. The museum features artifacts from the excavated ruins, and a self-guiding trail leads to them. The Farmington Museum has exhibits on the more recent cultural and pioneer history of the area.

• Navajo Indian Reservation

Shiprock—a volcanic monolith—rises more than 1,700 feet into the sky west of Farmington. The huge rock lies within the Navajo Indian Reservation, which takes up large parts of Arizona, Utah, and New Mexico. The rock is said by the resident natives to have spiritual properties. South of Farmington, Highway 371 passes across a high mesa where the Navajo farm an enormous tract of land, thanks to extensive amounts of irrigation water from the San Juan River.

Bandelier National Monument

On the Pajarito Plateau—10 miles from the town of Los Alamos—successive groups of prehistoric Indians lived, hunted, and farmed. The earliest occupation by natives is dated from about 2010 BC, with later development around 670 BC. The Archaic People, as they are known, were nomadic hunters, moving about in family groups. By AD 1300, the Anasazi had left the Four Corners region and some had moved into Frijoles Canyon. They built large pueblo structures in the canyon as well as small villages on the mesas where they grew crops. They also farmed on the bottomland of the canyon—beans, squash, and corn. With ample supplies of game and fertile farmlands, the Pajaritan culture survived here for 300 years. Cliff dwellings were carved out of volcanic tufa above the creek. These settlements comprise the area preserved in Bandelier National Monument.

There was much volcanic activity in the formation of the Jemez Mountains. Prime evidence of this is Vallee Grande, the huge caldera seen from Highway 4 west of Bandelier. There are several hot springs in the region, which add to the pleasure of a visit to this significant site.

How to Get There

The monument is 46 miles west of Santa Fe via U.S. 285/84 north to Pojoaque, and then west on N.M. Route 4 for another 24 miles. From Albuquerque, drive north on I-25 and U.S. Hwy. 85 to Santa Fe and take U.S. Route 285/84 and Highway 4. Total mileage from Albuquerque to the ruins is 105 miles. A longer but more scenic route through the Jemez Mountains is covered in the scenic drive that begins on page 308.

Things to See & Do

Bandelier National Monument contains fascinating ruins of the early Pueblo dwellers, including the Tyuonyi Pueblo, the Ceremonial Cave and—by a mile-long trail—the Frijolito Ruin. Named for one of the first European discoverers of the site, Adolph F. Bandelier, the monument attracts thousands of people each year. A businessman consumed with the study of native cultures, Bandelier became an explorer and researcher and is considered to be the first anthropologist of the Southwest region. Today's visitors are left in awe, as was Bandelier, at the complex culture that developed in Frijoles Canyon.

• Park Trails

The visitor center is located at the end of the entrance road, at the beginning of Frijoles Canyon, with the Tyuonyi Pueblo nearby. An interpretive trail leads to the cave dwellings, and the Ceremonial Cave is reached by climbing a series of ladders farther along. You can also hike in the canyon to the Rio Grande. Seventy miles of trails lead into the backcountry, giving hikers and backpackers entry to a huge wilderness area that is part of the monument preserve. Permits are required to travel these trails, which lead to

337

Destinations

remote canyons and additional ruins. A hike to the Stone Lions shrine offers a 12-mile round trip.

Painted Cave is reached via a 20-mile round trip.

• Tsankiwi Pueblo

A separate unit of the monument is located along Route 4, 11 miles north of the main entrance road. Tsankiwi is a mesa-top pueblo that has been left in an unexcavated state. A trail leads across these ruins and beside another set of cave dwellings.

• Camping and Services

There is a campground on the mesa at the main site (just below the entrance from Route 4), and there is a picnic area beside Frijoles Creek. The visitor center includes a small museum in addition to a snack bar and gift shop.

Carlsbad Caverns National Park

Combining the largest underground caves on the continent with spectacular desert backcountry, this park in the southeastern corner of the state attracts 750,000 visitors each year. The area lay in obscurity until Jim White, a 19-year-old cowboy who was wandering through the area, in 1901, and discovered a huge natural entrance to Carlsbad Cavern when he saw a cloud of bats rising from it. He descended into the cave and became enchanted. He stayed here for the rest of his life, becoming a guano miner and harvesting the bat droppings for the next 20 years.

A few months after his first tentative explorations, White traveled into the Big Room and the lower cave. He began escorting visitors through the caverns, using the mine hoist and guano buckets as an elevator for his tours. President Coolidge created the Carlsbad Cave National Monument in 1923, and the site was given national park status in 1930. New Cave was discovered at Slaughter Canyon in 1937. *National Geographic* magazine featured the caves, and throngs of tourists came during the 1940s. By then, passenger elevators had been built. The first self-guided tours began in 1972, and since then the caverns have become one of the most popular attractions in the state.

New Mexico

Both Carlsbad Caverns and New Cave are open to the public. They are accessed by different roads. The main road from the village of White's City leads to the visitor center and Carlsbad Cavern. County Road 418, off Hwy. 62 south of White's City, runs to a parking lot near the entrance to New Cave.

Things to See & Do

• Carlsbad Cavern Tours

The area of this huge set of caverns and passages stretches more than 20 miles. Visitors travel more than 800 feet below the surface with fanciful formations everywhere. The temperature here is always 56 degrees. Travelers through the caves are issued headphones for a narrative description of the tour, which proceeds along lighted trails. There are two tours from which to choose, depending on the time you have. The longer tour (Blue) provides a three-mile walk starting with a 2-mile descent on a trail which leads to the Big Room. Reserve about 2 hours for the Blue Tour.

The Red Tour enters the Big Room by elevator, descending 750 feet. The loop trail around the room is a little more than a mile long and takes an hour. Visitors on either tour may get food at the underground lunchroom. Both tours end with a ride to the entrance by elevator.

There's a museum with exhibits on the history of the cave and the surrounding desert landscape, as well as an observation tower, gift shop, day-care center, and pet kennel. Outside the visitor center is a half-mile nature trail that provides a self-guided walk over high ground, with displays of the region's flora and fauna.

• New Cave Tour

A trip through New Cave is more adventurous than the tours of the larger cavern. Here, visitors take a hike through the undeveloped cave in groups of 25 people, led by rangers. Reservations are necessary for this tour, and you are required to bring your own flashlight and water. The hour-long tour covers more than a mile of passageways, and the walk is fairly strenuous, with a climb of 500

Destinations

feet to return to the mouth of the cave and the parking lot. Rattlesnake Springs Picnic Area offers shaded picnic tables with water, grills, and toilets, beside the road that leads to New Cave.

• Bats in the Sky

From May through October, visitors gather in the park amphitheater at dusk to see thousands of bats flying out of the entrance, just as Jim White first saw the swarm of bats in 1901. The rodents swirl around and then fly to the Pecos River Valley to feed on insects. They are seen again at daybreak, returning to the cavern entrance—an area which is off-limits to humans.

• Walnut Canyon Drive

This is a 9.5-mile loop road which starts 1/2 mile from the Carlsbad Cavern entrance and proceeds along a ridge to Rattlesnake Canyon, returning to the visitor center through Upper Walnut Canyon. There's a guidebook available for full enjoyment of this fine tour.

• Nearby Parks & Attractions

Guadalupe Mountains National Park is south of the caverns, across the border in Texas. Guadalupe Peak is the highest mountain in Texas. This is a good place to camp while visiting the natural attractions of the area. Campgrounds are located at Pine Springs (off Route 62/180) and Dog Canyon a more remote site accessed via Route 137, which leads from U.S. 285 north of the town of Carlsbad). One of the most scenic parts of the park is McKittrick Canyon where high sheer rock walls protect a variety of plant species nurtured by a spring-fed creek. This is good birding territory, and from late October through mid-November, the oak and walnut trees are ablaze with brilliant colors. The canyon is at the end of a paved road off Route 62/180.

Living Desert State Park is located 4 miles north of Carlsbad, off Hwy. 285. The Chihauhuan Desert reserve is home to several dozen species of desert wildlife including birds and reptiles. An interpretive trail shows plants that live on the sand dunes. The **Desert Arboretum** features cacti from this and other desert regions

New Mexico

of the world. There's a small zoo with cougars, javalina, bobcats, kangaroo rats, and other animals of the area.

• Carlsbad

This small city takes advantage of the nearby natural attractions, providing services for tourists with a selection of modest motels and cafes. There are two golf courses and several nearby lakes for boating and fishing. Windsurfing is popular on **Lake Avalon**. There are campsites and picnic areas at **Brantley Lake State Park,** north of Carlsbad on Hwy. 285. A KOA campground and RV park is located nearby.

• White's City

Originally just one tourist court near the caverns, White's City has grown to three motels, the Velvet Garter Saloon and Restaurant, a hamburger joint, gas stations, a store (they do a great business selling flashlights and cameras), the Million Dollar Museum (a hugely popular commercial attraction), and RV parks. Granny's Opera House features old-fashioned melodramas.

Chaco Culture National Historic Park

About 800 years ago, the Anasazi departed from Chaco Canyon. No one knows why, and no one understands how the Anasazi managed to build the impressive structures in what is now recognized as the cultural center of these prehistoric Indian people. To visit this long, shallow canyon is to engage in both an historical search and an intense emotional experience—heightened by the enduring mystery of the Ancient Ones. This site is the location of the largest and most complicated architectural marvels of the Anasazi age.

How to Get There

Located in the northwestern corner of New Mexico, Chaco Canyon is in a remote location connected to the outside world by a gravel road, New Mexico Route 57. It is south of Farmington and Bloomfield and northeast of Gallup. Our scenic drive beginning on page 296 covers a route to the park from Aztec and Farmington, using county roads that cross the

Escabada Wash. For those with less yearning for backroad adventure, there are other, easy routes.

From the north, take N.M. Route 44 from Bloomfield (13 miles east of Farmington) and head south for 44 miles to Nageezi. Turn west and follow Route 57 to the park.

From the south, drive west from Gallup or east from Albuquerque on Interstate 40 and exit at Thoreau. Drive north on N.M. Route 371 and turn right (east) onto N.M. Route 57, then continue to the park (64 miles from I-40).

The Anasazi at Chaco Canyon

For more than 10,000 years, nomadic natives roamed the Four Corners area, passing through this canyon. The first long-term residents arrived about AD 700. The Basketmakers lived in the canyon, constructing small one-storey masonry pueblos. There is evidence that the Anasazi began building in Chaco Canyon around AD 900, constructing what later became Pueblo Benito, the largest of the community structures. By 1115, the Chaco culture had spread to more than 70 other pueblos, which had been established at some distance—as far as 60 miles away—and connected to the trading and cultural center by amazingly straight roads as much as 30 feet in width. Pueblo Bonito had expanded to contain more than 800 rooms, with adjoining plazas and ceremonial kivas. More than 2,000 people—perhaps as many as 5,000—lived in the canyon pueblos. Craftspeople of the region produced distinctive black-on-white glazed pottery in addition to turquoise ornaments including necklaces, bracelets, and pendants. Seashells were also strung into necklaces. Chaco traded with far-flung nations, including Mexico.

Then the Anasazi began to abandon their pueblos. First the outlying communities were deserted and by 1200 the towns in Chaco Canyon were empty. Drought may have been the reason for the evacuation. After moving to other places, the Anasazi faded into history, with the later Pueblo Indians carrying on some of the Anasazi architectural tradition.

After 1200, the Anasazi towns in the canyon sat and deteriorated for hundreds of years. For a while, Apache moved into the region, but they didn't stay at Chaco. Then, one of the Apache bands—the Navajo—established settlements in the area, and the remains of their homes are found on the nearby mesas. A few miles to the west is the boundary of the vast Navajo Indian Reservation. One-hundred miles due west is Canyon de Chelly, another reminder of the Anasazi tradition but occupied today by Navajo, who farm the river valley.

Chaco Canyon has no farming today, nor has it any residents except for a few Park Service employees. The canyon has been preserved for its unique role as the hub of a prehistoric civilization in North America and the center of an ancient culture that surpassed in complexity that of any other group of people in what is now the United States.

Things to See & Do

The road from the north passes through Cly Canyon, a narrow gorge on the drive into the historic park. After passing several Anasazi ruins, some of which are hidden from view, you'll find the one-way loop road that circles through Chaco Canyon, leading to the most important ruins. The visitor center is beyond this loop road, and the campground (the only place to stay in the area) is beyond the visitor center.

• Pueblo Bonito

The most impressive of the ruins, this large structure is located at the west end of the canyon. Built in stages, this huge pueblo eventually contained more than 600 rooms and had 40 round kivas (ceremonial chambers where rituals were carried out). It is considered the classic Anasazi group dwelling. If you have only a half-day to explore the park, this is the pueblo to see first.

Excavation started here at the turn of the century and this work continued through the 1920s. You'll be amazed at the intricate stone work—several storeys tall, most of it without mortar.

343

• Chetro Ketl

Located adjacent to Pueblo Bonito, Chetro Ketl has 500 rooms and 16 kivas. This pueblo dates from about 1054, and the structure was completed about 1100 or later. Visiting the two ruins will take about 90 minutes.

Destinations

• Casa Rinconada & Tsin Kletsin

Situated on the opposite side of the canyon, Casa Rinconada is one of the largest of the "great kivas" found in the Four Corners region. A short trail leads to this building, passing several small villages. The path continues, ascending to the mesa where stands Tsin Kletsin, a great house providing a fine panoramic view of the canyon and surrounding high points of land.

• Smaller Communities

Kin Kletso, located near the west end of the canyon, was supposedly built in two stages—the first from about 1125 and the remainder built about 1130. Archeologists say that it probably had three storeys on the north side and 100 rooms in all.

Slightly east of this site, beside the canyon road, is Pueblo del Arroyo. Built beside the wash, beginning in 1075, it was completed with the construction of the plaza about 1110. This building had about 280 rooms and at least 20 kivas. A smaller ruin, Una Vida, is reached by a short stroll from the visitor center. This partially excavated structure is thought to have had about 150 rooms.

• Trails

Hiking trails (including the path to Tsin Kletsin) lead to the mesa areas on both sides of the canyon. Pueblo Alta, sitting on the mesa above Pueblo Bonito, is an important site at the junction of several major Anasazi roads. Other trails lead to Casa Chiquita and Peñasco Blanco, at the extreme west end of the central canyon where the road descends into the park.

• Enjoying Your Chaco Canyon Visit

It pays to plan ahead to fully enjoy a visit to this remote place.

First, you need to consider that modern places to stay are some 60 to 80 miles away—to the north in Bloomfield and Farmington, or to the south at Crownpoint or farther still in Gallup. It is possible to spend 2 or 3 hours in the canyon and come away with something—at least a basic feeling for the importance of the communities that once flourished here.

New Mexico

A stay of 2 or 3 days is highly recommended if you are able to camp or stay in an RV or trailer. The park campground offers a place to stay although there are no hookups. Water is available from a tap at the visitor center, and there are restrooms in the campground. Trailers and RVs more than 30 feet long cannot be accommodated.

The nearest stores for supplies are in Nageezi and the Blanco Trading Post on N.M. Route 44. There is another store to the west on N.M. Route 371, near the village of Lake Valley (accessed via county roads). The best tactic is to purchase all the supplies you need before driving to the canyon.

The museum in the visitor center features displays on the history of the Anasazi. A ranger-led tour of the ruin sites is highly recommended. The visitor center has schedules for these tours as well as the evening interpretation sessions. There are booklets at the larger sites that provide walking tour information and historical background. The shop in the visitor center has a good supply of books on the history of the Anasazi and other Indian cultures.

Side Trips from Chaco Canyon
• To Bisti Badlands & Wilderness

Of course, the ideal thing to do is stay in the canyon for a few days and fully explore the sites in the canyon as well as nearby points of interest. These include the Bisti Badlands to the north, where weird, colored rock formations and petrified wood and fossils are seen in a desolate area on both sides of Gateway and Hunter's Washes. The Bisti Wilderness has no developed trails, and visitors are encouraged to walk across the stark wilderness areas—very much like what one would imagine walking on the moon would be like. The badlands are accessible from the east (the shortest route from Chaco Canyon) as well as from the west via N.M. Route 371. From Chaco Canyon, drive out to N.M. Route 44 and turn north toward Bloomfield. Then, take the road leading west at the El Huerfano Trading Post (County Road 7500). This dirt road leads beside the De-Na-Zin Wilderness Area, coming out at Highway

345

Destinations

371. Turn north and the Bisti Wilderness Road is a few minutes' drive. This road leads east to the old Bisti Trading Post and a rough parking lot that provides access to the badlands.

Another way to get to the badlands is by the network of county roads featured on our scenic drive (log on page 299).

• To Other Indian Ruins

Other prehistoric ruins in this general region include the **Salmon Ruins**, south of Farmington, and the **Aztec Ruins National Monument**, just north of Farmington in the town of Aztec. The more recently developed Zuni Pueblo is near the Salmon Ruins. Zuni are renowned for their silver and turquoise jewelry.

Canyon de Chelly National Monument is in Arizona, reached by taking U.S. Highway 191 north from Interstate 40 to the town of Chinle. The I-40 exit is just west of Sanders. Chinle is 67 miles from the interstate.

Chama

The village of Chama sits in the mountains close to the Colorado border, in a region of forests and towering peaks, looking much as it did at least 50 years ago. The community was founded in the mid-1800s when gold and silver attracted prospectors and the grazing lands enticed ranchers. The prospectors departed early but the ranchers stayed. Lumbering, ranching, and tourism are the mainstays of the local economy. Although there are a few modest motels in town, many visitors stay in several rustic mountain lodges, B & B inns, and guest ranches. The Chamber of Commerce Visitor Center is located at the junction of Highways 84 and 17 (call 800-477-0149 or write Box 306, Chama, N.M. 87520). Most travelers to Chama come here because of the railway.

Things to See & Do

• Cumbres & Toltec Scenic Railroad

The old steam engine chugs its way along the narrow gauge line, climbing to Cumbres Pass and drawing passengers along one of the most scenic routes and on the highest train line in North America.

This is the Cumbres & Toltec Scenic Railroad, an actual journey of 64 miles but—in the mind—a leap into the past amidst scenes of Rocky Mountain splendor.

Yes, the Rockies poke into New Mexico, and this railroad provides one of the best ways to see them. The line operates from Memorial Day weekend through mid-October from the depot in downtown Chama, traveling the 64 miles to Antonito, Colorado, and back again. A road joins the two communities, making it possible for visitors to take the train one way and return (or drive to Antonito) by car. You can also book a van ride for one-way transportation—either to or from Antonito. Osier is the high half-way point where the train stops and lunch is available. There are actually two trains that exchange at Osier and both have cars that are either fully-enclosed or open.

The line was built as the San Juan extension of the Denver & Rio Grande in 1880 to service the mining camps in the San Juan Mountains. It is now owned by the states of Colorado and New Mexico. Fares range from about $30 to $50, depending on the length of the ride and if you wish to have a one-way van ride. For information and reservations, call (505) 756-2151 or write Cumbres & Toltec Scenic Railroad, P.O. Box 789, Chama, N.M. 87520.

• City Slickers Adventure

An unusual tour combines travel on horseback, a wagon ride, camping, and a return train ride to and from Osier. Organized by Western Outdoor Adventures, their "City Slickers Package" involves taking the train to the top of the line, where you are met by cowboys who conduct the trail ride or give you a wagon ride to a camp on a wide mountain meadow.

347

There are private tents and several buildings including a dining hall. Evening meals are cooked around a campfire. The days are spent hiking, fishing, or relaxing. Two nights are spent at camp before returning to Osier for the train ride. For information and reservations, call (505) 756-2653.

Destinations

• Fishing

Trout fishing is available at Heron Lake and El Vado Lake, part of the Rio Brazos system. Several of the lodges and guest ranches in the area feature fishing (see the Places to Stay pages that follow).

• Chama Music Festival

For most of July, Chama features a festival that includes almost every type of music from chamber groups to jug bands, gospel, and cabaret performances. The festival is held at the Chama Valley Community Center and, in the past, has included a scenic mountain concert in Osier, with a train ride included. For information, call (505) 756-2197.

• Ghost Ranch Living Museum

Situated 45 miles south of Chama and 14 miles north of Abiquiu on U.S. Route 84, this small but fascinating museum is on the site of the old Ghost Ranch, the legendary farm where artist Georgia O'Keeffe painted some of her earliest and finest works. The museum houses a collection of native animals, and museum displays show the evolution of the geology of the region. Nearby at the actual Ghost Ranch (now owned by the Presbyterian Church) reconstructed dinosaur fossils found in the area are on display.

• Echo Amphitheater

A recreation site near the Ghost Ranch in the Santa Fe National Forest, this large rocky bowl offers a scenic campground and trails that explore this large forest and the rivers of the region.

• Jicarilla Apache Indian Reservation

West and south of Chama, this large reservation has several camping areas that are open to the public, as well as a large motor lodge in the town of Dulce. The drive from Santa Fe to Chama and then through the reservation is featured as part of our scenic drive beginning on page 292.

Permits are required for staying in the Apache campgrounds, and these are available in Dulce. The Little Beaver Roundup is held in July and the Stone Lake Fiesta in mid-September. Apache hunting guides are also available. Dulce is 30 miles west of Chama on Highway 64, on the route to Farmington and Shiprock. Highway 537 runs the full length of the reservation—from north to south—providing access to the sideroads that lead to Apache recreation areas. For information, call (505) 759-3255.

• Lodges, Guest Ranches, and Campgrounds

As mentioned above, the **Jicarilla Inn** (a Best Western) is located in Dulce, within the reservation. **Corkins Lodge** is a cabin resort overlooking the wild Brazos River next to the Brazos Cliffs, which rise to over 11,000 feet. Fishing is the main activity here. Call (505) 588-7261. **De Masters Lodge**, in Chama, is a modern/rustic place with meals available. Call (505) 756-2942.

Unser's Oso Ranch is operated by the Al Unsers (Jr. and Sr.). The lakes here are stocked with trout, and the ranch is popular with hunters looking for mountain lion and elk. During winter months, the ranch becomes a cross-country ski resort with ice-fishing available. Meals are served. For availabilities, call 800-882-5190 or (505) 756-2954.

Area motels are listed in the Places to Stay pages which follow.

Cloudcroft

Sitting 9,200 feet high in the Sacramento Mountains, this little village is a unique resort destination well worth the drive from Las Cruces (90 miles), Alamogordo (18 miles), or El Paso, Texas (95 miles). The drive from Las Cruces to Cloudcroft is featured in our scenic drive beginning on page 320.

Cloudcroft was founded as a railway town when the Southern Pacific Railroad built a spur line into the mountains to transport logs for railway ties and constructed a lodge for railroad workers and tourists. The railway has long since disappeared, and only a high wooden trestle remains. However, the workers' bunkhouse has become the renowned Cloudcroft Lodge, and it is as fine a resort inn as one could hope to encounter—anywhere in America. More about the lodge later.

Destinations

During winter months, the ski hill here provides the most southerly downhill experience in the lower 48 states. Cross-country skiing is a popular activity as well, in the Lincoln National Forest which sprawls throughout more than one million acres across the mountain range. In the summer, people flock here to fish, ride horses, hike and play golf on a spectacularly scenic course that is one of the highest courses in the west. The forest is a major attraction, providing hiking trails, riding (there are local stables with horse rentals), and several scenic drives (see below).

Things to See & Do

• Golfing

There are two courses: the high-level nine-hole course at the Cloudcroft Lodge, which offers fairways cutting through the pine forest—an experience that a golf magazine has described as "the most unique golfing experience this side of heaven"—and the nine-hole course (Ponderosa Pines) in Cox Canyon, nine miles southeast of Cloudcroft on New Mexico Route 130.

• Railroad Trestle

The only visible remains of the Sacramento Mountains railway line sits beside the highway on the west side of town. A trail leads down the hill to the bridge, which crosses a deep canyon.

• Snowmobiling & Winter Play

The Triple M Snow Play Area offers guided snowmobile tours in the high reaches of the Lincoln National Forest, as well as ice skating on a pond and inner tube sliding slopes (which have lifts to the top). Skate and tube rentals are available, and there is a snack bar. It is located south of town on Sunspot Road (Hwy. 130). Many snowmobile trails are available, using logging roads in the Lincoln National Forest. Ski Cloudcroft is located at the eastern edge of town on Hwy. 82. With 700 vertical feet, the ski area offers lifts, rentals and instruction. Lodging is less than 5 minutes' drive—in downtown Cloudcroft.

• Special Events

As with other summer and winter resort towns, Cloudcroft has a parade of special events and festivals throughout the year. The

New Mexico

annual Bluegrass Festival is held in June with groups from southern New Mexico and West Texas. The Sunday concert usually features gospel groups. June also brings the annual Western Roundup. This eclectic affair features an old-time fiddling contest, gun and knife show, a barbecue, pie auction, western street dance, and Mexican-style rodeo. Independence Day weekend features the July Jamboree, which combines a crafts fair with food stands, a horse-shoe tournament, another street dance, and other events.

In mid-August there's a spiritual singing festival, and the town has another street dance and barbecue on Labor Day weekend. Railroad/Logging Days (mid-September) features logging contests and an antique show among other events. Rodeo Weekend is in late September. As you might gather, there's something happening almost every week during the summer and fall period.

• The Lodge

I don't usually devote this much space to a single inn, but the Cloudcroft Lodge is special enough to plan a complete vacation trip around a stay here.

Built in 1899 by the railroad, the lodge is just as it was then: a grand Victorian structure with cozy rooms, an excellent dining room (with fine decor and fine dining), the 9,200-foot-high golf course, and the lodge's supreme natural setting on a hilltop above the little town.

The surrounding forest is thick with pine, blue spruce, and aspen. All rooms are filled with antique furnishings, and the lodge is such that it maintains the feeling of a private mansion rather than that of a hotel. **The Pavilion** is a separate bed and breakfast inn, located on the Lodge's entrance road. This is another restored historic lodge.

351

The dining room (**Rebecca's Restaurant and Lounge**) deserves special mention. The food is superb, and there is service to match. **Rebecca's Garden** is the outdoor dining deck, which is open during the summer and fall months for all three meals. The **Beach Bar and Grill** is beside the pool and is open from 10 AM to 4 PM.

Destinations

The **Red Dog Saloon** is a western bar, open daily from 5 PM to midnight, Wednesday through Saturday. Live entertainment is featured on weekends in the saloon, year-round.

Gila Cliff Dwellings National Monument

It is thought by archeologists that the modern pueblo culture in New Mexico had its origins with the people who are called the Mogollon (mug-ee-yone). These prehistoric peoples lived in small groups along the Little Colorado River system and as far south as Mexico. Following the evolution of the earlier Cochise people (5500 BC to AD 500), the Mogollon were influenced by the more highly-developed Anasazi who lived to the north in the Four Corners region. This was the period during which the Gila Cliff Dwellings were occupied—after AD 1000.

The earlier pit dwellings of the Mogollon have been destroyed by nature over the centuries. However, because they have been protected from the elements, the Gila Cliff Dwellings and a few other sites have survived. The dwellings and surrounding Gila Wilderness are national treasures.

How to Get There

Our route to these fascinating ruins is described in the scenic drive—the final drive in this book—that begins on page 324. The tour begins on Interstate 10, in Deming, a few miles north of the Mexico border, and leads beside the Mimbres River through the Gila National Forest, passing Lake Roberts. A more direct route (and the final part of the scenic drive) is via New Mexico Route 90, north from Lordsburg through Silver City and then by N.M. Route 15 to the monument.

Things to See & Do

• The Cliff Dwellings

After stopping at the main park visitor center, you proceed to the trailhead, which is a mile down the road. There's a parking lot and another smaller visitor center here. The trail is 1 mile long and leads across the west fork of the Gila River through Cliff Dwellers Canyon. After the climb, visitors can walk through the five deep caves—with 40 rooms in all. The caves are about 150 feet above

New Mexico

the floor of the canyon. You should plan for a 60- to 90-minute walk, including the tour of the dwellings. The walls of the community are well preserved, shaded from the rain and winds.

The national monument area comprises 533 acres, but it is placed within a much larger area—three million acres—of national forest, one of the most beautiful and wild regions and the first in the U.S. to be designated as a national wilderness area. In the immediate area surrounding the cliff dwellings are several hot springs which are accessible by a hiking trail.

The nearby village of Gila Hot Springs includes a store with gas, camping supplies, and horse rentals. Guided pack trips into the wilderness are also available. The Gila Wilderness is crossed by 2,000 miles of trails and is a magnet for cross-country hikers and backpackers, who rarely meet another human on their trips through this spectacular mountain region.

• Camping

Developed campsites are located near the cliff dwellings trailhead. The Scorpion Campgrounds (lower and upper) are located beside each other on the road to the cliff dwellings and are operated on a first come, first served basis. Water and flush toilets are available during summer months. Picnic tables, grills, and pit toilets are available year-round.

• Trails to Hot Springs and Other Places

There are several hot springs accessed via trails that begin near the monument visitor center. One, Little Fork Hot Springs, offers very hot soaking only 1/2 mile up the trail. Another hot spring is at the end of an 8-mile trail that leads through the Gila Wilderness.

353

Several popular day-hikes can be taken from the cliff dwellings. A scenic trail along the west and middle forks of the Gila River leads from the cliff dwellings parking lot, or from the middle fork trailhead parking lot. Another trail leaves from Woody's Corral and proceeds via the West Fork Loop and the Stock Bypass. This 4.5-mile hike has an ascent of 210 feet.

An 8-mile hike begins at Woody's Corral, 1 mile southeast of the cliff dwellings via Sideroad 15, and leads to the EE Canyon Loop, ending at the cliff dwellings parking lot.

Another trail begins at TJ Corral and leads to the West Fork Loop via the Zig-Zag Trail. This is an 11-mile walk, ending at the cliff dwellings parking lot. Trail guides and other material on the Gila Wilderness are available at the visitor center.

Las Cruces

The university and agricultural center for southeastern New Mexico, Las Cruces is located only 44 miles from El Paso, Texas. In the early 1800s, the town was a stopping point on the old Camino Real—the Spanish road that linked Santa Fe and Mexico City. In 1830, a caravan of travelers along the road was massacred by Apaches, and many crosses were placed in the burial grounds. Thus the city's name ("the crosses").

The Santa Fe Railroad came to town in 1881, and New Mexico State University was established here in 1888. The waters of the Rio Grande were used to irrigate the desert throughout this area, and Las Cruces became a major farming hub.

This is the place to visit if you're fascinated by chile peppers. The famed New Mexico green chile is grown here in abundance. The best place to shop for fresh green chiles, at roadside stands, is in Hatch, a little town 20 miles north of Las Cruces. Hatch chiles are found across the country in most of the restaurants that serve the popular southwestern cuisine.

Things to See & Do
• Outdoor Recreation

The Organ Mountains lie just to the east of the city, offering several places for hiking and picnicking, including the Aguirre Spring National Recreation Site.

Leasburg Dam State Park, near Hatch, is a popular place for canoeing and fishing on the Rio Grande. An irrigation dam backs up the river, making a small lake. There's a picnic area beside the

New Mexico

river, below the dam, and a campground is located on the desert overlooking the river. It's an ideal place to camp while visiting the area, just 15 miles north of Las Cruces via New Mexico Route 85.

• Fort Seldon State Monument

The historic site is 14 miles north of the city via Interstate 25. Established in 1865 and abandoned in 1891, Fort Seldon protected settlers and travelers against Indian raids. The site is open daily and a self-guided tour will take you to the adobe ruins of the fort from the visitor center. A small museum has historic exhibits, including displays of army uniforms and guns of the period when the fort was active. For information, call (505) 526-8911.

• State University

New Mexico State is situated three miles southeast of the downtown area, at University Avenue and Locust Street. The university offers free admission to its Museum of Regional History (open daily except Mondays). There is an art gallery on the campus, as well as an 18-hole golf course open to the public, daily, on a pay-for-play basis.

• Farmers Market

Every Wednesday and Saturday morning, throughout the year, the Downtown Mall on Main Street becomes a farmers market. You'll find fresh produce straight from local farms, plus baked goods, crafts, and jewelry. Hundreds of people flock to the market and it pays to get there early (around 8 AM).

• Scenic Drives

The most popular day-trip leads through the Organ Mountains to White Sands National Monument. This tour is featured in the scenic drive that begins on page 320. Other popular jaunts include the short drives to El Paso and into Mexico.

Where to Eat

Mexican and New-Mex food are the specialties here, and a couple of fine places to eat are **The Hacienda** (2605 Espina St.) in a historic home, serving updated Mexican dishes including blue corn tortillas, and **Nellie's**

Destinations

Cafe (1226 W. Hadley Ave.), said to be the best place in town for authentic Mexican food. This long time favorite cafe is closed on Sundays. For fine dining, the **Desert Rose** (1405 W. Picacho Ave.) serves adventurous dishes with tasty sauces in a candlelit setting. There are many other good places to eat in nearby Mesilla (see page 357).

Los Alamos

For a full appreciation of the wilderness and other attractions in this rather unknown part of northern New Mexico, I strongly recommend that you follow our scenic drive through the Jemez Mountains (page 308). If you had driven through this area in the 1940s and 1950s, you would not have been allowed to enter Los Alamos. The town was a closed area, created in 1942 as the nuclear laboratory that produced the atomic bombs that helped to end World War II.

The scientific facilities are still in Los Alamos but the town has been opened to the public and it serves as a center for tourists who wish to explore the historic sites and the wilderness opportunities in this remote area—90 miles north of Albuquerque and 35 miles from Santa Fe.

The most notable geological feature is Vallee Grande, an enormous caldera (collapsed volcano) situated 35 miles west of town. The Anasazi people who inhabited the region in prehistoric days carved their dwellings out of the volcanic cliffs. Bandelier National Monument—a few minutes' drive from Los Alamos—is an excellent example of Anasazi cliff dwelling and pueblo architecture (see page 336). There are several motels in town and in nearby White Rock.

Things to See & Do
• Historical Venues

Bandelier National Monument is 13 miles south of Los Alamos on N.M. Route 4. In addition to miles of hiking trails, this large protected area includes a campground and a picnic area beside Frijoles Creek. The major attraction here is the ruin of a prehistoric Anasazi community in Frijoles Canyon.

In town, the **Ray Bradbury Museum** is a showcase for the history

New Mexico

of nuclear development, including a collection of the original bomb casings as well as other atomic exhibits. Modern technology is not neglected, and the museum has interactive computer displays and exhibits of lasers and fiber optics. Films are shown on a regular basis. For information, call (505) 667-4444.

The **Los Alamos Historic Museum** (2132 Central Ave.) has exhibits relating to the evolution of the area—human, geological, and scientific. Admission is free. The complex includes the **Fuller Lodge Art Center**, an old log building with a regional art and crafts display. Many of the items here are for sale; call (505) 662-6272.

• A Day-Trip from Los Alamos

Vallee Grande and the Jemez Mountains are to the southwest of Los Alamos, providing the basis for a scenic day trip. The sunken caldera valley is 35 miles from town, about 15 miles in diameter, and 500 feet deep. The highway leads along the rim. A little farther west is the Jemez Falls Recreation Area, with camping and trails. Highway 4 continues to Jemez Springs, a small resort town, 40 miles from Los Alamos. It is noted for its two popular hot spring pools. You'll also find the Jemez National Monument, an Indian ruin with visitor center.

Mesilla

This charming, historic community is now a mere outskirt of Las Cruces. In earlier days, it was *the* important town in this whole region, founded by the Spanish in 1598 as a major stopover on the famed Camino Real—the Spanish high road that came north from Mexico City.

While the larger Las Cruces is a modern American city, Mesilla retains much of its original Spanish colonial ambience with a town square fronted by the mission church and many old adobe buildings. Some of the latter are now occupied by shops and restaurants.

It's interesting to note that Mesilla was the Confederate capital of the region during the Civil War. As a tourist town, Mesilla boasts art galleries, a fine museum and several bed and breakfast inns.

Destinations

As a place to eat, this little town is close to the top of our list of Southwest culinary adventure places.

Where to Eat

While the town is a small one, there are several fascinating restaurants which offer a warm Spanish atmosphere along with great food. The most historical of these is **La Posta de Mesilla**, located on the southeast corner of the Plaza. This is a large, spread-out adobe building that was originally an inn serving passengers on the stagecoaches that came through town. There are several dining rooms in the restaurant, one with an atrium, and a gift shop is attached. The house specializes in contemporary cuisine including red and green pepper enchiladas and other New-Mex dishes. The restaurant is closed on Mondays ($$).

Another fine restaurant is in a B & B inn, **Meson de Mesilla** (1803 Avenida de Mesilla). Open to the public (reservations required), the restaurant serves extremely fresh food with a menu that changes often. The focus here is on continental cuisine. The restaurant is open for lunch and dinner, Tuesday through Saturday ($$ to $$$). For reservations, call (505) 525-9212.

Back on the Plaza, **El Patio** is located on the southwest corner, serving New Mexican dishes as well as traditional Mexican food. There's a shaded patio for outdoor dining and a cantina-style bar ($$).

For fine dining, the **Double Eagle** offers French cuisine in an historic adobe building on the east side of the Plaza. There's a wonderful saloon complete with chandeliers and a fancy old backbar. The Maximilian Room is a large and stunningly appointed dining room. Matching the decor, the food here is fancy, as are the prices ($$$).

Ruidoso & Lincoln County

The Lincoln County War of 1878 pitted cowboys and ranchers against bankers and politicians. A three-day shootout resulted in several deaths and no victory for either side. William "Billy the Kid" Bonney was one of the cowboys who fled during the siege. Three years later, Billy was re-captured and brought back to Lincoln to be hanged.

He escaped from the Lincoln County Courthouse, killing two guards, only to be chased to Fort Sumner by Pat Garrett (the county sheriff) and shot to death. The spirit of the murderous events of 1878 still hovers over the area ,and the entire little town of Lincoln—still very much as it was then—has been designated the **Lincoln State Monument**.

Thirty-five miles southwest of Lincoln is **Ruidoso**, a town that is synonymous with quarter horses. Ruidoso Downs, the racetrack, is famed as the prime racing center for quarter horses and the site of the All-American Futurity, the world's richest horse race, which is held annually on Labor Day. A full season of quarter horse and thoroughbred racing is staged each summer, with horse sales taking place several times during the summer and fall.

Lincoln County lies in high country, north of Cloudcroft and east of Roswell. **Sierra Blanca Peak**, with an elevation of 12,003 feet, is the highest mountain in southern New Mexico. On its eastern slopes is the **Ski Apache** downhill ski area, which has a vertical rise of 1,800 feet and lots of powder skiing.

Things to See & Do
• Ruidoso Downs

Thoroughbreds and quarter horses race from May until Labor Day. Bleacher seating is free. The **Museum of the Horse**, located beside the racetrack, houses the extensive Anne C. Stradling Collection of horse art and memorabilia—from a Russian sleigh and an 1860 stagecoach to Remington statues and paintings by Charles Russell and many other Western artists. The museum is open daily and a fee is charged. For information, call (505) 378-4142.

• Smokey the Bear Historic Park

The Lincoln National Forest straddles the Sacramento Mountains, offering recreational opportunities. This park commemorates the original Smokey, a local forest resident who survived a fire and became famous as the symbol of forest fire prevention. Smokey died in 1976 and was buried in nearby Capitan. The park visitor center has exhibits on the beloved ursine and on forest firefighting.

Destinations

• Outdoor Attractions

Two River Park, located 2 miles from downtown Ruidoso on Sudderth Drive, is situated beside the Ruidoso River, with pine groves and a picnic area. **Bonito Lake**, 16 miles north of town on New Mexico Route 37, is a scenic forest lake that is popular with anglers and also offers a great site for a picnic. There are trails to old mine sites in the mountains. Horseback riding is a natural thing to do when visiting this horse-driven town. The **Inn of the Mountain Gods**, a resort complex, has a stable.

Where to Eat

There are several steak houses and informal Mexican restaurants. Try **Tinnie Silver Dollar** on U.S. Hwy. 70 for steaks in a Victorian setting ($$ to $$$). For more elaborate cuisine, we suggest the main dining room at the **Inn of the Mountain Gods** on Carrizo Canyon Rd. ($$ to $$$), or **La Loraine**, featuring French cuisine at 2523 Sudderth Dr., an elegant place for a romantic dinner ($$$).

Santa Fe

Before a single Englishman had set foot in the American West—before the landing at Plymouth Rock—Santa Fe was a capital city. For more than 380 years, this unique community has been a center of culture and government: first as the capital of the Spanish Kingdom of New Mexico, then as the Mexican province of Nuevo Mejico, and, since 1912, the State of New Mexico.

The cultural life of Santa Feans has been developing since the laying-out of the city in 1610 over the ruins of the Kaupoge Indian pueblo. Today, Santa Fe is the most desired vacation destination in all of the United States, and what draws visitors here is its symbiosis of the three dominating cultures: Indian, Spanish/Mexican, and Anglo. What surprises many visitors to Santa Fe is that this Southwest city is a mountain community. There are no cacti in Santa Fe except for those imported for garden landscaping. Situated at an elevation of 7,000 feet, at the southern edge of the Sangre de Cristo Mountains (the southernmost Rockies), the city is also at the edge of supreme outdoor adventure.

The Santa Fe Ski Basin is a half-hour's drive from downtown. North of the city is a land made for hikers, backpackers, and river rafters.

The modern big-city ambience of Albuquerque is an hour to the south. The small-town art community of Taos is an hour to the north. Within a day's travel of Santa Fe are most of the notable Indian pueblos in New Mexico—a continuing cultural presence in this fast-changing state. More than 20 Pueblo villages are within a 2-hour drive, and many exhibit a way of life which has been intact for 800 years.

There are two cultural subareas that make Santa Fe—to me and many other visitors—the most appealing city in the nation: architecture and food. The unique style of building called Santa Fe Style, or Pueblo, or Territorial, is an architecture blending the signatures of Spanish and Pueblo building design with modern adaptations to present a form of structure that is up-to-date yet blends with the terrain in a timeless way. These buildings—which can best be seen in the newest subdivisions on the Santa Fe outskirts—owe much to the original adobe brick homes of the first Spanish settlers.

The food of Santa Fe needs no extravagant praising here. New Mexico cuisine, now *au courant* across the U.S.A., originated in Santa Fe restaurants such as the Coyote Cafe, Le Tertulia, and La Casa Seña. These and less formal eateries including the Blue Corn Cafe continue to set the pace for the serving of super-fresh cuisine using regional foodstuffs in imaginative ways. Here too, the mingling of the three historic cultures produces a synergistic effect.

This city of 60,000 and its visitors support six fine museums and at least twenty art galleries. The city contains the country's oldest public building—the Palace of the Governors—situated along the north side of the Plaza. Now a museum, this Spanish adobe building has inspired the self-image of Santa Fe and the preservation of its historic districts. This early colonial office, called *Palacio Real,* was the site from which Governor Don Pedro de Peralta governed an empire that stretched from the Mississippi to the Pacific. It is a symbol of the past, but also of the present and future for this city, which always manages to excite the senses and inspire the imagination.

361

Destinations

Things to See & Do

• The Plaza

The heart and soul of Santa Fe, this park is surrounded by some of the earliest buildings to be constructed by the Spanish for their territorial capital. In the 1800s, the Plaza was the terminus for the Santa Fe Trail, the main trading route for the Spanish and Mexican settlers. Over the years, this historic center of culture for the territory (and later the state) saw the ebb and flow of political life, including the Pueblo Indian revolt, the re-conquering of the land by Spaniards, and attacks by other Indian tribes—Comanche, Apache, Navajo.

The park was laid out in a rectangular shape for protection and ceremonial purposes. It was a parade area for religious processions and was also used as a market and as the site of public executions. The Spanish reigned supreme from the Plaza between 1692 and 1821, when the Mexican period began. Soldiers for the Confederacy were based here for a few weeks in 1862.

The **Palace of the Governors** runs along the north side of the Plaza. This was the city's first building and the seat of Spanish and Mexican government. It is now the main site of the Museum of New Mexico, paying homage to that early era of settlement. It is the oldest public building in continuous use in the United States. It was the capitol until the 1860s, serving as a fortress in defense of the city against the Pueblo Revolt. It was then occupied by the new state government, and Governor Lew Wallace wrote most of his novel *Ben Hur* while occupying the Palace.

The other three sides of the Plaza are filled with shops and restaurants, while the historic ambience of the Plaza spills out over several blocks surrounding the park. The **La Fonda Hotel** and **St. Francis Cathedral** are both located here, and both are prime places to visit while strolling the Plaza. The cathedral, built in 1869, is in the French Romanesque style, seeming to be in stark contrast with the rest of the downtown area, but yet a major landmark. The church was constructed with local stone carved from nearby quarries and

New Mexico

from La Bajada Mesa west of town. Built on the site of a former Spanish church, *La Parroquia*—destroyed in the Pueblo Revolt—a few artifacts remain from the earlier period, notably the wooden statue of the Virgin, called *La Conquistadora*. The statue was first installed in the city in 1625 and was returned following the reconquest in 1692.

Only 600 yards from the Plaza is a hilltop ruin, the remains of Fort Marcy, the first American army outpost in the Southwest. The crumbled adobe walls are a testament to its military use from 1846 and its role in the development of modern Santa Fe, which spread out from around its base.

Shopping around the Plaza is always exciting. Some of Santa Fe's finest clothing and specialty stores are located in the old Victorian buildings looking out on the park. Local native artisans are often found at the Portal of the Palace of the Governors, selling exquisite Indian art and crafts including weavings and jewelry. The La Fonda Hotel is the scene of a monthly art and crafts fair. There are commercial galleries in the area and when you're tired of shopping, fine cafes are found around and near the plaza.

• Other Historic Districts

Seña Plaza is located on East Place Avenue, just a few minutes' walk from the main Plaza. Here, in this secluded historic district, is one of the best-preserved old homes in Santa Fe, built by Major Jose Seña about 1867. The huge house has 33 rooms enclosing a garden patio with trees and a fountain. The cathedral is across the street. A second storey was added to the hacienda in 1927 by artist William Penhallow Henderson, giving the building a new look and a new life.

A drive (or walk) along Old Santa Fe Trail will lead you past the **State Capitol**, looking like a Zia design representing the circle of life. Upstairs in the capitol building is the governor's office, which includes a public gallery featuring exhibits by New Mexican artists. Farther along Old Santa Fe Trail—across the river—is the **Barrio del Analco**, stretching along De Vargas Street. This is said to be the oldest residential neighborhood in the country, set on the ruins of a native pueblo. This section of the city was home to Santa Fe Indians and Spanish servants, who were directed by the Spanish conquistadors to live on the "other side of the river." The **Gregorio Crespin House** was built about 1720 and is purported to be the oldest home in the U.S.A.

• Museums

The **Museum of New Mexico** is the umbrella name for four separate museums in Santa Fe and five state monuments located across the state. Admission is $3.50 and a 2-day pass to all four museums is $6.00. Children under 16 years are admitted free. **Palacio Real** (Palace of the Governors) houses the History Museum—a regional collection with exhibits centered on the heritage of the Spanish, Mexican, and Indian past. For information, call (505) 827-6483.

The **Museum of Fine Arts** at 107 W. Palace Ave. features the work of recent and contemporary artists, including a substantial collection of paintings by Georgia O'Keeffe and the Taos Masters, as well as works by contemporary photographers, sculptors, and painters. More than 8,000 works are in the museum's permanent collection. The building, completed in 1917, was Santa Fe's first in the Pueblo revival style, influencing much of the city architecture to follow (505-827-4468). The **Museum of International Folk Art** houses a collection from more than 100 nations, with an emphasis on Hispanic folk art (including toys, textiles, and costumes). The museum also has a fine collection of religious art and artifacts. The Hispanic Heritage Wing features displays of Spanish–New Mexico colonial folk art. The building is located at 710 Camino Lejo (505-827-6350). The **Museum of Indian Arts and Culture**, at 710 Camino Lejo, focuses on the history and modern life of the Pueblo cultures. Opened in 1987, the museum features displays of southwestern artifacts from the nearby Laboratory of Anthropologists and of art, photographs, and artifacts of Pueblo existence over the centuries. For open hours, available tours and other information, call (505) 827-8000.

New Mexico

Nearby (at 704 Camino Lejo) is the **Wheelwright Museum of the American Indian**. Founded in 1937 by Mary Cabot Wheelwright, it was originally named the Museum of Navajo Ceremonial Art because of the influence upon the founder of the celebrated Navajo medicine man Hosteen Klah. The museum now includes works from varied North American Indian cultures. The unusual eight-sided structure is based on the shape of the traditional Navajo sand paintings and other Navajo ceremonial artifacts. Hours are Monday through Saturday from 10 AM to 5 PM and Sunday from 1 to 5 PM. For information, call (505) 982-4636.

In addition to these treasure houses of New Mexico history and culture, there are several more museums dedicated to preserving New Mexico traditions. **El Rancho de las Golondrinas** is a 400-acre town filled with buildings from the eighteenth and nineteenth centuries. The restored ranch features towers that were originally constructed in the 1850s. Demonstrations of colonial village life, including farming and domestic activity, take place during the summer months, particularly during festivals held at the site. The Rancho is open Wednesday through Sunday, with the special festivals held during June, August, and October. To get there, take Interstate 25 to exit 271 and follow signs to the village. For information, call (505) 471-2261.

The **Santa Fe Children's Museum** is approximately 1 mile south of the Plaza, at 1050 Old Pecos Trail. This is a great place for families, open Thursday through Saturday from 10 AM to 5 PM. For information, call (505) 989-8359. The **Institute of American Indian Arts Museum**, at Cathedral Place, features a national collection illustrating contemporary native cultural traditions; call (505) 988-6278. Put together, the Santa Fe museums serve to provide an exhaustive and stimulating look into the 500-year cultural history of New Mexico. In the walkable area close to the Plaza, one can savor the rich artistic heritage of the Southwest natives and enjoy the work of recent and contemporary emigrés who have added their own interpretations to the cultural mix.

• Santa Fe Opera

In a spectacular setting just north of the city, the Santa Fe Opera draws opera fans from around the world to its July/August season. Part of the excitement is in the outdoor amphitheater, which provides a perfect ambience for the music. The desert scene at sunset is an awe-inspiring vista.

Musical standards have always been very high, with noted conductors and singers coming to Santa Fe from the world's great opera companies. The Santa Fe Opera, now more than 40 years old, combines traditional operatic classics with premiers of modern operas, including new works by American composers.

The opera grounds are located near the Pueblo Indian villages of Tesuque and Nambe, via Highway 84/285. For advance information on the opera scene, write Santa Fe Opera, P.O. Box 2408, Santa Fe, NM 87504 or call (505) 982-3855 or 982-3851.

• Other Cultural Attractions

Santa Fe is almost a non-stop festival during the summer and fall months, and at other times of the year the city's institutions provide a full schedule of drama, music, and dance. These companies include the **Santa Fe Desert Chorale**, **Santa Fe Symphony**, **Serenata of Santa Fe** (a chamber ensemble), the **New Mexico Repertory Theater**, and the **Southwest Repertory Theater**.

The town of Madrid is only 30 minutes' drive south of Santa Fe. Here, in the old **Engine House Theatre**, two melodramas are staged in rotation from Memorial Day through Labor Day. The renowned **Santa Fe Chamber Music Festival** is held annually in July. The **Santa Fe Rodeo** is held during the second week of July.

• Markets

The **Spanish Market** has been held in the Plaza for more than 40 years—at the end of July. The **Indian Market** is more than 70 years old. Collectors of native art flock to the plaza each August to buy outstanding examples of native art and crafts and to eat Indian tacos and fry bread.

• Pueblos

Descendants of the Anasazi, the Pueblo Indians have lived and farmed in the valleys surrounding Santa Fe for many centuries. There are 19 pueblo villages in New Mexico today, and most are within an easy drive of the city. The villages are not only homes, they are also spiritual and ceremonial centers. Visitors may find feast observances, dancing, and other activities taking place. Tribal rules should be observed by all who visit the pueblos. There is sometimes a parking charge and a fee for photography (if allowed by the pueblo). Some forbid photography and sketching.

The **San Ildefonso Pueblo** is 21 miles north of Santa Fe via U.S. Hwy. 84/185 and off N.M. Route 502. There is a visitor center and museum; call (505) 455-2273.

Santa Clara Pueblo is 22 miles north of Santa Fe, on N.M. Highway 30. The Puyé Cliff Dwellings—at the entrance to the Santa Clara Canyon—provide a look into the past of this village. A self-guided tour will lead you through the cliff dwellings and escorted walking tours are available. As in most pueblos, there are shops and artists' studios in the village.

Tesuque and **Pojoaque** pueblos are located 9 and 15 miles north of the city, on N.M. Route 84/285. Tesuque Pueblo has a camp-ground and an ongoing bingo operation.

Nambe Pueblo (north of Santa Fe via U.S. 84/285 and N.M. 503) is a favorite for visitors and local residents, who picnic, fish, and camp at the pueblo and come to see Nambe Falls.

Where to Eat

When Mark Miller established the **Coyote Cafe** in Santa Fe, he set the standard for what has become known as Southwest cuisine. Miller has ventured east and even to Las Vegas to establish other restaurants with the same theme but, as owner, his influence is still intact at this landmark restaurant. The Coyote Cafe is a fairly noisy, gregarious place with modern decor and informal but efficient service. The food is super-fresh and the menu offers a variety of adventurous *prix-fixe* meals accompanied

Destinations

by a distinguished wine list. It is located near the Plaza, at 132 West Water Street; call (505) 983-1615. Reservations are necessary ($$$).

La Tertulia, at 416 Agua Fria, is another of the Santa Fe restaurants that has defined the Southwest cuisine genre. Open every day except Monday, La Tertulia offers fine American and southwestern dishes with attentive service ($$$).

La Casa Seña (125 E. Palace Ave.) is the third in this trio of influential downtown restaurants. Here, continental meets New Mexico in the historic district; call (505) 988-9232. You are advised to make reservations here ($$$).

For a more traditional approach to Mexican cuisine, served in a very informal setting, try the **Blue Corn Cafe** at 133 Water Street (across the street from the Coyote Cafe). Blue corn tortillas are washed down with margaritas and beer in this outstanding restaurant. For reservations, call (505) 984-1800 ($$). As a result of being a notable center of cuisine, the hotel restaurants in Santa Fe are better than in many other cities. The excellent dining rooms include the **Piñon Grill** in the Hilton (100 Sandoval St.) and **Los Rincones** in the Inn at Loretto at 211 Old Santa Fe Trail. Both hotel dining rooms are in the $$$ range.

Silver City

The former and present mining town is one of the great undiscovered places of the Southwest. It's a picturesque little community with a history, lying next to one of the most remarkable primitive areas in the country, the Gila Wilderness in the Gila National Forest. Silver City is featured in our loop tour of southeastern New Mexico, on page 324. The town is at an elevation of 5,850 feet, 44 miles northeast of Lordsburg. If you're traveling from Lordsburg, take New Mexico Route 90.

Tourism is just beginning to catch up with this early silver mining center, which began its existence in the 1880s. The silver boom lasted only ten years, but the state Normal School, built to train teachers and later becoming Western New Mexico University, was established by the time silver mining became uneconomical. Cattle ranching and lumber helped

New Mexico

save the community. The discovery of large copper deposits south of town gave new life to Silver City.

The town has an historic business district and close to downtown is a collection of Victorian houses and other buildings which are on the chamber of commerce self-guiding tour.

The town information center is located at 1103 N. Hudson Street (call 505-538-3785). There are a few places to stay in town including a couple of chain motels. There are two RV parks, and forest campgrounds are located north of town.

Things to See & Do
• In Silver City

There are two museums that provide information on the early mining days in this area as well as displaying art and artifacts. The **Western New Mexico University Museum** is at 12th and Virginia Streets and has collections of African folk art and Indian pottery and jewelry, as well as photographs showing life in the old mining camp. The **Silver City Museum** (312 W. Broadway St., downtown) is a preserved 1881 silver magnate's mansion that holds exhibits on the history of the mining town of Tyrone. There's a recently built annex that houses other exhibits on the region.

• Gila Cliff Dwellings National Monument

This remarkable historic site, 44 miles north on N.M. Route 15, offers a glimpse into prehistoric Mogollon Indian life. Seven natural caves hold more than 60 rooms built by the Mogollon about AD 1200. A 1-mile self-guided trail leads to the cliff dwellings from a trailhead a short drive from the monument visitor center.

There are two campgrounds and trails lead to two hot springs located along the west fork of the Gila River. For details, see page 352. The Gila Wilderness that surrounds the monument is one of the most pristine and beautiful natural areas in America. Information—on accessing the trails (including those that will lead you to the hot springs and others that lead into the Gila Wilderness)—is available at the visitor center.

Destinations

• Pinos Altos

This village is situated 7 miles north of Silver City, on the way to the Cliff Dwellings. It became a gold mining camp in 1860 and was the first county seat. The main street is a gallery of original buildings. **Santa Rita del Cobre Fort** is a three-quarter-scale reconstruction of a fort that sat at the Santa Rita copper mine in 1804 to protect the operation against hostile Apaches.

For atmospheric dining, head for the **Buckhorn Saloon and Opera House**. It's open daily except Sundays. Steaks are the focus of this historic adobe restaurant from the 1880s, with fireplaces and a perfect pioneer ambience—with class (**$$ to $$$**).

Taos

The haunting artistic temperament of Taos is best seen in two centers of activity. In the middle of downtown Taos is the Plaza—200 years old and Spanish in character. The Plaza is not large in comparison to other New Mexico plazas, but it has a quiet, serene ambience that complements the more recent cultural developments that have made this small community a magnet for visitors from around the world.

North of the modern town is a much more historic seat of culture—the oldest inhabited community in North America. **Taos Pueblo** is not only an amazing architectural marvel; it is a reminder that our modern cultural practices and history—derived from European development—are often rendered insignificant against the backdrop of the Pueblo Indians of the Southwest and the series of ancestor people (the Fremont, Mogollon, Anasazi, and others) who developed the indigenous culture of North America, long before the Europeans arrived.

At the time the Spanish explored the area and Hernando de Alvarado had come north to Taos in 1540, the Pueblo Indians had been living here for centuries. Together, the Indians and the Spanish occupied the area, farming the valley until the Pueblo Uprising of 1680, when the Indian pueblos united to drive out the Spanish. The Taos Indians were conquered in 1696 by Don Diego de Vargas, and the Spanish returned.

New Mexico

The legacies of both cultures are apparent throughout Taos, with the trademark Spanish/adobe architecture and festivals celebrating both cultures taking place year-round.

Taos lies 7,000 feet above sea level, nestled against the Sangre de Cristo Range of the Rocky Mountains. The air is crisp and summer skies are clear. The town is situated in the wide valley of the Rio Grande. The river flows south, through a dramatic gorge, a few miles to the west of the town.

The enchanting appeal of Taos is, first, in its shaded streets and buildings. You'll see a succession of old adobes with traditional walled courtyards, interspersed with the more modern quasi-adobe style of architecture, which mixes Spanish colonial touches with thick-walled adobe construction. The streets are lined with small boutiques and art galleries, cafes and crafts studios. All are within a short walk from each other in this city that has remained—in its feel—a small village.

Taos is a center for the arts, commemorated for all time by such groundbreaking Western artists as Georgia O'Keeffe and Ernest Blumenschein. Art museums and commercial galleries display the work of present-day Taos artists and other Southwest arts and crafts notables.

How to Get There
The scenic route between Santa Fe, Espanola, and Taos is featured in our scenic drive that begins on page 312. This is the historic High Road to Taos, the original wagon road between the two Spanish colonial centers. U.S. Highway 84 and New Mexico Route 68 offer a more direct and speedier drive from Santa Fe. Our recommendation is to take U.S. Highway 84 as far as Pojoaque (a pueblo town) or drive a little farther north to Espanola, and follow the scenic drive to complete the route via the old High Road.

Things to See & Do
• Taos Plaza
Located just west of the main street (Hwy. 64), the Plaza is the gathering place for the town, with original Spanish buildings (mostly homes) now converted to restaurants and shops.

You'll see chile ristras hanging in front of stores, the old Hotel La Fonda (related to but much less fancy and a lot more quirky than Santa Fe's La Fonda), and art galleries.

• Taos Pueblo

The pueblo is north of the main town via Hwy. 64 (turn onto the right-hand fork). Unlike many pueblos, this is not a ruin. It has been and is now occupied by families who live here year-round, and many others who have modern homes in the pueblo lands come here for ceremonial occasions. Some of the ground-floor "apartments" are now Indian bake shops and crafts stores. The two large, five-level structures have been here since about AD 1000.

The pueblo community has turned their apartment complex into something of a prime tourist attraction and commercial enterprise. Expect to pay when you drive your car into the pueblo parking lot. Expect to pay again if you wish to use your camera. Visit the bake shops and buy Indian bread and biscuits, and stroll through the crafts stores. There's an amazing collection of Indian art and memorabilia available here. The old Catholic mission church is open to the public, but the pueblo buildings are off-limits, except for the shops. Other than on a few ceremonial occasions (funerals, etc.) the pueblo is open every day.

• Ranchos de Taos

This village south of the main town has some fine restaurants and galleries, but the main attraction is St. Francis of Assisi Mission Church, a wonderful example of early Spanish mission architecture dating back to its completion in 1755. The interior features many art objects.

• Museums and Historic Homes

The **Millicent Rogers Museum** 4 miles north of Taos on N.M. Route 3) houses an outstanding collection of Indian art and crafts including the work of potter Maria Martînez in addition to Spanish-colonial art, furnishings, and artifacts. The museum overlooks the Rio Grande Valley. If there is one museum to visit when you're in the Taos area, this is the one.

New Mexico

The **Harwood Foundation Museum** is a cultural research center featuring public and research libraries as well as a gallery that features paintings by famous artists of the Southwest in addition to Spanish folk art.

The **Ernest Blumenschein Home and Museum** (13 Ledoux Street) is a national historic landmark and the home of the seminal Western artist who co-founded the Taos Society of Artists. The house was built in 1790 and has antique furnishings; it serves as a showcase for local artists.

The **Governor Bent House** was home to New Mexico's first American governor, from 1846. The old adobe house features a collection of Bent family artifacts and other local historical items. **Kit Carson**, the famous frontiersman, lived and died in Taos. His home, open to the public, is east of downtown on Kit Carson Street. The **Hacienda de Don Antonio Severino Martinez** is 2 miles west of town on N.M. Route 240. This Spanish hacienda has period furnishings and decor. A classic colonial home, it was built with security in mind and contains two enclosed courtyards. It's situated on the banks of the Rio Pueblo.

• Taos Ski Valley

With Mt. Wheeler looming overhead, this is New Mexico's best downhill ski area. It also serves as a base for outdoor activity in the summer, with hiking trails fanning out through the Carson National Forest. The vertical drop is 2,612 feet, and the longest run is a long 5.2 miles. At the base are condo accommodations, restaurants, and bars. To get there, drive north from Taos on N.M. Route 3 and turn right (east) onto N.M. Route 150. The ski area is 19.5 miles from downtown Taos.

• Angel Fire

Another noted ski area is located 26 miles east of Taos—via N.M. Route 68 and then south for 4 miles on N.M. Route 75. With a vertical drop of 2,180 feet, runs up to 3.5 miles, and a cross-country ski center, Angel Fire offers just about everything (including golf when the snow has disappeared).

Destinations

• Side Trips from Taos

Our scenic drive beginning on page 316 features the route around the Enchanted Circle, leading through the Carson National Forest, past the D. H. Lawrence Memorial to the rustic resort town of Red River, and then to Eagle Nest before returning to Taos. This drive is highly recommended, as is the longer Valle Vidal Circle route, which includes much of the Enchanted Circle. For details, visit the forest ranger station in Taos or see our highway log.

Where to Eat

While not as much a dining town as Santa Fe, Taos has excellent restaurants that are comfortable and relaxing places. **Doc Martin's** in the famed Taos Inn has several dining rooms with kiva-style fireplaces and a great collection of art. The specialties change regularly, and this fine restaurant serves both American and native dishes. The Adobe Bar is across the hotel lobby (\$\$ to \$\$\$).

Michael's Kitchen is a landmark among coffee shops, serving American and Southwest cuisine, including wonderful bakery items (\$ to \$\$). The **Garden Restaurant** on the north side of Taos Plaza is a distinctive Taos-style deli, with a focus on international dishes and baked goods. Open for three meals each day, this is a fine place to sit and people-watch (\$ to \$\$).

The **Double AA Grill** offers a pleasant surprise. You walk into what appears to be a modest cafe (to stay the least) only to find that the menu offers a wide selection of game dishes and fresh fish meals. Game dishes range from bear and buffalo to venison and elk. Mexican food is also served. There is a small but adequate wine list. It's on Paseo del Pueblo Sur (the main street—N.M. Route 64) south of the main business and shopping district (\$\$ to \$\$\$).

Roberto's Restaurant (East Kit Carson Rd.) is an excellent New Mexican restaurant that features intimate dining rooms in a building which is more than 150 years old. **Carl's French Quarter** restaurant (Ski Valley Road) is the place to eat if you're longing for Creole and Cajun cuisine. It's in the **Quail Ridge Inn**, which offers a well-appointed dining room with good service (\$\$ to \$\$\$).

New Mexico

ABIQUIU

The Abiquiu Inn
Box A, Highway 84
Abiquiu NM 87510
(505) 685-4378

A visit to the Abiquiu area makes it easy to see why the artist Georgia O'Keeffe was so inspired. The loveliness of this inn inspires the traveler to want to stay awhile. There are 12 rooms, some king, queen, double, and some with kitchenettes. The Cafe Abiquiu features Indian curries and Middle Eastern cuisine as well as New Mexican fare, and there is a gift shop selling native art and crafts (\$ to \$\$).

ALAMOGORDO

Desert Aire Motor Inn
1021 S. White Sands Blvd.
Alamogordo NM 88310
(505) 437-2110

This Best Western Inn has an outdoor pool with a mountain view, a restaurant, and a lounge with entertainment. King and queen beds are available (\$).

Holiday Inn
1401 S. White Sands Blvd.
Alamogordo NM 88310
(505) 437-7100

The largest of the town's accommodations with 107 units, this motor inn offers cable TV and movies, a heated pool and wading pool, and restaurant with lounge and entertainment (\$ to \$\$).

ALBUQUERQUE

Casas de Suenos
310 Rio Grande Blvd. SW
Albuquerque NM 87104
(505) 247-4560
or 800-242-8987

A charming bed & breakfast inn, located near Old Town, Casa de Suenos ("Houses of Dreams") was designed in the 1930s as an artists' compound and its creative design bespeaks its artistic origins: adobe construction, brick pathways through the gardens, antiques and art deco. Common rooms include a dining room with fireplace, living room, library, bar, and patio. A breakfast with Southwest touches is served. Eight rooms, suites, and casitas are available, all with private bath (\$\$ to \$\$\$).

NEW MEXICO • Places to Stay

375

Sheraton Old Town
800 Rio Grande Blvd. NW
Albuquerque NM 87104
(505) 843-6300
or 800-237-2133

Adjacent to museums and convenient to all of the Old Town attractions, this large 11-storey hotel complex has 20 suites and 170 rooms, pool, whirlpool, shops, restaurants, coffee shop, and a lounge which features entertainment (**$$ to $$$**).

La Posada de Albuquerque
125 2nd St. NW
Albuquerque NM 87012
(505) 242-9090
or 800-777-5732

Located in the heart of downtown, one block from the Convention Center, this 10-storey Spanish-style hotel is on the National Historic Register and was fully restored in recent years. It was built by Conrad Hilton in 1939. There are more than 100 rooms and a few suites, also the Lobby Bar and Eulalia's Restaurant, with New Mexican, American, and continental cuisine (**$ to $$**).

W. E. Mauger Estate
701 Roma Ave. NW
Albuquerque NM 87102
(505) 242-8755

Also on the National Register is this delightful B & B inn, a Queen Anne-style house built in 1897. There are six rooms (some are suites) some with views of the Sandia Mountains or of downtown. Continental breakfast is served (**$$**).

Casita Chamisa
850 Chamisal Rd. NW
Albuquerque NM 87017
(505) 897-4644

One of the things that sets this B & B apart from others is the fact that a thirteenth-century pueblo was found on the grounds when the owners, Kit and Arnold Sergeant, decided to dig a swimming pool! Kit is an archeologist and will be happy to talk about the dig. Arnold is renowned for his sour dough breakfast treats, made from 100-year-old starter. There is a two-room casita, a double room, private baths, plus the indoor pool and patio (**$$**).

Corrales Inn
P.O. Box 1361
Corrales NM 87048
(505) 897-4422

Although Corrales is 7 miles north of Albuquerque, it is close enough to serve as a base for exploring the area, and this inn had to be included. Each of the six rooms (all with private bath) has a different decor, and the Great Room is the setting for sherry and port in the evening. The Corrales Inn restaurant is particularly renowned for its wonderful country French and continental cuisine. The chef is co-owner Mary Briault (**$**).

New Mexico

Elaine's
#72 Snowline Rd.
P.O. Box 444
Cedar Crest NM 87008
(505) 281-2467
or 800-821-3092

For a mountain retreat near town, try this lovely 3-storey log bed and breakfast home located in the Sandia Mountains, just a few miles from the city on the historic Turquoise Trail. The 3rd-floor suite has a private bath and balcony, the second floor has two rooms with shared bath; also a living room with a large stone fireplace and a library for all the guests. Elaine serves a full breakfast, including fruit in season from her own trees. It's set on 4 acres adjacent to the Cibola National Forest, and Elaine guarantees that the full moon rises right over her balcony! ($$).

Friendship Inn
717 Central NW
Albuquerque NM 87102
(505) 247-1501

There are inexpensive accommodations available in the area, including representation from most of the budget chains. The Friendship Inn in the downtown area has 130 rooms and one suite, and also a lounge and restaurant—facilities that most budget motels do not have.

American RV Park
13500 Coronado
Freeway SW
Albuquerque NM 87121
(505) 831-3545

One of the state's top-rated RV parks with 156 full hookup sites, pool, propane, and convenience store. Take exit 149 from the freeway.

AZTEC

Aztec Residence Hotel
300 S. Main St.
Aztec NM 87410
(505) 334-3452

This quaint hotel is one of the many historic buildings on Aztec's main street (Hwy. 44 N) and is more than 100 years old, with stained glass and period furnishings. There are nine rooms available, all with TV and private bath, and five with kitchenettes (the hotel has no restaurant attached but the owners will recommend those nearby). Credit cards are not accepted ($$).

377

Enchantment Lodge
1800 W. Aztec Blvd.
Aztec NM 87410
(505) 334-6143

An outdoor pool, laundry, gift shop and morning coffee are some of the features at this budget motel. There are 20 units and they take credit cards but not pets ($).

Places to Stay

BLOOMFIELD

For motel accommodations, see listings for Aztec and Farmington.

KOA Campground
1900 E. Blanco Blvd.
Bloomfield NM 87413
(505) 632-8339

The amenities included with the 785 full hookups at this campground include showers, laundry, store, lounge, and swimming pool.

CARLSBAD

Cavern Inn
17 Carlsbad Cav. Hwy.
Box 128
White's City NM 88268
(505) 785-2291 or
1-800-CAVERNS

This Best Western motel is located not in downtown Carlsbad but in the community closest to Carlsbad Caverns National Park. It has 62 units (some with in-room whirlpool), 2 restaurants, cocktails, gift shop, grocery, museum, and more, including an RV park and campground ($ to $$).

Carlsbad Inn
601 S Canal
Carlsbad NM 88220
(505) 887-3541

The only full-service motel in downtown Carlsbad has 51 units in all (some housekeeping units and single to king rooms), a pool, restaurant, lounge, and entertainment ($).

CHAMA

Casa De Martinez
P.O. Box 96
Los Ojos NM 87551
(505) 588-7858

Located south of Chama in the village of Brazos near the fork of the Chama and Los Brazos Rivers (with a view of the El Chorro waterfall) is this historic double-adobe home run as a B & B operation by the great-granddaughter of the Martinez family, early settlers in the area. There is one suite with a fireplace plus six double rooms, three with private bath. There is also a dining room and a beautiful courtyard with a well and gardens. Open February–October ($$).

Corkins Lodge
P.O. Box 396
Chama NM 87520
(505) 588-7261

Also south of Chama on Hwy. 512 is this wonderful rustic lodge, which has been operating since 1929. If you love lake or river fishing, cross-country skiing, or just soaking up beautiful scenery, this may be your place. There are 15 cabins available, with sizes and prices varying. All have bath and

New Mexico

kitchen, so bring your own groceries or catch a few trout. There's a heated outdoor pool, game room, and 738 acres for hiking ($).

Gandy Dancer B & B
299 Maple St., Box 810
Chama NM 87520
(505) 756-2191
or 800-424-6702

Housed in a 1913 residence, this charming B & B offers a comfortable and elegant atmosphere full of art and antiques. A full breakfast is included with each of the three rooms, and dinner is also available for an additional charge. The hosts can arrange bicycle rentals or a hiking or fishing guide for a trip into the nearby Rio Grande National Forest—with a catered lunch ($ to $$).

Twin Rivers Trailer Park
and Campground
P.O. Box 155
Chama NM 87520
(505) 756-2218

The facility is located at the junction of U.S. 84 and State Route 17. There are pull-through sites with full hookups, showers, and laundromat. There is also a gas station and a supermarket adjacent to the campground.

CHIMAYO

Hacienda Rancho
de Chimayo
P.O. Box 11
Chimayo NM 87522
(505) 351-2222

Like many establishments in New Mexico, this hacienda and its related restaurant across the road are steeped in history. Both are the restored homes—built in the 1880s—of the Jaramillo brothers who come from a Chimayo family going back to the 1700s. Each of the seven rooms opens onto an open flower-filled and fountain-splashed courtyard. Furnishings here are antique Victorian, and some rooms sport balconies with mountain views. Continental breakfast is included, but try to have lunch or dinner in the restaurant, famous for its New Mexico food.

379

CLOUDCROFT

Summit Inn
P.O. Box 627
Cloudcroft NM 88317
(505) 687-3553

The inn offers rooms for one or two people, as well as three-room suites with kitchenettes, complete with utensils, and cottages that will house up to eight. There is a picnic area with grills ($).

Places to Stay

**Cloudcroft Lodge
& Pavilion**
P.O. Box 497
Cloudcroft NM 88317
(505) 682-2566 or
1-800-842-4216

The lodge, one of a few grand old railway resort lodges, was originally built in 1899, but it burned and was rebuilt in 1911. It features some gracious Victorian touches, such as glassed-in verandas and gabled windows, and sports a unique five-storey copper-clad tower. Recent additions to the property include The Retreat, a large four-bedroom mountain home built adjacent to The Lodge.

The Pavilion, a quaint bed and breakfast inn with 11 rooms with fireplaces. The guests at both of these facilities are welcome to use all of the amenities of the lodge, which include conference rooms, golf course, the award-winning Rebecca's Restaurant, and the Red Dog Saloon. There is also a pool, plus a whirlpool, sauna, and gift shop (**$$ to $$$+**).

Chalet Camper Village
Rte. 2, Box 2300
Cloudcroft NM 88317
(505) 687-3553

Located 5 miles east of Cloudcroft on Hwy. 82, this camper village has 95 trailer sites with full hookups as well as some tent sites.

FARMINGTON

Holiday Inn
600 E. Broadway
Farmington NM 87401
(505) 327-9811

As with many links in this chain, the Farmington Holiday Inn is large, with 150 units, and has many amenities such as a heated pool, sauna and exercise room, pay movies, cable TV, and phones. It also has a dining room and lounge. (**$ to $$**).

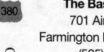

The Basin Lodge
701 Airport Drive
Farmington NM 87401
(505) 325-5061

This small (21-unit) budget motel is conveniently located and reasonably priced. Free local calls and cable TV are featured (**$**).

River Grove Trailer Park
801 E. Broadway
Farmington NM 87401
(505) 327-0974

The River Grove offers 28 full-service trailer sites and is conveniently located to Farmington and area attractions.

New Mexico

GALLUP

El Rancho Hotel & Motel
1000 East 66 Avenue
Gallup NM 87301
(505) 543-6351
or 800-863-9311

A famous motel, now on the National Register of Historic Places, it is billed as the Home of the Movie Stars and did indeed count many luminaries among its guests. And no wonder, since it was built by the brother of D. W. Griffiths, the legendary filmmaker, in 1937. It is now owned by another legend of the Southwest, Armando Ortega, owner of many Indian trading posts in the area, who has fully refurbished this gem. It is a must for Route 66 buffs too. There is a restaurant attached as well as the requisite Indian crafts store ($).

The Inn
3009 West Hwy. 66
Gallup NM 87301
(505) 722-2221
or 800-528-1234

The Inn is a Best Western facility with 124 oversized rooms, some with refrigerators, plus an indoor pool and whirlpool, pay TV, laundry, gift shop, and full-service restaurant and lounge ($$).

Travelers Inn
3304 W. Hwy. 66
Gallup NM 87301
(505) 722-7765
or 800-633-8300

For budget accommodations, this motel is a good bet. It has 108 units, a few with refrigerators, and even has a heated pool and whirlpool ($).

KOA Campground
West Hwy. 66, Exit 16
Gallup NM 87301
(505) 863-5021

Open year-round, this campground offers 170 spaces, full hookups, tenting sites, dump station, showers, gift shop, store, propane and recreation room.

LAS CRUCES

Holiday Inn de Las Cruces
201 E. University Ave.
Las Cruces NM 88004
(505) 526-4411

This beautifully landscaped motor hotel has 112 units, an indoor pool surrounded by lush gardens, a game room, shops, entertainment lounges, and dining rooms. One rarely finds a chain hotel this individually outfitted, and at a good price too. Each room boasts a floor-to-ceiling window and color TV with movies ($$).

381

Places to Stay

Inn of the Arts
618 S. Alameda Blvd.
Las Cruces NM 88005
(505) 526-3327

Gerald and Linda Lundeen have created at their inn an attractive mix of art gallery, architect's office (he's the architect and she runs the gallery), and gracious hospitality in their 2 suites and 13 double rooms. Each room is named for a famed Southwest artist and features original artwork as well as English and American antique furnishings. The Merienda Room (the guests' common room) joins two historic adobe homes. The Lundeens are also renowned for their energy and enthusiasm, as well as their wonderful Southwest food ($ to $$).

Meson de Mesilla
P.O. Box 1212
Mesilla NM 88046
(505) 525-9212

In nearby Mesilla, the historic Mexican town, can be found this lovely adobe B & B with 13 rooms, all with private bath. Bicycles are available to guests, as is a pool. A full gourmet breakfast is served and there is a restaurant on the premises that serves French cuisine at lunch and dinner most days and boasts a large wine list. Reservations are recommended for rooms and meals ($ to $$).

Hampton Inn
755 Avenida de Mesilla
Las Cruces NM 88005
(505) 527-2015

For a bargain motel, try this inn, which is found by taking exit 140 (the Mesilla exit) from I-10. There are 120 units, a pool, cable TV, and movies. Pets are allowed and weekly rates are available ($).

Las Cruces KOA
814 Weinrich Road
Las Cruces NM 88005
(505) 526-9030

This campground is set on a hill overlooking the valley and has 102 sites including tent sites, most with full hookups. There are BBQ pits and picnic tables. Take exit 135 off I-10 and go one mile east on Highway 70.

LOS ALAMOS

Orange Street Inn
3496 Orange Street
Los Alamos NM 87544
(505) 662-2651

Perched on one of the many area mountaintops, this small B & B (five rooms, all with private bath) offers a central location for visiting many of the region's attractions, such as Bandelier National Monument. The inn is famous for its wonderful New Mexico breakfasts, and guests may use the kitchen facilities for other meals ($$).

New Mexico

Hilltop House Hotel
2201 Trinity Drive
Los Alamos NM 87544
(505) 662-2411

This 87-unit motor inn features some rooms with kitchenettes and a glassed-in pool and atrium area. The adjacent restaurant serves three meals a day and guests receive a complimentary American breakfast ($$).

Los Alamos Inn
2210 Trinity Drive
Los Alamos NM 87544
(505) 662-7211
or 800-279-9279

The area's largest hotel, with 116 rooms, also offers an outdoor pool and whirlpool. There is a restaurant, Ashley's, serving three meals daily plus Sunday brunch and snacks. There are also meeting and banquet rooms here ($$).

RUIDOSO AREA

Inn of the Mountain Gods
P.O. Box 269
Mescallero NM 88340
(505) 257-5141
or 800-545-6040

Located about 3 miles from Ruidoso, off Highway 70, this resort is set on 460,000 acres and is open year-round. There are 250 rooms in the lodge plus restaurants, lounge, shops, and convention facilities. Among the many activities available here are boating, fishing, golf, riding, hunting, trap & skeet shooting, tennis, swimming, and skiing ($$ to $$$).

Sierra Mesa Lodge
P.O. Box 463
Alto NM 88312
(505) 336-4515

The five elegant guest rooms (all with private bath) at this B & B are beautifully appointed, each in a different decor such as Victorian or Oriental. The hosts, Larry and Lila Goodman, provide the extra touches that ensure a memorable stay, and breakfasts are bountiful. It's 6 miles from Ruidoso on Hwy. 48, then 2 miles on Fort Stanton Road($$).

Casa de Patron
P.O. Box 27
Lincoln NM 88338
(505) 653-4676

A claim to fame of this historic adobe B & B is that Billy the Kid slept here! A more recent claim is the delicious and generous breakfasts served by the owners, the Jordans. There are three rooms plus two 2-bedroom casitas—all but one room have private baths. Dinner is also available. This is a fine place from which to explore the history of the Lincoln County War and the adventures of Billy The Kid ($$).

383

Places to Stay

Dan Dee Cabins
310 Main, Box 844
Ruidoso NM 88345
(505) 257-2165

Billed as a "cottage resort" the cabins here are scattered over 5 rustic acres for maximum seclusion, yet they are close to all area recreation sites. Each has a fireplace, cable TV, full kitchen and barbecue, among other amenities (**$ to $$**).

Shadow Mountain Lodge
107 Main
Ruidoso NM 88345
(505) 257-4886 or
1-800-441-4331

Also in the scenic Upper Canyon area, this lodge is designed for couples, with king beds and fireplaces in each suite. Here you will find luxury in a romantic getaway for an affordable price. There is a spacious veranda and beautifully landscaped gardens (**$ to $$**).

SANTA FE

The Bishop's Lodge
Bishop's Lodge Road
P.O. Box 2367
Santa Fe NM 87504
(505) 983-6377

This fine resort is situated on the former ranch of the Archbishop Lamy, immortalized in Willa Cather's novel *Death Comes for the Archbishop.* It is set in a private valley just 3 miles north of town. Among the many amenities are an outdoor pool with a view of the gardens, whirlpool, and saunas. For an additional fee, one can play tennis, go horseback riding, and more (**$$$+**).

El Paradero
220 W. Manhattan Ave.
Santa Fe NM 87501
(505) 988-1177

This marvelous house started as a Spanish farmhouse and parts of it are more than 200 years old, while other parts reflect Victorian-era additions. Rooms (there are fourteen including two suites) contain original art and pine furniture with antique accents. Hearty breakfasts are served, along with afternoon tea and wine (**$ to $$**).

Alexander's Inn
529 East Palace Avenue
Santa Fe NM 87501
(505) 986-1431

Unusual for Santa Fe, this B & B is not adobe-style but is a brick and wood country inn. There are five rooms, three with private bath. Tea and cookies are served when you check in, as well as continental breakfast and afternoon tea during your stay. The innkeepers are very helpful in suggesting local restaurants, for example, or they will let you use their fridge for your own provisions. This is a no-smoking facility (**$$ to $$$**).

384

New Mexico

Grant Corner Inn
122 Grant Avenue
Santa Fe NM 87501
(505) 983-6678

Another charming B & B located near the Plaza, this inn is known for its extra welcoming touches and its bunny collection (stuffed and ceramic) as well as fine breakfasts. Complimentary wine and hors d'oeuvres are served in the evenings and pastries in the afternoons (**$$ to $$$**).

Hotel St. Francis
210 Don Gaspar Avenue
Santa Fe NM
(505) 983-5700

Dating from the 1920s, the Hotel St. Francis is now on the National Historic Register. A recent remodeling offers the best of the old charm with modern amenities, including suites. It is centrally located and has a bar and restaurant (**$$ to $$$**).

Hotel Santa Fe
1501 Paseo de Paralta
Santa Fe NM 87501
(505) 982-1200
or 800-825-9876

If a large modern hotel is more to your taste, this hotel, built in the Pueblo revival style, is also centrally located in the historic district. It offers 131 rooms, all with microwaves and mini-bars. There is complimentary parking (**$$ to $$$+**).

Hotel La Fonda
100 E. San Francisco
Santa Fe NM 87501
(505) 982-5511
or 800-523-5002

The La Fonda is a must-see, even if you don't stay here, but if you can, do! Known as the Inn at the End of the Santa Fe Trail, it is the latest of the inns on the present site going back to the founding of Santa Fe in 1610. It is located right on the Plaza, and the whole place is a showcase of Southwest decor. Features include a year-round outdoor pool, seasonal patio bar, and roof garden restaurant. Or try the enclosed skylit courtyard restaurant, La Plazuela. Being at La Fonda is a phsychic experience. **$$$ to $$$+**).

Preston House
106 Faithway
Santa Fe NM 87501
(505) 982-3465

Unusual in that it is the only Queen Anne-style house in the state, this B & B also sports an antique staircase: of gold and black lacquer built by Chinese laborers (the house was constructed in 1886). Now there is an adjoining adobe building so that guests have a choice of decor. There are 15 guest rooms sharing 14 baths, a parlor and a large dining room in which a generous breakfast is served. There is also an afternoon snack. (**$ to $$$**).

385

Places to Stay

**Stage Coach
Motor Inn**
3360 Cerrillos Road
Santa Fe NM 87501
(505) 471-0707

This is a small, older motel with comfortable rooms, convenient to downtown Santa Fe, offering very reasonable rates.

Cerrillos Road is known as "motel row" for good reason. If you are looking for other budget accommodations, all of the major motel chains are represented along the strip: Days Inn, Holiday Inn, Howard Johnson, La Quinta, Motel 6, etc., etc. This is definitely not one of the more outstanding sections of town from an historic or aesthetic viewpoint, but it leads to the downtown area.

SILVER CITY

**Bear Mountain
Guest Ranch**
P.O. Box 1163
Silver City NM 88062
(505) 538-2538

One of the finest attributes of this guest ranch is the energy and enthusiasm of its owner, Myra McCormick. She has instituted a Lodge & Learn program, providing classes in birding, for example. Excursions to nearby attractions such as the Gila Cliff Dwellings are also popular with guests. All rooms (15, including some suites) have private baths, and the ranch is open all year ($$).

Copper Manor Motel
710 Silver Heights Blvd.
Silver City NM 88062
(505) 538-5392

This modern motel has 68 units, with color TV and phones in each room, in addition to an indoor pool, whirlpool, a cafe and lounge ($)

Holiday Motor Hotel
3420 Hwy. 120E
Silver City NM 88061
(505) 538-3711

A pool and coin laundry are two of the features of this Best Western facility. It also has a restaurant which serves beer and wine. There are 79 units available here at a reasonable rate ($).

TAOS

**American Artists
Gallery House**
132 Frontier Road
Taos NM 87571
(505) 758-4446

In keeping with the artistic ambience which permeates Taos, this inn is a gallery in itself, hung with the works of many well-known artists of the Southwest. The owners, Ben and Myra Carp, are former educators and their love of learning shows

New Mexico

in many areas of their hospitality. There are five rooms, including one suite and one cottage, all with private bath. Breakfasts here are lavish (Myra has published a cookbook on them) and dessert is served in the evening ($$).

Brooks Street Inn
207 Brooks Street
P.O. Box 4954
Taos NM 87571
(505) 758-1489

Built in the 1950s in the traditional adobe manner, this inn offers a location convenient to the Taos Plaza, Kit Carson State Park, and other attractions. There are seven rooms, five with private bath. Each room is named for a native tree and is eclectically furnished ($ to $$).

Casa Benavides
137 Kit Carson Road
Taos NM 87571
(505) 758-3934

This inn was the family home of owner (along with her husband and son) Barbara McCarthy, a Taos native. This, combined with other neighboring adobe buildings, has resulted in 22 guest rooms, all with private bath and TV and some with kitchenettes. All rooms are authentically decorated in New Mexican style with kiva fireplaces and tile. Breakfast might include eggs with green chile and cheese and homemade flour tortillas ($$ to $$$).

Casa de la Chimeneas
405 Cordoba Road
P.O. Box 5303
Taos NM 87571
(505) 758-4777

Named for the chimneys adorning the kiva fireplaces found in each room, this B & B is well known for the extra touches provided by owner Susan Vernon: sheepskin mattress covers and luxury bed linens, to name two. The grounds are well landscaped, and there is a fountain among the flowers. There are two double rooms and one suite, all with private bath and TV ($$ to $$$).

Hacienda del Sol
109 Mabel Dodge Lake
P.O. Box 177
Taos NM 87571
(505) 758-0287

The old adobe house was originally bought by art patron Mabel Dodge Luhan as a hideaway for her Taos Indian husband Tony. Georgia O'Keeffe painted her *Sunflowers* here. The home adjoins the Taos Pueblo and has a beautiful view of Taos Mountain from the outdoor hot tub! There are seven rooms, four with private bath and all furnished with authentic Southwest decor including

Places to Stay

kiva fireplaces and original art. The owners, Marcine and John Landon, serve afternoon wine and cheese as well as breakfast ($ to $$$).

Sagebrush Inn
P.O. Box 557
Taos NM 87571
(505) 758-2254

Another of the places where Georgia O'Keeffe painted is this lovely pueblo-style inn built in 1929. There are 63 rooms in all, most on two stories and one on the top floor; all have private baths. There are many facilities, including two hot tubs, tennis courts, and swimming pool. There is a steak house, a restaurant, and a bar with live entertainment ($ to $$$).

Taos Inn
P.O. Drawer N
Taos NM 87571
(505) 748-2233

The Taos Inn is an utterly charming hotel whose lobby sits on the former Taos town square, with parts of the building dating back to the 1600s. The old town well still adorns the room but is now a sitting place near the hotel's wonderful watering hole, the Adobe Bar. Also located off the lobby is Doc Martin's Restaurant, serving three meals daily. There are now 40 rooms in the inn, all with private bath, TV, and phone ($$ to $$$++).

New Mexico

The listings in this index cover the drives, cities, towns and significant attractions which are found in the Destinations pages for California, Nevada, Utah, Arizona and New Mexico. When information on attractions is included in the Scenic Drives section for each state, these attractions are also included in the index with page numbers shown in bold type. Parks along the scenic routes are listed in the highway logs which accompany maps in the Drives pages.

Index

Index

Index